Cambridge
International AS and A Level

Economics

Peter Smith

HODDER
EDUCATION
AN HACHETTE UK COMPANY

Unless otherwise acknowledged, the questions that appear in this book and CD were written by the author.

Although every effort has been made to ensure that website addresses are correct at time of going to press, Hodder Education cannot be held responsible for the content of any website mentioned in this book. It is sometimes possible to find a relocated web page by typing in the address of the home page for a website in the URL window of your browser.

Hachette UK's policy is to use papers that are natural, renewable and recyclable products and made from wood grown in sustainable forests. The logging and manufacturing processes are expected to conform to the environmental regulations of the country of origin.

Orders: please contact Bookpoint Ltd, 130 Milton Park, Abingdon, Oxon OX14 4SB. Telephone: (44) 01235 827827. Fax: (44) 01235 400401. Lines are open 9.00–5.00, Monday to Saturday, with a 24-hour message answering service. Visit our website at www.hoddereducation.com

© Peter Smith 2014
First published in 2014 by
Hodder Education,
An Hachette UK Company
Carmelite House,
50 Victoria Embankment,
London EC4Y 0DZ

Impression number   3
Year   2016

All rights reserved. Apart from any use permitted under UK copyright law, no part of this publication may be reproduced or transmitted in any form or by any means, electronic or mechanical, including photocopying and recording, or held within any information storage and retrieval system, without permission in writing from the publisher or under licence from the Copyright Licensing Agency Limited. Further details of such licences (for reprographic reproduction) may be obtained from the Copyright Licensing Agency Limited, Saffron House, 6–10 Kirby Street, London EC1N 8TS.

Cover photo Jean-Pierre Pieuchot/Photographer's Choice/Getty Images
Illustrations by Aptara, Inc.
Typeset in 9/12 ITC Garamond by Aptara, Inc.
Printed in Slovenia

A catalogue record for this title is available from the British Library
ISBN: 978 1444 181 364

Contents

Contents

Contents

Contents

Contents

Student's CD contents

Interactive tests

Glossary

Chapter summaries

Answers to exercises

Revision checklist and resource assessment

Acknowledgements

I would like to thank those who kept me organised during the production of this book, especially Kate Gentles and Chris Bessant, and Eleanor Miles and Nina Konrad at Hodder Education. Their efficiency and encouragement were invaluable. I would also like to thank my wife Maureen for her support and patience when I spent my time with this book instead of with her.

The Publishers would like to thank the following for permission to reproduce copyright material:

Photo credits: p.2 © Deyan Georgiev – Fotolia; **p.9** © Heartland – Fotolia; **p.19** © Moreno Soppelsa – Fotolia; **p.21** © anankml – Fotolia; **p.23** © lefebvre_jonathan – Fotolia; **p.32** © Siegfried Schnepf – Fotolia; **p.34** © Thomas Cockrem/Alamy; **p.44** © WoodyStock/Alamy; **p.52** © Peter Treanor/Alamy; **p.55** Elvert Barnes Protest Photography/http://www.flickr.com/photos/perspective/7096365867/http://creativecommons.org/licenses/by-sa/2.0/deed.en_GB/11Dec2012; **p.65** © Kimpin – Fotolia; **p.78** © Eléonore H – Fotolia; **p.79** © Thierry Hoarau – Fotolia; **p.100** © David Gee/Alamy; **p.105** © kornpoj – Fotolia; **p.106** © Micah Hanson/Alamy; **p.110** © Fancy/Alamy; **p.116** © GFC Collection/Alamy; **p.126** © RIA Novosti/TopFoto; **p.131** © andrey89 – Fotolia; **p.134** ©Allan Tannenbaum/The Image Works/TopFoto; **p.136** © Big Cheese Photo LLC/Alamy; **p.141** © Andy Chang – Fotolia; **p.144** © Igor Kali – Fotolia; **p.146** © Kristoffer Tripplaar/Alamy; **p.147** © artstudio_pro – Fotolia; **p.152** © David Pearson/Alamy; **p.160** © Shariff Che'Lah – Fotolia; **p.168** © dbimages/Alamy; **p.170** © wong yu liang – Fotolia; **p.180** © pressmaster – Fotolia; **p.183** © bst2012 – Fotolia; **p.184** © Paul Keevil/Actionplus/TopFoto; **p.202** © chungking – Fotolia; **p.205** © Lou-Foto/Alamy; **p.211** © Bark Fahnestock/Alamy; **p.215** © Cifotart – Fotolia; **p.220** ©Lilliput/Planet News/TopFoto; **p.225** © Tengku Mohd Yusof/Alamy; **p.229** © Asim Hafeez/Bloomberg via Getty Images; **p.233** © fkruger – Fotolia **p.236** © Borderlands/Alamy; **p.238** © liew0227 – Fotolia **p.252** © Asianet-Pakistan/Alamy; **p.269** © Eric Isselée – Fotolia

Text acknowledgements: Past examination questions reproduced by permission of Cambridge International Examinations.

Many of the UK data series shown in figures in this book were drawn from raw data obtained from the National Statistics website: *www.statistics.gov.uk*. Crown copyright material is reproduced with the permission of the Controller of HMSO.

Other raw data were from various sources, including OECD, World Bank, United Nations Development Programme and other sources as specified. The International Monetary Fund data was abstracted from their online database via the Economic and Social Data Service (www.esds.ac.uk). Data from the OECD is based on data from 'Government expenditure by function (COFOG)' http://stats.oecd.org/Index.aspx?DataSetCode=SNA_TABLE11 from OECD.StatExtracts http://stats.oecd.org/.

p.46 © Farmgate prices of milk USA; www.clal.it; 2 September 2009; **p.85** © *Annual Report 2007/2008*; Data from the Balance of Payments and Trade commentary; Central Bank of Swaziland; **p.109** © Diamonds Prices Fall in November; IDEX Online Research, International Diamond Exchange; http@//diafon.net/blog/?=475; 10 April 2009; **p.156** © adapted from an article by Judi Bevan, *Royal Society of Arts Journal*, pp.40–43, June 2005; **p.247** © *Wall Street Journal*, p.3, 15–17 June 2007; **p.248** *Financial Times* 12 June 2009. Table: *Economist,* p105, 18–24 April 2009; **p.270** Q1 Harold Goodwin; *Development Magazine*, Issue 27, 2004, Q3 © *The Guardian*, p.21, 6 September 2006; **p.271** Q4 *Developments*, p.25, Issue 38, Department for International Development 2007, Q6 © *The Times Business Section*; page 44–4; 1 November 2007

Every effort has been made to trace all copyright holders, but if any have been inadvertently overlooked the Publishers will be pleased to make the necessary arrangements at the first opportunity.

Introduction

This textbook provides an introduction to economics. It has been tailored explicitly to cover the content of the Cambridge International Examinations specification for AS and A Level Economics, module by module. The text provides the foundation for studying Cambridge Economics, but you will no doubt wish to keep up to date by referring to additional topical sources of information about economic events. This can be done by reading the serious newspapers, visiting key sites on the internet, and by reading such magazines as *Economic Review*.

The core content of the text follows closely the layout of the Cambridge syllabus.

The text features the following:

- a statement of the intended learning outcomes for each chapter
- clear and concise but comprehensive explanation and analysis of economic terms and concepts
- definitions of key terms
- examples to show these concepts applied to real world situations
- exercises to provide active engagement with economic analysis
- a selection of past examination questions.

Assessment objectives

In common with other economics specifications, Cambridge economics entails five assessment objectives. Candidates will thus be expected to:

- Demonstrate knowledge and understanding of the specified content.
- Interpret economic information presented in verbal, numerical or graphical form.
- Explain and analyse economic issues and arguments, using relevant economic concepts, theories and information.
- Evaluate economic information, arguments, proposals and policies, taking into consideration relevant information and theory, and distinguishing facts from hypothetical statements and value judgements.
- Organise, present and communicate economic ideas and informed judgements in a clear, logical and appropriate form.

(See the Cambridge Economics syllabus at *www.cie.org.uk.*)

Economics

Economics is different from many other A Level subjects in that relatively few students will have studied it before embarking on the AS course. The text thus begins from the beginning, and provides a thorough foundation in the subject and its applications. By studying this book, you should develop an awareness of the economist's approach to issues and problems, and the economist's way of thinking about the world.

Recent and historical data about the UK economy can be found at the website of the Office for National Statistics (ONS) at: *www.statistics.gov.uk*. Also helpful is the site of HM Treasury at: *www.hm-treasury.gov.uk.*

The Bank of England site is well worth a visit, especially the Inflation Report and the Minutes of the Monetary Policy Committee: *www.bankofengland.co.uk.*

The Institute for Fiscal Studies offers an independent view of a range of economic topics: *www.ifs.org.uk.*

For information about other countries, visit the following:

- www.oecd.org
- europa.eu
- www.worldbank.org
- www.undp.org

Individual countries also have national statistics websites that can provide useful data:

China	www.stats.gov.cn/english
Brunei Darussalam	www.depd.gov.bn/dept_dos.html
Malaysia	www.statistics.gov.my/portal/index.php?lang=en
Mauritius	www.gov.mu/portal/site/cso
Nepal	cbs.gov.np
New Zealand	www.stats.govt.nz
Pakistan	www.pbs.gov.pk
Zimbabwe	www.zimstat.co.zw

Another way of keeping up to date with economic topics and events is to read *Economic Review*, a magazine specifically written for A Level economics students, published by Philip Allan Updates.

How to study economics

There are two crucial aspects of studying economics. The first stage is to study the theory, which helps us to explain economic behaviour. However, in studying AS and A2 economics it is equally important to be able to apply the theories and concepts that you meet, and to see just how these relate to the real world.

If you are to become competent at this, it is vital that you get plenty of practice. In part, this means carrying out the exercises that you will find in this text. However, it also means thinking about how economics helps us to explain news items and data that appear in the newspapers and on the television. Make sure that you practise as much as you can.

In economics, it is also important to be able to produce examples of economic phenomena. In reading this text, you will find some examples that help to illustrate ideas and concepts. Do not rely solely on the examples provided here, but look around the world to find your own examples, and keep a note of these ready for use in essays and exams. This will help to convince the examiners that you have understood economics. It will also help you to understand the theories.

Enjoy economics

Most important of all, I hope you will enjoy your study of economics. I have always been fascinated by the subject, and hope that you will capture something of the excitement and challenge of learning about how markets and the economy operate. I also wish you every success with your AS/A Level studies.

Peter Smith

A new feature of the syllabus is Key concepts. These are the essential ideas, theories, principles or mental tools that help learners to develop a deep understanding of their subject, and make links between different topics. An icon indicates where each Key concept is covered:

Scarcity and choice
The fundamental problem in economics is that resources are scarce and wants are unlimited, so there is always a choice required between competing uses for the resources.

The margin and change
Decision-making by individuals, firms and governments is based on choices at the margin; that is, once behaviour has been optimised, any change will be detrimental as long as conditions remain the same.

Equilibrium and efficiency
Prices are set by markets, are always moving in to and out of equilibrium, and can be both efficient and inefficient in different ways and over different time periods.

Regulation and equity
There is a trade-off between freedom for firms and individuals in unregulated markets, and greater social equality and equity through the government regulation of individuals and markets.

Progress and development
Economics studies how societies can progress in measurable money terms and develop in a wider more normative sense.

1 Introducing economics

Welcome to economics. Many of you opening this book will be meeting economics for the first time, and you will want to know what is in store for you as you set out to study the subject. This opening chapter sets the scene by introducing you to some key ideas and identifying the scope of economic analysis. As you learn more of the subject, you will find that economics is a way of thinking that will broaden your perspective on the world around you.

Learning outcomes

This chapter will introduce you to:
- the nature and scope of economic analysis
- the importance of scarcity
- the concept of opportunity cost
- market, centrally planned and mixed economies
- the distinction between microeconomics and macroeconomics
- the notion of factors of production
- the role of models and assumptions in economics
- the production possibility curve
- the concept of the division of labour
- how specialisation can improve productivity
- the role of markets
- the importance of money and exchange in an economy
- positive and normative statements
- private goods and public goods
- merit goods and demerit goods.

1.1 The economic problem

The fundamental economic problem faced by any society in the world is that of **scarcity**. For countries in sub-Saharan Africa or parts of South Asia, it seems obvious that there is scarcity. However, it is also true of relatively prosperous economies such as those of Switzerland, the USA or the UK.

> **Key term**
>
> **Scarcity**: a situation that arises because people have unlimited wants in the face of limited resources.

It is true in the sense that all societies have *finite resources*, but people have *unlimited wants*. A big claim? Not really. There is no country in the world in which all wants can be met, and this is clearly true at the global level.

Talking about *scarcity* in this sense is not the same as talking about *poverty*. Poverty might be seen as an extreme form of scarcity, in which individuals lack the basic necessities of life – whereas even relatively prosperous people face scarcity because resources are limited.

Scarcity and choice

The key issue that arises from the existence of scarcity is that it forces people to make choices. Each individual must choose which goods and services to consume. In other words, everyone needs to prioritise the consumption of whatever commodities they need or would like to have, as they cannot satisfy all their wants. Similarly, at the national level, governments have to make choices between alternative uses of resources.

It is this need to choose that underlies the subject matter of economics. Economic analysis is about analysing those choices made by individual people, firms or governments.

Opportunity cost

This raises one of the most important concepts in all of economic analysis – the notion of **opportunity cost**. When an individual chooses to consume one good, he or she does so at the cost of the item that would have been next in their list of priorities. For example, suppose you have enough money in your pocket either for a can of cola or for a snack from a street vendor. If you choose the cola, the opportunity cost of the cola is the snack that you could have had instead. In other words, the opportunity cost is the value of the next-best alternative forgone.

Key term

Opportunity cost: in decision-making, the value of the next-best alternative forgone.

This important notion can be applied in many different contexts because, whenever you make a decision, you reject an alternative in favour of your chosen option. You have chosen to read this book, when instead you could be out with your friends.

Exercise 1.1

Abdul has just started his AS courses, and has chosen to take economics, mathematics, geography and French. Although he was certain about the first three, it was a close call between French and English. What is Abdul's opportunity cost of choosing French?

As you move further into studying economics, you will encounter the notion of opportunity cost again and again. For example, firms take decisions about the sort of economic activity in which to engage. A farmer with limited land available has to decide whether to plant onions or sweet potatoes; if he decides to grow onions, he has to forgo the opportunity to grow sweet potatoes. From the government's point of view, if it decides to devote more resources to the provision of healthcare, it will have fewer resources available for, say, defence.

If a farmer decides to grow sweet potatoes, he will have fewer resources available to grow onions

The coordination problem

With so many different individuals and organisations (consumers, firms, governments) all taking decisions, a major question is how it all comes together. How are all these separate decisions coordinated so that the overall allocation of resources in a society is coherent? In other words, how can it be ensured that firms produce the commodities that consumers wish to consume? And

how can the distribution of these products be organised? These are some of the basic questions that economics sets out to answer.

A **market economy** is one in which market forces are allowed to guide the allocation of resources within a society. Prices play a key role in this sort of system, providing signals and incentives to producers and consumers. Consumers express changes in their preferences by their decisions to buy (or not to buy) at the going price. This is then a signal to firms, which are able to respond to changes in consumer demand, given the incentive of profitability, which is related to price.

The government's role in a free market economy is limited, but nonetheless important. A basic framework of *property rights* is essential, together with a basic legal framework. However, the state does not intervene in the production process directly. Secure property rights are significant, as this assures the incentives for the owners of capital.

Within such a system, consumers try to maximise the satisfaction they gain from consuming a range of products, and firms seek to maximise their profits by responding to consumer demand through the medium of price signals.

In contrast, a **centrally planned economy** is one in which the government undertakes the coordination role, planning and directing the allocation of resources. Given the complexity of modern economies, reliance on central planning poses enormous logistical problems. In order to achieve a satisfactory allocation of resources across the economy, the government needs to make decisions on thousands of individual matters.

One example of this emerges from the experience of central planning in Russia after the Revolution. Factories were given production targets to fit in with the overall plan for the development of the economy. These targets then had to be met by the factory managers, who faced strong incentives to meet those targets. Factories producing nails were given two sorts of targets. Some factories were given a target to produce a certain number of nails, whereas others were given targets in weight terms. The former responded by producing large numbers of very small nails; the latter produced a very small number of very big nails. Neither were what the planners had in mind!

Micromanagement on this sort of scale proved costly to implement administratively. The collapse of the Soviet bloc in the 1990s largely discredited this approach, although a small number of countries (such as North Korea and Cuba) continue to stick with central planning. China moved away from pure central planning by beginning to allow prices to be used as signals.

Most economies now operate a **mixed economy** system, in which prices provide signals to firms and consumers, but in which the government intervene by providing market infrastructure and by influencing the allocation of resources by a pattern of taxes and expenditure and by regulation. As this course progresses, you will see a variety of ways in which such intervention takes place, and will come to understand the reasoning that underpins such intervention – especially in situations where the free market fails to produce the best possible allocation of resources.

It has been argued that any such state intervention should be *market-friendly*: in other words, when governments do intervene in the economy, they should do so in a way that helps markets to work, rather than trying to have the government replace market forces.

Key terms

Market economy: market forces are allowed to guide the allocation of resources within a society.

Centrally planned economy: decisions on resource allocation are guided by the state.

Mixed economy: resources are allocated partly through price signals and partly on the basis of direction by government.

The transition from a centrally planned economy to a mixed economy can be painful. This was seen in the initial break-up of the Soviet bloc, when countries in eastern Europe went through a difficult time both economically and politically. During the transition period, both firms and consumers need to become accustomed to the idea that they have increased freedom to make decisions, and that prices need to adjust and take a more active role in providing signals and incentives. People and firms needs to get used to the idea that they need to take risk, rather than depending on the State to take decisions for them. Governments need to move away from trying to micro-manage economic decision-making and allow market forces to take over the coordination role.

Decision-making at the margin

The notion of 'the margin' is important in much of economic analysis. Decision-makers – whether they be firms or consumers – are seen to take decisions with reference to small changes in behaviour. For example, a firm may decide whether to increase its output by an extra unit by checking whether the additional revenue that it would receive from selling the extra unit will compensate for the additional cost of producing it. A consumer may decide whether the extra benefit of consuming an additional can of cola is worth the price to be paid for it.

Notice that the timescale over which decisions are made is important. Firms and consumers may not be able to adjust their behaviour very much in the short run, as they may be committed to decisions already made. In the long run, they may be able to be more flexible – for example, firms can hire more labour and install new capital. In the very long run, whole industries and markets may be able to adjust.

Factors of production

People in a society play two quite different roles. On the one hand, they are the consumers, the ultimate beneficiaries of the process of production. On the other, they are a key part of the production process in that they are instrumental in producing goods and services.

More generally, it is clear that both *human resources* and *physical resources* are required as part of the production process. These productive resources are known as the **factors of production**.

Key term

Factors of production: resources used in the production process; *inputs* into production, including labour, capital, land and enterprise.

The most obvious human resource is *labour*. Labour is a key input into production. Of course, there are many different types of labour, encompassing different skill levels and working in different ways. *Enterprise* (or 'entrepreneurship') is another human resource that is seen as increasingly important in the economy. An entrepreneur is someone who organises production and identifies potentially profitable projects to be undertaken, bearing the risk of the activity. Enterprise provides dynamism and innovation in an economy, especially within the sector dominated by small and medium-sized firms. Many governments in countries around the world have looked for ways of encouraging an enterprise culture as a key component of a mixed economy.

Management is also sometimes classified as a human resource, although it might be seen as a particular form of labour. *Natural resources* are also inputs into the production process. In particular, all economic activities require some use of *land*, and most use some raw materials. An important distinction here is between *renewable resources* such as forests, and *non-renewable resources* such as oil or coal.

There are also *produced resources* – inputs that are the product of a previous manufacturing process. If you like, these can be regarded as a stock of past production used to aid current production. For example, machines are used in the production process; they are resources manufactured for the purpose of producing other goods. These inputs are referred to as *fixed capital*, which includes things like factory buildings and transport equipment as well as plant and machinery. Firms also need *working capital*, made up of goods that are used up during the production process.

The way in which these inputs are combined in order to produce output is another important part of the allocation of resources. Firms need to take decisions about the mix of inputs used in order to produce their output. Such decisions are required in whatever form of economic activity a firm is engaged.

When a worker supplies the factor of production labour, it is in return for wages, and the wage can be seen as the reward to labour. Similarly, rent is the reward for the supply of land, and profits are the reward to the owners of capital and the entrepreneurs that determine how the factors of production are used.

Exercise 1.2

Classify each of the following as human, natural (renewable or non-renewable) or produced resources:

a timber
b services of a window cleaner
c natural gas
d solar energy
e a combine harvester
f a computer programmer who sets up a company to market his software
g a computer

By now you should be getting some idea of the subject matter of economics. The US economist Paul Samuelson (who won the Nobel Prize for Economic Sciences in 1970) identified three key questions that economics sets out to investigate:

1 *What?* What goods and services should be produced in a society from its scarce resources? In other words, how should resources be allocated among producing DVD players, potatoes, banking services and so on?
2 *How?* How should the productive resources of the economy be used to produce these various goods and services?
3 *For whom?* Having produced a range of goods and services, how should these be allocated among the population for consumption?

Exercise 1.3

With which of Samuelson's three questions (what, how, for whom) would you associate the following?

a A firm chooses to switch from producing CD players in order to increase its output of DVD recorders.
b The government reduces the highest rate of income tax.
c Faced with increased labour costs, a firm introduces labour-saving machinery.
d There is an increase in social security benefits.
e The owner of a curry house decides to close down and take a job in a local factory.

Summary

- The fundamental problem faced by any society is scarcity, because resources are finite but wants are unlimited. As a result, choices need to be made.
- Each choice has an opportunity cost – the value of the next-best alternative.
- Decisions need to be coordinated within a society, either by market forces or by state intervention, or a mixture of the two.
- The amount of output produced in a period depends upon the inputs of factors of production.
- Economics deals with the questions of what should be produced, how it should be produced, and for whom.

1.2 The production possibility curve

Models and assumptions

Economics sets out to tackle some complex issues concerning what is a very complex real world. This complexity is such that it is essential to simplify reality in some way; otherwise the task would be overwhelming. Economists thus work with **models**. These are simplified versions of reality that are more tractable for analysis, allowing economists to focus on some key aspects of the world.

Key term

Model: a simplified representation of reality used to provide insight into economic decisions and events.

Often this works by allowing them to focus on one thing at a time. A model almost always begins with assumptions that help economists to simplify their questions. These assumptions can then be gradually relaxed so that the effect of each one of them can be observed. In this way, economists can gradually move towards a more complicated version of reality.

In evaluating a model, it is not a requirement that it be totally realistic. The model's desired objectives may be to predict future behaviour, or test empirical evidence collected from the real world. If a model provides insights into how individuals take decisions or helps to explain economic events, then it has some value, even if it seems remote from reality.

However, it is always important to examine the assumptions that are made, and to ask what happens if these assumptions do not hold.

Opportunity cost and the production possibility curve

Economists rely heavily on diagrams to help in their analysis. In exploring the notion of opportunity cost, a helpful diagram is the **production possibility curve** (*PPC*), also sometimes known as the production possibility frontier or the production transformation curve. This shows the maximum combinations of goods that can be produced with a given set of resources.

Key term

Production possibility curve: a curve showing the maximum combinations of goods or services that can be produced in a set period of time given available resources.

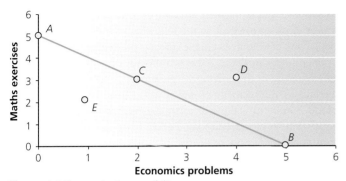

Figure 1.1 The production possibility curve

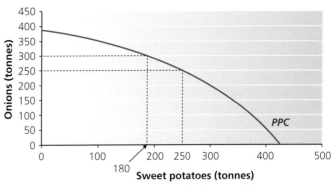

Figure 1.2 Opportunity cost and the production possibility curve

First consider a simple example. In Exercise 1.1, Abdul was studying for his AS. Suppose now that he has got behind with his homework. He has limited time available, and has five economics questions to answer and five maths exercises to do. An economics question takes the same time to answer as a maths exercise.

What are the options? Suppose he knows that in the time available he can either tackle all of the maths and none of the economics, or all of the economics and none of the maths. Alternatively, he can try to keep both teachers happy by doing some of each. Figure 1.1 shows his options.

He can devote all of his efforts to maths, and leave the economics for another day. He will then be at point *A* in the figure. Alternatively, he can do all the economics exercises and no maths, and be at point *B*. The line joining these two extreme points shows the intermediate possibilities. For example, at *C* he does two economics exercises and three maths problems.

The line shows the maximum combinations that Abdul can tackle – which is why it is sometimes called a 'frontier'. There is no way he can manage to be beyond the frontier (for example, at point *D*), as he does not have the time (i.e. resources) to do so. However, he could end up *inside* the frontier, at a point such as *E*. This could happen if he gives up, and squanders his time by watching television; that would be an inefficient use of his resources – at least in terms of tackling his homework.

As Abdul moves down the line from left to right, he is spending more time on economics and less on maths. The opportunity cost of tackling an additional economics question is an additional maths exercise forgone.

Figure 1.2 shows how the *PPC* provides information about opportunity cost. Suppose we have a farmer with 10 hectares of land who is choosing between growing sweet potatoes and onions. The *PPC* shows the combinations of the two crops that could be produced. For example, if the farmer produces 300 tonnes of onions on part of the land, then 180 tonnes of sweet potatoes could be produced from the remaining land. In order to increase production of potatoes by 70 tonnes from 180 to 250, 50 tonnes of onions must be given up. Thus, the opportunity cost of 70 extra tonnes of sweet potatoes is seen to be 50 tonnes of onions.

Consumption and investment

To move from thinking about an individual to thinking about an economy as a whole, it is first necessary to simplify reality. Assume that an economy produces just two types of good: capital goods and consumer goods. Capital goods are goods that are to be used to increase the future capacity of the economy. For example, you might think of machinery, trucks or factory buildings that will be used to produce other goods in the future. Expenditure on such goods is known as **investment**. In contrast, consumer goods are for present use. They are goods that people consume, such as apples, televisions or private cars. This sort of expenditure is known as **consumption**.

> ## Key terms
>
> **Investment**: expenditure undertaken by firms to add to the capital stock; an increase in the capital stock.
> **Consumption**: household spending on goods and services in the economy.

Figure 1.3 illustrates society's options in a particular period. Given the resources available, society can produce any combination of capital and consumer goods along the *PPC*. Thus,

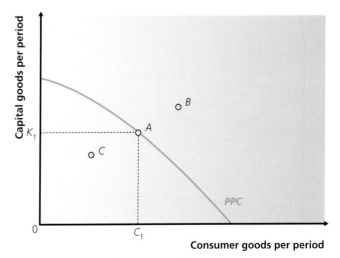

Figure 1.3 Capital and consumer goods

5

point *A* represents one possible combination of outputs, in which the economy produces C_1 consumer goods and K_1 capital goods.

As with the simpler examples, if society were to move to the right along the *PPC*, it would produce more consumer goods – but at the expense of capital goods. Thus, it can be seen that the opportunity cost of producing consumer goods is in terms of forgone opportunities to produce capital goods. Notice that the *PPC* has been drawn as a curve instead of a straight line. This is because not all factors of production are equally suited to the production of both sorts of good. When the economy is well balanced, as at *A*, the factors can be allocated to the uses for which they are best equipped. However, as the economy moves towards complete specialisation in one of the types of good, factors are no longer being best used, and the opportunity cost changes. For example, if nearly all of the workers are engaged in producing consumer goods, it becomes more difficult to produce still more of these, whereas those workers producing machinery find they have too few resources with which to work. In other words, the more consumer goods are being produced, the higher is their opportunity cost.

It is now possible to interpret points *B* and *C*. Point *B* is unreachable given present resources, so the economy cannot produce that combination of goods. This applies to any point outside the *PPC*. On the other hand, at point *C* society is not using its resources efficiently. In this position there is *unemployment* of some resources in the economy. By making better use of the resources available, the economy can move towards the frontier, reducing unemployment in the process.

Economic growth

Figure 1.2 focused on a single period. However, if the economy is producing capital goods, then in the following period its capacity to produce should increase, as it will have more resources available for production. How can this be shown on the diagram? An expansion in the available inputs suggests that in the next period the economy should be able to produce more of both goods. This is shown in Figure 1.4.

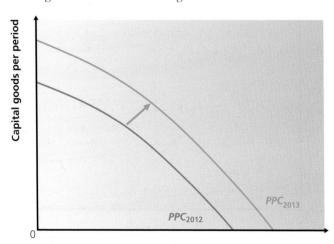

Figure 1.4 Economic growth

Suppose that in the year 2012 the production possibility curve was at PPC_{2012}. However, in the following year the increased availability of resources enables greater production, and the frontier moves to PPC_{2013}. This is a process of **economic growth**, an expansion of the economy's productive capacity through the increased availability of inputs. Notice that the decision to produce more capital goods today means that fewer consumer goods will be produced today. People must choose between consuming more now or having more to consume in the future.

> ### Key term
>
> **Economic growth**: an expansion in the productive capacity of the economy.

Total output in an economy

Remember that the *PPC* is a model: a much simplified version of reality. In a real economy there are many different goods and services produced by a wide range of different factors of production – but it is not possible to draw diagrams to show all of them. The total output of an economy is measured by its **gross domestic product (GDP)**.

> ### Key term
>
> **Gross domestic product (GDP)**: a measure of the economic activity carried out in an economy during a given time period.

> ### Exercise 1.4
>
>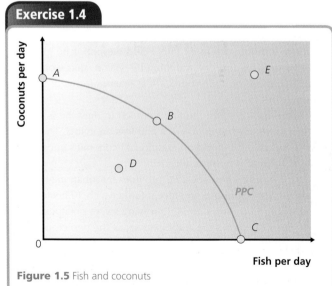
>
> **Figure 1.5** Fish and coconuts
>
> Bijal has been cast away on a desert island, and has to survive by spending her time either fishing or climbing trees to get coconuts. The *PPC* in Figure 1.5 shows the maximum combinations of fish and coconuts that she can gather during

a day. Which of the points *A* to *E* represents each of the following?

a A situation where Bijal spends all her time fishing.

b An unreachable position.

c A day when Bijal goes for a balanced diet – a mixture of coconuts and fish.

d A day when Bijal does not fancy fish, and spends all day collecting coconuts.

e A day when Bijal spends some of the time trying to attract the attention of a passing ship.

Summary

- The production possibility curve shows the maximum combinations of goods or services that can be produced in a period by a given set of resources.
- At any point on the *PPC*, society is making full use of all resources.
- At any point inside the *PPC*, there is unemployment of some resources.
- Points beyond the *PPC* are unattainable.
- In a simple society producing two goods (consumer goods and capital goods), the choice is between consumption and investment for the future.
- As society increases its stock of capital goods, the productive capacity of the economy increases, and the production possibility curve moves outwards: this may be termed 'economic growth'.

1.3 Some key economic ideas

Specialisation

How many workers does it take to make a pin? The eighteenth-century British economist Adam Smith figured that ten was about the right number. He argued that when a worker was producing pins on his own, carrying out all the various stages involved in the production process, the maximum number of pins that could be produced in one day was 20 – given the technology of his day, of course. This would imply that ten workers could produce about 200 pins if they worked in the same way as the lone worker. However, if the pin production process were broken into ten separate stages, with one worker specialising in each stage, the maximum production for a day's work would be a staggering 48 000. This is known as **division of labour**.

Key term

Division of labour: a process whereby the production procedure is broken down into a sequence of stages, and workers are assigned to particular stages.

The division of labour is effective because individual workers become skilled at performing specialised tasks. By focusing on a particular stage, they can become highly adept, and thus more efficient, at carrying out that task. In any case, people are not all the same, so some are better at certain activities. Furthermore, this specialisation is more efficient because workers do not spend time moving from one activity to another. Specialisation may also enable firms to operate on a larger scale of production. You will see later that this may be advantageous.

This can be seen in practice in many businesses today, where there is considerable specialisation of functions. Workers are hired for particular tasks and activities. You do not see Wayne Rooney pulling on the goalkeeper's jersey at half time because he fancies a change. Earlier in the chapter, it was argued that 'labour' is considered a factor of production. This idea will now be developed further by arguing that there are different types of labour, having different skills and functions.

Although we refer to the division of labour, we can extend these arguments to consider specialisation among firms, or even among nations. For example, consider car manufacturing. The process of mass producing cars does not all take place within a single firm. One firm may specialise in producing tyres; another may produce windscreens; another may focus on assembling the final product. Here again, specialisation enables efficiency gains to be made.

At national level, specialisation again takes place, simply because some countries are better equipped to produce some products than others. For example, it would not make sense for the UK to go into commercial production of pineapples, or mangoes. There are other countries with climatic conditions that are much more suitable for producing these products. On the other hand, most Formula 1 racing teams have their headquarters in the UK, and there are benefits from this specialisation.

The benefits from specialisation

Everyone is different. Individuals have different natural talents and abilities that make them good at different things. Indeed, there are some lucky people who seem to be good at everything.

Consider this example. Ali and Ayesha supplement their incomes by making pots and bracelets to sell at the market. Depending on how they divide their time, they can make differing combinations of these goods; some of the possibilities are shown in Table 1.1.

Table 1.1 Ali and Ayesha's production

Ali	
Pots	Bracelets
12	0
9	3
6	6
3	9
0	12
Ayesha	
Pots	Bracelets
18	0
12	12
6	24
3	30
0	36

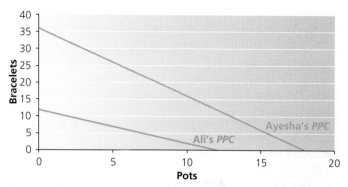

Figure 1.6 Ali and Ayesha's production possibilities

The first point to notice is that Ayesha is much better at both activities than Ali. If they each devote all their time to producing pots, Ali produces only 12 to Ayesha's 18. If they each produce only bracelets, Ali produces 12 and Ayesha, 36. There is another significant feature of this table. Although Ayesha is better at producing both goods, the difference is much more marked in the case of bracelet production than pot production. So Ayesha is relatively more proficient in bracelet production: in other words, she faces a lower opportunity cost in making bracelets. If Ayesha switches from producing pots to producing bracelets, she gives up 6 pots for every 12 additional bracelets that she makes. The opportunity cost of an additional bracelet is thus 6/12 = 0.5 pots. For Ali, there is a one-to-one trade-off between the two, so his opportunity cost of a bracelet is 1 pot.

More interesting is what happens if the same calculation is made for Ali and pot making. Although Ayesha is absolutely better at making pots, if Ali increases his production of pots, his opportunity cost in terms of bracelets is still 1. But for Ayesha the opportunity cost of making pots in terms of bracelets is 12/6 = 2, so Ali has the lower opportunity cost.

Why does this matter? It illustrates the potential benefits to be gained from specialisation. Suppose that both Ali and Ayesha divide their time between the two activities in such a way that Ali produces 6 pots and 6 bracelets, and Ayesha produces 6 pots and 24 bracelets. Between them, they will have produced 12 pots and 30 bracelets. However, if they each specialise in the product in which they face the lower opportunity cost, their joint production will increase. If Ali devotes all his time to pottery, he produces 12 pots, while Ayesha, focusing only on bracelets, produces 36. So between them they will have produced the same number of pots as before – but 6 extra bracelets.

One final point before leaving Ali and Ayesha: Figure 1.6 shows their respective production possibility curves. You can check this by graphing the points in Table 1.1 and joining them up. In this case the PPCs are straight lines. You can see that because Ayesha is better at both activities, her PPC lies entirely above Ali's. The differences in opportunity

cost are shown by the fact that the two *PPC*s have different slopes, as the opportunity cost element is related to the slope of the *PPC* – the rate at which one good is sacrificed for more of the other.

Although there may be many disadvantages that flow from specialisation, it is also important to realise that there may be a downside if individuals, firms or countries overspecialise. If Ali spends all of his time producing pots while Ayesha only produces bracelets, they may each get bored, and begin to lose concentration and job satisfaction. This may be even more of a danger in the case of Adam Smith's pin production. If workers find themselves carrying out the same task day after day, the tedium of it may lead them to become careless and inefficient.

If a firm focuses on production of a very narrow range of products and then finds that demand is falling for those products, then it will face difficulties. It may thus be advisable to maintain some diversity in the output range, in the hope that demand will not fall for all products simultaneously. Complete specialisation may not always be the best way for a firm to become successful in the long run.

Nations may also find problems if they overspecialise. For example, it could be argued that all nations should retain some agricultural activity for strategic reasons. If a nation were to be completely dependent on imported foodstuffs, and then became engage in a war, this could leave the country in a very vulnerable position. Indeed, this was one of the motivations for the establishment of what would become the European Union.

Markets

You will find that in economics the term **market** is used frequently, so it is important to be absolutely clear about what is meant by it.

> ## Key term
>
> **Market**: a set of arrangements that allows transactions to take place.

Adam Smith

A market need not be a physical location (although it could be – you might regard a village market as an example of 'a set of arrangements that allows transactions to take place'). With the growth of the internet, people are becoming accustomed to ways of buying and selling that do not involve direct physical contact between buyer and seller, so the notion of an abstract market should not be too alien a concept. In relation to a particular product, a market brings together potential buyers and sellers. This will be explored in the next chapter.

Markets are very important in the process of resource allocation, with prices acting as a key signal to potential buyers and sellers. If a firm finds that it cannot sell its output at the price it has chosen, this is a signal about the way that buyers perceive the product. Price is one way that firms find out about consumers and their willingness to pay for a particular product. This will be explored more carefully in Chapter 4.

Money and exchange

Imagine a world without money. It is lunchtime, and you fancy a banana. In your bag you have an apple. Perhaps you can find someone with a banana who fancies an apple? But the only person with a banana available fancies an ice cream. The problem with such a *barter economy* is that you need to find someone who wants what you have and who has what you want – a *double coincidence of wants*. If this problem were to be faced by a whole economic system, undertaking transactions would be so inefficient as to be impossible. Hence the importance of *money* as a *medium of exchange*.

In order to fulfil this role, money must be something that is acceptable to both buyers and sellers. Nobody would accept money in payment for goods or services if they did not trust that they could proceed to use money for further transactions. Money must thus also act as a *store of value*: it must be possible to use it for future transactions. This quality of money means that it can be used as one way of storing wealth for future purchases. Money also allows the value of goods, services and other assets to be compared – it provides a *unit of account*. In this sense, prices of goods reflect the value that society places on them, and must be expressed in money terms. Notice that money may be in the form of banknotes or coins, but other accepted methods of payments can also be classed as money. For example, a *cheque* drawn against a bank account becomes money if it is accepted as a means of payment.

A further role for money is that it acts as a *standard of deferred payment*. For example, a firm may wish to agree a contract for the future delivery of a good, or may wish to hire a worker to be paid at the end of the month. Such contracts are typically agreed in terms of a money value.

All of these *functions of money* are important to the smooth operation of markets, and are crucial if prices are to fulfil their role in allocating resources within society. This will become apparent as you learn more about economics.

Microeconomics and macroeconomics

The discussion so far has focused sometimes on individual decisions, and sometimes on the decisions of governments, or of 'society' as a whole. Economic thinking is applied in different ways, depending on whether the focus is on the decisions taken by individual agents in the economy or on the interaction between economic variables at the level of the whole economy.

Microeconomics deals with individual decisions taken by households or firms, or in particular markets.

Macroeconomics examines the interactions between economic variables at the level of the aggregate economy. For example, it might examine the effect of a change in income taxes on the level of unemployment, or of the interest rate on total demand and the rate of inflation.

In some ways the division between the two types of analysis is artificial. The same sort of economic reasoning is applied in both types, but the focus is different.

Key terms

Microeconomics: the study of economic decisions taken by individual economic agents, including households and firms.
Macroeconomics: the study of the interrelationships between economic variables at an aggregate (economy-wide) level.

Exercise 1.5

Think about the following, and see whether you think each represents a macroeconomic or microeconomic phenomenon.

a The overall level of prices in an economy.
b The price of ice cream.
c The overall rate of unemployment in an economy.
d The unemployment rate amongst catering workers in Karachi.
e The average wage paid to construction workers in Kuala Lumpur.

Positive and normative statements

Economics tries to be objective in analysis. However, some of its subject matter requires careful attention in order to retain an objective distance. In this connection, it is important to be clear about the difference between **positive** and **normative statements**.

Key terms

Positive statement: a statement about what *is*, i.e. about *facts*.
Normative statement: a statement about what *ought to be*.

In short, a positive statement is about *facts*. In contrast, a normative statement is about *what ought to be*. Another way of looking at this is that a statement becomes normative when it involves a *value judgement*.

Suppose the government is considering raising the tax on cigarettes. It may legitimately consult economists to discover what effect a higher tobacco tax will have on the consumption of cigarettes and on government revenues. This would be a *positive* investigation, in that the economists are being asked to use economic analysis to forecast what will happen when the tax is increased.

A very different situation will arise if the government asks whether it *should* raise the tax on cigarettes. This moves the economists beyond positive analysis because it entails a value judgement – so it is now a *normative* analysis. There are some words that betray normative statements, such as 'should' or 'ought to' – watch for these.

Most of this book is about positive economics. However, you should be aware that positive analysis is often called upon to inform normative judgements. If the aim of a policy is to stop people from smoking (which reflects a normative judgement about what *ought* to happen), then economic analysis may be used to highlight the strengths and weaknesses of alternative policy measures in a purely positive fashion.

Critics of economics often joke that economists always disagree with one another: for example, it has been said that if you put five economists in a room together, they will come up with at least six conflicting opinions. However, although

economists may arrive at different value judgements, and thus have differences when it comes to normative issues, there is much greater agreement when it comes to positive analysis.

Summary

- Adam Smith introduced the notion of division of labour, which suggests that workers can become more productive by specialising in stages of the production process.
- Specialisation opens up the possibility of trade.
- The gains from specialisation and trade result from differences in opportunity cost.
- A market is a set of arrangements that allows transactions to take place.
- A barter economy is a highly inefficient way of conducting transactions; hence the importance of money in enabling exchange to take place.
- Money plays key roles as a medium of exchange, a store of value, a unit of account, and a standard of deferred payment.
- By fulfilling these various roles, money enables the smooth operation of markets, and allows prices to act as a guide in allocating resources.
- Microeconomics deals with individual decisions made by consumers and producers, whereas macroeconomics analyses the interactions between economic variables in the aggregate – but both use similar ways of thinking.
- Positive statements are about what *is*, whereas normative statements are about what *ought to be*.

1.4 Types of goods and services

Private goods

Most of the goods that individuals consume are **private goods,** sometimes known as economic goods. You buy a can of cola, you drink it, and it's gone. You may choose to share it with a friend, but you do not have to: by drinking it you can prevent anyone else from doing so. Furthermore, once it is gone, it's gone: nobody else can subsequently consume that cola.

The two features that characterise a private good are:

- other people can be excluded from consuming it
- once consumed by one person, it cannot be consumed by another.

The first feature can be described as *excludability*, whereas the second feature might be described by saying that consumption of a private good is *rivalrous*: the act of consumption uses up the good.

Public goods

Not all goods and services have these two characteristics. There are goods that, once provided, are available to all. In other words, people cannot be excluded from consuming such goods. There are other goods that do not diminish through consumption, so they are non-rivalrous in consumption. Goods that have the characteristics of *non-excludability* and *non-rivalry* are known as **public goods**.

> ## Key terms
>
> **Private good**: a good that, once consumed by one person, cannot be consumed by somebody else; such a good has excludability and is rivalrous.
>
> **Public good**: a good that is non-exclusive and non-rivalrous – consumers cannot be excluded from consuming the good, and consumption by one person does not affect the amount of the good available for others to consume.

Examples of public goods that are often cited include street lighting, a lighthouse and a nuclear deterrent. For example, once street lighting has been provided in a particular street, anyone who walks along that street at night benefits from the lighting – no one can be excluded from consuming it. So street lighting is non-exclusive. In addition, the fact that one person has walked along the street does not mean that there is less street lighting left for later walkers. So street lighting is also non-rivalrous.

The key feature of such a market is that, once the good has been provided, there is no incentive for anyone to pay for it – so the market will fail, as no firm will have an incentive to supply the good in the first place. This is often referred to as the **free-rider problem**, as individual consumers can free-ride and avoid having to pay for the good if it is provided.

> ## Key term
>
> **Free-rider problem**: when an individual cannot be excluded from consuming a good, and thus has no incentive to pay for its provision.

> ## Exercise 1.6
>
> For each of the following goods, think about whether they have elements of non-rivalry, non-excludability, both or neither:
>
> **a** a national park
> **b** a playground
> **c** a theatre performance
> **d** an apple
> **e** a television programme
> **f** a firework display
> **g** police protection
> **h** a lecture
> **i** a DVD recording of a film
> **j** the national defence

Merit goods

There are some goods that the government believes will be undervalued by consumers, so that too little will be consumed in a free market. In other words, individuals do not fully perceive the benefits that they will gain from consuming such goods. These are known as **merit goods**.

> ## Key term
>
> **Merit good**: a good that brings unanticipated benefits to consumers, such that society believes that it will be under-consumed in a free market.

One situation in which the merit good phenomenon arises is where the government is in a better position than individuals to take a long-term view of what is good for society. In particular, governments may need to take decisions on behalf of future generations as well as the present. Resources need to be used wisely in the present in order to protect the interests of tomorrow's citizens. Notice that this may require decision-makers to make normative judgements about the appropriate weighting to be given to the present as opposed to the future.

There is a strong political element involved in identifying the goods that should be regarded as merit goods: this is because there is a subjective or normative judgement involved, since declaring a good to be a merit good requires the decision-maker to make a choice on behalf of the population, which may be seen as being paternalistic.

At the heart of the notion of a merit good, therefore, is the notion that consumers have imperfect information.

Demerit goods

There is also a category of goods that governments think will be over-consumed in a free market. These are known as **demerit goods** – or sometimes as 'merit bads'. Obvious examples are hard drugs and tobacco. Here the argument is that individual consumers overvalue the benefits from consuming such a good.

> ## Key term
>
> **Demerit good:** a good that brings less benefit to consumers than they expect, such that too much will be consumed by individuals in a free market.

Summary

- A private good is one that, once consumed by one person, cannot be consumed by anyone else – it has characteristics of excludability and rivalry.

- A public good is non-exclusive and non-rivalrous.

- Because of these characteristics, public goods tend to be underprovided by a free market.

- One reason for this is the free-rider problem, whereby an individual cannot be excluded from consuming a public good, and thus has no incentive to pay for it.

- A merit good is one that society believes should be consumed by individuals whether or not they have the means or the willingness to do so.

- There is a strong normative element in the identification of merit goods.

- Demerit goods (or 'merit bads') are goods that society believes should not be consumed by individuals even if they wish to do so.

- In the case of merit and demerit goods, 'society' (as represented by government) believes that it has better information than consumers about these goods, and about what is good (or bad) for consumers.

Examination questions

1 a Explain how division of labour can affect labour productivity. [8]

  b Discuss how the operation of a barter economy would be affected by the introduction of money. [12]

Cambridge AS and A Level Economics 9708, Paper 21, Q2, June 2010

2 a Explain the functions of an economic system. [8]

  b Discuss possible reasons why mixed economic systems have replaced most of the former planned economic systems. [12]

Cambridge AS and A Level Economics 9708, Paper 21, Q2, June 2011

2 The nature of demand

The demand and supply model is perhaps the most famous of all pieces of economic analysis; it is also one of the most useful. It has many applications that help explain the way markets work in the real world. It is thus central to understanding economics. This chapter introduces the 'demand' side of the model. Chapter 3 will introduce supply. Chapter 4 brings demand and supply together to analyse market equilibrium.

Learning outcomes

After studying this chapter, you should:

- be familiar with the notion of the demand for a good or service
- be aware of the relationship between the demand for a good and its price
- be familiar with the demand curve and the law of demand
- understand the distinction between a movement along the demand curve and a shift in its position
- be aware of the distinction between normal and inferior goods
- understand the other influences that affect the position of the demand curve.

2.1 The demand curve

Individual demand

Consider an individual consumer. Think of yourself, and a product that you consume regularly. What factors influence your **demand** for that product? Put another way, what factors influence how much of the product you choose to buy?

> **Key term**
>
> **Demand**: the quantity of a good or service that consumers choose to buy at any possible price in a given period.

When thinking about the factors that influence your demand for your chosen product, common sense will probably mean that you focus on a range of different points. You may think about why you enjoy consuming the product. You may focus on how much it will cost to buy the product, and whether you can afford it. You may decide that you have consumed a product so much that you are ready for a change; or perhaps you will decide to try something advertised on TV, or being bought by a friend.

Whatever the influences you come up with, they can probably be categorised under four headings that ultimately determine your demand for a good. First, the *price* of the good is an important influence on your demand for it, and will affect the quantity of it that you choose to buy. Second, your *income* will determine how much of the good you can afford to purchase. Third, the *price of other goods* may be significant. Finally, almost any other factor that you may have thought of can be listed as part of your *preferences*. Notice that however much you like a particular product, your effective demand is constrained by the prices of goods and the income that you have to devote to it. This reflects the notion of scarcity that was introduced in Chapter 1, and also applies across the whole market for a good.

This common-sense reasoning provides the basis for the economic analysis of demand. You will find that a lot of economic analysis begins in this way, by finding a way to construct a model that is rooted in how we expect people or firms to behave.

Market demand

A similar line of argument may apply if we think in terms of the demand for a particular product – say, DVDs. The market for DVDs can thus be seen as bringing together all the potential buyers (and sellers) of the product, and market demand can be analysed in terms of the factors that influence all potential buyers of that good or service. In other words, market demand can be seen as the total quantity of a good or service that all potential buyers would choose to buy at any given price. The same four factors that influence your own individual decision to buy will also influence the total market demand for a product. In addition, the number of potential buyers in the market will clearly influence the size of total demand at any price.

Demand and the price of a good

Assume for the moment that the influences mentioned above, other than the price of the good, are held constant, so that the focus is only on the extent to which the price of a good influences the demand for it. This is a common assumption in economics, which is sometimes expressed by the Latin phrase **ceteris paribus**, meaning 'other things being equal'. Given the complexity of the real world, it is often helpful to focus on one thing at a time.

Key term

Ceteris paribus: a Latin phrase meaning 'other things being equal'; it is used in economics when we focus on changes in one variable while holding other influences constant.

This ceteris paribus assumption is used a lot in economics, and is a powerful tool. Focusing on one influence at a time is a way of coping with the complexities of the real world and makes the analysis of economic issues much clearer than if we try to analyse everything at once. You will see many instances of it as the course proceeds.

So how is the demand for DVDs influenced by their price? Other things being equal (ceteris paribus), you would expect the demand for DVDs to be higher when the price is low and lower when the price is high. In other words, you would expect an inverse relationship between the price and the quantity demanded. This is such a strong phenomenon that it is referred to as the **law of demand**. It is one of a small number of 'laws' in economics – in other words, it is always expected to hold true.

If you were to compile a list that showed how many DVDs would be bought at any possible price and plot these on a diagram, this would be called the **demand curve**. Figure 2.1 shows what this might look like. As it is an inverse relationship, the demand curve slopes downwards. Notice that this need not be a straight line: its shape depends upon how consumers react at different prices. According to this curve, if price were to be set at $40, the quantity demanded would be 20 000 per period. However, if the price were only $20, the demand would be higher, at 60 000.

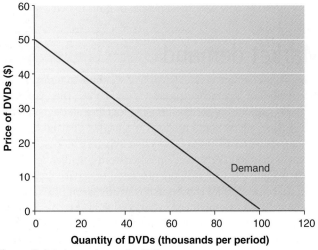

Figure 2.1 A demand curve for DVDs

Exercise 2.1

Table 2.1 shows how the demand for oojits varies with their price. Draw the demand curve.

Table 2.1 The demand for oojits

Price	Quantity
100	0
90	3
80	7
70	15
60	25
50	40
40	60
30	85
20	120

Key terms

Law of demand: a law that states that there is an inverse relationship between quantity demanded and the price of a good or service, ceteris paribus.

Demand curve: a graph showing how much of a good will be demanded by consumers at any given price.

Extension: income and substitution effects

An analysis of why the demand curve should be downward sloping would reveal that there are two important forces at work. At a higher price, a consumer buying a DVD has less income left over. This is referred to as the *real income effect* of a price increase. In addition, if the price of DVDs goes up, consumers may find other goods more attractive and choose to buy something else instead of DVDs. This is referred to as the *substitution effect* of a price increase.

As the price of a good changes, a movement along the demand curve can be observed as consumers adjust their buying pattern in response to the price change.

Notice that the demand curve has been drawn under the ceteris paribus assumption. In other words, it was assumed that all other influences on demand were held constant in order to focus on the relationship between demand and price. There are two important implications of this procedure.

First, the price drawn on the vertical axis of a diagram such as Figure 2.1 is the *relative* price – it is the price of DVDs under the assumption that all other prices are constant.

Second, if any of the other influences on demand change, you would expect to see a shift of the whole demand curve. It is very important to distinguish between factors that induce a movement *along* a curve, and factors that induce a shift *of* a curve. This applies not only in the case of the demand curve – there are many other instances where this is important.

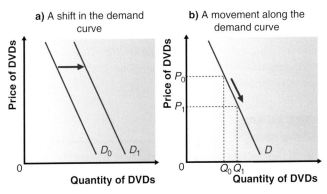

Figure 2.2 A shift in the demand curve and a movement along it

The two parts of Figure 2.2 show this difference. In part **a**, the demand curve has shifted to the right because of a change in one of the factors that influences demand. In part **b**, the price of DVDs falls from P_0 to P_1, inducing a movement along the demand curve as demand expands from Q_0 to Q_1.

Snob effects

It is sometimes argued that for some goods a 'snob effect' may lead to the demand curve sloping upwards. The argument is that some people may value certain goods more highly simply because their price is high, especially if they know that other people will observe them consuming these goods; an example might be Rolex watches. In other words, people gain value from having other people notice that they are rich enough to afford to consume a particular good. There is thus a *conspicuous consumption* effect, which was first pointed out by Thorstein Veblen at the end of the nineteenth century.

However, although there may be some individual consumers who react to price in this way, there is no evidence to suggest that there are whole markets that display an upward-sloping demand curve for this reason. In other words, most consumers would react normally to the price of such goods.

Summary

- The market demand for a good depends upon the price of the good, the price of other goods, consumers' incomes and preferences and the number of potential consumers.
- The demand curve shows the relationship between demand for a product and its price, ceteris paribus.
- The demand curve is downward sloping, as the relationship between demand and price is an inverse one.

2.2 The determinants of demand

Demand and consumer incomes

The second influence on demand is consumer incomes. For a **normal good**, an increase in consumer incomes will, ceteris paribus, lead to an increase in the quantity demanded at any given price. Foreign holidays are an example of a normal good because, as people's incomes rise, they will tend to demand more foreign holidays at any given price.

Figure 2.3 illustrates this. D_0 here represents the initial demand curve for foreign holidays. An increase in consumers' incomes causes demand to be higher at any given price, and the demand curve shifts to the right – to D_1.

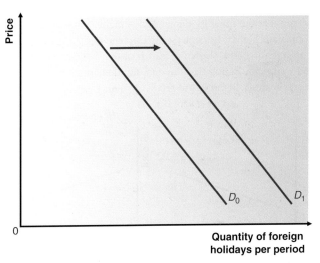

Figure 2.3 A shift in the demand curve following an increase in consumer incomes (a normal good)

However, demand does not always respond in this way. For example, think about bus journeys. As incomes rise in a society, more people can afford to have a car, or to use taxis. This means that, as incomes rise, the demand for bus journeys may tend to fall. Such goods are known as **inferior goods**.

Key terms

Normal good: one where the quantity demanded increases in response to an increase in consumer incomes.

Inferior good: one where the quantity demanded decreases in response to an increase in consumer incomes.

This time an increase in consumers' incomes in Figure 2.4 causes the demand curve to shift to the left, from its initial position at D_0, to D_1 where less is demanded at any given price.

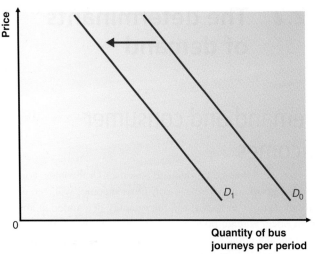

Figure 2.4 A shift in the demand curve following an increase in consumer incomes (an inferior good)

The relationship between quantity demanded and income can be shown more directly on a diagram. Part **a** of Figure 2.5 shows how this would look for a normal good. It is upward sloping, showing that the quantity demanded is higher when consumer incomes are higher. In contrast, the income demand curve for an inferior good, shown in part **b** of the diagram, slopes downwards, indicating that the quantity demanded will be lower when consumer incomes are relatively high.

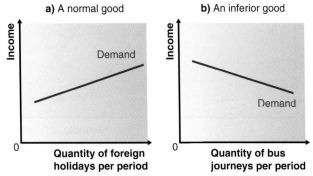

Figure 2.5 Demand and income

Extension: Giffen goods

Remember that a consumer's response to a change in the price of a good is made up of a substitution effect and a real income effect (see the extension point on page 14). The substitution effect always acts in the opposite direction to the price change: in other words, an increase in the price of a good always induces a switch *away* from the good towards other goods. However, it can now be seen that the real income effect may operate in either direction, depending on whether it is a normal good or an inferior good that is being considered.

Suppose there is a good that is *very* inferior. A fall in the price of a good induces a substitution effect towards the good, but the real income effect works in the opposite direction.

The fall in price is equivalent to a rise in real income, so consumers will consume less of the good. If this effect is really strong, it could overwhelm the substitution effect, and the fall in price could induce a *fall* in the quantity demanded: in other words, for such a good the demand curve could be upward sloping.

Such goods are known as *Giffen goods*, after Sir Robert Giffen, who pointed out that this could happen. However, in spite of stories about the reaction of demand to a rise in the price of potatoes during the great Irish potato famine, there have been no authenticated sightings of Giffen goods. The notion remains a theoretical curiosity.

Exercise 2.2

Identify each of the following products as being either a normal good or an inferior good:

a digital camera
b magazine
c potatoes
d bicycle
e new car
f second-hand car

Demand and the price of other goods

The demand for a good may respond to changes in the price of other related goods, of which there are two main types. On the one hand, two goods may be **substitutes** for each other. For example, consider two different (but similar) breakfast cereals. If there is an increase in the price of one of the cereals, consumers may switch their consumption to the other, as the two are likely to be close substitutes for each other. Not all consumers will switch, of course – some may be deeply committed to one particular brand – but some of them are certainly likely to change over.

On the other hand, there may also be goods that are **complements** – for example, products that are consumed jointly, such as breakfast cereals and milk, or cars and petrol. Here a fall in the price of one good may lead to an increase in demand for *both* products.

Key terms

Substitutes: two goods are said to be substitutes if consumers regard them as alternatives, so that the demand for one good is likely to rise if the price of the other good rises.

Complements: two goods are said to be complements if people tend to consume them jointly, so that an increase in the price of one good causes the demand for the other good to fall.

Whether goods are substitutes or complements determines how the demand for one good responds to a change in the price of another. Figure 2.6 shows the demand curves (per period) for two goods that are substitutes – tea and coffee.

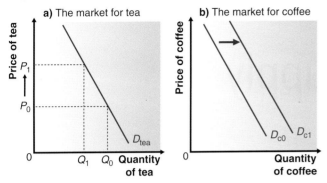

Figure 2.6 A shift in the demand curve following an increase in the price of a substitute good

If there is an increase in the price of tea from P_0 to P_1 in part **a**, more consumers will switch to coffee and the demand curve in part **b** will shift to the right – say, from D_{c0} to D_{c1}.

For complements the situation is the reverse: in Figure 2.7 an increase in the price of tea from P_0 to P_1 in part **a** causes the demand curve for milk to shift leftwards, from D_{m0} to D_{m1}.

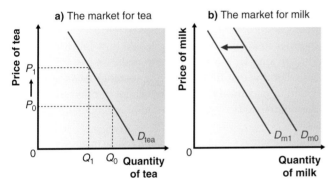

Figure 2.7 A shift in the demand curve following an increase in the price of a complementary good

Demand, consumer preferences and other influences

The discussion has shown how the demand for a good is influenced by the price of the good, the price of other goods, and by consumer incomes. It was stated earlier that almost everything else that determines demand for a good can be represented as 'consumer preferences'. In particular, this refers to whether you like or dislike a good. There may be many things that influence whether you like or dislike a product. In part it simply depends upon your own personal inclinations – some people like dark chocolate, others prefer milk chocolate. However, firms may try to influence your preferences through advertising, and sometimes they succeed. Or you might be one of those people who get so irritated by television advertising that you compile a blacklist of products that you will never buy! Even this is an influence on your demand.

In some cases your preferences may be swayed by other people's demand – again, this may be positive or negative.

Fashions may influence demand, but some people like to buck (or lead) the trend.

You may also see a movement of the demand curve if there is a sudden surge in the popularity of a good – or, indeed, a sudden collapse in demand.

Exercise 2.3

Sketch some demand curves for the following situations, and think about how you would expect the demand curve to change (if at all).

a The demand for chocolate following a campaign highlighting the dangers of obesity.
b The demand for oranges following an increase in the price of apples.
c The demand for oranges following a decrease in the price of oranges.
d The demand for DVDs following a decrease in the price of DVD players.
e The demand for simple mobile phones following a decrease in the price of smartphones.
f The demand for private transport following an increase in consumer incomes.
g The demand for public transport following an increase in consumer incomes.

The above discussion has covered most of the factors that influence the demand for a good. However, in some cases it is necessary to take a time element into account. Not all of the goods bought are consumed instantly. In some cases, consumption is spread over long periods of time. Indeed, there may be instances where goods are not bought for consumption at all, but are seen by the buyer as an investment, perhaps for resale at a later date. In these circumstances, expectations about future price changes may be relevant. For example, people may buy antiques or works of art in the expectation that prices will rise in the future. There may also be goods whose prices are expected to fall in the future. This has been common with many hi-tech products; initially a newly launched product may sell at a high price, but as production levels rise, costs may fall, and prices also. People may therefore delay purchase in the expectation of future price reductions.

Summary

- A change in price induces a movement along the demand curve, whereas a change in the other determinants of demand induces a shift of the demand curve.
- When the demand for a good rises as consumer incomes rise, that good is referred to as a normal good; when demand falls as income rises, the good is referred to as an inferior good.
- A good or service may be related to other goods by being either a substitute or a complement.
- For some products, demand may be related to expected future prices.

3 The nature of supply

The previous chapter introduced you to the demand curve. The other key component of the demand and supply model is, of course, supply. For any market transaction, there are two parties: buyers and sellers. The question to be considered in this chapter is what determines the quantity that sellers will wish to supply to the market.

Learning outcomes

After studying this chapter, you should:
- be familiar with the notion of the supply of a good or service
- be aware of the relationship between the supply of a good and its price in a competitive market
- understand what is meant by the supply curve and the factors that influence its shape and position
- be able to distinguish between shifts *of* the supply curve and movements *along* it
- be aware of the effect of taxes and subsidies on the supply curve.

3.1 The supply curve

In discussing demand, the focus of attention was on consumers, and on their willingness to pay for goods and services. In thinking about supply, attention switches to firms, as it is firms that take decisions about how much output to supply to the market. It is important at the outset to be clear about what is meant by a 'firm'. A **firm** exists to organise production: it brings together various factors of production, and organises the production process in order to produce output.

> ### Key term
> **Firm**: an organisation that brings together factors of production in order to produce output.

The organisation of a firm can take various forms. A firm could be a *sole proprietor*: probably a small business such as a newsagent where the owner of the firm also runs the firm. A firm could be a *partnership* – for example, a dental practice in which profits (and debts) are shared between the partners in the business. Larger firms may be organised as private or public *joint-stock companies*, owned by shareholders. The difference between private and public joint-stock companies is that the shares of a public joint-stock company are traded on the stock exchange, whereas this is not the case with the private company.

In order to analyse how firms decide how much of a product to supply, it is necessary to make an assumption about what it is that firms are trying to achieve. Assume that they aim to maximise their profits, where 'profits' are defined as the difference between a firm's total revenue and its total costs.

As discussed in Chapter 2, the demand curve shows a relationship between quantity demanded and the price of a good or service. A similar relationship between the quantity supplied by firms and the price of a good can be identified in relation to the behaviour of firms in a **competitive market** – that is, a market in which individual firms cannot influence the price of the good or service that they are selling, because of competition from other firms.

> ### Key term
> **Competitive market**: a market in which individual firms cannot influence the price of the good or service they are selling, because of competition from other firms.

In such a market it may well be supposed that firms will be prepared to supply more goods at a high price than at a lower one (ceteris paribus), as this will increase their profits. The **supply curve** illustrates how much the firms in a market will supply at any given price, as shown in Figure 3.1. As firms are expected to supply more goods at a high price than at a lower price, the supply curve will be upward sloping, reflecting this positive relationship between quantity and price.

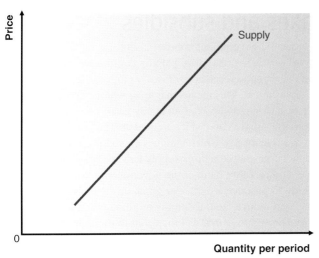

Figure 3.1 A supply curve

Key term

Supply curve: a graph showing the quantity supplied at any given price.

Exercise 3.1

Table 3.1 shows how the supply of oojits varies with their price. Draw the supply curve.

Table 3.1 The supply of oojits

Price	Quantity
100	98
90	95
80	91
70	86
60	80
50	70
40	60
30	50
20	35
30	18

Notice that the focus of the supply curve is on the relationship between quantity supplied and the price of a good in a given period, ceteris paribus – that is, holding other things constant. As with the demand curve, there are other factors affecting the quantity supplied. These other influences on supply will determine the position of the supply curve: if any of them changes, the supply curve can be expected to shift.

Summary

- Other things being equal, firms in a competitive market can be expected to supply more output at a higher price.
- The supply curve traces out this positive relationship between price and quantity supplied.

3.2 The determinants of supply

We can identify five important influences on the quantity that firms will be prepared to supply to the market at any given price:

- production costs
- the technology of production
- taxes and subsidies
- the price of related goods
- firms' expectations about future prices.

Costs and technology

If firms are aiming to maximise profits, an important influence on their supply decision will be the costs of production that they face. Chapter 1 explained that in order to produce output, firms need to use inputs of the factors of production – labour, capital, land, etc. If the cost of those inputs increases, firms will in general be expected to supply less output at any given price. The effect of this is shown in Figure 3.2, where an increase in production costs induces firms to supply less output at each

Improved technology, such as digital textile printing, means firms can reduce their production costs

price. The curve shifts from its initial position at S_0 to a new position at S_1. For example, suppose the original price was $10 per unit; before the increase in costs, firms would have been prepared to supply 100 units of the product to the market. An increase in costs of $6 per unit that shifted the supply curve from S_0 to S_1 would mean that, at the same price, firms would now supply only 50 units of the good. Notice that the vertical distance between S_0 and S_1 is the amount of the change in cost per unit.

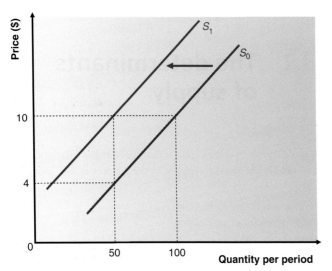

Figure 3.2 The supply curve shifts to the left if production costs increase

In contrast, if a new technology of production is introduced, which means that firms can produce more cost effectively, this could have the opposite effect, shifting the supply curve to the right. This is shown in Figure 3.3, where improved technology induces firms to supply more output at any given price, and the supply curve shifts from its initial position at S_0 to a new position at S_1. Thus, if firms in the initial situation were supplying 50 units with the price at $10 per unit, then a fall in costs of $6 per unit would induce firms to increase supply to 100 units (if the price remained at $10).

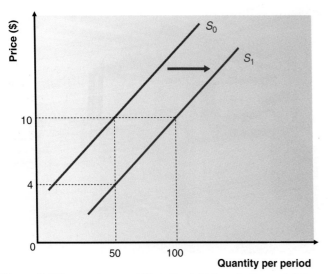

Figure 3.3 The supply curve shifts to the right if production costs fall

Taxes and subsidies

Suppose the government imposes a sales tax such as VAT on a good or service. The price paid by consumers will be higher than the revenue received by firms, as the tax has to be paid to the government. This means that firms will (ceteris paribus) be prepared to supply less output at any given market price. Again, the supply curve shifts to the left. This is shown in part **a** of Figure 3.4, which assumes a fixed per unit tax. The supply curve shifts, as firms supply less at any given market price. On the other hand, if the government pays firms a subsidy to produce a particular good, this will reduce their costs, and induce them to supply more output at any given price. The supply curve will then shift to the right, as shown in part **b**.

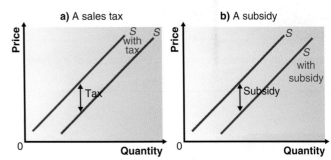

Figure 3.4 The effects of taxes and subsidies on supply

Prices of other goods

It was shown earlier that from the consumers' perspective, two goods may be substitutes for each other, such that if the price of one good increases, consumers may be induced to switch their consumption to substitute goods. Similarly, there may be substitution on the supply side. A firm may face a situation in which there are alternative uses to which its factors of production may be put: in other words, it may be able to choose between producing a range of different products. A rise in the price of a good raises its profitability, and therefore may encourage a firm to switch production from other goods. This may happen even if there are high switching costs, provided the increase in price is sufficiently large. For example, a change in relative prices of sweet potatoes and onions might encourage a farmer to stop planting sweet potatoes and grow onions instead.

In other circumstances, a firm may produce a range of goods jointly. Perhaps one good is a by-product of the production process of another. An increase in the price of one of the goods may mean that the firm will produce more of both goods. This notion of joint supply is similar to the situation on the demand side where consumers regard two goods as complements.

Expected prices

Because production takes time, firms often take decisions about how much to supply on the basis of expected future prices. Indeed, if their product is one that can be stored, there may be times when a firm will decide to allow stocks of a product to build up in anticipation of a higher price in the future, perhaps by holding back some of its production from current sales.

In some economic activities, expectations about future prices are crucial in taking supply decisions because of the length of time needed in order to increase output. For example, a firm producing palm oil, rubber or mangoes needs to be aware that newly planted trees will take several years to mature before they are able to yield their product.

Newly planted fruit trees, like those in this plantation in Thailand, take years to mature before they are able to yield their product

Movements along and shifts of the supply curve

As with the demand curve, it is very important to remember that there is a distinction between movements *along* the supply curve, and shifts *of* the supply curve. If there is a change in the market price, this induces a movement along the supply curve. After all, the supply curve is designed to reveal how firms will react to a change in the price of the good. For example, in Figure 3.5, if the price is initially at P_0 firms will be prepared to supply the quantity Q_0, but if the price then increases to P_1 this will induce a movement along the supply curve as firms increase supply to Q_1.

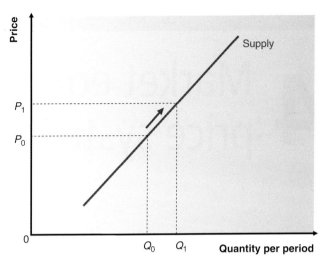

Figure 3.5 A movement along a supply curve in response to a price change

In contrast, as seen in the previous section, a change in any of the other influences on supply will induce a shift of the whole supply curve, as this affects the firms' willingness to supply at any given price.

Exercise 3.2

For each of the following, decide whether the demand curve or the supply curve will move, and in which direction.

a Consumers are convinced by arguments about the benefits of organic vegetables.
b A new process is developed that reduces the amount of inputs that firms need in order to produce bicycles.
c There is a severe frost in Brazil that affects the coffee crop.
d The government increases the rate of value added tax.
e Real incomes rise.
f The price of tea falls: what happens in the market for coffee?
g The price of sugar falls: what happens in the market for coffee?

Summary

- Changes in the costs of production, technology, taxes and subsidies or the prices of related goods may induce shifts of the supply curve, with firms being prepared to sell more (or less) output at any given price.
- Expectations about future prices may affect current supply decisions.

4 Market equilibrium and the price system

The previous chapters introduced the notions of demand and supply, and it is now time to bring the demand and supply curves together in order to meet the key concept of market equilibrium. The model can then be further developed to see how it provides insights into how markets operate. You will encounter demand and supply in a wide variety of contexts, and begin to glimpse some of the ways in which the model can help to explain how the economic world works.

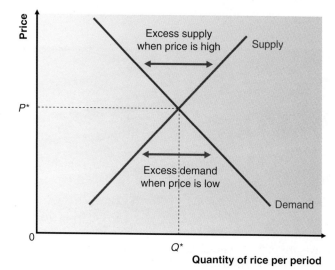

Figure 4.1 Bringing demand and supply together

Learning outcomes

After studying this chapter, you should:

- understand the notion of equilibrium and its relevance in the demand and supply model
- be aware of what is meant by comparative static analysis
- understand the concept of elasticity measures and appreciate their importance and applications
- have an overview of how the price mechanism works to allocate resources
- understand the meaning and significance of consumer surplus
- be able to see how prices provide incentives to producers
- understand the meaning and significance of producer surplus.

4.1 Market equilibrium

The previous chapters in this section have described the components of the demand and supply model. It only remains to bring them together, for this is how the power of the model can be appreciated. Figure 4.1 shows the demand for and supply of rice.

Suppose that the price were to be set at a relatively high price (above P^*). At such a price, firms wish to supply lots of rice to the market. However, consumers are not very keen on rice

at such a high price, so demand is not strong. Firms now have a problem: they find that their stocks of rice are building up. What has happened is that the price has been set at a level that exceeds the value that most consumers place on rice, so they will not buy it. There is *excess supply*. The only thing that the firms can do is to reduce the price in order to clear their stocks.

Suppose they now set their price relatively low (below P^*). Now it is the consumers who have a problem, because they would like to buy more rice at the low price than firms are prepared to supply. There is *excess demand*. Some consumers may offer to pay more than the going price in order to obtain their rice supplies, and firms realise that they can raise the price.

How will it all end? When the price settles at P^* in Figure 4.1, there is a balance in the market between the quantity that consumers wish to demand and the quantity that firms wish to supply, namely Q^*. This is the **market equilibrium**. In a free market, the price can be expected to converge on this equilibrium level, through movements along both demand and supply curves.

Key term

Market equilibrium: a situation that occurs in a market when the price is such that the quantity that consumers wish to buy is exactly balanced by the quantity that firms wish to supply.

Exercise 4.1

Identify the equilibrium market price if demand and supply are as in Figure 4.2.

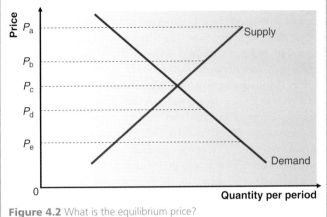

Figure 4.2 What is the equilibrium price?

Summary

- Bringing demand and supply together, you can identify the market equilibrium.
- The equilibrium price is the unique point at which the quantity demanded by consumers is just balanced by the quantity that firms wish to supply.
- In a free market, natural forces can be expected to encourage prices to adjust to the equilibrium level.

4.2 Examples of markets

The markets that have been discussed so far are product markets, such as the market for DVDs, tea or rice. However, the model is much more widely applicable than this, as is shown by the examples that follow.

Tea picking in China

The labour market

Within the economy, firms demand labour and employees supply labour – so why not use demand and supply to analyse the market? This can indeed be done.

From the firms' point of view, the demand for labour is a *derived demand*. In other words, firms want labour not for its own sake, but for the output that it produces. When the 'price' of labour is low, firms will tend to demand more of it than when the 'price' of labour is high. The wage rate can be regarded as this 'price' of labour. On the employee side, it is argued that more people tend to offer themselves for work when the wage is relatively high.

On this basis, the demand for labour is expected to be downward sloping and the supply of labour upward sloping, as in Figure 4.3.

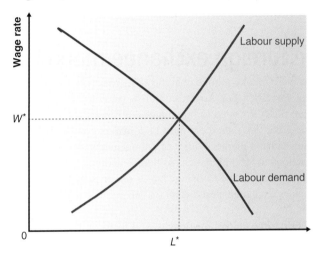

Figure 4.3 A labour market

As usual, the equilibrium in a free market will be at the intersection of demand and supply, so firms will hire L^* labour at a wage rate of W^*.

The consequences of such a market being away from equilibrium are important. Consider Figure 4.4.

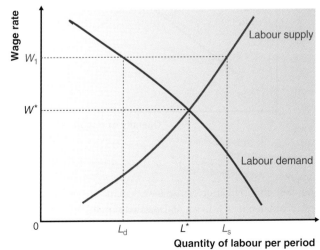

Figure 4.4 A labour market out of equilibrium

Suppose the wage rate is set above the equilibrium level at W_1. The high wage rate encourages more people to offer themselves for work – up to the amount of labour L_s. However, at this wage rate employers are prepared to hire only up to L_d labour. Think about what is happening here. There are people offering themselves for work who cannot find employment: in other words, there is **unemployment**. Thus, one possible cause of unemployment is a wage rate that is set above the equilibrium level.

Key term

Unemployment: results when people seeking work at the going wage cannot find a job.

The foreign exchange market

If you were to take a holiday in the USA, you would need to buy dollars. Equally, when American tourists travel to visit Malaysia or Mauritius, they need to buy ringgits or rupees. If there is buying going on, then there must be a market – remember from Chapter 1 that a market is a set of arrangements that enable transactions to be undertaken. So here is another sort of market to be considered. The exchange rate is the price at which two currencies exchange, and it can be analysed using demand and supply.

Consider the market for ringgits, and focus on the exchange rate between ringgits and dollars, as shown in Figure 4.5.

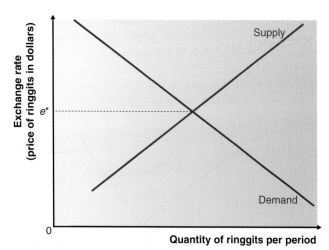

Figure 4.5 The market for ringgits

Think first about what gives rise to a demand for ringgits. It is not just Americans who visit Malaysia who need dollars to spend on holiday: anyone holding dollars who wants to buy Malaysian goods needs ringgits in order to pay for them. So the demand for ringgits comes from people outside Malaysia who want to buy Malaysian goods or services – or, indeed, assets. When the exchange rate for ringgits in terms of dollars is high, potential buyers of American goods get relatively few ringgits per dollar, so the demand will be relatively low, whereas if the dollar per ringgit rate is relatively low, they get more for their money. Hence the demand curve is expected to be downward sloping.

One point to notice from this is that foreign exchange is another example of a derived demand, in the sense that people want ringgits not for their own sake, but for the goods or services that they can buy. One way of viewing the exchange rate is as a means by which to learn about the international competitiveness of exports from the USA. When the exchange rate (dollars per ringgit) is high, Malaysian goods are less competitive in the USA, ceteris paribus. Notice the ceteris paribus assumption here. This is important because the exchange rate is not the only determinant of the competitiveness of Malaysian goods: this also depends on the relative price levels in Malaysia and the USA.

How about the supply of ringgits? Ringgits are supplied by Malaysians wanting dollars to buy goods or services from the USA. From this point of view, when the dollar/ringgit rate is high, Malaysia residents get more dollars for their ringgits and therefore will tend to supply more ringgits.

If the exchange market is in equilibrium, the exchange rate will be at e^*, where the demand for ringgits is matched by the supply.

The money market

Chapter 1 highlighted the importance of money in enabling exchange to take place through the operation of markets. This implies that people have a demand for money. This **demand for money** is associated with the functions of money set out on pages 8–9 – as a medium of exchange, store of value, unit of account and standard of deferred payment. If there is a demand for money, then perhaps there should also be a market for money?

We can think of the demand for money depending on a number of factors – in particular, upon the number of transactions that people wish to undertake, which probably depends upon income. But is there a price of money? The price of money can be viewed in terms of opportunity cost. When people choose to hold money, they incur an opportunity cost, which can be seen as the next best alternative to holding money. For example, instead of holding money, you could decide to purchase a financial asset that would provide a rate of return, represented by the rate of interest. This rate of interest can thus be interpreted as the price of holding money.

How about the supply of money? This will be discussed much later in the course, but for now, it can be assumed that the supply of money is determined by the central bank, and it can be assumed that this money supply will not depend upon the rate of interest. Figure 4.6 illustrates the market for money.

The demand for money is shown to be downward sloping, as the higher the rate of interest, the greater the return that is

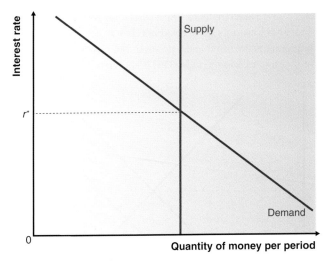

Figure 4.6 The market for money

sacrificed by holding money, so the smaller will be the demand for money. The supply of money does not depend upon the rate of interest (by assumption), so is shown as a vertical line. The market is in equilibrium when the rate of interest is at r^*, the level at which the demand and supply of money are equal.

Summary

- In the labour market, equilibrium is achieved through the wage rate. If the wage rate is set too high, it leads to unemployment.
- Demand and supply enable you to examine how the foreign exchange rate is determined.
- The model can also be applied to analyse the money market.

4.3 Comparative statics

In order to make good use of the demand and supply model, it is necessary to introduce another of the economist's key tools – comparative static analysis. You have seen the way in which a market moves towards equilibrium between demand and supply through price adjustments and movements along the demand and supply curves. This is called static analysis, in the sense that a ceteris paribus assumption is imposed by holding constant the factors that influence demand and supply, and focusing on the way in which the market reaches equilibrium.

In the next stage, one of these background factors is changed, and the effect of this change on the market equilibrium is then analysed. In other words, beginning with a market in equilibrium, one of the factors affecting either demand or supply

is altered, and the new market equilibrium is then studied. In this way, two static equilibrium positions – before and after – will be compared. This approach is known as **comparative static analysis**.

Key term

Comparative static analysis: examines the effect on equilibrium of a change in the external conditions affecting a market.

A market for dried noodles

Begin with a simple market for dried noodles, a basic staple foodstuff that is widely obtainable. Figure 4.7 shows the market in equilibrium.

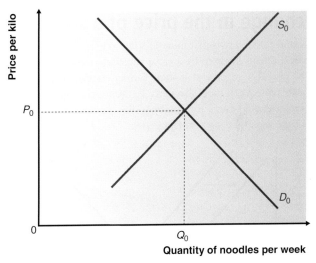

Figure 4.7 A market for noodles

D_0 represents the demand curve in this initial situation, and S_0 is the supply curve. The market is in equilibrium with the price at P_0, and the quantity being traded is Q_0. It is equilibrium in the sense that noodles producers are supplying just the amount of noodles that consumers wish to buy at that price. This is the 'before' position. Some experiments will now be carried out with this market by disturbing the equilibrium.

A change in consumer preferences

Suppose that a study is published highlighting the health benefits of eating noodles, backed up with an advertising campaign. The effect of this is likely to be an increase in the demand for noodles at any given price. In other words, this change in consumer preferences will shift the demand curve to the right, as shown in Figure 4.8.

The market now adjusts to a new equilibrium, with a new price P_1, and a new quantity traded at Q_1. In this case, both price and quantity have increased as a result of the change in preferences.

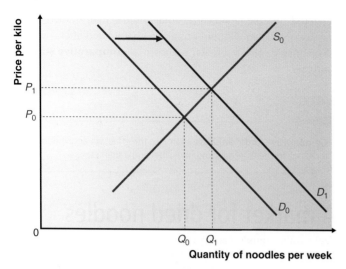

Figure 4.8 A change in consumer preferences for noodles

A change in the price of a substitute

A second possibility is that there is a fall in the price of fresh noodles. This is likely to be a close substitute for dried noodles, so the probable result is that some former consumers of dried noodles will switch their allegiance to the fresh variety. This time the demand curve for dried noodles moves in the opposite direction, as can be seen in Figure 4.9.

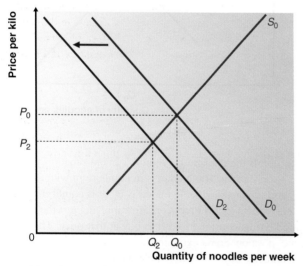

Figure 4.9 A change in the price of a substitute for dried noodles

Here the starting point is the original position, with market equilibrium at price P_0 and a quantity traded of Q_0. After the shift in the demand curve from D_0 to D_2, the market settles again with a price of P_2 and a quantity traded of Q_2. Both price and quantity traded are now lower than in the original position.

An improvement in noodles technology

Next, suppose that a new noodles-making machine is produced, enabling dried noodles makers to produce at a lower cost than

before. This advance reduces firms' costs, and consequently they are prepared to supply more dried noodles at any given price. The starting point is the same initial position, but now it is the supply curve that moves – to the right. This is shown in Figure 4.10.

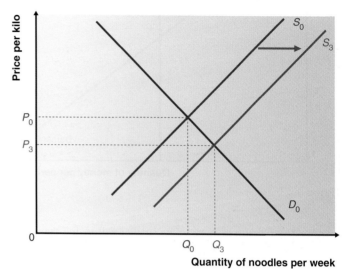

Figure 4.10 New noodles-making technology

Again, comparative static analysis can be undertaken. The new market equilibrium is at price P_3, which is lower than the original equilibrium, but the quantity traded is higher at Q_3.

An increase in labour costs

Finally, suppose that noodles producers face an increase in their labour costs. Perhaps the Noodle Workers' Union has negotiated higher wages, or the noodles producers have become subject to stricter health and safety legislation, which raises their production costs. Figure 4.11 starts as usual with equilibrium at price P_0 and quantity Q_0.

The increase in production costs means that noodles producers are prepared to supply fewer dried noodles at any

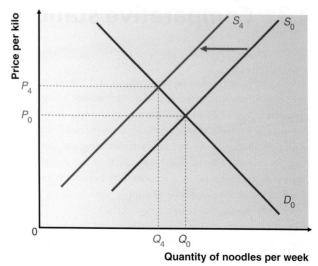

Figure 4.11 An increase in labour costs

given price, so the supply curve shifts to the left – to S_4. This takes the market to a new equilibrium at a higher price than before (P_4), but with a lower quantity traded (Q_4).

Exercise 4.2

For each of the following market situations, sketch a demand and supply diagram, and undertake a comparative static analysis to see what happens to the equilibrium price and quantity. Explain your answers.

a An increase in consumer incomes affects the demand for bus travel.

b New regulations on environmental pollution force a firm making paint to increase outlay on reducing its emission of toxic fumes.

c A firm of accountants brings in new, faster computers, which have the effect of reducing the firm's costs.

d An outbreak of bird flu causes consumers of chicken to buy burgers instead. (What is the effect on both markets?)

Exercise 4.3

Profits and superships

In August 2001 the *Financial Times* reported that ship-owners were facing serious problems. Shipping rates (the prices that ship-owners charge for carrying freight) had fallen drastically in the second quarter of 2001. For example, on the Europe–Asia route, rates fell by 8% eastbound and 6% westbound, causing the ship-owners' profits to be squeezed. Here are some relevant facts and issues:

- New 'superships', having been ordered a few years earlier, were coming into service with enhanced capacity for transporting freight.
- A worldwide economic slowdown was taking place; Japan was in lengthy recession and the US economy was also slowing, affecting the growth of world trade.
- Fuel prices were falling.
- The structure of the industry was fragmented, with ship-owners watching each other's orders for new ships.
- New ships take a long time to build.
- Shipping lines face high fixed costs with slender margins.

Assume that this is a competitive market. (This will allow you to draw supply and demand curves for the market.) There is some evidence for this, as shipping lines face 'slender margins' (see the last point above). This suggests that the firms face competition from each other, and are unable to use market power to increase profit margins.

a How would you expect the demand and supply curves to move in response to the first three factors listed? Sketch a diagram for yourself.

b Why should the shipping lines undertake a large-scale expansion at a time of falling or stagnant demand?

Summary

- Comparative static analysis enables you to analyse the way in which markets respond to external shocks, by comparing market equilibrium before and after a shock.
- All you need to do is to figure out whether the shock affects demand or supply, and in which direction.
- The size and direction of the movements of the demand and supply curves determine the overall effect on equilibrium price and quantity traded.

4.4 Elasticity: the sensitivity of demand and supply

Both the demand for and the supply of a good or service can be expected to depend upon its price as well as other factors. It is often interesting to know just how sensitive demand and/or supply will be to a change in either price or one of the other determinants – for example, in predicting how market equilibrium will change in response to a change in the market environment. The sensitivity of demand or supply to a change in one of its determining factors can be measured by its **elasticity**.

The price elasticity of demand

The most common elasticity measure is the **price elasticity of demand (PED)**. This measures the sensitivity of the quantity demanded of a good or service to a change in its price. The elasticity is defined as the percentage change in quantity demanded divided by the percentage change in the price.

We define the percentage change in price as $100 \times \Delta P/P$ (where Δ means 'change in' and P stands for 'price'). Similarly, the percentage change in quantity demanded is $100 \times \Delta Q/Q$.

Key terms

Elasticity: a measure of the sensitivity of one variable to changes in another variable.

Price elasticity of demand (PED): a measure of the sensitivity of quantity demanded to a change in the price of a good or service. It is measured as:

$$\frac{\% \text{ change in quantity demanded}}{\% \text{ change in price}}$$

When the demand is highly price sensitive, the percentage change in quantity demanded following a price change will be large relative to the percentage change in price. In this case,

PED will take on a value that is numerically greater than 1. For example, suppose that a 2% change in price leads to a 5% reduction in quantity demanded; the elasticity is then −5 divided by 2 = −2.5. When the elasticity is numerically greater than 1, demand is referred to as being *price elastic*.

There are two important things to notice about this. First, because the demand curve is downward sloping, the elasticity will always be negative. This is because the changes in price and quantity are always in the opposite direction. Second, you should try to calculate the elasticity only for a relatively small change in price, as it becomes unreliable for very large changes.

When demand is not very sensitive to price, the percentage change in quantity demanded will be smaller than the original percentage change in price, and the elasticity will then be numerically less than 1. For example, if a 2% change in price leads to a 1% reduction in quantity demanded, then the value of the elasticity will be −1 divided by 2 = −0.5. In this case, demand is referred to as being *price inelastic*.

An example

Figure 4.12 shows a demand curve for pencils. When the price of a pencil is 40c, the quantity demanded will be 20. If the price falls to 35c, the quantity demanded will rise to 30. The percentage change in quantity is 100 × 10/20 = 50 and the percentage change in price is 100 × −5/40 = −12.5. Thus, the elasticity can be calculated as (50/−12.5) = −4. At this price, demand is highly price elastic.

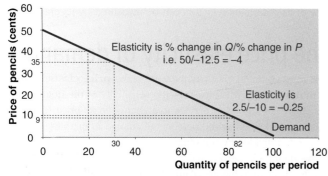

Figure 4.12 A demand curve for pencils

At a lower price, the result is quite different. Suppose that the price is initially 10c, at which price the quantity demanded is 80. If the price falls to 9c, demand increases to 82. The percentage change in quantity is now 100 × 2/80 = 2.5, and the percentage change in price is 100 × −1/10 = −10, so the elasticity is calculated as 2.5/−10 = −0.25, and demand is now price inelastic.

This phenomenon is true for any straight-line demand curve: in other words, demand is price elastic at higher prices and inelastic at lower prices. At the halfway point the elasticity is exactly −1, which is referred to as *unit elasticity*.

Why should this happen? The key is to remember that elasticity is defined in terms of the percentage changes in price and quantity. Thus, when price is relatively high, a 1c change in price is a small percentage change, and the percentage change

in quantity is relatively large – because when price is relatively high, the initial quantity is relatively low. The reverse is the case when price is relatively low. Figure 4.13 shows how the elasticity of demand varies along a straight-line demand curve.

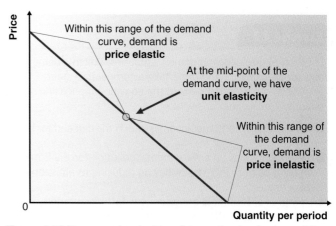

Figure 4.13 The own-price elasticity of demand varies along a straight line

Demand curves need not always be straight lines, of course. For example, a demand curve could be drawn such that there was unitary elasticity at every point – such a curve would be a *rectangular hyperbola*.

The price elasticity of demand and total revenue

One reason why firms may have an interest in the price elasticity of demand is that, if they are considering changing their prices, they will be eager to know the extent to which demand will be affected. For example, they may want to know how a change in price will affect their total revenue. As it happens there is a consistent relationship between the price elasticity of demand and total revenue.

Total revenue is given by price multiplied by quantity. In Figure 4.14, if price is at P_0, quantity demanded is at Q_0 and total revenue is given by the area of the rectangle OP_0AQ_0. If price

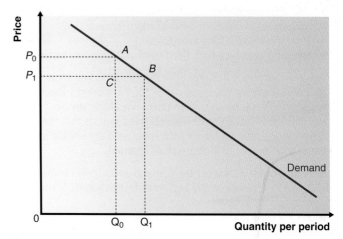

Figure 4.14 Demand and total revenue

falls to P_1 the quantity demanded rises to Q_1, and you can see that total revenue has increased, as it is now given by the area OP_1BQ_1. This is larger than at price P_1, because in moving from P_0 to P_1 the area P_1P_0AC is lost, but the area Q_0CBQ_1 is gained, and the latter is the larger. As you move down the demand curve, total revenue at first increases like this, but then decreases – try sketching this for yourself to check that it is so.

For the case of a straight-line demand curve, the relationship is illustrated in Figure 4.15.

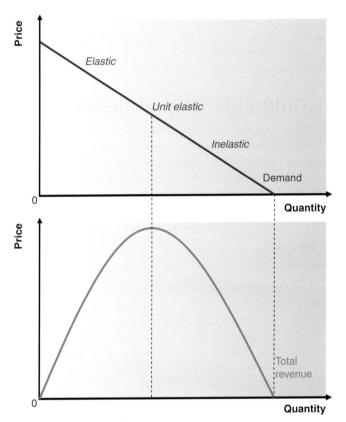

Figure 4.15 Elasticity and total revenue

Remember that demand is price elastic when price is relatively high. This is the range of the demand curve in which total revenue rises as price falls. This makes sense, as in this range the quantity demanded is sensitive to a change in price and increases by more (in percentage terms) than the price falls. This implies that, as you move to the right in this segment, total revenue rises. The increase in quantity sold more than compensates for the fall in price. However, when the mid-point is reached and demand becomes unit elastic, total revenue stops rising – it is at its maximum at this point. The remaining part of the curve is inelastic: that is, the increase in quantity demanded is no longer sufficient to compensate for the decrease in price, and total revenue falls. Table 4.1 summarises the situation.

Thus, if a firm is aware of the price elasticity of demand for its product, it can anticipate consumer response to its price changes, which may be a powerful strategic tool.

Table 4.1 Total revenue, elasticity and a price change

Price elasticity of demand	For a price increase, total revenue …	For a price decrease, total revenue …
Elastic	falls	rises
Unit elastic	does not change	does not change
Inelastic	rises	falls

One very important point must be made here. If the price elasticity of demand varies along a straight-line demand curve, such a curve cannot be referred to as either elastic or inelastic. To do so is to confuse the elasticity with the *slope* of the demand curve. It is not only the steepness of the demand curve that determines the elasticity, but also the point on the curve at which the elasticity is measured.

Two extreme cases of the price elasticity of demand should also be mentioned. Demand may sometimes be totally insensitive to price, so that the same quantity will be demanded whatever price is set for it. In such a situation, demand is said to be *perfectly inelastic*. The demand curve in this case is vertical – as in D_i in Figure 4.16. In this situation, the numerical value of the price elasticity is zero, as quantity demanded does not change in response to a change in the price of the good.

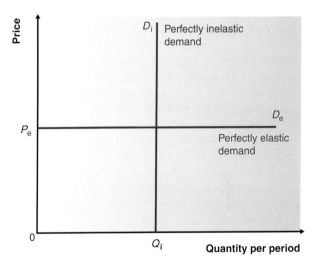

Figure 4.16 Perfectly elastic and inelastic demand

The other extreme is shown on the same figure, where D_e is a horizontal demand curve and demand is *perfectly elastic*. The numerical value of the elasticity here is infinity. Consumers demand an unlimited quantity of the good at price P_e. No firm has any incentive to lower price below this level, but if price were to rise above P_e, demand would fall to zero.

An example

A study carried out in Pakistan found that the price elasticity of demand for household electricity was -0.63. This means that demand for electricity was inelastic. If the price of electricity were to increase by 10%, there would be a fall of just 6.3% in the quantity of electricity demanded.

Influences on the price elasticity of demand

A number of important influences on the price elasticity of demand can now be identified. The most important is the availability of substitutes for the good or service under consideration. For example, think about the demand for cauliflower. Cauliflower and broccoli are often seen as being very similar, so if the price of cauliflower is high one week, people might quite readily switch to broccoli. The demand for cauliflower can be said to be price sensitive (elastic), as consumers can readily substitute an alternative product. On the other hand, if the prices of all vegetables rise, demand will not change very much, as there are no substitutes for vegetables in the diet. Thus, goods that have close substitutes available will tend to exhibit elastic demand, whereas the demand for goods for which there are no substitutes will tend to be more inelastic.

Associated with this is the question of whether an individual regards a good or service as a necessity or as a luxury item. If a good is a necessity, then demand for it will tend to be inelastic, whereas if a good is regarded as a luxury, consumers will tend to be more price-sensitive. This is closely related to the question of substitutes, as by labelling a good as a necessity, one is essentially saying that there are no substitutes for it.

A second influence on the price elasticity of demand is the relative share of the good or service in overall expenditure. You may tend not to notice small changes in the price of an inexpensive item that is a small part of overall expenditure, such as salt. This tends to mean that demand for that good is relatively inelastic. On the other hand, an item that figures large in the household budget will be seen very differently, and consumers will tend to be much more sensitive to price when a significant proportion of their income is involved.

Finally, the time period under consideration may be important. Consumers may respond more strongly to a price change in the long run than to one in the short run. An increase in the price of petrol may have limited effects in the short run; however, in the long run, consumers may buy smaller cars or switch to diesel. Thus, the elasticity of demand tends to be more elastic in the long run than in the short run. Habit or commitment to a certain pattern of consumption may dictate the short-run pattern of consumption, but people do eventually adjust to price changes.

Exercise 4.4

Examine Table 4.2, which shows the demand for tomato ketchup at different prices.

a Draw the demand curve.
b Calculate the price elasticity of demand when the initial price is $4.

Table 4.2 Demand for tomato ketchup

Price ($)	Quantity demanded (bottles per week)
5	20
4	40
3	60
2	80
1	100

c Calculate the price elasticity of demand when the initial price is $3.
d Calculate the price elasticity of demand when the initial price is $2.

Income elasticity of demand

Elasticity is a measure of the sensitivity of a variable to changes in another variable. In the same way as the price elasticity of demand is determined, an elasticity measure can be calculated for any other influence on demand or supply. **Income elasticity of demand (YED)** is therefore defined as:

$$YED = \frac{\% \text{ change in quantity demanded}}{\% \text{ change in consumer income}}$$

Key term

Income elasticity of demand (YED): a measure of the sensitivity of quantity demanded to a change in consumer incomes.

Unlike the price elasticity of demand, the income elasticity of demand may be either positive or negative. Remember the distinction between normal and inferior goods? For normal goods the quantity demanded will increase as consumer income rises, whereas for inferior goods the quantity demanded will tend to fall as income rises. Thus, for normal goods the YED will be positive, whereas for inferior goods it will be negative.

Suppose you discover that the YED for magazines is +0.7. How do you interpret this number? If consumer incomes were to increase by 10%, the demand for magazines would increase by $10 \times 0.7 = 7\%$. This example of a normal good may be helpful information for newsvendors, if they know that consumer incomes are rising over time.

On the other hand, if the YED for coach travel is −0.3, that means that a 10% increase in consumer incomes will lead to a 3% fall in the demand for coach travel – perhaps because more people are travelling by car. In this instance, coach travel would be regarded as an inferior good.

In some cases the YED may be very strongly positive. For example, suppose that the YED for digital cameras is +2. This implies that the quantity demanded of such cameras will increase by 20% for every 10% increase in incomes. An increase in income is encouraging people to devote more of their incomes to this product, which increases its share in total expenditure. Such goods are referred to as **luxury goods**.

Key term

Luxury good: one for which the income elasticity of demand is positive, and greater than 1, such that as income rises, consumers spend proportionally more on the good.

Cross elasticity of demand

Another useful measure is the **cross elasticity of demand (XED)**. This is helpful in revealing the interrelationships between goods. Again, this measure may be either positive or negative, depending on the relationship between the goods. It is defined as:

$$XED = \frac{\%\text{ change in quantity demanded of good X}}{\%\text{ change in price of good Y}}$$

Key term

Cross-price elasticity of demand (XED): a measure of the sensitivity of quantity demanded of a good or service to a change in the price of some other good or service.

If the *XED* is seen to be positive, it means that an increase in the price of good Y leads to an increase in the quantity demanded of good X. For example, an increase in the price of apples may lead to an increase in the demand for pears. Here apples and pears are regarded as substitutes for each other; if one becomes relatively more expensive, consumers will switch to the other. A high value for the *XED* indicates that two goods are very close substitutes. This information may be useful in helping a firm to identify its close competitors.

On the other hand, if an increase in the price of one good leads to a fall in the quantity demanded of another good, this suggests that they are likely to be complements. The *XED* in this case will be negative. An example of such a relationship is that between coffee and sugar, which tend to be consumed together.

Examples

Suppose you found that the *XED* for sugar with respect to a change in the price of coffee was −0.087. This would imply that a 10% increase in the price of coffee would lead to a 0.87% fall in the demand for sugar, suggesting that coffee and sugar are complements. If the *XED* for pineapples with respect to a change in the prices of mangoes was +0.532, this would suggest that a 10% increase in the price of pineapples would lead to a 5.32% increase in the demand for mangoes, suggesting that pineapples and mangoes are substitutes.

Price elasticity of supply

As elasticity is a measure of sensitivity, its use need not be confined to influences on demand, but can also be turned to evaluating the sensitivity of quantity *supplied* to a change in its determinants – in particular, its price.

It was argued in Chapter 3 that the supply curve is likely to be upward sloping, so the price elasticity of supply can be expected to be positive. In other words, an increase in the market price will induce firms to supply more output to the market. The **price elasticity of supply (PES)** is defined as:

$$PES = \frac{\%\text{ change in quantity supplied}}{\%\text{ change in price}}$$

Key term

Price elasticity of supply (PES): a measure of the sensitivity of quantity supplied of a good or service to a change in the price of that good or service.

So, if the price elasticity of supply is 0.8, an increase in price of 10% will encourage firms to supply 8% more. As with the price elasticity of demand, if the elasticity is greater than 1, supply is referred to as being elastic, whereas if the value is between 0 and 1, supply is considered inelastic. *Unit elasticity* occurs when the price elasticity of supply is exactly 1, so that a 10% increase in price induces a 10% increase in quantity supplied.

The value of the elasticity will depend on how willing and able firms are to increase their supply. For example, if firms are operating close to the capacity of their existing plant and machinery, they may be unable to respond to an increase in price, at least in the short run. So here again, supply can be expected to be more elastic in the long run than in the short run. Figure 4.17 illustrates this.

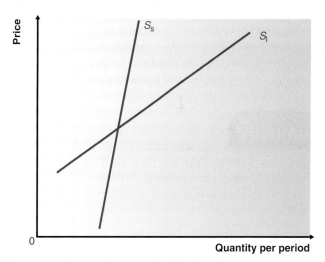

Figure 4.17 Short- and long-run elasticity of supply

In the short run, firms may be able to respond to an increase in price only in a limited way, and so supply may be relatively inelastic, as shown by S_s in the figure. However, firms can become more flexible in the long run by installing new machinery or building new factories, so supply can then become more elastic, moving to S_l.

There are two limiting cases of supply elasticity. For some reason, supply may be fixed such that, no matter how much price increases, firms will not be able to supply any more. For example, it could be that a certain amount of fish is available in a market, and however high the price goes, no more can be obtained. Equally, if the fishermen know that the fish they do not sell today cannot be stored for another day, they have an incentive to sell, however low the price goes. In these cases, supply is perfectly inelastic. At the other extreme is perfectly elastic supply, where firms would be prepared to supply any amount of the good at the going price.

The supply of fresh fish to this market in Bangkok is inelastic

These two possibilities are shown in Figure 4.18. Here S_i represents a perfectly inelastic supply curve: firms will supply Q_i whatever the price, perhaps because that is the amount available for sale. Supply here is vertical. At the opposite extreme, if supply is perfectly elastic then firms are prepared to supply any amount at the price P_e, and the supply curve is given by the horizontal line S_e.

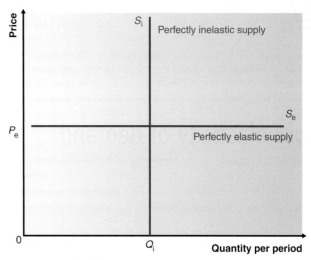

Figure 4.18 Perfectly elastic and inelastic supply

Exercise 4.5

Imagine the following scenario. You are considering a pricing strategy for a bus company. The economy is heading into recession, and the company is running at a loss. Your local rail service provider has announced an increase in rail fares. How (if at all) do you use the following information concerning the elasticity of bus travel with respect to various variables to inform your decision on price? Do you raise or lower price?

price elasticity of demand	−1.58
income elasticity of demand	−2.43
cross-price elasticity of demand with respect to rail fares	+2.21
your price elasticity of supply	+1.15

Summary

- The price elasticity of demand measures the sensitivity of the quantity of a good demanded to a change in its price.
- As there is an inverse relationship between quantity demanded and price, the price elasticity of demand is always negative.
- Where consumers are sensitive to a change in price, the percentage change in quantity demanded will exceed the percentage change in price. The elasticity of demand then takes on a value that is numerically greater than 1, and demand is said to be elastic.
- Where consumers are not very sensitive to a change in price, the percentage change in quantity demanded will be smaller than the percentage change in price. Elasticity of demand then takes on a value that is numerically smaller than 1, and demand is said to be inelastic.
- When demand is elastic, a fall (rise) in price leads to a rise (fall) in total revenue.
- When demand is inelastic, a fall (rise) in price leads to a fall (rise) in total revenue.

- The size of the price elasticity of demand is influenced by the availability of substitutes for a good, the relative share of expenditure on the good in the consumer's budget and the time that consumers have to adjust.
- The income elasticity of demand (*YED*) measures the sensitivity of quantity demanded to a change in consumer incomes. It serves to distinguish between normal, luxury and inferior goods.
- The cross-price elasticity of demand (*XED*) measures the sensitivity of the quantity demanded of one good or service to a change in the price of some other good or service. It can serve to distinguish between substitutes and complements.
- The price elasticity of supply (*PES*) measures the sensitivity of the quantity supplied to a change in the price of a good or service. The price elasticity of supply can be expected to be greater in the long run than in the short run, as firms have more flexibility to adjust their production decisions in the long run.

5 Prices and resource allocation

Now that you are familiar with the use of the demand and supply model, it is time to take a wider view of the process of resource allocation within society. This chapter examines how prices can act as market signals to guide resource allocation, and introduces notions of consumer and producer surplus.

Learning outcomes

After studying this chapter, you should:
- have an overview of how the price mechanism works to allocate resources
- understand the meaning and significance of consumer surplus
- be able to see how prices provide incentives to producers
- understand the meaning and significance of producer surplus
- be aware of the effects of the entry and exit of firms into and out of a market.

5.1 The role of prices in allocating resources

The coordination problem

As Chapter 1 indicated, all societies face the fundamental economic problem of scarcity. Because there are unlimited wants but finite resources, it is necessary to take decisions on which goods and services should be produced, how they should be produced and for whom they should be produced. For an economy the size of the UK, there is thus an immense coordination problem. Another way of looking at this is to ask how consumers can express their preferences between alternative goods so that producers can produce the best mix of goods and services.

Some alternative possibilities for handling this problem will now be considered. In a **free-market economy**, market forces are allowed to allocate resources. At the other extreme, in a centrally planned economy the state plans and directs resources into a range of uses. In between there is the mixed economy. In order to evaluate these alternatives, it is necessary to explore how each of them operates.

Key term

Free-market economy: one in which resource allocation is guided by market forces without intervention by the state.

In a free-market economy, prices play the key role; this is sometimes referred to as the *laissez-faire* approach to resource allocation.

Summary

- Societies face the fundamental economic problem of scarcity.
- In a free-market economy there needs to be a mechanism that coordinates the allocation of resources.
- Prices play a key role in this process.

5.2 Prices and consumers

Prices and preferences

How can consumers signal their preferences to producers? Demand and supply analysis provides the clue. Figure 5.1 shows the demand and supply for laptop computers. Over time there has been a rightward shift in the demand curve – in the figure, from D_0 to D_1. This simply means that consumers are placing a higher value on these goods; they are prepared to demand more at any given price. The result, as you know from comparative static analysis, is that the market will move to a new equilibrium, with price rising from P_0 to P_1 and quantity traded from Q_0 to Q_1: there is a movement along the supply curve.

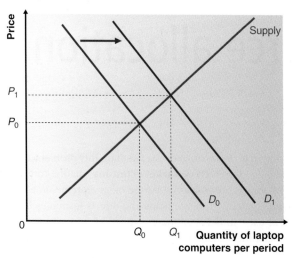

Figure 5.1 The market for laptop computers

The shift in the demand curve is an expression of consumers' preferences; it embodies the fact that they value laptop computers more highly now than before. The price that consumers are willing to pay represents their valuation of laptop computers.

Consumer surplus

Think a little more carefully about what the demand curve represents. Figure 5.2 again shows the demand curve for laptop computers. Suppose that the price is set at P^* and quantity demanded is thus Q^*. P^* can be seen as the value that the last customer places on a laptop. In other words, if the price were even slightly above P^*, there would be one consumer who would choose not to buy: this individual will be referred to as the *marginal consumer*.

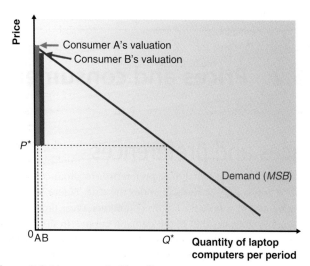

Figure 5.2 Price as marginal benefit

To that marginal consumer, P^* represents the marginal benefit derived from consuming this good – it is the price that just reflects the consumer's benefit from a laptop, as it is the price that just induces her to buy. Thinking of the society as a whole (which is made up of all the consumers within it), P^* can be regarded as the **marginal social benefit** (MSB) derived from consuming this good. The same argument could be made about any point along the demand curve, so the demand curve can be interpreted as the marginal benefit to be derived from consuming laptop computers.

A display of laptop computers in a store in Kuala Lumpur. Consumers now value laptop computers more highly than before

Key term

Marginal social benefit: the additional benefit that society gains from consuming an extra unit of a good.

In most markets, all consumers face the same prices for goods and services. This leads to an important concept in economic analysis. P^* may represent the value of laptops to the *marginal* consumer, but what about all the other consumers who are also buying laptops at P^*? They would all be willing to pay a higher price for a laptop. Indeed, consumer A in Figure 5.2 would pay a very high price indeed, and thus values a laptop much more highly than P^*. When consumer A pays P^* for a laptop, he gets a great deal, as he values the good so much more highly – as represented by the vertical green line on Figure 5.2. Consumer B also gains a surplus above her willingness to pay (the purple line).

If all these surplus values are added up, they sum to the total surplus that society gains from consuming laptops. This is known as the **consumer surplus**, represented by the shaded triangle in Figure 5.3. It can be interpreted as the welfare that society gains from consuming the good, over and above the price that has to be paid for it.

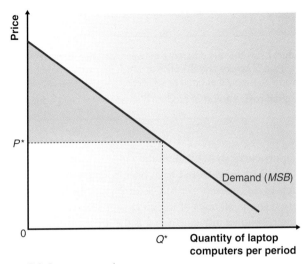

Figure 5.3 Consumer surplus

Prices as signals and incentives

From the producers' perspective, the question is how they receive signals from consumers about their changing preferences. Price is the key. Figure 5.1 showed how an increase in demand for laptop computers leads to an increase in the equilibrium market price. The shift in the demand curve leads to an increase in the equilibrium price, which encourages producers to supply more computers – there is a movement *along* the supply curve. This is really saying that producers find it profitable to expand their output of laptop computers at that higher price. The price level is thus a signal to producers about consumer preferences.

Notice that the price signal works equally well when there is a *decrease* in the demand for a good or service. Figure 5.5, for example, shows the market for video recordings.

Key term

Consumer surplus: the value that consumers gain from consuming a good or service over and above the price paid.

Exercise 5.1

Figure 5.4 shows a demand curve.

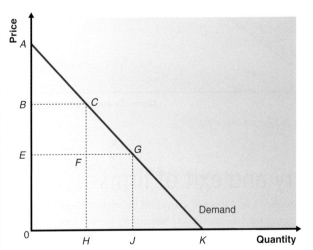

Figure 5.4 Consumer surplus when price changes

a Identify the area that represents consumer surplus if the price of the good is OE.

Suppose that the price increases to OB.

b Identify the consumer surplus at this new price.
c Which area represents the change in consumer surplus between the two positions?
d Which area shows how total welfare in the society has changed?

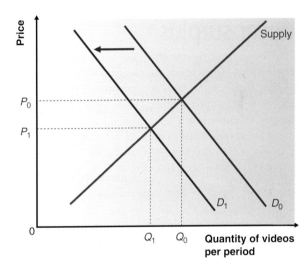

Figure 5.5 The market for video recordings

With the advent of DVDs, there has been a large fall in the demand for video recordings, so the demand for them has shifted to the left – consumers are demanding fewer videos at any price. Thus, the demand curve shifts from D_0 to D_1. Producers of video recordings are beginning to find that they cannot sell as many videos at the original price as before, so they have to reduce their price to avoid an increase in their unsold stocks. They have less incentive to produce videos, and will supply less. There is a movement *along* the supply curve to a lower equilibrium price at P_1, and a lower quantity traded at Q_1. You may like to think of this as a movement along the firm's production possibility curve for DVDs and videos.

Thus, you can see how existing producers in a market receive signals from consumers in the form of changes in the equilibrium price, and respond to these signals by adjusting their output levels.

Summary

- If market forces are to allocate resources effectively, consumers need to be able to express their preferences for goods and services in such a way that producers can respond.
- Consumers express their preferences through prices, as prices will adjust to equilibrium levels following a change in consumer demand.
- Consumer surplus represents the benefit that consumers gain from consuming a product over and above the price they pay for that product.

Key terms

Producer surplus: the difference between the price received by firms for a good or service and the price at which they would have been prepared to supply that good or service.

Marginal cost: the cost of producing an additional unit of output.

5.3 Prices and producers

Producer surplus

Parallel to the notion of consumer surplus is the concept of **producer surplus**. Think about the nature of the supply curve: it reveals how much output firms are prepared to supply at any given price in a competitive market. Figure 5.6 depicts a supply curve. Assume the price is at P^*, and that all units are sold at that price. P^* represents the value to firms of the marginal unit sold. In other words, if the price had been set slightly below P^*, the last unit would not have been supplied, as firms would not have found this profitable.

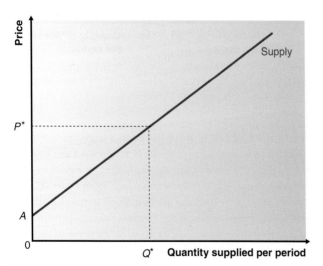

Figure 5.6 A supply curve

Notice that the threshold at which a firm will decide it is not profitable to supply is the point at which the price received by the firm reaches the cost to the firm of producing the last unit of the good. Thus, in a competitive market the supply curve reflects **marginal cost**.

The supply curve shows that, in the range of prices between point A and P^*, firms would have been willing to supply positive amounts of this good or service. So at P^*, they would gain a surplus value on all units of the good supplied below Q^*. The total area is shown in Figure 5.7: it is the area above the supply curve and below P^*, shown as the shaded triangle.

One way of defining this producer surplus is as the surplus earned by firms over and above the minimum that would have kept them in the market. It is the reason for which firms exist.

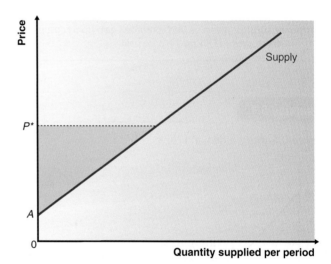

Figure 5.7 Producer surplus

Entry and exit of firms

The discussion so far has focused on the reactions of existing firms in a market to changes in consumer preferences. However, this is only part of the picture. Think back to Figure 5.1, where there was an increase in demand for laptop computers following a change in consumer preferences. The equilibrium price rose, and existing firms expanded the quantity supplied in response. Those firms are now earning a higher producer surplus than before. Other firms not currently in the market will be attracted by these surpluses, perceiving this to be a profitable market in which to operate.

If there are no barriers to entry, more firms will join the market. This in turn will tend to shift the supply curve to the right, as there will then be more firms prepared to supply. As a result, the equilibrium market price will tend to drift down again, until the market reaches a position in which there is no further incentive for new firms to enter the market. This will occur when the rate of return for firms in the laptop market is no better than in other markets.

Figure 5.8 illustrates this situation. The original increase in demand leads, as before, to a new equilibrium with a higher price P_1. As new firms join the market in quest of producer surplus, the supply curve shifts to the right to S_2, pushing the price back down to P_0, but with the quantity traded now up at Q_2.

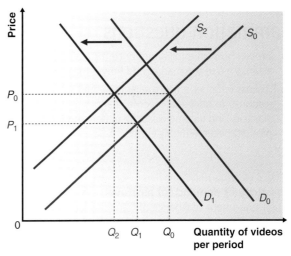

Figure 5.9 The market for video recordings revisited

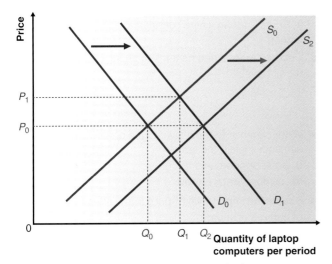

Figure 5.8 The market for laptop computers revisited

If the original movement in demand is in the opposite direction, as it was for video recordings in Figure 5.5, a similar long-run adjustment takes place. As the market price falls, some firms in the market may decide that they no longer wish to remain in production, and will exit from the market altogether. This will shift the supply curve to the left in Figure 5.9 (to S_2) until only firms that continue to find it profitable will remain in the market. In the final position, price is back to P_0, and quantity traded has fallen to Q_2.

Exercise 5.2

a Sketch a demand and supply diagram and mark on it the areas that represent consumer and producer surplus.
b Using a demand and supply diagram, explain the process that provides incentives for firms to adjust to a decrease in the demand for fountain pens in a competitive market.
c Think about how you could use demand and supply analysis to explain recent movements in the world price of oil.

Summary

- Producer surplus represents the benefit gained by firms over and above the price at which they would have been prepared to supply a product.
- Producers have an incentive to respond to changes in prices. In the short run this occurs through output adjustments of existing firms (movements along the supply curve), but in the long run firms will enter the market (or exit from it) until there are no further incentives for entry or exit.

Examination questions

1 a Explain how an equilibrium price for a product is established in the market and how it may change. [8]

b Discuss whether a firm's revenue would increase, in response to price and income changes, if the price elasticity and income elasticity of demand for its product became highly elastic. [12]

Cambridge AS and A Level Economics 9708, Paper 2, Q2, November 2007

2 Elasticity of demand for air travel

The Department of Finance of Canada examined 21 studies of elasticity of demand for air travel. These were mainly based on behaviour in the USA. It produced a summary of what it thought were the most accurate estimates of elasticity for different segments of the market. Some of these findings are given in Figures 1 and 2.

	YED value
Total market	+1.1

Figure 1 Income elasticity of demand (*YED*) for air travel

Market segment	*PED* value
Long-distance international business flights	−0.3
Long-distance international leisure flights	−1.0
Short-distance business flights	−0.7
Short-distance leisure flights	−1.5

Figure 2 Price elasticity of demand (*PED*) for air travel

a i) State the formula used to calculate income elasticity of demand. [2]

ii) What can be concluded about air travel from Figure 1? [2]

b Using Figure 2, explain a likely reason for the different price elasticity values for

i) business flights compared with leisure flights [3]

ii) long-distance flights compared with short-distance flights. [3]

c Explain the significance of the price elasticity values in Figure 2 for an airline considering a policy of fare cutting. [4]

d Discuss the costs and benefits of an increased demand for air travel. [6]

Cambridge AS and A Level Economics 9708, Paper 21, Q1, November 2009

3 a With reference to the relevant type of elasticity of demand, explain the terms

i) inferior good, and

ii) complementary good. [8]

b Discuss the importance of price in the effective operation of a mixed economy. [12]

Cambridge AS and A Level Economics 9708, Paper 22, Q3, November 2010

6 The government in the microeconomy

If markets are to be effective in guiding the allocation of resources in society, a precondition is that market prices are able to reflect the full costs and benefits associated with market transactions. However, there are situations in which the government may see that there is a need to intervene to influence markets. This chapter looks at ways in which governments intervene, either to improve the workings of markets or to affect the way in which resources are allocated – for example by influencing the distribution of income in society.

Learning outcomes

After studying this chapter, you should:
- be familiar with ways in which the government intervenes in markets
- appreciate the effects on a market if controls are placed on prices
- understand the effects of taxes and subsidies in a market
- be familiar with the Canons of Taxation
- understand the rationale for governments to redistribute income and wealth, and policies that can be used for this purpose
- be aware of how governments may intervene through direct provision of goods and services
- understand what is meant by nationalisation and privatisation and recognise the effects they have on markets.

6.1 Minimum and maximum prices

Most governments see it as their responsibility to ensure that markets allocate resources efficiently. However, some policies have unintended effects that may not culminate in successful elimination of market failure. Indeed, in some cases government intervention may introduce new market distortions, leading to a phenomenon known as **government failure**. One way in which governments may intervene is through direct control of prices in some markets: that is, through regulation.

> **Key term**
>
> **Government failure**: a misallocation of resources arising from government intervention.

A minimum wage

One way in which governments have often intervened in markets is by the introduction of a **minimum wage**. To illustrate how this works, Figure 6.1 represents the labour market for office cleaners. Employers demand labour according to the wage rate – the lower the wage, the higher the demand for the labour of office cleaners. On the supply side, more workers will offer themselves for work when the wage rate is relatively high. If the market is unregulated, it will reach equilibrium with a wage rate W^* and quantity of labour L^*.

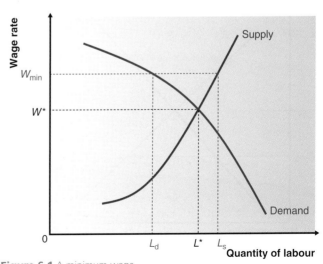

Figure 6.1 A minimum wage

Key term

Minimum wage: legislation under which firms are not allowed to pay a wage below some threshold level set by the government.

Suppose now that the government comes to the view that W^* is not sufficiently high to provide a reasonable wage for cleaners. One response is to impose a minimum wage, below which employers are not permitted to offer employment – say, W_{min} on the figure. This will have two effects on the market situation. First, employers will demand less labour at this higher wage, so employment will fall to L_d. Second, more workers will be prepared to offer themselves for employment at the higher wage, so labour supply will rise to L_s. However, the net effect of this is that there is an excess supply of labour at this wage and hence unemployment, with more workers offering themselves for work than there are jobs available in the market.

What is happening here is that, with the minimum wage in effect, *some* workers (those who manage to remain in employment) are better off, and now receive a better wage. However, those who are now unemployed are worse off. It is not then clear whether the effect of the minimum wage is to make society as a whole better off – some people will be better off, but others will be worse off.

Notice that this analysis rests on some assumptions that have not been made explicit. In particular, it rests on the assumption that the labour market is competitive. Where there are labour markets in which the employers have some market power, and are able to offer lower wages to workers than would be obtained in a free-market equilibrium situation, it is possible that the imposition of a minimum wage will increase employment.

Rent controls

Another market in which governments have been tempted to intervene is the housing market. Figure 6.2 represents the market for rented accommodation. The free-market equilibrium would be where demand and supply intersect, with the equilibrium rent being R^* and the quantity of accommodation traded being Q^*.

If the government regards the level of rent as excessive, to the point where households on low incomes may be unable to afford rented accommodation, then, given that housing is one of life's necessities, it may regard this as unacceptable.

The temptation for the government is to move this market away from its equilibrium by imposing a maximum level of rent that landlords are allowed to charge their tenants. Suppose that this level of rent is denoted by R_{max} in Figure 6.2. Again, there are two effects that follow. First, landlords will no longer find it profitable to supply as much rental accommodation, and so will reduce supply to Q_s. Second, at this lower rent there will be more people looking for accommodation, so that demand for rented accommodation will move to Q_d. The upshot of the rent controls, therefore, is that there is less accommodation available, and more homeless people.

It can be seen that the well-meaning rent control policy, intended to protect low-income households from being exploited by landlords, merely has the effect of reducing the amount of accommodation available. This is not what was supposed to happen.

Summary

- Government failure can occur when well-meaning intervention by governments has unintended effects.
- Governments may intervene by using direct controls on prices in some markets.
- One example of this is where the government impose a minimum wage to protect low-paid workers.
- In some circumstances, this may result in a rise in unemployment.
- Governments may also set maximum prices, as in the case of rent controls.

6.2 Indirect taxes and subsidies

Governments need to raise funds to finance the expenditure that they undertake. One way of doing this is through taxes on expenditure, such as a sales tax.

The effects of a sales tax can be seen in a demand and supply diagram. An **indirect tax** is paid by the seller, so it affects the supply curve for a product. Figure 6.3 illustrates the case of a *fixed rate* or **specific tax** – a tax that is set at a constant amount per pack of cigarettes. Without the tax, the market equilibrium is at the intersection of demand and supply with a price of P_0

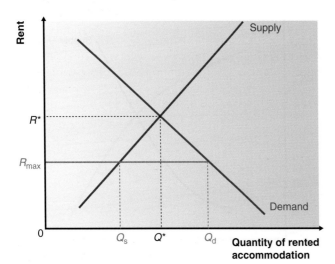

Figure 6.2 Rent controls

and a quantity traded of Q_0. The effect of the tax is to reduce the quantity that firms are prepared to supply at any given price – or, to put it another way, for any given quantity of cigarettes, firms need to receive the amount of the tax over and above the price at which they would have been prepared to supply that quantity. The effect is thus to move the supply curve upwards by the amount of the tax, as shown in the figure. We get a new equilibrium with a higher price at P_1 and a lower quantity traded at Q_1.

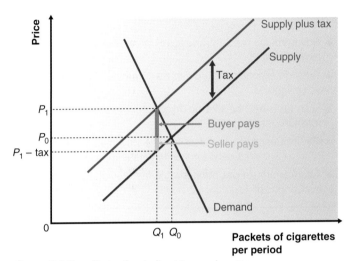

Figure 6.3 The effects of an indirect tax on cigarettes

> ### Key terms
>
> **Indirect tax**: a tax levied on expenditure on goods or services (as opposed to a direct tax, which is a tax charged directly to an individual based on a component of income).
>
> **Specific tax**: a tax of a fixed amount imposed on purchases of a commodity.

An important question is: who bears the burden of the tax? If you look at the diagram, you will see that the price difference between the with-tax and without-tax situations (i.e. $P_1 - P_0$) is *less* than the amount of the tax, which is the vertical distance between the with-tax and without-tax supply curves. Although the seller may be responsible for the mechanics of paying the tax, part of the tax is effectively passed on to the buyer in the form of the higher price. In Figure 6.3, the **incidence of the tax** falls partly upon the seller, but most of the tax is borne by the buyer.

The price elasticity of demand determines the incidence of the tax. If demand were perfectly inelastic, then the sellers would be able to pass the whole burden of the tax on to the buyers through an increase in price equal to the value of the tax, knowing that this would not affect demand. However, if demand were perfectly elastic, then the sellers would not be able to raise the price at all, so they would have to bear the entire burden of the tax.

> ### Exercise 6.1
>
> Sketch demand and supply diagrams to confirm that the statements in the previous paragraph are correct – that is, that if demand is perfectly inelastic, then the tax falls entirely on the buyers, whereas if demand is perfectly elastic, it is the sellers who have to bear the burden of the tax.

If the tax is not a constant amount, but a percentage of the price (known as an **ad valorem** tax), the effect is still on the supply curve, but the tax steepens the supply curve, as shown in Figure 6.4. Here, the free-market equilibrium would be where demand equals supply, with price at P_0 and the quantity traded at Q_0. With an *ad valorem* tax in place, the price rises to P_1, with quantity falling to Q_1.

> ### Key terms
>
> **Incidence of a tax**: the way in which the burden of paying a sales tax is divided between buyers and sellers.
>
> **Ad valorem tax**: a tax on expenditure set at a percentage of the price.

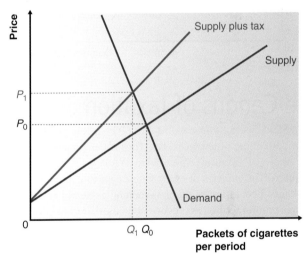

Figure 6.4 The effects of an *ad valorem* tax on cigarettes

In some situations, the government may wish to encourage production of a particular good or service, perhaps because it views a good as having strategic significance to the country. One way it can do this is by giving **subsidies**.

> ### Key term
>
> **Subsidy**: a grant given by the government to producers to encourage production of a good or service.

Subsidies are used to encourage producers to increase their output of particular goods. Subsidies have been especially common in agriculture, which is often seen as being of strategic significance. In recent years, the USA has come under pressure to reduce the subsidies that it grants to cotton producers. Analytically, we can regard a subsidy as a sort of negative indirect tax that shifts the supply curve down – as shown in Figure 6.5. Without the subsidy, market equilibrium is at a price P_0 and the quantity traded is Q_0. With the subsidy in place, the equilibrium price falls to P_1 and quantity traded increases to Q_1.

Again, notice that because the price falls by less than the amount of the subsidy, the benefits of the subsidy are shared between the buyers and sellers – depending on the elasticity of demand. If the aim of the subsidy is to increase production, it is only partially successful; the degree of success also depends upon the elasticity of demand.

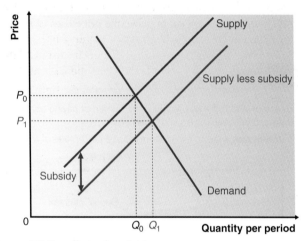

Figure 6.5 The effects of a subsidy

The Canons of Taxation

Adam Smith set out four maxims that he believed should form the underpinning of any good tax. These later became known as the 'Canons of Taxation'. These were as follows:

- **Equity:** 'The subjects of every state ought to contribute towards the support of the government, as nearly as possible, in proportion to their respective abilities; that is, in proportion to the revenue which they respectively enjoy under the protection of the state.'
- **Certainty:** 'The tax which each individual is bound to pay ought to be certain, and not arbitrary.'
- **Convenience:** 'Every tax ought to be levied at the time, or in the manner, in which it is likely to be convenient for the contributor to pay it.'
- **Economy:** 'Every tax ought to be contrived as both to take out and to keep out of the pockets of people as little as possible over and above what it brings into the public treasury of the state.'

Source: Adam Smith (1776): *An Inquiry into the Nature and Causes of the Wealth of Nations* (Book V, Chapter 2)

These desirable characteristics of a tax would still command widespread support today, although the focus would normally be on the incidence of a tax and whether the tax is implemented in a way that is efficient. In this context, efficiency would be seen not only in terms of the cost of collection, but also in

relation to the impact that it may have on resource allocation. This will be examined in more detail in Chapter 19. In a modern economy, it may also be important to see that levels of taxation reflect changing prices in an inflationary environment. Where countries have close trade links with other countries (and especially when they are part of regional trade agreements), it is also important to ensure that tax rates are compatible with those of their trading partners.

Summary

- Governments need to raise funds to finance their expenditure.
- Taxes on expenditure (indirect taxes) provide one way of achieving this.
- Such taxes may be specific (fixed rate) or *ad valorem* (proportional to price).
- The incidence of a tax identifies the way in which the burden of a tax is shared between consumers and producers.
- Adam Smith set out the desirable features of a good tax in his Canons of Taxation.

6.3 Government intervention to redistribute income

There are a number of ways in which government intervention influences the distribution of income in a society, although not all of these interventions are expressly intended to do so. Most prominent is the range of transfer payments and taxation that has been implemented. Another example is the minimum wage legislation discussed earlier, which was also intended to protect the poor.

Benefits

Governments in many countries make **transfer payments** to poor households. These may be in the form of cash benefits, such as income support, child benefit, incapacity benefit and working families tax credit. These benefits are designed to protect families in certain circumstances whose income would otherwise be very low. Second, there are benefits in kind, such as health and education. These benefits accrue to individual households depending on the number of members of the household and their age and gender. Some benefits may be **means-tested**: that is, paid only to those whose income falls below a certain level. Others may be **universal**, and paid to all, regardless of income. Some benefits are funded through contributions. For example, in Pakistan an old age pension is paid to those above the retirement age who have made at least 15 years of contributions to the Social Insurance system. However, any shortfall must be covered by the government, partly through tax revenues.

Key terms

Transfer payment: occurs where the government provides benefits (in cash or in kind) to poor households; hence there is a transfer from taxpayers to the recipients of the benefits.

Means-tested benefit: a benefit (in cash or in kind) paid to people or households whose income falls below a certain level.

Universal benefit: a benefit (in cash or in kind) paid without reference to the income of the receiving person or household.

Taxation

There are two main forms of taxation – **direct taxes** levied on various forms of income, and indirect taxes that are levied on expenditure.

Key term

Direct tax: a tax levied directly on income.

Direct taxes (taxes on incomes) tend to be **progressive**: in other words, higher income groups pay tax at a higher rate. Direct taxes include income tax, corporation tax (paid by firms on profits) and capital gains tax (paid by individuals who sell assets at a profit). There may also be taxes levied by local authorities on property, such as the UK's Council Tax.

With a tax such as income tax, its progressive nature is reflected in the way that the percentage rates payable increase as an individual moves into higher income ranges. In other words, the **marginal tax rate** increases as income increases. The progressive nature of the tax ensures that it does indeed contribute to reducing inequality in the income distribution. This may be further enhanced by the use of *tax credits*, which act rather like a negative income tax, reducing the tax liability of those on low incomes.

The effect of indirect taxes can sometimes be **regressive**: in other words, indirect taxes may impinge more heavily on lower-income households. Indirect taxes are taxes that are paid on items of expenditure, rather than on income.

Key terms

Progressive tax: a tax in which the marginal rate rises with income.

Marginal tax rate: tax on additional income, defined as the change in tax payments divided by the change in taxable income.

Regressive tax: a tax bearing more heavily on the relatively poorer members of society.

An example of an indirect tax is value-added tax (VAT), which is charged on most goods and services sold in the UK. However, there are also tobacco taxes, excise duties on alcohol and oil duties. These specific taxes are levied per unit sold. More discussion of this issue will be found in Chapter 19.

Benefits and incentives

In setting levels of benefits, the government faces a tricky dilemma. On the one hand, it wishes to protect the poor, and to provide a safety net for those who cannot earn enough. On the other hand, it wants to provide good incentives for people to make the best of themselves. In a system in which individuals can receive benefits but face a progressive income tax system, there is a danger that some will fall into a **poverty trap**. An individual who is receiving social security benefits may find that their after-tax pay in a job would be less than the amount they receive in benefits. Their incentive to take up a job is thus low.

Key term

Poverty trap: a situation in which an individual has no incentive to take a job, because any additional income will be taken away in taxes and lost benefits, thus leaving them worse off.

Summary

- Government action influences the pattern of income distribution, with the net effect being a reduction in inequality.
- Most effective in this is the provision of cash benefits to low-income households.
- Direct taxes tend to be progressive, and help to redistribute income towards poorer households.
- Some indirect taxes, however, can be regressive in their impact.
- It is important to keep a balance between protecting the low-paid and providing incentives for those in work.

6.4 Direct provision of goods and services by government

The notion of public goods was introduced in Section 1.4 of Chapter 1. It was noted that a free market for public goods (or services) will not operate effectively because of the *free-rider problem*. An important question is whether the government needs to intervene in such circumstances by producing the good or service directly?

Note that public goods are called 'public goods', not because they are publicly provided, but because of their characteristics.

The free-rider problem makes it difficult to charge for a public good, so the private sector will be reluctant to supply such goods. In fact, pure public goods are relatively rare, but there are many goods that have some but not all of the required characteristics. On the face of it, the lighthouse service seems to be a good example of a public good. Once the lighthouse has been constructed and is sending out its signal, all boats and ships that pass within the range of its light can benefit from the service: that is, it is non-excludable. Moreover, the fact that one ship has seen the lighthouse signal does not reduce the amount of light available to the next ship, so it is also non-rivalrous.

However, this does not mean that ships cannot be charged for their use of lighthouse services. In 2002 an article in *The Guardian* reported that ships in the UK were complaining about the high charges to which they were subjected for lighthouse services. Ships of a certain size must pay 'light dues' every time they enter or leave UK ports, and the fees collected are used to fund lighthouses, buoys and beacons around the coast. In principle, it could be argued that this renders lighthouses excludable, as ships can be prevented from sailing if they have not paid their dues, and so could not consume the lighthouse services. At the heart of the complaints from the shipping companies was the fact that leisure craft below a certain threshold did not have to pay the charges, and they made more use of the lighthouses than the larger vessels. This is one example of the way in which it becomes necessary to design a charging system to try to overcome the free-rider problem associated with the provision of public goods.

Lighthouses, such as this one in the Baltic Sea, are a good example of a public good

In fact, there are many goods that are either non-rivalrous or non-excludable, but not both. One example of this is a football match. If I go to watch a football match, my 'consumption' of the match does not prevent the person sitting next to me from also consuming it, so it is non-rivalrous. However, if I go

along without my season ticket (or do not have a ticket), I can clearly be excluded from consuming the match, so it is *not* non-exclusive.

A stretch of road may be considered non-exclusive, as road users are free to drive along it. However, it is not non-rivalrous, in the sense that as congestion builds up, consumption is affected. This example is also imperfect as a public good because, by installing toll barriers, users can be excluded from consuming it.

Where goods have some features of a public good, the free market may fail to produce an ideal outcome for society. Exercise 1.6 on page 11 provides some examples of goods: to what extent may each of these be considered to be non-rivalrous or non-excludable?

Tackling the public goods problem

For some public goods, the failure of the free market to ensure provision may be regarded as a serious problem – for example, in such cases as street lighting or law and order. Some government intervention may thus be needed to make sure that a sufficient quantity of the good or service is provided. Notice that this does not necessarily mean that the government has to provide the good itself, although it may choose to do so. It may be that the government will raise funds through taxation in order to ensure that street lighting is provided, but could still make use of private firms to supply the good through some sort of subcontracting arrangement. In some countries, it may be that the government delegates the responsibility for provision of public goods to local authorities, which in turn may subcontract to private firms.

Nationalisation and privatisation

Nationalisation occurs when a government chooses to take an industry into public ownership in order to safeguard the supply of a good or service. In many countries, utilities such as water, electricity or gas supply are examples of industries that have been taken into public ownership. One reason for this concerns the cost conditions that prevail in these industries, which make it difficult to foster competition, as will be seen in Chapter 19. The danger here is that an unregulated market operating as a private monopoly may be in a position to abuse its market power, and restrict the supply of these key utilities.

However, nationalised industries have not always been seen to operate effectively. State-owned enterprises have often been criticised for becoming inefficient, as they are not exposed to the discipline that competition with other firms can provide. Underpinning this criticism is the observation that managers of state-owned enterprises could be thought to be insufficiently accountable for their actions, and might not face the right incentives to be cost-efficient in their decision-making. This led to widespread attempts from the 1980s onwards to transfer nationalised industries back into the private sector, and to expose them to competition. This process was known as **privatisation**. A recent example in the UK was in 2013, when the Royal Mail postal service was privatised.

The most successful privatisations have been in those markets where it is possible to encourage effective competition between suppliers.

Key terms

Nationalisation: a process whereby an enterprise is taken into state ownership.

Privatisation: a process whereby an enterprise is transferred from public into private ownership.

Costs of intervention

Some roles are critical for a government to perform if a mixed economy is to function effectively. A vital role is the provision by the government of an environment in which markets can operate effectively. There must be stability in the political system if firms and consumers are to take decisions with confidence about the future. And there must be a secure system of property rights, without which markets could not be expected to work.

In addition, there are sources of market failure that require intervention. This does not necessarily mean that governments need to substitute markets with direct action. However, it does mean that they need to be more active in markets that cannot operate effectively, while at the same time performing an enabling role to encourage markets to work well whenever this is feasible.

Such intervention entails costs. There are costs of administering, and costs of monitoring the policy to ensure that it is working as intended. This includes the need to look out for the unintended distortionary effects that some policies can have on resource allocation in a society. It is therefore important to check that the marginal costs of implementing and monitoring policies do not exceed their marginal benefits.

Summary

- Governments may intervene through direct provision of some goods and services.
- One rationale for this is where there are public goods, which would not be effectively provided by the free market.
- The government may choose to pay private firms to provide public goods or services, financing this out of taxation, rather than engaging in direct production.
- Some industries (especially utilities) have been taken into state ownership through a process of nationalisation.
- Some nationalised industries were seen to become inefficient over time.
- Privatisation is the process whereby state-owned enterprises are transferred into private ownership.
- Privatisation has been most successful when it has been possible to foster effective competition.
- Government failure can occur when well-meaning intervention by governments has unintended effects.
- In some circumstances a minimum wage intended to protect the low paid may aggravate their situation by increasing unemployment.
- Rent controls may have the effect of reducing the amount of accommodation available.
- A sales tax imposes an excess burden on society.
- Prohibition may also have unintended effects.

Examination questions

1 a Explain, with the help of an example, the effects when a government introduces a maximum price for a good or service. [8]

  b With the help of a diagram, discuss how desirable it is for a government to pay subsidies to producers. [12]

Cambridge AS and A Level Economics 9708, Paper 22, Q3, June 2009

2 **Problems for dairy farmers in the United States**

Milk is used to make a range of products, including butter, cheese and ice cream, as well as serving as a drink. This was of no help to US dairy farmers in 2009 when they faced a falling price for their milk. Figure 1 shows the extent of the price change in recent years. While consumers purchase milk by volume (litres), farmers are paid by weight (kilograms).

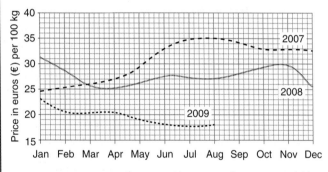

Source: www.clal.it

Figure 1 Average milk price paid to farmers in the US, January 2007 to August 2009

A price fall was also experienced by New Zealand as shown in Table 1.

Table 1 Average annual milk price (€ per 100 kg) in the US and New Zealand, 2007–2009

	2007	2008	2009
US	30.69	27.49	19.30
New Zealand	22.48	25.17	16.21

US farmers blamed their problems on the global recession, the strength of the US$ and high cattle feed prices. At the same time, New Zealand and Australia increased their exports and the European Union (EU) reintroduced its export subsidies on milk products. The world milk industry has often had support from governments that have paid subsidies to farmers and supplied free milk to young children. US farmers were hoping for extra government intervention.

a i) Compare the average milk price paid to farmers in the US in August 2008 with that in August 2009. [2]

  ii) How far does Figure 1 suggest that the price of milk is subject to regular seasonal influences? [2]

b i) Compare the changes in milk prices in the US and in New Zealand between 2007 and 2009. [2]

  ii) Explain **two** possible reasons for the different level of milk prices in the US and New Zealand. [4]

c Explain how one group, other than dairy farmers, would lose from lower milk prices and how another group would gain from lower milk prices. [4]

d Discuss the case for the use of government subsidies for the production of milk. [6]

Cambridge AS and A Level Economics 9708, Paper 21, Q1, June 2011

3 a Explain how a government's approach to making a decision about a construction project might differ from that of a private firm. [8]

  b Discuss whether economists would classify healthcare and national defence in the same way. [12]

Cambridge AS and A Level Economics 9708, Paper 21, Q2, November 2011

7 Aggregate demand, aggregate supply and macroeconomic equilibrium

This part of the book switches attention to macroeconomics. Macroeconomics has much in common with microeconomics, but focuses on the whole economy, rather than on individual markets and how they operate. Although the way of thinking about issues is similar, and although similar tools are used, now it is interactions between economic variables at the level of the whole economy that are studied. The starting point is to consider the components of aggregate demand. The way in which the levels of these components are determined in practice is an important key to the operation of the economy when considered at the aggregate level. It is also important to examine aggregate supply and the factors that influence it. Macroeconomic equilibrium is seen to occur at the intersection of aggregate demand and aggregate supply.

Learning outcomes

After studying this chapter, you should:
- understand what is meant by aggregate demand
- be able to identify the components of aggregate demand
- be familiar with the notion of the aggregate demand curve
- understand what is meant by aggregate supply
- be able to identify the factors that influence aggregate supply
- be familiar with the notion of the aggregate supply curve
- understand the nature of equilibrium in the macroeconomy
- be able to undertake comparative static analysis of external shocks affecting aggregate demand and aggregate supply.

7.1 Aggregate demand

Macroeconomics deals with relationships between economic variables at the aggregate level – that is, in the economy viewed as a whole. In building a theory to explain those relationships, the starting point is to consider **aggregate demand**. This represents the total amount of effective demand in the economy as a whole. Aggregate demand in this sense can be seen to come from various sources. First, it includes the combined spending of households (on consumer goods) and firms (on investment goods). In addition, it is necessary to include international trade (exports and imports) and spending by government in this measure.

> **Key term**
>
> **Aggregate demand:** the total amount of effective demand in the economy.

The components of aggregate demand
Consumption

The largest component of aggregate demand is household spending on goods and services produced in the domestic economy, often known as consumption (C). The main factor that will influence the size of consumption expenditure is likely to be the level of real income that households have at their disposal. When real incomes are relatively high, households will tend to spend more than when real incomes are low. Notice that people may not choose to spend all of their income on domestically produced goods: some expenditure may be on imported goods, and they may choose to save part of their income against future needs.

Investment

A second key part of aggregate demand is spending by firms – in particular, spending on investment goods (*I*). For example, firms may choose to invest in new machinery or transport equipment. This is important not only because it contributes to aggregate demand in the current period, but because investment in new machinery enables higher production of goods in the future. The amount of investment that firms will wish to undertake will depend upon a number of factors. For example, it may be influenced by whether firms are optimistic or pessimistic about future demand for their products. If their expectations are high, they are more likely to invest in order to meet future demand. However, investment expenditure needs to be financed, so the level of investment may also depend upon the availability of finance. If firms have made good profits, then this may provide a fund for investment. However, if firms need to borrow, then the cost of borrowing will also be important, so the rate of interest will be important.

Government expenditure

The government plays an important role in the macroeconomy. It spends on goods and services, both to allow it to carry on its normal operations and to provide improved facilities that will allow the economy to develop in the future or to protect vulnerable members of society. In other words, government expenditure (*G*) may be partly consumption and partly investment.

International trade

Most economies are open to international trade, and transactions between the domestic economy and the rest of the world will affect aggregate demand. Domestic residents and firms may spend on *imports* (*M*), bringing in goods and services that are produced elsewhere in the world. At the same time, foreign consumers and firms may purchase goods and services in the domestic economy in the form of *exports* (*X*). The contribution of these transactions to domestic aggregate demand will depend on the balance between exports and imports, known as the **trade balance**.

Key term

Trade balance: the balance between expenditure on exports and on imports.

Figure 7.1 shows the components of aggregate expenditure in Pakistan in 2011. This highlights the relative size of these components. Consumption is by far the largest component, amounting to more than 86% of aggregate demand in 2011. Government current expenditure accounted for about 8%, but you should realise that this somewhat understates the importance of government in overall spending, as it excludes public spending on investment, which is treated together with private sector investment in the data. Combined public and private sector investment made up just over 13% of total GDP; this includes changes in the inventory holdings of firms. Notice that imports were higher than exports, indicating a negative balance of trade in goods and services.

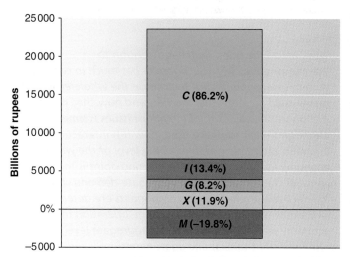

Note: *I* includes changes in inventory holdings.
Source: International Monetary Fund

Figure 7.1 The components of aggregate demand in Pakistan in 2011

Exercise 7.1

Suppose there is an economy in which the following values apply (all measured in $ million):

Consumption	75
Profits	60
Investment	30
Government expenditure	25
Exports	50
Private saving	50
Imports	55

a Calculate the level of aggregate demand.
b Calculate the trade balance.

The aggregate demand curve

The key relationship to help in explaining the macroeconomy is the **aggregate demand curve (*AD*)**, which shows the relationship between aggregate demand and the overall price level. Formally, this curve shows the total amount of goods and services demanded in an economy at any given overall level of prices.

Key term

Aggregate demand curve (*AD*): a curve showing the relationship between the level of aggregate demand in an economy and the overall price level; it shows planned expenditure at any given overall price level.

It is important to realise that this is a very different sort of demand curve from the microeconomic demand curves that were introduced in Chapter 2, where the focus was on an individual product and its relationship with its own price. Here the relationship is between the *total* demand for goods and services and the *overall* price level. Thus, aggregate demand is made up of all the components discussed above, and price is an average of all prices of goods and services in the economy.

Figure 7.2 shows an aggregate demand curve. The key question is why it slopes downwards. To answer this, it is necessary to determine the likely influence of the price level on the various components of aggregate demand that have been discussed in this chapter, as prices have not been mentioned explicitly. First, then, the discussion needs to be cast in terms of the price *level*.

When the overall level of prices is relatively low, the purchasing power of income is relatively high. In other words, low overall prices can be thought of as indicating relatively high real income. Furthermore, when prices are low, this raises the real value of households' wealth. For example, suppose a household holds a financial asset such as a bond with a fixed money value of $100. The relative (real) value of that asset is higher when the overall price level is relatively low. From the above discussion, this suggests that, ceteris paribus, a low overall price level means relatively high consumption.

A second argument relates to interest rates. When prices are relatively low, interest rates also tend to be relatively low, which would encourage both investment and consumption expenditure, as interest rates can be seen as representing the cost of borrowing to households and firms.

A third argument concerns exports and imports. It can be argued that, ceteris paribus, when prices at home are relatively low compared with the rest of the world, this will increase the competitiveness of domestically produced goods, leading to an increase in foreign demand for exports, and a fall in the demand for imports into the economy as people switch to buying home goods and services.

All of these arguments support the idea that the aggregate demand curve should be downward sloping. In other words, when the overall price level is relatively low, aggregate demand will be relatively high, and when prices are relatively high, aggregate demand will be relatively low.

There are other factors that will affect the *position* of the *AD* curve. This point will be explored after the introduction of the other side of the coin – the aggregate supply curve.

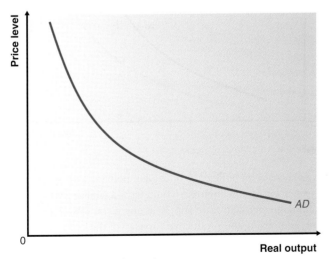

Figure 7.2 An aggregate demand curve

Summary

- Aggregate demand is the total demand in an economy, made up of consumption, investment, government spending and net exports.
- Consumption is the largest of these components and is determined by income and other influences, such as interest rates, wealth and expectations about the future.
- Investment leads to increases in the capital stock and is influenced by interest rates, past profits and expectations about future demand.
- Government expenditure may be regarded as largely autonomous.
- Trade in goods and services (exports and imports) is determined by the competitiveness of domestic goods and services compared with the rest of the world, which in turn is determined by relative inflation rates and the exchange rate. Imports are also affected by domestic income, and exports are affected by incomes in the rest of the world.
- The aggregate demand curve shows the relationship between aggregate demand and the overall price level.

7.2 Aggregate supply

Key term

Short-run aggregate supply curve: a curve showing how much output firms would be prepared to supply in the short run at any given overall price level.

The previous section discussed the notion of aggregate demand and introduced the aggregate demand curve. In order to analyse the overall macroeconomic equilibrium, it is necessary to derive a second relationship: that between aggregate supply and the price level. It is important to remember that the level of aggregate supply covers the output of all sorts of goods and services that are produced within an economy during a period of time. However, it is not simply a question of adding up all the individual supply curves from individual markets. Within an individual market, an increase in price may induce higher supply of a good because firms will switch from other markets in search of higher profits. What you now need to be looking for is a relationship between the *overall* price level and the total amount supplied, which is a completely different thing.

The total quantity of output supplied in an economy over a period of time depends upon the quantities of factors of production employed: that is, the total amounts of labour, capital and other factors used. The ability of firms to vary output in the short run will be influenced by the degree of flexibility that the firms have in varying inputs. This suggests that it is necessary to distinguish between short-run and long-run aggregate supply.

In the short run, firms may have relatively little flexibility to vary their inputs. Money wages are likely to be fixed, and if firms wish to vary output, they may need to do so by varying the intensity of utilisation of existing inputs. For example, if a firm wishes to expand output, the only way of doing so in the short run may be by paying its existing workers overtime, and it will be prepared to do this only in response to higher prices. This suggests that in the short run, aggregate supply may be upward sloping, as shown in Figure 7.3, where *SAS* represents **short-run aggregate supply**.

Firms will not want to operate in this way in the long run. It is not good practice to be permanently paying workers overtime. In the long run, therefore, firms will adjust their working practices and hire additional workers to avoid this situation.

What factors influence the position of aggregate supply? Given that aggregate supply arises from the use of inputs of factors of production, one important influence is the availability and effectiveness of factor inputs.

As far as labour is concerned, an increase in the *size of* the workforce will affect the position of aggregate supply. In practice, the size of the labour force tends to change relatively slowly unless substantial international migration is taking place. However, another important factor is the *level of skills* in the workforce. An increase in the skills that workers have will increase the amount of aggregate output that can be produced and lead to a shift in the aggregate supply curve.

For example, in Figure 7.4 aggregate supply was originally at SAS_0. An increase in the skills of the workforce means that firms are prepared to supply more output at any given overall price level, so the aggregate supply curve moves to SAS_1.

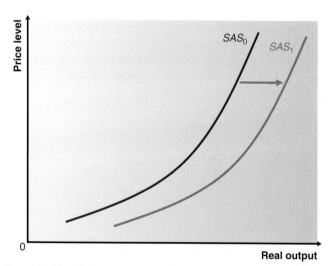

Figure 7.4 A shift in aggregate supply

An increase in the efficiency of capital, perhaps arising from improvements in technology, would have a similar effect, enabling greater aggregate supply at any given overall price level, and raising the productive capacity of the economy.

An increase in the quantity of capital will also have this effect, by increasing the capacity of the economy to produce. However, such an increase requires firms to have undertaken investment activity. In other words, the balance of spending between consumption and investment may affect the position of the aggregate supply curve in future periods.

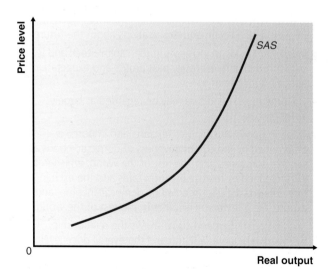

Figure 7.3 Aggregate supply in the short run

Summary

- The total quantity of output that can be produced in an economy depends upon the use of factors of production.
- The flexibility of firms to adjust output in the short run depends upon their ability to vary the inputs of factors of production.
- The aggregate supply (SAS) curve shows the relationship between aggregate supply and the overall price level.
- The position of the AS curve depends upon the availability and effectiveness of factor inputs.

7.3 Macroeconomic equilibrium

Bringing aggregate demand and aggregate supply together, the overall equilibrium position for the macroeconomy can be identified. In Figure 7.5, with aggregate supply given by SAS and aggregate demand by AD, equilibrium is reached at the real output level Y, with the price level at P.

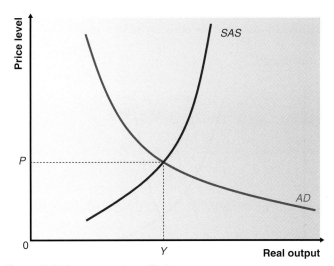

Figure 7.5 Macroeconomic equilibrium

This is an equilibrium, in the sense that if nothing changes then firms and households will have no reason to alter their behaviour in the next period. At the price P, aggregate supply is matched by aggregate demand.

Can it be guaranteed that the macroeconomic equilibrium will occur at the full-employment level of output? In other words, can we be sure that the equilibrium will be such that all workers who would like to have a job can obtain one? For example, suppose that in Figure 7.6 the output level Y^* corresponds to the full-employment level of output – that is, the level of output that represents productive capacity when all factors of production are fully employed. It may be possible to produce more than this in the short run, but only on a temporary basis, perhaps by the use of overtime. If aggregate demand is at AD^*, the macroeconomic equilibrium is at this full-employment output Y^*. However, if the aggregate demand curve is located at AD_1 the equilibrium will occur at Y_1, which is below the full-employment level, so there is surplus capacity in the economy.

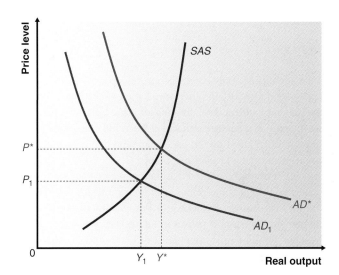

Figure 7.6 Will macroeconomic equilibrium be at full employment?

An increase in aggregate demand

Having identified macroeconomic equilibrium, it is possible to undertake some comparative static analysis. The position of the aggregate demand curve depends on the components of aggregate demand: consumption, investment, government spending and net exports. Factors that affect these components will affect the position of aggregate demand.

Consider Figure 7.7. Suppose that the economy begins in equilibrium with aggregate demand at AD_0. The equilibrium output level is Y_0, and the price level is P_0. An increase in government expenditure will affect the position of the aggregate demand curve, shifting it to AD_1. The economy will move to a new equilibrium position, with a higher output level Y_1 and a higher price level P_1.

This seems to suggest that the government can always reach full employment, simply by increasing its expenditure. However, you should be a little cautious in reaching such a conclusion, as the effect on equilibrium output and the price level will depend upon how close the economy is to the full-employment level. Notice

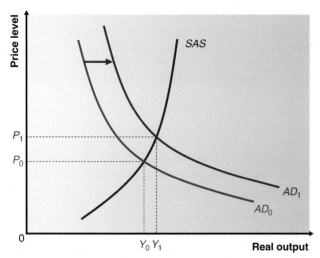

Figure 7.7 A shift in aggregate demand

The effect of a supply shock

The *AD/AS* model can also be used to analyse the effects of an external shock that affects aggregate supply. For example, suppose there is an increase in oil prices arising from a disruption to supplies in the Middle East. This raises firms' costs, and leads to a reduction in aggregate supply. Comparative static analysis can again be employed to examine the likely effects on equilibrium.

A disruption in the Middle East could lead to an increase in oil prices

that the aggregate supply curve becomes steeper as output and the price level increase. In other words, the closer the economy is to the full-employment level, the smaller is the elasticity of supply, so an increase in aggregate demand close to full employment will have more of an effect on the price level (and hence potentially on inflation) than on the level of real output.

Indeed, it might be argued that the aggregate supply curve becomes vertical at some point, as there is a maximum level of output that can be produced given the factors of production available. Such a curve is shown in Figure 7.8, where Y^* represents the full-employment level of real output. In this case, the economy has settled into an equilibrium that is below potential capacity output. We may regard this as a longer-run aggregate supply curve (*AS*), since the only way that real output can be beyond Y^* is through the temporary use of overtime, which could not be sustained in the long run.

Figure 7.9 analyses the situation. The economy begins in equilibrium with output at Y_0 and the overall level of prices at P_0. The increase in oil prices causes a movement of the aggregate supply curve from SAS_0 to SAS_1, with aggregate demand unchanged at *AD*. After the economy returns to equilibrium, the new output level has fallen to Y_1 and the overall price level has increased to P_1.

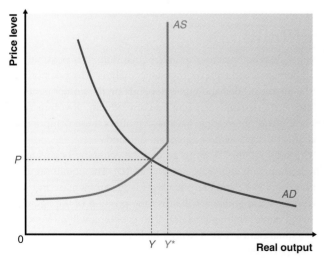

Figure 7.8 Macroeconomic equilibrium revisited

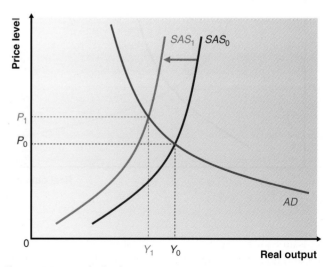

Figure 7.9 A supply shock

At the time of the first oil price crisis back in 1973/74, the UK government of the day tried to maintain the previous level of real output by stimulating aggregate demand. This had the effect of pushing up the price level, but did not have any noticeable effect on real output. Such a result is not unexpected, given the steepness of the aggregate supply curve. Indeed, in Figure 7.9 the previous output level Y_0 cannot be reached with aggregate supply in its new position.

movement *along* the other. For example, if the *AS* curve shifts as a result of a supply shock, the response is a movement *along* the *AD* curve, and vice versa. Thus, in trying to analyse the effects of a shock, the first step is to think about whether the shock affects *AD* or *AS*, and the second is to analyse whether the shock is positive or negative: that is, which way the relevant curve will shift. The move towards a new equilibrium can then be investigated.

Exercise 7.2

For each of the following, decide whether the change affects aggregate demand or aggregate supply, and sketch a diagram to illustrate the effects on equilibrium real output and overall price level. Undertake this exercise first for a starting position in the steep part of the *SAS* curve, and then repeat the exercise for an initial position further to the left, where *SAS* is more elastic.

a An advancement in technology that improves the efficiency of capital.
b A global financial crisis that reduces the demand for exports.
c An improvement in firms' expectations about future demand, such that investment expenditure increases.
d The introduction of new health and safety legislation that raises firms' costs.

Exercise 7.3

For each of the changes that you analysed in Exercise 7.2, indicate whether the result is a shift of or a movement along the *AD* and *AS* curves.

Shifts of and movements along the *AD* and *AS* curves

It is important to be aware of the distinction between shifts *of* the *AD* and *AS* curves, and movements *along* them. Typically, if a shock affects the position of one of the curves, it will lead to a

---

Summary

- Macroeconomic equilibrium is reached at the intersection of *AD* and *AS*.
- Comparative static analysis can be used to analyse the effects of changes in the factors that influence aggregate demand and aggregate supply.
- Changes in the components of aggregate demand shift the aggregate demand curve. Within the vertical segment of *AS*, changes in *AD* affect only the overall price level, but below full employment both price and real output will be affected.
- Changes in the factors affecting aggregate supply alter the long-run potential productive capacity of the economy.

8 Macroeconomic performance and inflation

In monitoring the performance of an economy, attention tends to focus on key macroeconomic issues – notably inflation, unemployment and the balance of payments. Inflation is regarded as one of the most serious afflictions that can affect a macroeconomy. In this chapter, the causes and consequences of inflation are explored.

Learning outcomes

After studying this chapter, you should:

- understand the distinction between real and nominal variables
- be familiar with the use of index numbers and the calculation of growth rates
- be aware of the meaning of the general price level, and ways of measuring it
- understand what is meant by inflation
- be aware of the varying experience of inflation in different parts of the world
- understand the quantity theory of money and its implications for macroeconomic stability
- be aware of alternative explanations for the cause of inflation
- understand the consequences of inflation for an economy.

8.1 Macroeconomic performance

In a modern economy, there are many separate markets and it is difficult to get an overall picture of how well the economy is working. So, when it comes to monitoring its overall performance, the focus tends to be on the macroeconomic aggregates – for example, total unemployment in an economy, or total spending on goods and services – rather than, say, unemployed workers in a particular occupation, or spending on a particular good.

There are a number of dimensions in which the economy as a whole can be monitored. One prime focus of economic policy in recent years has been the inflation rate, as it has been argued that maintaining a stable economic environment is crucial to enabling markets to operate effectively. A second focus has been unemployment, which has been seen as an indicator of whether the economy is using its resources to the full – in other words, whether there are factors of production that are not being fully utilised. In addition, of course, there may be concern that the people who are unemployed are being disadvantaged.

Perhaps more fundamentally, there is an interest in economic growth. Is the economy expanding its potential capacity as time goes by, thereby making more resources available for members of society? In fact, it might be argued that this is the most fundamental objective for the economy, and the most important indicator of the economy's performance. Issues surrounding economic growth will be explored in the A-level part of the book.

Other concerns may also need to be kept in mind. In particular, there is the question of how the economy interacts with the rest of the world. This aspect of macroeconomic performance needs to be monitored too. This is done through the balance of payments accounts, which are introduced in Chapter 9.

The importance of data

In order to monitor the performance of the economy, it is crucial to be able to observe how the economy is functioning, and for this you need data. Remember that economics, especially macroeconomics, is a non-experimental discipline. It is not possible to conduct experiments to see how the economy reacts to various stimuli in order to learn how it works. Instead, it is necessary to observe the economy, and to come to a judgement about whether or not its performance is satisfactory, and whether macroeconomic theories about how the economy works are supported by the evidence. So, a reliable measure is needed for tracking each of the variables mentioned above, in order to observe how the economy is evolving through time.

Most of the economic statistics used by economists are collected and published by various government agencies. Such data are published by national statistics offices. Data on countries around the world are also published by the International Monetary Fund (IMF), the World Bank and the United Nations. There is little alternative to relying on such sources because the accurate collection of data is an expensive and time-consuming business.

The IMF Headquarters in Washington DC, USA

Care needs to be taken in the interpretation of economic data. It is important to be aware of how the data are compiled, and the extent to which they are indicators of what economists are trying to measure. It is also important to remember that the economic environment is ever changing, and that the economic events that are observed can rarely be attributed to single causes. This is because the ceteris paribus condition that underlies so much economic analysis is rarely fulfilled in reality. In other words, you cannot rely on 'other things remaining constant' when using data about the real world.

It is also important to realise that even the government statistical agencies cannot observe with absolute accuracy. Indeed, some data take so long to be assembled that early estimates are provisional in nature and subject to later revision as more information becomes available. Data used in international comparisons must be treated with even greater caution.

Real and nominal measurements

The measurement of economic variables poses many dilemmas for statisticians. Not least is the fundamental problem of what to use as units of measurement. Suppose economists wish to measure total output produced in an economy during successive years. In the first place, they cannot use volume measures. They may be able to count how many computers, passenger cars, tins of paint and cauliflowers the economy produces – but how do they add all these different items together to produce a total?

An obvious solution is to use the money values. Given prices for all the items, it is possible to calculate the money values of all these goods and thus produce a measurement of the total output produced in an economy during a year in terms of pounds sterling. However, this is just the beginning of the problem because, in order to monitor changes in total output between two years, it is important to be aware that not only do the volumes of goods produced change, but so too do their prices. In effect, this means that, if pounds sterling or dollars are used as the unit of measurement, the unit of measurement will change from one year to the next as prices change.

This is a problem that is not faced by most of the physical sciences. After all, the length of a metre does not alter from one year to the next, so if the length of something is being measured, the unit is fixed. Economists, however, have to make allowance for changing prices when measuring in money terms.

Measurements made using prices that are current at the time a transaction takes place are known as measurements of **nominal values**. When prices are rising, these nominal measurements will always overstate the extent to which an economic variable is growing through time. Clearly, to analyse performance, economists will be more interested in '**real**' **values** – that is, the quantities produced after having removed the effects of price changes. One way in which these real measures can be obtained is by taking the volumes produced in each year and valuing these quantities at the prices that prevailed in some base year. This then enables allowance to be made for the changes in prices that take place, permitting a focus on the real values. These can be thought of as being measured at *constant prices*.

For example, suppose that last year you bought a tub of ice cream for $2, but that inflation has been 10%, so that this year you had to pay $2.20 for the same tub. Your *real* consumption of the item has not changed, but your spending has increased. If you were to use the value of your spending to measure changes in consumption through time, it would be misleading, as you know that your *real* consumption has not changed at all (so it is still $2), although its *nominal* value has increased to $2.20.

Key terms

Nominal value: the value of an economic variable based on current prices, taking no account of changing prices through time.

Real value: the value of an economic variable taking account of changing prices through time.

Index numbers

In some cases there is no apparent unit of measurement that is meaningful. For example, if you wished to measure the general level of prices in an economy, there is no meaningful unit of measurement that could be used. In such cases the solution is to use **index numbers**, which is a form of ratio that compares the value of a variable with some base point.

Key term

> **Index number**: a device for comparing the value of a variable in one period or location with a base observation (e.g. the retail price index measures the average level of prices relative to a base period).

For example, suppose the price of a kilo of oranges last year was $0.80, and this year it is $0.84. How can the price between the two periods be compared? One way of doing it is to calculate the percentage change:

$$100 \times (84 - 80) \div 80 = 5\%$$

(Note that this is the formula for calculating any growth rate in percentage terms. The change in the variable is always expressed as a percentage of the initial value, not the final value.)

An alternative way of doing this is to calculate an index number. In the above example, the current value of the index could be calculated as $100 \times 84 \div 80 = 105$. In other words, the current value is divided by the base value and multiplied by 100. The resulting number gives the current value relative to the base value. This turns out to be a useful way of expressing a range of economic variables where you want to show the value relative to a base period.

One particular use for this technique is when you want to show the average level of prices at different points in time. For such a general price index, one procedure is to define a typical basket of commodities that reflects the spending pattern of a representative household. The cost of that bundle can be calculated in a base year, and then in subsequent years. The cost in the base year is set to equal 100, and in subsequent years the index is measured relative to that base date, thereby reflecting the change in prices since then. For example, if in the second year the weighted average increase in prices were 2.5%, then the index in year 2 would take on the value 102.5 (based on year 1 = 100). Such a general index of prices could be seen as an index of the *cost of living* for the representative household, as it would give the level of prices faced by the average household relative to the base year.

Notice that there is a crucial distinction between such measurements of the general price *level* and the notion of *inflation*, which is a key economic indicator frequently discussed in the media. A price index such as those described above measures the average level of prices at a particular moment in time. Inflation, on the other hand, is the rate of change of the price index – it measures the rate of which prices are changing through time. These two different things should not be confused with each other, although clearly they are related.

Exercise 8.1

Table 8.1 provides data on consumer prices for Malaysia, the USA and Pakistan.

Table 8.1 Consumer prices

	Malaysia consumer price index	Mauritius consumer price index	Pakistan consumer price index
2001	93.0	82.3	80.3
2002	94.7	87.6	82.9
2003	95.7	91.0	85.3
2004	97.1	95.3	91.7
2005	100.0	100.0	100.0
2006	103.6	108.9	107.9
2007	105.7	118.5	116.1
2008	111.5	130.1	139.7
2009	112.1	133.4	158.7
2010	114.0	137.2	180.8
2011	117.6	146.2	202.3

Source: International Monetary Fund

a Calculate the annual inflation rate for each of the countries from 2002 to 2011.
b Plot these three inflation series on a graph against time.
c By what percentage did prices increase in each country over the whole period – that is, between 2001 and 2011?
d Which economies do you judge to have experienced most and least stability in the inflation rate?

Summary

- Macroeconomics is the study of the interrelationships between economic variables at the level of the whole economy.
- Some variables are of particular interest when monitoring the performance of an economy – for example, inflation, unemployment and economic growth.
- As economists cannot easily conduct experiments in order to test economic theory, they rely on the use of economic data: that is, observations of the world around them.
- Data measured in money terms need to be handled carefully, as prices change over time, thereby affecting the units in which many economic variables are measured.
- Index numbers are helpful in comparing the value of a variable with a base date or unit.

8.2 Measuring the price level

In any economy, prices of different goods and services change at a different rate through time. This is partly in response to changes in demand and supply – if a good becomes popular, excess demand will tend to push up the price of the good as the market moves to a new equilibrium, whilst some other goods may face the opposite effect so that prices rise less steeply. A price index designed to represent the general level of prices in an economy is based on taking a weighted average of individual prices, as described above. With prices changing at different rates, the choice of which goods and services to include in the index – and with what weights – is an important step. For example, it is likely that different groups in a society choose to consume different combinations of goods and services, so may experience inflation at different rates. A first step in measuring the general price level is thus to find a representative bundle of commodities, together with the relative weighting to be applied to each. The experience of the UK can be used to illustrate some of the issues that arise.

The consumer price index

The most important general price index in the UK is the **consumer price index (CPI)**, which has been used by the government in setting its inflation target since the beginning of 2004. This index is based on the prices of a bundle of goods and services measured at different points in time. 180 000 individual price quotes on 680 different products are collected by ONS each month, by visits to shops, and using the telephone and internet. Data on spending from the *Household Final Monetary Consumption Expenditure* is used to compile the weights for the items included in the index. These weights are updated each year, as changes in the consumption patterns of households need to be accommodated if the index is to remain representative. A criticism of the index has been that it excludes housing costs of owner occupiers and a new index was launched in March 2013 to remedy this. The index is known as CPIH and is published alongside the CPI.

Key terms

Consumer price index (CPI): a measure of the general level of prices in the UK, adopted as the government's inflation target since December 2003.

Inflation: the rate of change of the average price level: for example, the percentage annual rate of change of the CPI.

As noted in the previous section, it is important to remember that the CPI provides a measurement of the *level* of prices in the economy. This is not inflation: **inflation** is the *rate of change* of prices, and the percentage change in the CPI provides one estimate of the inflation rate.

Being able to calculate percentage changes is a useful skill. Going back to the example of the ice cream from page 55, remember that you had bought a tub of ice cream for $2 last year, but now have to pay $2.20. The percentage change in the price is obtained by dividing the *change* in price by the original price and multiplying by 100. Thus, the percentage change is $100 \times 0.20/2.00 = 10\%$.

Alternative measurements of inflation

The traditional measure of inflation in the UK for many years was the **retail price index (RPI)**, which was first calculated (under another name) in the early twentieth century to evaluate the extent to which workers were affected by price changes during the First World War. When the British government first set an explicit inflation target in 1997, it chose the RPIX, which is the RPI excluding mortgage interest payments. This was felt to be a better measure of the effectiveness of macroeconomic policy. It was argued that if interest rates are used to curb inflation, then including mortgage interest payments in the inflation measure will be misleading.

Key term

Retail price index (RPI): a measure of the average level of prices in the UK.

The CPI replaced RPIX partly because it is believed to be a more appropriate indicator for evaluating policy effectiveness. In addition, it has the advantage of being calculated using the same methodology as is used in other countries within the European Union, so that it is more useful than the RPIX for making international comparisons of inflation.

The CPI and RPI are based on a similar approach, although there are some significant differences in the detail of the calculation. Both measures set out to calculate the overall price level at different points in time. Each is based on calculating the overall cost of a representative basket of goods and services at different points in time relative to a base period. Both are produced by combining some 120 000 individual prices, which are collected each month for around 650 representative items. The result of these calculations is an index that shows how the general level of prices has changed relative to the base year. The rate of inflation is then calculated as the percentage rate of change of the price index, whether it be the CPI or the RPI.

The indexes share a common failing, arising from the fixed weights used in calculating the overall index. Suppose the price of a particular item rises more rapidly than other prices during the year. One response by consumers is to substitute an alternative, cheaper, product. As the indices are based on fixed weights, they do not pick up this substitution effect, and therefore tend to overstate the price level in terms of the cost of living. Some attempt is made to overcome this problem by changing the weights on an annual basis in order to limit the impact of major changes. This includes incorporating new items when appropriate – for example, digital cameras were included in the CPI calculations for the first time in 2004, reflecting a change in consumer spending patterns.

The CPI and RPI differ for a number of reasons, partly because of differences in the content of the basket of goods and services that are included, and partly in terms of the population of people who are covered by the index. For example, in calculating the weights, the RPI excludes pensioner households and the highest-income households, whereas the CPI does not. There are also some other differences in the ways that the calculations are carried out.

Figure 8.1 shows data for the rates of change of the RPI, RPIX and the CPI since March 1997. These rates have been calculated on a monthly basis, computing the percentage rate of change of each index relative to the value 12 months previously.

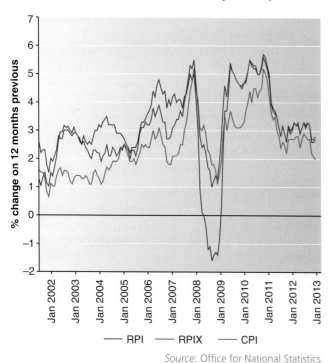

Source: Office for National Statistics

Figure 8.1 Alternative inflation measures in the UK, 2002–2013

A noticeable characteristic of Figure 8.1 is that for much of the period the CPI has shown a lower rate of change than the RPI. In part this reflects the way in which the prices are combined, but it also reflects the fact that different items and households are covered.

Summary

- In order to monitor the performance of an economy at the macroeconomic level, it is necessary to measure some key economic variables.
- There is an important distinction between real and nominal measurements.
- A key macroeconomic variable is the general, or average, price level in an economy.
- The general price level is calculated as a weighted average of the prices of goods and services prevailing in the economy.
- The retail price index (RPI) is the best-known measure of the average price level in the UK.
- In December 2003 the British government adopted the consumer price index (CPI) as its preferred measure of the price level.
- Inflation is defined as the rate of change of the general price level.

8.3 The experience of inflation

Economies have experienced inflation to varying degrees in the past. Figure 8.2 shows how inflation affected the world in the period since 1970, and how advanced and developing countries were affected in different ways.

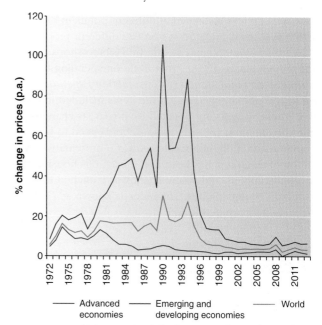

Note: p.a. stands for 'per annum', meaning each year
Source: International Monetary Fund

Figure 8.2 World inflation since 1972 (% change in consumer prices)

For the world as a whole, inflation had been steady (below 10% per year) through most of the 1960s until the mid-1970s, when there was an acceleration following the first oil-price crisis in 1973/74. Average inflation then remained relatively high until the period of relative stability in the late 1990s and early 2000s. The figure also shows that in the advanced countries, inflation decelerated relatively quickly from about 1980 onwards, whereas emerging and developing countries experienced acceleration and instability during the 1980s and 1990s.

In part, this was a regional phenomenon, with Latin America being especially prone to very high inflation during this period. When inflation reaches such high levels, it is known as **hyperinflation**. This can be seen in Figure 8.3, which contrasts inflation in Latin America ('Western Hemisphere') with that in developing Asian economies and the world as a whole. Notice the scale of the vertical axis – in order to show average inflation across the Western Hemisphere, the other series on the graph get compressed to the axis. Average inflation in the Western Hemisphere peaked at 515% in 1990, but this conceals the wide variation in inflation between countries. In 1990, Argentina was experiencing inflation of 2314% (down from 3079% in 1989), Brazil was suffering 2947% and Peru 7482%. Bolivia had experienced inflation at 11 750% in 1985.

Key term

Hyperinflation: occurs when inflation is very high, sometimes defined as being above 50% per month.

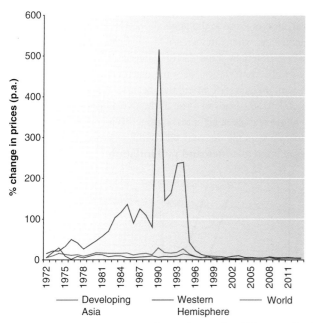

Figure 8.3 Inflation in Latin America and Asia since 1972 (% change in consumer prices)

Source: International Monetary Fund

In contrast, Figure 8.4 shows inflation in developing countries in Asia and in sub-Saharan Africa over the same period. Again, notice that the vertical scale of the graph has changed radically. The figure reveals that these countries in Asia experienced

inflation below the world average for much of the period, although the spike at the time of the 1973/74 oil price hike is more marked. Notice that countries in sub-Saharan Africa suffered from higher inflation from the 1990s onwards.

It should not be assumed that prices always increase, all the time. There have been countries (e.g. Japan) that have experienced periods in which the general level of prices has fallen. Such a situation is known as **deflation**.

Key term

Deflation: a period in which the general level of prices in an economy falls.

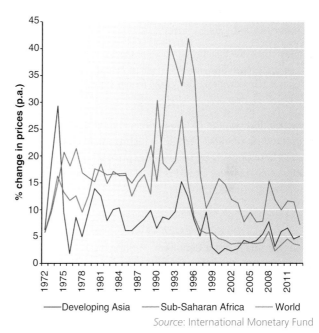

Source: International Monetary Fund

Figure 8.4 Inflation in Asia and sub-Saharan Africa since 1972 (% change in consumer prices)

Exercise 8.2

Find out the current rate of inflation in the country in which you live. Discuss whether this is likely to cause problems for the economy.

Summary

- The control of inflation has been the major focus of macroeconomic policy in many countries in recent years.
- Experience with inflation has varied in different regions and countries around the world.
- Some countries, especially in Latin America and parts of sub-Saharan Africa, have experienced hyperinflation.
- At the other extreme, some countries have experienced deflation.

8.4 Causes of inflation

The quantity theory of money

A starting point for discussion is the so-called quantity theory of money. This requires a new concept, that of the velocity of circulation. If the **money stock** is defined as the quantity of money (notes and coins) in circulation in the economy, the **velocity of circulation** is defined as the speed with which that money stock changes hands. It is defined as the volume of transactions divided by the money stock.

> ### Key terms
>
> **Money stock:** the quantity of money in the economy.
> **Velocity of circulation:** the rate at which money changes hands: the volume of transactions divided by the money stock.

In practice, the volume of transactions is seen as being represented by nominal income, which is the level of real income (Y) multiplied by the average price level (P). If V is the velocity of circulation, and M is the size of the money stock, then the following equation holds:

$$V = PY/M$$

Notice that this is just a definition. Multiplying both sides of the equation by M gives:

$$MV = PY$$

This is still based on a definition, so is not a theory. However, the Monetarist school of economists argued that the velocity of circulation (V) would be constant – or at least would be stable over time. They also argued that real output would always tend rapidly towards a natural rate. These assumptions together with the equation $MV = PY$ provide us with a direct link between money (M) and the overall price level (P). This relationship suggests that prices can only increase persistently if money stock itself increases persistently.

Even if we allow real output to vary through time, the equation still shows that persistent inflation can arise only when money stock persistently grows more rapidly than real output. This provides the backdrop for the discussion of inflation.

Supply shocks

Inflation occurs when there is a rise in the general price level. However, it is important to distinguish between a one-off increase in the price level and a sustained rise over a long period of time. For example, a one-off rise in the price of oil may have an effect on the price level by shifting aggregate supply, thus affecting the equilibrium price level – as shown in Figure 8.5

(reproducing Figure 7.9). However, this takes the economy to a new equilibrium price level, and if nothing else were to change, there would be no reason for prices to continue to rise beyond P_1.

This is one reason why prices may begin to increase. Inflation thus may be initiated on the supply side of the macroeconomy, arising from an increase in the costs faced by firms. This is sometimes referred to as **cost-push inflation**, as the increase in the overall level of prices is cost-driven.

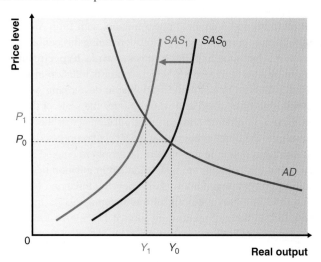

Figure 8.5 A supply shock

An increase in aggregate demand

In terms of the AD/AS model, it is clear that an alternative explanation of a rise in the general price level could come from the demand side, where an increase in aggregate demand leads to a rise in prices, especially if the AS curve becomes so steep in the long run as to become vertical, as some macroeconomists believe. This is shown in Figure 8.6, where the increase in aggregate demand from AD_0 to AD_1 leads to a rise in the overall price level from P_0 to P_1 with no change at all in real output. An increase in the price level emanating from the demand side of the macroeconomy is sometimes referred to as **demand-pull inflation**.

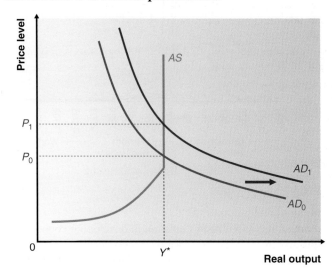

Figure 8.6 An increase in aggregate demand

Key terms

Cost-push inflation: inflation initiated by an increase in the costs faced by firms, arising on the supply side of the economy.

Demand-pull inflation: inflation initiated by an increase in aggregate demand.

Summary

- Inflation can be initiated on either the supply side of an economy or the demand side.
- However, sustained inflation can take place only if there is also a sustained increase in money supply.

8.5 Consequences of inflation

A crucial question is why it matters if an economy experiences inflation. The answer is that very high inflation gives rise to a number of costs. In particular, unanticipated inflation means that decision-makers will take poor decisions based on their mistaken expectations of inflation. For example, people may choose to hold more money as cash, or in low- or no-interest bank accounts, rather than investing in assets that bring a higher return. People holding assets that offer a fixed return or who live on fixed incomes may find that they have lost out when inflation is higher than expected.

The fact that firms have to keep amending their price lists raises the costs of undertaking transactions. These costs are often known as the *menu costs* of inflation; however, this should not be expected to be significant unless inflation really is very high. A second cost of very high inflation is that it discourages people from holding money because, at the very high nominal interest rates that occur when inflation is high, the opportunity cost of holding money becomes great. People therefore try to keep their money in interest-bearing accounts for as long as possible, even if it means making frequent trips to the bank – for which reason these are known as the *shoe leather costs* of inflation.

This reluctance to use money for transactions may inhibit the effectiveness of markets. For example, there was a period in the early 1980s when inflation in Argentina was so high that some city parking fines had to be paid in litres of petrol rather than in cash. Markets will not work effectively when people do not use money and the economy begins to slip back towards a barter economy. The situation may be worsened if taxes or pensions are not properly indexed so that they do not keep up with inflation.

However, these costs are felt mainly when inflation reaches the hyperinflation stage. This has been rare in developed countries in recent years, although it was noted earlier that Latin America was prone to hyperinflation for a period in the 1980s, and some of the transition economies also went through very high inflation periods as they began to introduce market reforms; one example of this was the Ukraine, where inflation reached 10 000% per year in the early 1990s. Another example is the African country of Zimbabwe, where it was reported that inflation reached around 24 411% per year in 2007 before going off the scale.

However, there may be costs associated with inflation even when it does not reach these heights, especially if inflation is volatile. If the rate of change of prices cannot be confidently predicted by firms, the increase in uncertainty may be damaging, and firms may become reluctant to undertake the investment that would expand the economy's productive capacity. Firms can take decisions taking into account anticipated inflation, but when unanticipated inflation occurs, this can impose costs on society.

Furthermore, as Chapter 5 emphasised, prices are very important in allocating resources in a market economy. Inflation may consequently inhibit the ability of prices to act as reliable signals in this process, leading to a wastage of resources and lost business opportunities.

It is these last reasons that have elevated the control of inflation to one of the central planks of government macroeconomic policy in many countries. However, it should be noticed that the target for inflation has not necessarily been set at zero. The reasoning here is twofold. One argument is that it has to be accepted that measured inflation will overstate actual inflation, partly because it is so difficult to take account of quality changes in products such as computers, where it is impossible to distinguish accurately between a price change and a quality change. Second, wages and prices tend to be sticky in a downward direction: in other words, firms may be reluctant to lower prices and wages. A modest rate of inflation (e.g. 2%) thus allows relative prices to change more readily, with prices in some sectors rising by more than in others. This may help price signals to be more effective in guiding resource allocation.

Exercise 8.3

Suppose that next year inflation in the economy in which you live suddenly takes off, reaching 60% per annum – in other words, prices rise by 60% – but so do incomes. Discuss how this would affect your daily life. Why would it be damaging for the economy as a whole?

Summary

- High inflation imposes costs on society and reduces the effectiveness with which markets can work.
- Low inflation reduces uncertainty, and may encourage investment by firms.

9 The balance of payments and the exchange rate

Most economies in the world are open economies – they engage in international trade, exporting and importing goods and services, albeit to varying degrees. This chapter analyses these transactions, and explores ways in which the domestic economy can be influenced by the international environment. This requires discussion of the balance of payments and the foreign exchange (Forex) market.

Learning outcomes

After studying this chapter, you should:
- be familiar with the role and importance of the balance of payments
- be able to explain how a deficit or surplus on the current account of the balance of payments may arise
- be aware of the consequences of a surplus or deficit on the current account of the balance of payments
- understand how exchange rates are determined
- be aware of how changes in the exchange rate influence the macroeconomy through export and import prices and aggregate demand.

9.1 The balance of payments

When a country engages in international trade, it is important to be able to keep track of the various transactions that take place between the residents of a country and the rest of the world. The **balance of payments** is the set of accounts that monitors these transactions. For an individual household it is important to monitor incomings and outgoings, as items purchased must be paid for in some way – either by using income or savings, or by borrowing. In a similar way, a country has to pay for goods, services or assets that are bought from other countries. The balance of payments accounts enable the analysis of such international transactions.

Key term

Balance of payments: a set of accounts showing the transactions conducted between residents of a country and the rest of the world.

As with the household, transactions can be categorised as either incoming or outgoing items. For example, if a car made in Malaysia is exported (i.e. purchased by a non-resident of Malaysia), this is an 'incoming' item, as the payment for the car is a credit to Malaysia. On the other hand, the purchase of Thai pineapples (an import) is a debit item.

Similarly, all other transactions entered into the balance of payments accounts can be identified as credit or debit items, depending upon the direction of the payment. In other words, when money flows into the country as the result of a transaction, that is a credit; if money flows out, it is a debit. As all items have to be paid for in some way, the overall balance of payments when everything is added together must be zero. However, individual components can be positive or negative.

In line with international standards (as set out by the IMF), the accounts are divided into three categories: the **current account**, the **capital account** and the **financial account**. In addition, it is important to identify transactions in **reserve assets**. Taken together, these items should all sum to zero, as the overall balance of payments must always be in balance. However, because it is not possible to record everything accurately, a final item called 'errors and omissions' or the 'balancing item' ensures overall balance.

Key terms

Current account of the balance of payments: an account identifying transactions in goods and services between the residents of a country and the rest of the world.

Financial account of the balance of payments: an account identifying transactions in financial assets between the residents of a country and the rest of the world.

Capital account of the balance of payments: an account identifying transactions in (physical) capital between the residents of a country and the rest of the world.

Reserve assets: stocks of foreign assets (e.g. foreign currency or gold) owned by the central bank of a country to enable it to meet any mismatch between the demand and supply of the country's currency.

Table 9.1 summarises the key components of the balance of payments accounts for Pakistan in 2010.

Table 9.1 The balance of payments accounts, Pakistan 2010 (US$ million)

Exports of goods		21 469
Imports of goods		32 915
Visible balance		−11 446
Services (credits)		6 593
Services (debits)		7 106
Invisible balance		−513
Income (balance)		−3 187
Transfers (balance)		13 778
	Current account balance	−1 368
	Capital account balance	125
Direct investment (balance)		1 975
Portfolio investment (balance)		−108
Other investment (balance)		1 076
	Financial account balance	2 943
	Errors and omissions	−1 006
	Overall balance	694
	Reserves and related items	−694

Source: International Monetary Fund

The current account

The current account identifies transactions in goods and services, together with income payments and international transfers. Income payments here include the earnings of residents from employment abroad and payments of investment income. Transfers are mainly transactions between governments. Flows of bilateral aid and social security payments abroad are also included here.

Commentators in the media often focus on the current account. Three main items appear on this account. First,

there is the balance of trade in goods and services – in other words, the balance between exports and imports of goods and services. If domestic residents buy foreign cars, this is an import and counts as a negative entry on the current account; on the other hand, if someone abroad buys a domestically produced car, this is an export and constitutes a positive entry. Trade in goods is known as visible trade, and the **visible balance** is the balance between exports and imports of goods. On the other hand, the **invisible balance** is the balance between exports and imports of services.

Key terms

Visible trade: trade in goods.
Invisible trade: trade in services.

The second item in the current account is income. Part of this represents employment income, but the major item is made up of profits, dividends and interest arising from domestic ownership of overseas assets – and, of course, payments of income arising from foreign ownership of domestic assets, whether from foreign direct investment or portfolio investment. The income balance for Pakistan in 2010 showed a deficit.

Finally, there are international transfers – either transfers through central government or transfers made or received by private individuals. This includes taxes and social contributions received from non-resident workers and businesses, bilateral aid flows and military grants. For Pakistan in 2010, this part of the current account showed a strong surplus, an important element of which was remittances of income from Pakistan nationals working abroad.

It is important to realise that the overall balance on the current account arises from combining the balances on all of these items. An overall current account deficit arises when the deficit items outweigh the surplus items in the accounts.

It is also important to realise that a deficit on the current account must be balanced by a surplus on the financial and capital accounts. In the short run, it may be possible to finance a trade deficit by selling domestic financial assets to foreigners, or by borrowing from overseas. However, this might not be regarded as being desirable in the longer term, if this affects the overall ownership pattern of assets in the longer term. For this reason, the current account cannot be viewed in isolation from the rest of the balance of payments.

The capital account

The capital account is relatively small for most countries. It contains capital transfers, the largest item of which is associated with migrants. When a person changes status from a non-resident to resident of a country, any assets owned by that person are transferred to being domestically owned.

The financial account

The financial account measures transactions in financial assets, including direct and portfolio flows.

The trend towards globalisation means that both inward and outward investment increased substantially during the 1990s for many countries, although there was a dip after the terrorist attacks on the USA. However, foreign investment flows recovered quite quickly, only to be affected again by the global recession of the late 2000s.

An important question is whether it is sustainable in the long run to finance a current account deficit by running a financial account surplus. Selling assets or borrowing abroad has future implications for the current account, as there will be outflows of investment income, and debt repayments in the future following today's financial surplus. It also has implications for interest rate policy. If the authorities hold interest rates high relative to the rest of the world, this will tend to attract inflows of investment, again with future implications for the current account. This will be explained in Chapter 27.

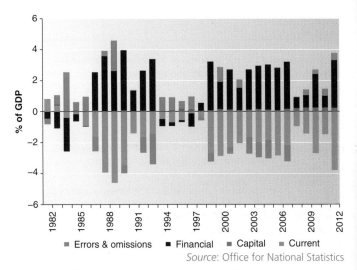

Source: Office for National Statistics

Figure 9.1 The UK balance of payments, 1982–2012

Exercise 9.1

Find out what are the most significant components of the balance of payments accounts in your own country. Discuss ways in which this may affect the development of the economy.

Exercise 9.2

Allocate each of the following items to the current, financial or capital account, and calculate the balances for each account. Check that (together with errors and omissions) the total is zero. All data refer to 2012, at current prices in $ billion.

a	Trade in goods	−68.79
b	Migrants' transfers	+1.94
c	Total net direct investment	+57.80
d	Investment income	+26.35
e	Current transfers	−12.01
f	Transactions in reserve assets	+0.43
g	Trade in services	+24.61
h	Other capital transfers	−0.45
i	Compensation of employees	−0.61
j	Net portfolio investment	−29.46
k	Other transactions in financial assets	+11.91
l	Errors and omissions	−11.95

Summary

- The balance of payments is a set of accounts that contains details of the transactions that take place between the residents of an economy and the rest of the world.
- The accounts are divided into three sections: the current, financial and capital accounts.
- The current account identifies transactions in goods and services, together with income payments and international transfers.
- The financial account measures transactions in financial assets, including investment flows.
- The capital account, which is relatively small, contains capital transfers.
- Transactions in reserve assets complete the accounts.
- The overall balance of payments must always be zero.

Summary

- The balance of payments is a set of accounts that contains details of the transactions that take place between the residents of an economy and the rest of the world.
- The accounts are divided into three sections: the current, financial and capital accounts.
- The current account identifies transactions in goods and services, together with some income payments and international transfers.
- The financial account measures transactions in financial assets, including investment flows and central government transactions in foreign reserves.
- The capital account, which is relatively small, contains capital transfers.
- The overall balance of payments must always be zero.

Figure 9.1 shows the relative magnitude of the main accounts of the UK balance of payments since 1980. This shows very clearly that the key accounts are the current and financial accounts, with a persistent deficit on the current account being balanced by a persistent surplus on the financial account, and the capital account being of minor significance. Notice that the account balances in the figure have been expressed as a percentage of GDP.

9.2 The exchange rate and international competitiveness

Closely associated with the balance of payments is the **exchange rate** – the price of one currency in terms of another. The exchange rate is important because it influences the prices that domestic consumers must pay for imported goods, services and assets, and also the price that foreigners pay for domestically produced goods, services and assets. Chapter 4 introduced the notion of the demand and supply of foreign currency, reproduced as Figure 9.2.

This uses ringgits as an example, with the vertical axis representing the price of Malaysian ringgits in terms of US dollars. The demand for ringgits arises from people holding US dollars wanting to purchase Malaysian goods, services or assets, whereas the supply emanates from holders of ringgits wanting to purchase US goods, services or assets. The connection is that the balance of payments accounts itemise these transactions, which entail the demand for and supply of ringgits. Notice that the demand for currency is a *derived demand* – thus ringgits are demanded when people holding dollars or other currencies want to buy Malaysian goods, services or assets. Similarly, ringgits are supplied when Malaysians want to buy foreign goods, services or assets.

> ### Key term
>
> Exchange rate: the price of one currency in terms of another.

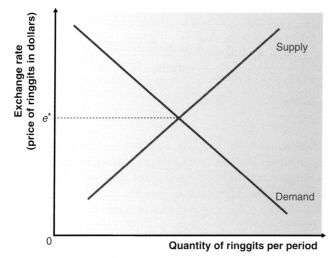

Figure 9.2 The market for ringgits

Malaysia's biggest exports, palm oil and oil, create a demand for local currency

In analysing the balance of payments, the relative competitiveness of domestically produced goods and services is an important issue. The exchange rate plays a key role in this process. If a country persistently shows a deficit on the current account, does that imply that the goods that it produces are uncompetitive in international markets?

Consider the situation from the perspective of the Malaysian economy. The demand for Malaysian exports in world markets depends upon a number of factors. In some ways, it is similar to the demand for a good. In general, the demand for a good depends on its price, on the prices of other goods, and on consumer incomes and preferences. In a similar way, you can think of the demand for Malaysian exports as depending on the price of Malaysian goods, the price of other countries' goods, incomes in the rest of the world and foreigners' preferences for Malaysian goods over those produced elsewhere. However, in the case of international transactions the exchange rate is also relevant, as this determines the purchasing power of Malaysian incomes in the rest of the world. Similarly, the demand for imports into Malaysia depends upon the relative prices of domestic and foreign goods, incomes in Malaysia, preferences for foreign and domestically produced goods and the exchange rate. These factors will all come together to determine the balance of demand for exports and imports.

The exchange rate plays a key role in influencing the levels of both imports and exports, and thus affects the balance of payments, so the way it changes over time and the way in which it is determined is important.

Figure 9.3 shows the time path of the US$/£ exchange rate. The period should be seen in two sections. Until 1971, the UK government managed the exchange rate. From 1949 until 1967, the exchange rate was pegged at $2.80 per pound. The peg changed to $2.40 per pound in 1967, a policy intervention known as 'devaluation', which will be discussed later in the chapter. Since then the rate has been left to the market. The graph shows some fluctuations between 1971 and the late 1980s, around a declining trend. Since then the exchange rate seems to have remained fairly steady. Nonetheless, there was a fall from a peak of $2.50 to the pound in 1972 to $1.50 some 30 years later. Other things being equal, this suggests an improvement in the competitiveness of UK products. In other words, Americans wanting to buy UK goods got more pounds for their dollars in 2002 than in 1972, and thus would have tended to find UK goods more attractive.

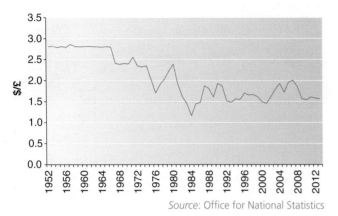

Source: Office for National Statistics

Figure 9.3 The sterling exchange rate

Figure 9.4 shows the $/ringgit exchange rate. This also reveals some 'flat' periods, when the ringgit was pegged against the dollar – namely between 1952 and 1971, and again for a period after the Asian financial crisis of 1997. Again, the changes shown in the graph suggest (other things being equal) that there were changes in the international competitiveness of Malaysian goods over time.

However, some care is needed because other things do not remain equal. In particular, remember that the competitiveness of domestic goods in overseas markets depends not only on the exchange rate, but also on movements in the prices of goods over time, so this needs to be taken into account – which is why Figure 9.4 refers to the **nominal exchange rate**. In other words, if the prices of Malaysian goods have risen more rapidly than prices in the USA, this will have partly offset the downward movement in the exchange rate.

Source: International Monetary Fund

Figure 9.4 The nominal ringgit exchange rate

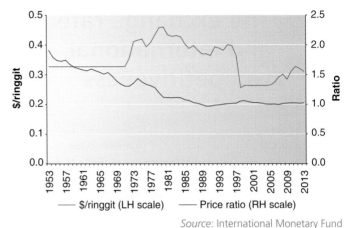

Source: International Monetary Fund

Figure 9.5 The nominal ringgit exchange rate and the ratio of consumer prices

Figure 9.5 shows the nominal exchange rate again, but also the ratio of consumer prices in Malaysia relative to the USA (plotted using the right-hand scale). This reveals that in fact prices in Malaysia rose much less steeply than those in the USA until about 1990. Thus, the movement in relative prices until 1990 improved the competitiveness of Malaysian goods, as inflation was lower in Malaysia than in the USA, as is confirmed in Figure 9.6. After 1990, the ratio settles down, indicating that the two countries were experiencing inflation at very similar rates in this period.

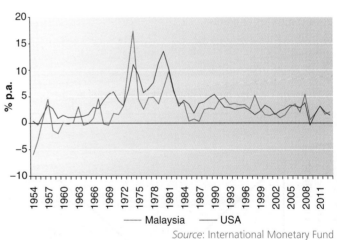

Source: International Monetary Fund

Figure 9.6 Inflation in Malaysia and the USA

In order to assess the overall competitiveness of Malaysian goods compared with the USA, it is necessary to calculate the **real exchange rate**, which is defined as the nominal exchange rate multiplied by the ratio of relative prices.

The real exchange rate is shown in Figure 9.7, superimposed on the nominal rate. Remember that (other things being equal) a fall in the exchange rate means an improvement in competitiveness, so the fall in the real exchange rate during the 1950s and 1960s (when the nominal rate was pegged) shows how Malaysia's competitiveness gradually improved during that period. The closeness of the two series after 1990 reflects the similarities in the inflation rates of Malaysia and the USA.

Notice that the series in Figure 9.7 relates only to competitiveness relative to the USA, as it is the real US$/ringgit exchange rate. An alternative measure is the **effective exchange rate**, shown in Figure 9.8. This shows the strength of the ringgit relative to a weighted average of exchange rates of Malaysia's trading partners.

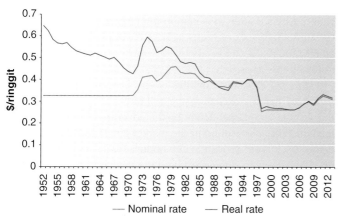

Source: International Monetary Fund

Figure 9.7 The ringgit exchange rate

Source: International Monetary Fund

Figure 9.8 The ringgit effective exchange rate

Key terms

Nominal exchange rate: the price of one currency in terms of another, with no account being taken of changes in relative prices in the two countries.

Real exchange rate: the nominal exchange rate adjusted for differences in relative inflation rates between countries.

Effective exchange rate: the exchange rate for a country relative to a weighted average of currencies of its trading partners.

Exercise 9.3

Table 9.2 provides data for the exchange rate for the Pakistan rupee (PKR) against the US dollar, expressed as $ per rupee. Also provided is the consumer price index for Pakistan and for the USA. Use these data to calculate the real exchange rate for the period, and comment on the effect that any movement will have had on the competitiveness of Pakistani goods and services relative to the USA.

Table 9.2 Competitiveness of Pakistan compared to the USA

	Nominal exchange rate ($/PKR)	Consumer price index (2000 = 100)	
		Pakistan	USA
2004	0.017168	91.7	96.7
2005	0.016802	100.0	100.0
2006	0.016594	107.9	103.2
2007	0.016464	116.1	106.2
2008	0.014358	139.7	110.2
2009	0.012243	158.7	109.9
2010	0.011739	180.8	111.7
2011	0.011585	202.3	115.2

Source: International Monetary Fund

The exchange rate and the financial account

The discussion is still incomplete. The exchange rate is influenced by the demand and supply for the home currency relative to other currencies, which reflects the demand from foreigners for domestic goods, services and assets, and the supply of currency from residents wanting to buy foreign goods, services and assets. So far, the discussion has focused on the current account – that is, on the demand and supply of goods and services. However, it is also important to be aware that international transactions in financial assets also influence (and are influenced by) the exchange rate.

Suppose that interest rates in the UK are high relative to those that prevail in the USA. American investors looking for a good return may be attracted by the prospect of investing in the UK, so there will thus tend to be an inflow of funds into the UK. This will then lead to an increase in the financial account surplus, helping to fund a current account deficit.

A further twist in the story is that if high interest rates do attract such financial inflows, this means that there is an increase in the demand for pounds, because foreign investors have to buy pounds in order to pay for the British assets that they want to acquire. This will then put upward pressure on the exchange rate, which in turn affects the international competitiveness of UK goods and services. There is therefore a link between movements in the exchange rate and the level of aggregate demand in the economy.

This close interrelationship between the current account, the financial account and the exchange rate is critical in the design of macroeconomic policy.

Summary

- The exchange rate is the price of one currency in terms of another.
- The level of the exchange rate is one influence on the competitiveness of domestic goods, services and assets in international markets, but this also depends upon relative prices in the home economy and the rest of the world.
- The real exchange rate is a measure of the international competitiveness of an economy's goods.
- The effective exchange rate measures the relative strength of a national currency compared with a weighted average of the exchange rates of the country's trading partners.
- There is a complex, but important, interrelationship between the exchange rate and the current and financial accounts of the balance of payments.

9.3 The determination of exchange rates

The way in which a country's exchange rate is determined has important implications for the balance of payments, and for macroeconomic policy. Viewing the foreign exchange market as a variant of the demand and supply model seems to suggest that the exchange rate will be determined by the interaction of demand and supply. If the market were to be left to find its way to equilibrium, this is exactly what would happen, and where this is permitted to happen, it is known as a **floating exchange rate system**. However, the exchange rate is so important for the economy that governments may see the exchange rate as being too important to be left to the market, and may thus intervene, either through a **managed float**, or by operating a **fixed exchange rate system**.

Key terms

Floating exchange rate system: a system in which the exchange rate is permitted to find its own level in the market.

Managed floating exchange rate system: a system under which the exchange rate is permitted to find its own level in the market, but within limits, with the government intervening in certain situations.

Fixed exchange rate system: a system in which the government commits to maintaining the exchange rate at a specific level against another currency.

A fixed exchange rate system

In the Bretton Woods conference at the end of the Second World War, it was agreed to establish a fixed exchange rate system, under which countries would commit to maintaining the price of their currencies in terms of the US dollar. This system remained in place until the early 1970s. For example, from 1950 until 1967 the sterling exchange rate was set at $2.80, and the British government was committed to making sure that it stayed at this rate. This system became known as the *dollar standard*. Occasional changes in exchange rates were permitted after consultation if a currency was seen to be substantially out of line – as happened for the UK in 1967. During the period up to about 1971 most countries in the world followed this approach.

Figure 9.9 illustrates how this works. Suppose the authorities announce that the exchange rate will be set at e_f. Given that this level is set independently by the government, it cannot be guaranteed to correspond to the market equilibrium, and in Figure 9.9 it is set above the equilibrium level. At this exchange rate, the supply of ringgits exceeds the demand for ringgits. This can be interpreted in terms of the overall balance of payments. If there is an excess supply of ringgits, the implication is that residents of Malaysia are trying to buy more US goods, services and assets than Americans are trying to buy Malaysian: in other words, there is an overall deficit on the balance of payments.

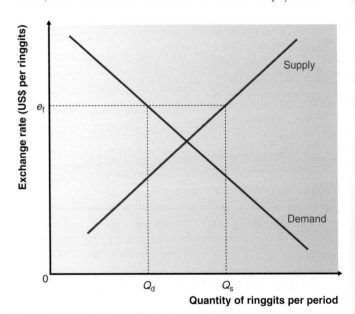

Figure 9.9 Maintaining a fixed exchange rate

In a free market, you would expect the exchange rate to adjust until the demand and supply of ringgits came back into equilibrium. However, with the authorities committed to maintaining the exchange rate at e_f, such an adjustment cannot take place. As Malaysia owes the USA for the excess goods, services and assets that its residents have purchased, the authorities then have to sell **foreign exchange reserves** in order to make the books balance.

In terms of Figure 9.9, Q_d represents the demand for ringgits at e_f and Q_s represents the supply. The difference represents the amount of foreign exchange reserves that the authorities have to sell to preserve the balance of payments.

> **Key term**
>
> Foreign exchange reserves: stocks of foreign currency and gold owned by the central bank of a country to enable it to meet any mismatch between the demand and supply of the country's currency.

Notice that the *position* of the demand and supply curves depends on factors other than the exchange rate that can affect the demand for Malaysian and US goods, services and assets in the respective countries. It is likely that through time these will shift in position. For example, if the preference of Americans for Malaysian goods changes through time, this will affect the demand for ringgits.

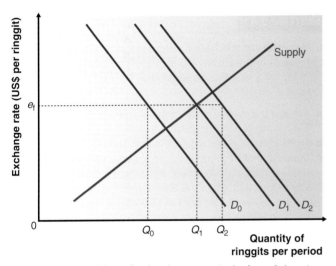

Figure 9.10 Maintaining a fixed exchange rate in the face of changing demand for ringgits

Consider Figure 9.10. For simplicity, suppose that the supply curve remains fixed, but demand shifts through time. Let e_f be the value of the exchange rate that the Malaysian monetary authorities have undertaken to maintain. If the demand for ringgits is at D_1, the chosen exchange rate corresponds to the market equilibrium, and no action by the authorities is needed. If demand is at D_0, then with the exchange rate at e_f there is an excess supply of ringgits (as was the case in Figure 9.9). The monetary authorities in Malaysia need to buy up the excess supply by selling foreign exchange reserves. Conversely, if the demand for ringgits is strong, say because Americans have developed a preference for Malaysian pewter goods, then demand could be at D_2. There is now excess demand for ringgits, and the Malaysian monetary authorities supply additional ringgits in return for US dollars. Foreign exchange reserves thus accumulate.

In the long term, the system will operate successfully for the country as long as the chosen exchange rate is close to the average equilibrium value over time, so that the central bank is neither running down its foreign exchange reserves nor accumulating them.

A country that tries to hold its currency away from equilibrium indefinitely will find this problematic in the long run. For example, in the first few years of the twenty-first century, China and some other Asian economies were pegging their currencies against the US dollar at such a low level that they were accumulating reserves. In the case of China, it was accumulating substantial amounts of US government stock. The low exchange rate had the effect of keeping the exports of these countries highly competitive in world markets. However, such a strategy relies on being able to continue to expand domestic production to meet the high demand; otherwise inflationary pressure will begin to build.

During the period of the dollar standard, the pound was probably set at too high a level, which meant that UK exports were relatively uncompetitive, and in 1967 the UK government announced a **devaluation** of the pound from $2.80 to $2.40.

> **Key terms**
>
> Devaluation: a process whereby a country in a fixed exchange rate system reduces the price of its currency relative to an agreed rate in terms of a foreign currency.
>
> Revaluation: a process whereby a country in a fixed exchange rate system raises the price of the domestic currency in terms of a foreign currency.

During the period of the dollar standard, the UK economy went through what became known as a 'stop–go' cycle of growth. When the government tried to stimulate economic growth, the effect was to suck in imports, as when incomes rise, UK consumers spend part of the increase on imported goods. The effect of this was to generate a deficit on the current account of the balance of payments, which then needed to be financed by selling foreign exchange reserves.

This process has two effects. First of all, in selling foreign exchange reserves, domestic money supply increases, which then puts upward pressure on prices, threatening inflation. In addition, the Bank of England has finite foreign exchange reserves, and cannot allow them to be run down indefinitely. This meant that the government had to rein in the economy, thereby slowing the rate of growth again; hence the label 'stop–go'.

An important point emerges from this discussion. The fact that intervention to maintain the exchange rate affects domestic money supply means that, under a fixed exchange rate regime, the monetary authorities are unable to pursue an independent monetary policy. In other words, money supply and the exchange rate cannot be controlled independently of one another. Effectively, the money supply has to be targeted to maintain the value of the currency. Governments may be tempted to use tariffs or non-tariff barriers to reduce a current account deficit, but this has been shown to be distortionary.

If you look back at the figures showing the ringgit exchange rate over time, you will see that Malaysia seems to have gone through a devaluation in 1998. The reasons for this were very different from the British devaluation of 1967. During the Asian financial crisis of 1997, the ringgit came under pressure from currency speculators, forcing a depreciation of the currency. In 1998 the Malaysian government intervened to peg the ringgit against the dollar and avoid further falls in the value of the currency.

The effects of devaluation

During the stop–go period in the UK, there were many debates about whether there should be a devaluation. The effect of devaluation is to improve competitiveness. At a lower value of the currency, you would expect an increase in the demand for exports and a fall in the demand for imports, ceteris paribus. In other words, the *AD* curve would be expected to shift to the right.

However, this does not necessarily mean that there will be an improvement in the current account. One reason for this concerns the elasticity of supply of exports and import substitutes. If domestic producers do not have spare capacity, or if there are time lags before production for export can be increased, then exports will not expand quickly in the short run, and so the impact of this action on exports will be limited. Similar arguments apply to producers of goods that are potential substitutes for imported products, which reinforces the sluggishness of adjustment. In the short run, therefore, it may be that the current account will worsen rather than improve, in spite of the change in the competitiveness of domestic firms.

This is known as the *J-curve effect* and is shown in Figure 9.11. Time is measured on the horizontal axis, and the current account is initially in deficit. A devaluation at time *A* initially pushes the current account further into deficit because of the inelasticity of domestic supply. Only at time *B*, when domestic firms have had time to expand their output to meet the demand for exports, does the current account move into surplus.

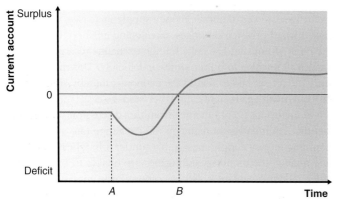

Figure 9.11 The J-curve effect of a devaluation

A second consideration relates to the elasticity of demand for exports and imports. Again, if competitiveness improves but demand does not respond strongly, there may be a negative impact on the current account. If the demand for exports is price

inelastic, a fall in price will lead to a fall in revenue. Indeed, the *Marshall–Lerner condition* states that a devaluation will have a positive effect on the current account only if the sum of the elasticities of demand for exports and imports is negative and numerically greater than 1.

The Bretton Woods dollar standard broke down in the early 1970s. Part of the reason for this was that such a system depends critically on the stability of the base currency (i.e. the US dollar). During the 1960s the US need to finance the Vietnam War meant that the supply of dollars began to expand, one result of which was accelerating inflation in the countries that were fixing their currency in terms of the US dollar. It then became increasingly difficult to sustain exchange rates at fixed levels. The UK and many other countries withdrew from the dollar standard in 1972. Following this, the pound fell steadily for the next five years or so. In Malaysia, the opposite happened, and the ringgit rose in value after leaving the dollar standard.

Exercise 9.4

A firm wants to purchase a machine tool which is obtainable in the UK for a price of £125 000, or from a US supplier for $300 000. Suppose that the exchange rate is fixed at £1 = $3.

a What is the sterling price of the machine tool if the firm chooses to buy in the USA?
b From which supplier would the firm be likely to purchase?
c Suppose that between ordering the machine tool and its delivery the UK government announces a devaluation of sterling, so that when the time comes for the firm to pay up the exchange rate is £1 = $2. What is the sterling price of the machine tool bought from the USA?
d Comment on how the competitiveness of UK goods has been affected.

Floating exchange rates

Under a floating exchange rate system, the value of the currency is allowed to find its own way to equilibrium. This means that the overall balance of payments is automatically assured, and the monetary authorities do not need to intervene to make sure it happens. In practice, however, governments have tended to be wary of leaving the exchange rate entirely to market forces, and there have been occasional periods in which intervention has been used to affect the market rate.

An example of this in the UK was the **Exchange Rate Mechanism (ERM)**, which was set up by a group of European countries in 1979 with the objective of keeping member countries' currencies relatively stable against each other. This was part of the European Monetary System (EMS). Each member nation agreed to keep its currency within 2.25% of a weighted average of the members' currencies (known as the European Currency Unit, or ECU). This was an *adjustable peg* system. Eleven realignments were permitted between 1979 and 1987.

Key term

Exchange Rate Mechanism (ERM): a system which was set up by a group of European countries in 1979 with the objective of keeping member countries' currencies relatively stable against each other.

The UK opted not to join the ERM when it was first set up, but started shadowing the Deutschmark in the mid-1980s, aiming to keep the rate at around DM3 to the pound, as you can see in Figure 9.12.

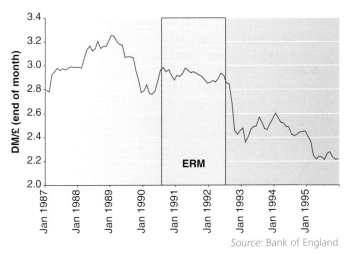

Source: Bank of England

Figure 9.12 The nominal DM/£ exchange rate, 1987–95

The UK finally decided to become a full member of the ERM in September 1990, agreeing to operate within a 6% band. However, the rate at which sterling had been set against the Deutschmark was relatively high, and the situation was worsened by the effects of German reunification, which led to substantial capital flows into Germany, reinforcing the overvaluation of sterling. Once it became apparent that sterling was overvalued, speculative attacks began, and the Bank of England's foreign exchange reserves were depleted; in 1992 the pound left the ERM. You can see in Figure 9.12 that the value of the pound fell rapidly after exit.

What determines exchange rates?

If the foreign exchange market is left free to find its own way to equilibrium, it becomes important to consider what factors will influence the level of the exchange rate. Notice that under a floating exchange rate system, a fall in the value of a currency is known as a **depreciation**, whereas an increase is known as an **appreciation**.

Key terms

Depreciation: a fall in the exchange rate within a floating exchange rate system.
Appreciation: a rise in the exchange rate within a floating exchange rate system.

Exchange rate equilibrium also implies a zero overall balance of payments. If the exchange rate always adjusts to the level that ensures this, it might be argued that the long-run state of the economy is one in which the competitiveness of domestic firms remains constant over time. In other words, you would expect the exchange rate to adjust through time to offset any differences in inflation rates between countries. The **purchasing power parity theory of exchange rates** argues that this is exactly what should be expected in the long run.

However, in the short run the exchange rate may diverge from its long-run equilibrium. An important influence on the exchange rate in the short run is speculation. So far, the discussion of the exchange rate has stressed mainly the current account of the balance of payments. However, the financial account is also significant, especially since regulation of the movement of financial capital was removed. Some of these capital movements are associated with direct investment. However, sometimes there are also substantial movements of what has come to be known as **hot money**: that is, stocks of funds that are moved around the globe from country to country in search of the best return. The size of the stocks of hot money is enormous, and can significantly affect exchange rates in the short run. The precise amount of such funds is not known with any precision, but some have claimed that the daily foreign exchange market turnover can reach up to $1.5 trillion.

Key terms

Purchasing power parity theory of exchange rates: a theory stating that, in the long run, exchange rates (in a floating rate system) are determined by relative inflation rates in different countries. It argues that the exchange rate will always adjust to maintain the real competitiveness of domestic goods and services.
Hot money: stocks of funds that are moved around the globe from country to country in search of the best return.

Such movements can influence the exchange rate in the short run. The returns to be gained from such capital flows depend on the relative interest rate in the country targeted, and on the expected exchange rate in the future, which in turn may depend on expectations about inflation.

Suppose you are an investor holding assets denominated in US dollars, and the UK interest rate is 2% higher than that in the USA. You may be tempted to shift the funds into the UK in order to take advantage of the higher interest rate. However, if you believe that the exchange rate is above its long-run equilibrium, and therefore is likely to fall, this will affect your expected return on holding a UK asset. Indeed, if investors holding UK assets expect the exchange rate to fall, they are likely to shift their funds out of the country as soon as possible, which may then have the effect of pushing down the exchange rate. In other words, this may be a self-fulfilling prophecy. However, speculators may also react to news in an unpredictable way, so not all speculative capital movements act to influence the exchange rate towards its long-run equilibrium value.

Speculation was a key contributing factor in the unfolding of the Asian financial crisis of 1997. Substantial flows of capital had moved into Thailand in search of high returns, and speculators came to believe that the Thai currency (the baht) was overvalued. Outward capital flows put pressure on the exchange rate, and although the Thai central bank tried to resist, it eventually ran down its reserves to the point where it had to devalue. This then sparked off capital flows from other countries in the region, including South Korea.

Summary

- After the Bretton Woods conference at the end of the Second World War, the dollar standard was established, under which many countries agreed to maintain the value of their currencies in terms of US dollars.
- In order to achieve this, the monetary authorities engaged in foreign currency transactions to ensure that the exchange rate was maintained at the agreed level, accumulating foreign exchange reserves to accommodate a balance of payments surplus and running down the reserves to fund a deficit.
- Occasional realignments were permitted, such as the devaluation of sterling in 1967.
- Under a fixed exchange rate system, monetary policy can only be used to achieve the exchange rate target.
- A devaluation has the effect of improving international competitiveness, but the effect on the current account depends upon the elasticity of demand for exports and imports.
- The current account may deteriorate in the short run if the supply response is sluggish.
- The Bretton Woods system broke down in the early 1970s.
- Under a floating exchange rate system, the value of a currency is allowed to find its own way to equilibrium without government intervention.
- This means that an overall balance of payments of zero is automatically achieved.
- The purchasing power parity theory argues that the exchange rate will adjust in the long run to maintain international competitiveness, by offsetting differences in inflation rates between countries.
- In the short run, the exchange rate may diverge from this long-run level, particularly because of speculation.
- The exchange rate is thus influenced by relative interest rates and expected inflation, as well as by news about the economic environment.

9.4 Balance of payments problems

Lists of macroeconomic policy objectives invariably include equilibrium on the balance of payments as a key item, alongside low inflation and unemployment. However, why should disequilibrium in the balance of payments be a problem that warrants policy action?

Think back to the market for ringgits that was discussed early in the chapter. The demand for ringgits was said to arise from overseas when people and firms want to buy Malaysian goods, services and assets, whereas the supply arises from domestic residents wanting to buy goods, services and assets from elsewhere. If the exchange rate is at its equilibrium level, this implies that the demand for ringgits (i.e. the foreign demand for domestic goods, services and assets) is equal to the supply of ringgits (i.e. the domestic demand for goods, services and assets from elsewhere).

In a free foreign exchange market, the exchange rate can be expected to adjust in order to bring about this equilibrium position. Even under a fixed exchange rate system in which the government pledges to hold the exchange rate at a particular level, any discrepancy between the demand and supply of the domestic currency would have to be met by the monetary authorities buying or selling foreign exchange reserves. Thus, the overall balance of payments is always in equilibrium. So why might there be a problem?

A fixed exchange rate regime

Suppose first of all that the government of an economy is operating a fixed exchange rate. In order to maintain the exchange rate at the agreed level, the authorities are committed to intervening by buying or selling foreign exchange reserves. There is a limit to how long the authorities could continue to hold the exchange rate away from equilibrium, as foreign exchange reserves are finite.

A floating exchange rate regime

Under floating exchange rates, the problem arises not with the *overall* balance of payments, but with an imbalance between components of the balance of payments. In particular, attention focuses on the balance of the current account, which shows the balance in the trade in goods and services together with investment income flows and current transfers.

If the current account is in deficit, domestic residents are purchasing more in imports of goods and services than the economy is exporting. In other words, earnings from exports are not sufficient to pay for imports. This is a bit like a household spending beyond its income, which can be sustained only by selling assets or by borrowing.

The concern for the economy is that a large and sustained deficit on the current account implies that the financial account must be in a large and sustained surplus. This in turn means that the country is effectively exporting assets. And this means that overseas residents are buying up domestic assets, which in turn may mean a leakage of investment income in the future. Alternatively, overall balance could be achieved through the sale of foreign exchange reserves. This soaks up the excess supply of domestic currency that arises because residents are supplying more currency in order to buy imports than overseas residents are demanding in order to buy exports from the home economy.

However the current account deficit is financed, a large deficit cannot be sustained indefinitely. This begs the question of what is meant by a 'large' deficit. Figure 9.1 showed the UK's current account balance as a percentage of GDP, which gives some idea of the relative magnitude of the deficit. This shows that, although the current account has been in deficit every year since 1984, the deficit has been less than 4% of GDP since 1990. This might be regarded as tolerable. Equally, running a persistent surplus on the current account can create difficulties. China showed a persistent surplus on current account during its period of rapid economic growth, when exports were expanding rapidly. Domestically, this was only possible because the economy was able to expand so quickly in order to supply exports, but this was probably at the expense of domestic consumption. It also meant political pressure from the USA, which perceived that China's undervalued currency was creating an unfair competitive advantage.

A critical issue for a deficit country is whether home assets will remain attractive to foreign buyers. Running a sustained deficit on current account requires running a surplus on financial account. If foreign buyers of domestic assets become reluctant to buy, interest rates in the home economy might have to rise in order to make assets more attractive. A by-product of this would be a curb in spending by domestic firms and consumers. Given that part of this reduction in spending would have an impact on imports, this would begin to reduce the current account deficit.

Causes of a deficit on current account

The quantity of exports of goods and services from an economy depends partly on income levels in the rest of the world and partly on the competitiveness of domestically produced goods and services, which in turn depends partly on the exchange rate and partly on relative price levels at home and abroad. Similarly, the level of imports depends partly on domestic income and partly on the international competitiveness of domestic and foreign goods and services.

This suggests that a fundamental cause of a deficit on the current account is a lack of competitiveness of domestic goods and services, arising from an overvalued exchange rate or from high relative prices of home-produced goods and services. There may thus be a need to improve the efficiency of production in order to compete more effectively with foreign producers. Alternatively, domestic incomes may be rising more rapidly than those in the rest of the world.

Summary

- If the exchange rate is free to reach its equilibrium value, the overall balance of payments will always be zero.
- However, a deficit on the current account of the balance of payments must always be balanced by a corresponding surplus on the financial account.
- A persistent deficit on current account means that in the long run domestic assets are being sold to overseas buyers, or that foreign exchange reserves are being run down. Neither situation can be sustained in the long run.
- A key cause of a deficit on the current account is the lack of competitiveness of domestic goods and services.

10 Trade and specialisation

The world economy is becoming increasingly integrated, and it is no longer possible to think of any single economy in isolation. The UK economy is no exception. It relies on international trade, engaging in exporting and importing activity, and many UK firms are increasingly active in global markets. This situation has created opportunities for UK firms to expand and become global players, and for UK consumers to have access to a wider range of goods and services. However, there is also a downside: global shocks, whether caused by increases in oil prices, financial crises or the emergence of China as a world economic force, can reverberate throughout economies in all parts of the world. It is also apparent that, although economic analysis suggests that there are potential gains to be reaped from international trade, it is still the case that many countries interfere with freedom of trade and try to protect their domestic markets. These are some of the issues that will be explored in this chapter.

Learning outcomes

After studying this chapter, you should:

- understand the distinction between absolute and comparative advantage
- be able to analyse the effects of international trade
- be familiar with the pattern of global trade
- be aware of the significance of the terms of trade
- be able to evaluate the case for and against protectionism
- be aware of the different forms that economic integration may take: free trade areas, customs unions, common markets and economic and monetary union
- know the features of these alternative forms of integration and understand the distinction between them
- be aware of the potential importance of trade creation and trade diversion.

10.1 The importance of international trade

The central importance of international trade for growth and development has been recognised since the days of Adam Smith and David Ricardo. For example, during the Industrial Revolution a key factor was that Britain could bring in raw materials from its colonies for use in manufacturing activity. Today, consumers in the UK are able to buy and consume many goods that simply could not be produced within the domestic economy. From the point of view of economic analysis, Ricardo showed that countries could gain from trade through a process of *specialisation*.

Absolute and comparative advantage

The notion of specialisation was introduced in Chapter 1, where you were introduced to Ali and Ayesha, who produced pots and bracelets with varying levels of effectiveness. Ali and Ayesha's relative skill levels in producing these two goods can now be extended. Table 10.1 reminds you of Ali and Ayesha's production possibilities.

Table 10.1 Ali and Ayesha's production

Ali	
Pots	**Bracelets**
12	0
9	3
6	6
3	9
0	12
Ayesha	
Pots	**Bracelets**
18	0
12	12
6	24
3	30
0	36

You may remember that Ayesha was much better at both activities than Ali. If they each devote all their time to producing pots, Ali produces only 12 to Ayesha's 18. If they each produce only bracelets, Ali produces 12 and Ayesha, 36.

This illustrates **absolute advantage**. Ayesha is simply better than Ali at both activities. Another way of looking at this is that, in order to produce a given quantity of a good, Ayesha needs less labour time than Ali.

There is another significant feature of this table. Although Ayesha is better at producing both goods, the difference is much more marked in the case of bracelet production than for pot production. So Ayesha is relatively more proficient in bracelet production: in other words, she has a **comparative advantage** in making bracelets. This is reflected in differences in opportunity cost. If Ayesha switches from producing pots to producing bracelets, she gives up 6 pots for every 12 additional bracelets that she makes. The opportunity cost of an additional bracelet is thus $6/12 = 0.5$ pots. For Ali, there is a one-to-one trade-off between the two, so his opportunity cost of a bracelet is 1 pot.

More interesting is what happens if the same calculation is made for Ali and pot making. Although Ayesha is absolutely better at making pots, if Ali increases his production of pots, his opportunity cost in terms of bracelets is still 1. But for Ayesha the opportunity cost of making pots in terms of bracelets is $12/6 = 2$, so Ali has the lower opportunity cost. Although Ayesha has an *absolute* advantage in pot making, Ali has a *comparative* advantage. It was this difference in comparative advantage that gave rise to the gains from specialisation that were set out in Chapter 1.

The **law of comparative advantage** states that overall output can be increased if all individuals specialise in producing the goods in which they have a comparative advantage.

Key terms

Absolute advantage: the ability to produce a good more *efficiently* (e.g. with less labour).

Comparative advantage: the ability to produce a good relatively more efficiently (i.e. at lower opportunity cost).

Law of comparative advantage: a theory stating that there may be gains from trade arising when countries (or individuals) specialise in the production of goods or services in which they have a comparative advantage.

Gains from international trade

This same principle can be applied in the context of international trade. Suppose there are two countries – call them Overthere and Elsewhere. Each country can produce combinations of agricultural goods and manufactures. However, Overthere has a comparative advantage in producing manufactured goods, and Elsewhere has a comparative advantage in agricultural goods. Their respective *PPC*s are shown in Figure 10.1.

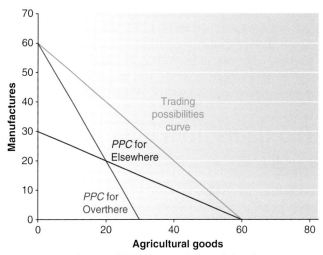

Figure 10.1 Trading possibilities for Overthere and Elsewhere

The pattern of comparative advantage held by the two countries is reflected in the different slopes of the countries' *PPC*s. In the absence of trade, each country is constrained to consume along its *PPC*. For example, if Elsewhere wants to consume 20 units of manufactures, it can consume a maximum of 20 units of agricultural goods.

However, suppose that each country were to specialise in producing the product in which it has a comparative advantage. Overthere could produce 60 units of manufactures and Elsewhere could produce 60 units of agricultural goods. If each country were to specialise completely in this way, and if trade were to take place on a one-to-one basis (i.e. if one unit of manufactures is exchanged for one unit of agricultural goods), then it can be seen that this expands the consumption possibilities for both countries. The **trading possibilities curve** in Figure 10.1 shows the potential consumption points for each country in this situation.

For example, if Elsewhere still wishes to consume 20 units of manufactures, it could now produce 60 units of agricultural goods, and exchange 20 units of them for 20 units of manufactures. It would then have its 20 units of manufactures, but have more agricultural goods than without trade. In this particular exchange, Overthere would now have 40 units of manufactures and 20 units of agricultural goods, and would also be better off than without trade.

Key term

Trading possibilities curve: shows the consumption possibilities under conditions of free trade.

It can be seen that in this situation trade may be mutually beneficial. Notice that this particular result of trading has assumed that the countries exchange the goods on a one-to-one basis. Although this exchange rate makes both better off, it is not the only possibility. It is possible that exchange will take place at different prices for the goods, and clearly, the prices at which exchange takes place will determine which of the countries gains most from the trade that occurs.

In the above example, specialisation and trade are seen to lead to higher overall production of goods. Although the examples have related to goods, you should be equally aware that services too may be a source of specialisation and trade.

Who gains from international trade?

Specialisation can result in an overall increase in total production. However, one of the fundamental questions of economics is 'for whom?' So far nothing has been said about which of the countries will gain from trade. It is possible that exchange can take place between countries in such a way that both countries are better off. But whether this will actually happen in practice depends on the prices at which exchange takes place.

In particular, specialisation may bring dangers and risks, as well as benefits. One obvious way in which this may be relevant is that, by specialising, a country allows some sectors to run down. For example, suppose a country came to rely on imported food, and allowed its agricultural sector to waste away. If the country then became involved in a war, or for some other reason was unable to import its food, there would clearly be serious consequences if it could no longer grow its own foodstuffs. For this reason, many countries have in place measures designed to protect their agricultural sectors – or other sectors that are seen to be strategic in nature.

Over-reliance on some commodities may also be risky. For example, the development of artificial substitutes for rubber had an enormous impact on the demand for natural rubber; this was reflected in falls in its price and caused difficulties for countries such as Malaysia that had specialised in producing rubber.

A key factor that determines which of the countries will gain from trade – and whether trade will take place at all – is the relative prices at which trade takes place, known as the terms of trade. In practice, the relative prices are set in world markets, although it is possible that for some commodities there are countries large enough to influence prices.

The terms of trade

One of the factors that determines who gains from international trade is the **terms of trade**, defined as the ratio of export prices to import prices.

> ### Key term
>
> Terms of trade: the ratio of export prices to import prices.

Suppose that both export and import prices are rising through time, but import prices are rising more rapidly than export prices. This means that the ratio of export to import prices will fall – which in turn means that a country must export a greater volume of its goods in order to acquire the same volume of imports. In other words, a fall in the terms of trade makes a country worse off.

In recent years, concerns have been raised about the effect of changes in the terms of trade for less developed countries (LDCs). One problem faced by LDCs that export primary products is that they are each too small as individual exporters to be able to influence the world price of their products. In other words, the problem for LDCs is that they have little market power in world markets, so they cannot influence the terms of trade that they face in their international transactions. They must accept the prices that are set in world commodity markets.

The terms of trade change over time as the prices of exports and imports change. Economic analysis suggests that there are reasons to expect the terms of trade to be volatile in the short run, and to follow trends in the longer run. Neither of these may prove favourable for many LDCs.

Short-run volatility

In the case of agricultural goods, demand tends to be relatively stable over time, but supply can be volatile, varying with weather and climatic conditions from season to season. Figure 10.2 shows a typical market in two periods. In period 1 the global harvest of this commodity is poor, with supply given by S_1: equilibrium is achieved with price at P_1 and quantity traded at Q_1. In period 2 the global harvest is high at S_2, so that prices plummet to P_2 and quantity traded rises to Q_2.

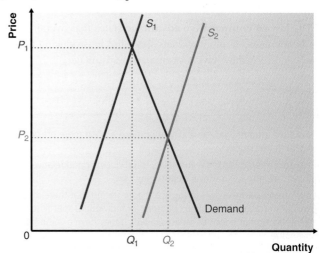

Figure 10.2 Volatility in supply

Notice that in this case the movement of prices is relatively strong compared with the variation in quantity. This reflects the price elasticity of demand, which is expected to be relatively inelastic for many primary products. From the consumers' point of view, the demand for foodstuffs and other agricultural goods will tend to be inelastic, as demand will not be expected to respond strongly to changes in prices.

For many minerals and raw materials, however, the picture is different. For such commodities, supply tends to be stable over time, but demand fluctuates with the economic cycle in developed countries, which are the importers of raw materials. Figure 10.3 illustrates this. At the trough of the economic cycle, demand is low, at D_1, and so the equilibrium price will also be low, at P_1. At the peak of the cycle, demand is more buoyant, at D_2, and price is relatively high, at P_2.

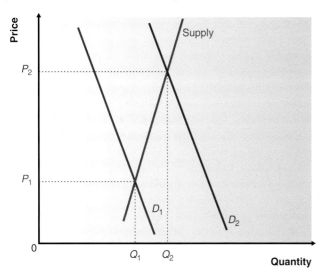

Figure 10.3 Volatility in demand

From an individual country's point of view, the result is the same: the country faces volatility in the prices of its exports. From this perspective it does not matter whether the instability arises from the supply side of the market or from the demand side. The problem is that prices can rise and fall quite independently of conditions within the domestic economy.

Instability of prices also means instability of export revenues, so if the country is relying on export earnings to fund its development path, to import capital equipment or to meet its debt repayments, such volatility in earnings can constitute a severe problem: for example, if export earnings fall such that a country is unable to meet its commitments to repaying debt.

Long-run deterioration

The nature of the demand for primary products may be expected to influence the long-run path of relative prices. In particular, the income elasticity of demand is an important consideration. As real incomes rise in the developed countries, the demand for agricultural goods can be expected to rise relatively slowly. Ernst Engel pointed out that at relatively high income levels, the proportion of expenditure devoted to foodstuffs tends to fall and the demand for luxury goods rises. This suggests that the demand for agricultural goods shifts relatively slowly through time.

In the case of raw materials, there have been advances in the development of artificial substitutes for many commodities used in manufacturing. Furthermore, technology has changed over time, improving the efficiency with which inputs can be converted into outputs. This has weakened the demand for raw materials produced by LDCs.

Furthermore, if some LDCs are successful in boosting output of these goods, there will be an increase in supply over time. Figure 10.4 shows the result of such an increase. Suppose that the market begins with demand at D_0 and supply at S_0. Market equilibrium results in a price of P_0 and quantity of Q_0. As time goes by, demand moves to the right a little to D_1, and supply shifts to S_1. The result is a fall in the price of the commodity to P_1.

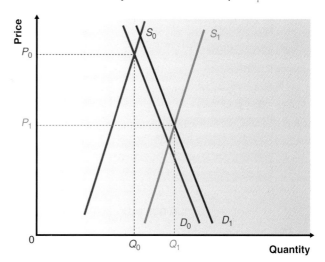

Figure 10.4 Long-term movements of demand and supply

It is thus clear that, not only may LDCs experience short-run volatility in prices, but the terms of trade may also deteriorate in the long run.

In the light of these twin problems, it is perhaps no surprise that many LDCs see themselves as trapped by their pattern of comparative advantage, rather than being in a position to exploit it. They are therefore reluctant to continue in such a state of dependency on (non-fuel) primary products, but the process of diversification into a wide range of products has been difficult to achieve.

A potential change in this pattern was seen in 2007 and 2008, with food prices rising rapidly. This included the prices of some staple commodities such as maize and rice. The net effect of this on LDCs was not clear. Countries in a position to export these commodities would benefit from the rise in prices – that is, an increase in their terms of trade. However, there are many LDCs that need to import these staple commodities and for them the terms of trade deteriorated. These trends were interrupted by the onset of recession in many developed countries in 2008.

The pattern of global trade

Countries all around the world engage in international trade. This is partly for obvious reasons: tropical crops will not grow in temperate climates; not all countries have natural resources such as gold or oil. International trade thus enables individuals to consume goods that cannot be easily produced domestically. It makes sense for mangoes to be produced in countries where the relative opportunity cost is low.

The extent to which countries engage in international trade varies enormously, as can be seen in Figure 10.5, which shows total trade (exports plus imports) as a percentage of GDP. In some cases, the extent of dependence on trade reflects the availability of natural resources in a country, but it may also reflect political attitudes towards trade.

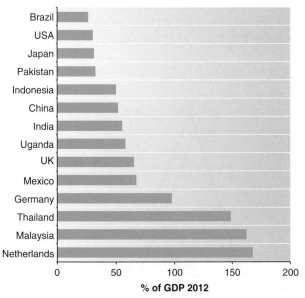

Source: World Bank

Figure 10.5 Trade as a percentage of GDP, 2012

The USA has a large and diverse economy, with a wealth of natural resources, and does not depend so heavily on trade.

China has now opened up to international trade to stimulate economic growth

Brazil, India and Pakistan have a similar level of dependence, but this partly reflects a conscious policy over many years to limit the extent to which their economies have to rely on external trade. At the other extreme, countries such as Malaysia and Thailand have followed policies that promote exports, believing that this will allow more rapid economic growth. China has been in a process of transition, having been closed to international trade for a long period and now not only opening up, but also relying heavily on exporting in order to stimulate economic growth. The share of trade in GDP for China has expanded rapidly.

The degree to which a country or region engages in trade depends upon several factors. One important influence is the extent to which a country has the resources needed to trade – in other words, whether it can produce the sorts of goods that other countries wish to buy. However, it also depends upon the policy

stance adopted by a country. Some countries have been very open to international trade. For example, a number of countries in South East Asia built success in economic growth on the basis of promoting exports. In contrast, there are countries such as India that in the past have been less eager to trade, and have introduced policies that have hindered their engagement with trade.

Two Swedish economists, Eli Heckscher and Bertil Ohlin, argued that a country's comparative advantage would depend crucially on its relative endowments of factors of production. They argued that the optimal techniques for producing different commodities varied. Some commodities are most efficiently produced using labour-intensive techniques, whereas others could be more efficiently produced using relatively capital-intensive methods. This suggests that if a country has abundant labour but scarce capital, then its natural comparative advantage would lie in the production of goods that require little capital but lots of labour. In contrast, a country with access to capital but facing a labour shortage would tend to have a comparative advantage in capital-intensive goods or services.

Under these arguments, it would seem to make sense for LDCs to specialise in labour- or land-intensive activities such as agriculture or other primary production. More developed countries could specialise in more capital-intensive activities such as manufacturing activity or financial services. By and large, this describes the way in which the pattern of world trade developed. However, the pattern is not static and there have been changes over time. For example, countries in South East Asia, such as Hong Kong, Singapore and Taiwan, encouraged the structure of their economies to change over time, switching away from labour-intensive activities as the access to capital goods improved over time. Their success then induced changes in the structure of activity in more developed countries as the availability of imported manufactured goods allowed the expansion of service sector activity. In more recent years, China's economy has been undergoing even further structural change, with a rapid expansion of the manufacturing sector, supported by an exchange rate policy that has made its exports highly competitive in global markets.

Whether it is good for countries to rely on this pattern of natural comparative advantage is a different matter – for example, in the light of the changing patterns of relative prices reflected in the evolution of the terms of trade over time. This suggests that there may be potential for countries to seek to alter the pattern of their comparative advantage by diversifying their economies and developing new specialisms in the face of changing patterns of global consumer demand. This is not an easy path for an economy to travel, and it may be tempting to turn instead to a more inward-looking protectionist strategy. These policy options will be examined later in the chapter.

Exercise 10.1

Discuss where you think your country's natural comparative advantage lies. How would you expect this pattern to differ from that which would apply to countries such as France, India, China, Brazil or a country in sub-Saharan Africa?

Summary

- Specialisation opens up the possibility of trade.
- The theory of comparative advantage shows that even if one country has an absolute advantage in the production of goods and services, trade may still increase total output if each country specialises in the production of goods and services in which it has a comparative advantage.
- Who gains from specialisation and trade depends crucially on the prices at which exchange takes place.
- The terms of trade are measured as the ratio of export prices to import prices.
- When the terms of trade deteriorate for a country, it needs to export a greater volume of goods to be able to maintain the same volume of imports.
- The terms of trade have tended to be volatile in the short run, and to deteriorate over the longer term for countries that rely heavily on non-fuel primary production.
- The pattern of comparative advantage that characterises a country may depend upon the relative endowments of the factors of production.
- There is a choice to be made between seeking to exploit this natural comparative advantage, and diversifying the economy in an attempt to develop new specialisms.

10.2 Trade liberalisation or protectionism?

The process of globalisation

The term '**globalisation**' has been much used in recent years, especially by protest groups that have demonstrated against it. It is therefore important to be clear about what the term means before seeking to evaluate the strengths and weaknesses of the phenomenon.

Ann Krueger, the first deputy managing director of the International Monetary Fund (IMF), defined globalisation as 'a phenomenon by which economic agents in any given part of the world are much more affected by events elsewhere in the world'. Joseph Stiglitz, the Nobel laureate and former chief economist at the World Bank, defined it as follows:

Fundamentally, [globalisation] is the closer integration of countries and peoples of the world which has been brought about by the enormous reduction of costs of transportation and communication, and the breaking down of artificial barriers to the flows of goods, services, capital, knowledge, and (to a lesser extent) people across borders.

J. Stiglitz, *Globalisation and its Discontents* (Penguin, 2004)

Key term

Globalisation: a process by which the world's economies are becoming more closely integrated.

On this basis, globalisation is crucially about the closer integration of the world's economies. Critics have focused partly on the environmental effects of rapid global economic growth, and partly on the opportunities that powerful nations and large corporations have for exploiting the weak.

The quotation from the book by Joseph Stiglitz not only defines what is meant by globalisation, but also offers some reasons for its occurrence.

Transportation costs

One of the contributory factors to the spread of globalisation has undoubtedly been the rapid advances in the technology of transportation and communications.

Improvements in transportation have enabled firms to fragment their production process to take advantage of varying cost conditions in different parts of the world. For example, it is now possible to site labour-intensive parts of a production process in areas of the world where labour is relatively plentiful, and thus relatively cheap. This is one way in which **multinational corporations** (MNCs) arise, in some cases operating across a wide range of countries.

Improvements in transportation have enabled firms to sell their goods all over the world

Furthermore, communications technology has developed rapidly with the growth of the worldwide web and e-commerce, enabling firms to compete more easily in global markets.

These technological changes have augmented existing economies of scale and scope, enabling firms to grow. If the sizes of firms were measured by their gross turnover, many of them would be found to be larger in size than a lot of the countries in which they operate (when size is measured by GDP): for instance, on this basis General Motors is bigger than Hong Kong or Norway.

Key term

Multinational corporation: a company whose production activities are carried out in more than one country.

Reduction of trade barriers

A second factor that has contributed to globalisation has been the successive reductions in trade barriers during the period since the Second World War, first under the auspices of the **General Agreement on Tariffs and Trade (GATT)**, and later under the **World Trade Organization (WTO)**, which replaced it.

Key terms

General Agreement on Tariffs and Trade (GATT): the precursor of the WTO, which organised a series of 'rounds' of tariff reductions.

World Trade Organization (WTO): a multilateral body responsible for overseeing the conduct of international trade.

In addition to these trade-liberalising measures, there has been a trend towards the establishment of free trade areas and customs unions in various parts of the world, with the European Union being just one example.

By facilitating the process of international trade, such developments have encouraged firms to become more active in trade, and thus have added to the impetus towards globalisation.

Deregulation of financial markets

Hand in hand with these developments, there have been moves towards removing restrictions on the movement of financial capital between countries. Many countries have removed capital controls, thereby making it much easier for firms to operate globally. This has been reinforced by developments in technology that enable financial transactions to be undertaken more quickly and efficiently.

Arguments for protectionism

In spite of the well-known gains from trade, countries often seem reluctant to open their economies fully to international trade, and tend to intervene in various ways to protect their domestic producers.

There are good and bad reasons for implanting protectionist policies. A reason often given is the *infant industry* argument. The idea here is that a new industry cannot become fully established, and ready to participate in world markets, without being protected in its early years. A new industry needs to learn the business, and grow in order to take advantage of economies of scale in production. If exposed to international competition from well-established producers at too early a stage, it will not be able to cope. In principle, this sounds a sensible argument,

but there are dangers. All too often such infant industries are over-protected, so do not ever grow up enough to compete in global markets.

It is also sometimes argued that domestic firms need to be protected against the 'dumping' of goods by foreign firms that have found themselves with unsalable surpluses. This again may be said to be unfair competition for local firms. However, it is difficult to judge when a firm is dumping, and when it is actually much more efficient than domestic firms.

Protectionist policies
Tariffs

A policy instrument commonly used in the past to give protection to domestic producers is the imposition of a **tariff**. Tariff rates have been considerably reduced in the period since the Second World War, but nonetheless are still in place.

Key term

Tariff: a tax imposed on imported goods.

Figure 10.6 shows how a tariff is expected to operate. D represents the domestic demand for a commodity, and S_{dom} shows how much domestic producers are prepared to supply at any given price. The price at which the good can be imported from world markets is given by P_w. If dealing with a global market, it is reasonable to assume that the supply at the world

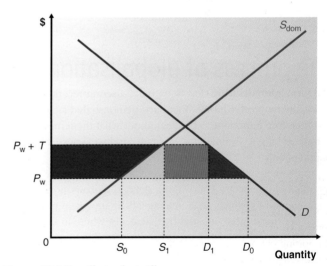

Figure 10.6 The effects of a tariff

price is perfectly elastic. So, in the absence of a tariff, domestic demand is given by D_0, of which S_0 is supplied within the domestic economy and the remainder $(D_0 - S_0)$ is imported. If the government wishes to protect this industry within the domestic economy, it needs to find a way of restricting imports and encouraging home producers to expand their capacity.

By imposing a tariff, the domestic price rises to $P_w + T$, where T is the amount of the tariff. This has two key effects. One is to reduce the demand for the good from D_0 to D_1; the second is to encourage domestic producers to expand their output of this good from S_0 to S_1. As a consequence, imports fall substantially to $(D_1 - S_1)$. On the face of it, the policy has achieved its objective. Furthermore, the government has been able to raise some tax revenue (given by the green rectangle).

However, not all the effects of the tariff are favourable for the economy. Consumers are certainly worse off, as they have to pay a higher price for the good; they therefore consume less, and there is a loss of consumer surplus. Some of what was formerly consumer surplus has been redistributed to others in society. The government has gained the tariff revenue, as mentioned. In addition, producers gain some additional producer surplus, shown by the dark blue area. There is also a deadweight loss to society, represented by the red and pale-blue triangles. In other words, overall society is worse off as a result of the imposition of the tariff.

Effectively, the government is subsidising inefficient local producers, and forcing domestic consumers to pay a price that is above that of similar goods imported from abroad.

Some would try to defend this policy on the grounds that it allows the country to protect an industry, thus saving jobs that would otherwise be lost. However, this involves sacrificing the benefits of specialisation. In the longer term it may delay structural change. For an economy to develop new specialisations there needs to be a transitional process in which old industries contract and new ones emerge. Although this process may be painful, it is necessary in the long run if the economy is to remain competitive. Furthermore, the protection that firms enjoy that allows them to reap extra producer surplus from the tariff may foster complacency and an inward-looking attitude. This is likely to lead to inefficiency, and an inability to compete in the global market.

Even worse is the situation that develops where nations respond to tariffs raised by competitors by putting up tariffs of their own. This has the effect of further reducing the trade between countries, and everyone ends up worse off, as the gains from trade and specialisation are sacrificed.

Quotas

An alternative policy that a country may adopt is to limit the imports of a commodity to a given volume. For example, a country may come to an agreement with another country that only a certain quantity of imports will be accepted by the importing country. Such arrangements are sometimes known as **voluntary export restraints** (VERs).

> ### Key term
>
> **Voluntary export restraint:** an agreement by a country to limit its exports to another country to a given quantity (quota).

Figure 10.7 illustrates the effects of a quota. D represents the domestic demand for this commodity, and S_{dom} is the quantity that domestic producers are prepared to supply at any given price. Suppose that, without any agreement, producers from country A would be prepared to supply any amount of the product at a price P_A. If the product is sold at this price, D_0 represents domestic demand, of which S_0 is supplied by domestic producers and the remainder $(D_0 - S_0)$ is imported from country A.

By imposing a quota, total supply is now given by S_{total}, which is domestic supply plus the quota of imports allowed into the economy from country A. The market equilibrium price rises to P_1 and demand falls to D_1, of which S_1 is supplied by domestic producers and the remainder is the agreed quota of imports.

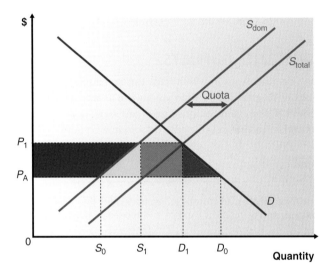

Figure 10.7 The effects of a quota

Figure 10.7 shows who gains and who loses by this policy. Domestic producers gain by being able to sell at the higher price, so (as in the case of the tariff) they receive additional surplus given by the dark blue area. Furthermore, the producers exporting from country A also gain, receiving the green rectangle (which, in the case of the tariff, was tax revenue received by the government). As in the case of the tariff, the two triangles (red and pale blue) represent the loss of welfare suffered by the importing country.

Such an arrangement effectively subsidises the foreign producers by allowing them to charge a higher price than they would have been prepared to accept. Furthermore, although domestic producers are encouraged to produce more, the protection offered to them is likely to lead to inefficiency and weak attitudes towards competition.

There are a number of examples of such agreements, especially in the textile industry. For example, for a long time the USA and China had long-standing agreements on quotas for a range of textile products. Ninety-one such quotas expired at the end of 2004 as part of China's accession to the World Trade Organization. As you might expect, this led to extensive lobbying by producers in the USA, especially during the run-up to the 2004 presidential election. Trade unions in the USA supported the producers, arguing that 350 000 jobs had been lost since the expiry of earlier quota agreements in 2002. In the case of three of these earlier agreements, some restraint had been reinstated for bras, dressing gowns and knitted fabrics. Producers in other countries, such as Sri Lanka, Bangladesh, Nepal, Indonesia, Morocco, Tunisia and Turkey, were lobbying for the quotas to remain, regarding China as a major potential competitor. However, for the USA at least, it can be argued that the removal of the quotas would allow domestic consumers to benefit from lower prices, and would allow US textile workers to be released for employment in higher-productivity sectors, where the USA maintains a competitive advantage.

Similar problems arose in connection with the dismantling of quotas for Chinese textile products being imported into Europe. This led to problems in 2005 when warehouses full of fashion products were prohibited from entry into the EU following a late agreement to delay the dismantling of the quotas.

Non-tariff barriers

There are other ways in which trade can be hampered, one example being the use of what are known as **non-tariff barriers**. These often comprise rules and regulations that control the standard of products that can be sold in a country.

> ### Key term
>
> **Non-tariff barrier:** an obstacle to free trade other than a tariff – for example, quality standards imposed on imported products.

This is a grey area, as some of the rules and regulations may seem entirely sensible and apply equally to domestic and foreign producers. For example, laws that prohibit the sale of refrigerators that contain CFCs are designed to protect the ozone layer, and may be seen to be wholly appropriate. In this case, the regulation is for purposes other than trade restriction.

However, there may be other situations in which a regulation is more clearly designed to limit trade. For example, the USA specifies a larger minimum size for vine-ripened tomatoes than for green tomatoes, thereby raising costs for the former. This has to do with trade because vine-ripened tomatoes are mainly imported from Mexico, but green tomatoes are mainly grown in Florida. Thus, the regulation gives Florida producers an advantage.

Such rules and regulations may operate against producers in less developed countries, who may find it especially difficult to meet demanding standards of production or to cope with excessive administrative burdens ('red tape'). This applies in particular where such countries are trying to develop new skills and specialisations to enable them to diversify their exports and engage more actively in international trade.

Evaluating trade liberalisation and protectionism

Although the theory of comparative advantage outlined above seems to suggest that there are potential gains from specialisation and trade, there must be some explanation for the widespread use of tariff and non-tariff barriers. The reasons may be partly political: for example, it may be that the people responsible for running protected sectors have accumulated political power and influence. They will be keen to try to avoid incurring the costs that emerge when protection is removed. However, there are some important economic issues as well.

One issue concerns the relative market power of trading partners. Although two partners may be jointly better off as the result of trade, the theory does not spell out how those gains are likely to be shared between the countries engaging in trade. If one partner has market power, it may be able to appropriate a large share of the potential gains.

It may also be the case that the gains from more openness in international trade arise where low-productivity sectors are able to release resources that can be redeployed in an expanding export sector. These gains will be the greatest when the economy is in full employment, so that the export sector before liberalisation is unable to obtain the resources needed for expansion. However, for many less developed countries, this is not the situation, as there is high unemployment and underemployment. The danger then is that by opening up to international competition, the low-productivity sectors merely release resources that then become unemployed, leaving the overall economy worse off than before the liberalisation of trade. In addition, it may be that the sorts of resources (such as skilled labour) that are needed for the expansion of exports are not available in some countries.

These factors suggest that the arguments for and against trade liberalisation are not as straightforward as the simple theory predicts, and careful consideration needs to be given to the arguments on both sides, to figure out under what conditions a country will benefit from a process of trade liberalisation.

> ### Exercise 10.2
>
> Discuss the arguments for and against the use of protectionist measures for your country.

> ## Summary
>
> - Countries can potentially gain from international trade by specialising in the production of goods or services in which they have a lower opportunity cost of production.
> - In spite of these possible gains, countries have often introduced protectionist measures to restrict trade, including tariffs, quotas and non-tariff barriers.
> - There may be political and economic reasons for doubting that trade liberalisation is always good in all circumstances.

10.3 Economic integration

Economies are becoming more interdependent over time. One aspect of this process deserves close attention, namely the growing formal integration of economies in regional groupings. This has been a gradual process, but it has accelerated as the technology of transport and communications has been transformed and as markets have been deregulated – especially financial markets; a process which has allowed the increased free movement of financial capital between countries.

There are many examples of such regional trade agreements. The European Union is perhaps one of the most prominent – and one of the furthest advanced – but there are also examples in the Americas (NAFTA, MERCOSUR), Asia (ASEAN, APEC), Africa (COMESA) and elsewhere. These agreements are at varying stages in the integration process. In addition, there has been a proliferation of regional trade agreements, and the World Trade Organization has estimated that some 400 agreements were scheduled to be implemented by 2010. This may partly reflect the slow progress made in the latest round of trade negotiations – the Doha Development Agenda. There has been much debate as to whether these agreements are stepping stones to further global cooperation, or whether they may turn out to be obstacles to that process.

The process of regional trade integration entails four successive stages, under which countries link their economies more closely together. The stages are as follows:

- free trade area
- customs union
- common market
- economic and monetary union.

These successive stages reflect different degrees of closeness. The underlying motivation for integration is to allow trading partners to take advantage of the potential gains from international trade, as illustrated by the law of comparative advantage. By reducing the barriers to trade, this specialisation can be encouraged, and there should be potential gains from the process. In practice, there may be other economic and political forces at work that affect the nature of the gains and the extent to which integration will be possible – and beneficial.

Free trade areas

The first level of integration is the formation of a so-called **free trade area**. The notion of a free trade area is that countries within the area agree to remove internal tariff and quota restrictions on trade between them, while still allowing member countries to impose their own pattern of tariffs and quotas on non-members. The lack of a common external tariff wall may cause problems within the member countries. If one country has lower tariffs than the rest, the natural tendency will be for imports into the area to be channelled through that country, with goods then being resold to other member countries. This may distort the pattern of trade and cause unnecessary transaction

costs associated with trading activity. It is worth noting that free trade areas are normally concerned with enabling free trade in goods and do not cover the movement of labour.

> ### Key term
>
> **Free trade area**: a group of countries that agree to remove tariffs, quotas and other restrictions on trade between the member countries, but have no agreement on a common barrier against non-members.

In spite of these problems, a free trade area does allow member countries to increase their degree of specialisation, and may bring gains. In South East Asia, the Association of South-East Asian Nations (ASEAN) began to create a free trade area in 1993. This involved six nations (Brunei, Indonesia, Malaysia, the Philippines, Singapore and Thailand). The group was later expanded to include Cambodia, Laos, Myanmar and Vietnam. Progress towards eliminating tariffs in this group has been relatively slow, but intense competition from the rapidly growing Chinese economy provides a strong motivation for accelerating the process.

Another major trading group operating a free trade area is the North American Free Trade Association (NAFTA), which covers the USA, Canada and Mexico. The agreement was signed in 1992 and launched in 1994, and has led to an expansion of trade between those countries. Unlike in Europe, there is as yet no stated intention that NAFTA should evolve into anything more than a free trade area.

Customs unions

A **customs union** is one notch up from a free trade area, in the sense that in addition to eliminating tariffs and quotas between the member nations, a common external tariff wall is set up against non-member nations. Again, the prime reason for establishing a customs union is to encourage trade between the member nations.

Such increased trade is beneficial when there is **trade creation**. This is where the formation of the customs union allows countries to specialise more, and thus to exploit their comparative advantage. The larger market for the goods means that more economies of scale may be available, and the lower prices that result generate additional trade between the member nations. These lower prices arise partly from the exploitation of comparative advantage, but also from the removal of tariffs between the member nations.

> ### Key terms
>
> **Customs union**: a group of countries that agree to remove restrictions on trade between the member countries, and set a common set of restrictions (including tariffs) against non-member states.
>
> **Trade creation**: the replacement of more expensive domestic production or imports with cheaper output from a partner within the trading bloc.

However, it is also important to be aware that becoming a member of a customs union may alter the pattern of trading relationships. A country that is part of a customs union will be more inclined to trade with other members of the union because of the agreement between them, and because of the absence of internal tariffs. However, given the common external tariff, it is quite possible that members of the union are not the most efficient producers on the global stage. So there may be a situation of **trade diversion**. This occurs where a member country of a customs union imports goods from other members *instead* of from more efficient producers elsewhere in the world. This may mean that there is no net increase in trade, but simply a diversion from an external source to a new source within the union. In this situation, there are not necessarily the same gains from trade to be made.

> ### Key term
>
> Trade diversion: the replacement of cheaper imported goods by goods from a less efficient trading partner within a bloc.

There are some further disadvantages of customs unions. Certainly, the transaction costs involved in administering the union cannot be ignored, and where there are traditional rivalries between nations there may be political sensitivities to overcome. This may impede the free working of the union, especially if some member nations are more committed to the union than others, or if some countries have close ties with non-member states.

It is also possible that a geographical concentration of economic activity will emerge over time within the union. This may result where firms want to locate near the centre of the area in order to minimise transportation costs. Alternatively, it may be that all firms will want to locate near the richest part of the market. Over time, this could mean that firms tend to concentrate in certain geographical areas, while the countries that are more remote, or which have smaller populations or lower average incomes, become peripheral to the centre of activity. In other words, over time, there may be growing inequality between regions within the union.

These disadvantages must be balanced against the benefits. For example, it may be that it is the smaller countries in the union that have the most to gain from tapping economies of scale that would not be accessible to them if they were confined to selling only within their domestic markets.

In addition to these internal economies of scale, there may be external economies of scale that emerge over time as the transport and communications infrastructure within the union improves. Furthermore, opening up domestic markets to more intense competition may induce efficiency gains, as firms will only be able to survive in the face of international competition by adopting best practice techniques and technologies. Indeed, another advantage of a customs union is that technology may be disseminated amongst firms operating within the union.

Common markets

It may be that the countries within a customs union wish to move to the next stage of integration, by extending the degree of cooperation between the member nations. A **common market** adds to the features of a customs union by harmonising some aspects of the economic environment between them. In a pure common market, this would entail adopting common tax rates across the member states, and a common framework for the laws and regulations that provide the environment for production, employment and trade. A common market would also allow for the free movement of factors of production between the member nations, especially in terms of labour and capital (land is less mobile by its nature!). Given the importance of the public sector in a modern economy, a common market would also set common procurement policies across member governments, so that individual governments did not favour their own domestic firms when purchasing goods and services. The Single European Market has encompassed most of these features, although tax rates have not been harmonised across the countries that are included.

> ### Key term
>
> Common market: a set of trading arrangements in which a group of countries remove barriers to trade among them, adopt a common set of barriers against external trade, establish common tax rates and laws regulating economic activity, allow free movement of factors of production between members and have common public sector procurement policies.

Economic and monetary union

Moving beyond a common market, there is the prospect of full **economic and monetary union**. This entails taking the additional step of adopting fixed exchange rates between the member states. This in turn requires member states to follow a common monetary policy, and it is also seen as desirable to harmonise other aspects of macroeconomic policy across the union.

> ### Key term
>
> Economic and monetary union: a set of trading arrangements the same as for a common market, but in addition having fixed exchange rates between the member countries and a common monetary policy.

The adoption of fixed exchange rates is a contentious aspect of proposals for economic and monetary union. With fixed exchange rates, governments are no longer able to use monetary policy for internal domestic purposes. This is because monetary variables become subservient to the need to maintain the exchange rate, and it is not possible to set independent targets for the rate of interest or money supply if the government has to maintain the value of the currency on the foreign exchange market. This is all very well if all countries in the union are following a similar business cycle, but if one country becomes poorly synchronised with the others, there may be major problems.

For example, it could be that the union as a whole is enjoying a boom, and setting interest rates accordingly. For an individual member country suffering a recession, this could mean deepening and prolonging the recession, as it would not be possible to relax interest rates in order to allow aggregate demand to recover.

A successful economic and monetary union therefore requires careful policy coordination across the member nations. Notice that economic and monetary union involves fixed exchange rates between the member countries, but does not necessarily entail the adoption of a common currency, although this may follow at some stage.

Summary

- Economic integration can take a variety of forms, of differing degrees of closeness.
- A free trade area is where a group of countries agree to remove restrictions on trade between them, but without having a common external tariff.
- A customs union is a free trade area with an agreed common set of restrictions on trade with non-members.
- A customs union can entail trade creation, in which member countries benefit from increased trade and specialisation.
- However, there may also be trade diversion, in which countries divert their trading activity from external trade partners to countries within the union.
- Trade diversion does not always bring gains, as the producers within the union are not necessarily more efficient than external producers.
- A common market is a customs union in which the member countries also agree to harmonise their policies in a number of key respects.
- Economic and monetary union entails fixed exchange rates between member countries, but not necessarily agreement to adopt a common currency.

Examination questions

1 a Explain how the rate of inflation is measured. [8]

b Discuss how a rapid rate of inflation might affect different groups within an economy. [12]

Cambridge AS and A Level Economics 9708, Paper 2, Q3, June 2007

2 The current account of Swaziland's balance of payments

Swaziland is a small, landlocked economy in southern Africa. The Swazi currency is the lilangeni (plural emalangeni) and the currency is pegged to the South African rand at a fixed rate of one to one. The country has faced changing international conditions in recent years, as is shown in its current account statistics.

Table 1 Swaziland's current account components, selected years, millions emalangeni

	2003	2005	2007
Balance on goods	957.9	−1641.3	−1910.1
Balance on services	−1090.2	−765.0	−367.6
Net income	−317.4	1133.8	449.3
Net current transfers	1136.4	619.8	1366.6

The Central Bank of Swaziland's report on the 2007 export performance identified the following.

- Exports grew by 8.4% with a positive performance by some manufacturing companies.
- Successful exports included sugar, sugar-based products, soft drink concentrates, wood pulp and timber products, textiles and garments, citrus and canned fruits and meat products.
- Global demand and rising export prices led to increased export revenue.

Export performance was helped by the depreciation of the domestic currency against the US$ and the currencies of other trading partners outside of the Southern African Customs Union (SACU)and Common Monetary Area (CMA), of which Swaziland is a member. In addition, exports of meat and meat products to the European Union (EU) resumed in 2007 after the EU lifted its ban on Swaziland's beef exports. This ban was originally imposed because of Swaziland's failure to comply with the required quality standards.

Data source: Central Bank of Swaziland Annual Report 2007/08

a In Swaziland's current account between 2003 and 2007,

i) which component showed a continuous improvement, and

ii) which component showed a continuous worsening? [2]

b How did the current account balance change between 2003 and 2007? [3]

c **i)** What is comparative advantage? [2]

    ii) In the light of the Central Bank of Swaziland's report what might be concluded about the nature of Swaziland's comparative advantage and the factors on which it is based? [4]

d Explain the conditions necessary for the depreciation of a country's currency to increase its export revenue. [3]

e Discuss the case for and against the use of tariffs by Swaziland to retaliate when the EU banned imports of Swaziland's beef. [6]

Cambridge AS and A Level Economics 9708, Paper 22, Q1 November 2010

3 **a** How might opportunity cost help to explain the pattern of international trade? [8]

b Discuss whether the formation of regional trading groups, such as ASEAN and NAFTA, is desirable. [12]

Cambridge AS and A Level Economics 9708, Paper 2, Q4, November 2008

4 **a** Explain the 'infant industry' and anti-dumping arguments for the introduction of tariffs. [8]

b Discuss whether the trade arrangements, such as the European Union or the South Asian Free Trade Area, encourage or discourage the benefits of free trade. [12]

Cambridge AS and A Level Economics 9708, Paper 22, Q4, June 2009

5 **a** With the aid of a diagram, explain why an economy's floating exchange rate may depreciate. [8]

b Discuss whether a current account deficit is always a serious economic problem for a country. [12]

Cambridge AS and A Level Economics 9708, Paper 21, Q4, June 2010

11 Macroeconomic policies

Inevitably, there is a policy dimension to the study of the performance of the macroeconomy. Indeed, in evaluating such performance, it is the success of macroeconomic policy that is under scrutiny. However, the success of macroeconomic policy can be judged only if you are aware of what it is that the policy is trying to achieve. This chapter introduces and analyses the main objectives of policy at the macroeconomic level, and discusses policies aimed at tackling inflation and problems with the balance of payments.

Learning outcomes

After studying this chapter, you should:

- be familiar with the principal objectives of macroeconomic policy
- understand the reasons for setting these policy objectives
- be aware of the main types of macroeconomic policy
- be familiar with policies designed to combat inflation and to correct balance of payments disequilibrium or influence the exchange rate
- be aware of some potential obstacles that may inhibit the achievement of the targets
- appreciate that the targets may sometimes conflict with each other.

11.1 Targets of macroeconomic policy

So far, the discussion of macroeconomics has centred on ways of measuring – and thus monitoring – the performance of an economy at the aggregate level. If macroeconomic performance is found to be wanting in some way, then it is reasonable to ask whether some policy intervention might improve the situation. This chapter considers aspects of the macroeconomy that might be regarded as legitimate targets for policy action, and explores policies to tackle inflation and balance of payment problems.

Price stability

One of the most prominent objectives of macroeconomic policy in recent years has been the need to control inflation. Inflation was discussed in Chapter 8, which explored the causes and consequences of a persistent rise in the general price level.

A number of costs of inflation were identified, which may justify the introduction of a policy to control inflation. In particular, if prices are increasing at a very rapid rate, then markets will not be able to operate effectively, and thus the economy will be damaged. Furthermore, if inflation is unpredictable, then this may affect firms' expectations of the future and discourage investment, which has repercussions for the overall productive capacity of the economy.

Full employment

For an economy to be operating on the production possibility curve, the factors of production need to be fully employed. From society's point of view, surplus capacity in the economy represents waste. In the macroeconomic policy arena, attention in this context focuses on unemployment. For example, Figure 11.1 shows that it is possible for the economy to be in macroeconomic equilibrium at a level of output Y_1 that is below the potential full-employment level at Y^*. This may be seen as an unnecessary waste of potential output. In addition, there may be a cost suffered by the people who are unemployed in this situation and who could have been productively employed.

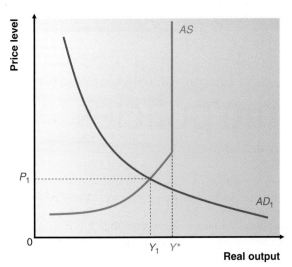

Figure 11.1 Macroeconomic equilibrium below full employment

The balance of payments

Lists of macroeconomic policy objectives include equilibrium on the balance of payments as a key item. Chapter 9 explained the interconnections that exist between the balance of payments and the exchange rate. Disequilibrium on the balance of payments has implications for the exchange rate, and the way in which this affects the macroeconomy depends critically on whether the economy is operating with fixed or floating exchange rates. The policy implications of this are discussed below.

Economic growth

If the ultimate aim of a society is to improve the well-being of its citizens, then in economic terms this means that the resources available within the economy need to expand through time in order to widen people's choices. From a theoretical point of view, economic growth can be thought of as an expansion of the productive capacity of an economy. If you like, it is an expansion of the potential output of the economy, or an outward shift of the production possibility curve.

Concern for the environment

International externalities pose problems for policy design because they require coordination across countries. If pollution caused by forest fires in Indonesia causes smog in Singapore or Malaysia, then Indonesia is imposing costs on other countries that are not fully reflected in market prices. Furthermore, there may be effects that cross generations. If the environment today is damaged, it may not be enjoyed by future generations – in other words, there may be intergenerational externality effects.

There is a macroeconomic dimension to these issues. If policy were only designed to achieve economic growth, regardless of the consequences for the environment, these externality effects could be severe, and for this reason they cannot be tackled solely at the microeconomic level of individual markets.

Income redistribution

The final macroeconomic policy objective to be mentioned concerns attempts to influence the distribution of income within a society. This may entail transfers of income between groups in society – that is, from richer to poorer – in order to protect the latter. Income redistribution may work through progressive taxation (whereby those on high incomes pay a higher proportion of their income in tax) or through a system of social security benefits.

The focus of this chapter is on inflation and the balance of payments; the other macroeconomic policy targets will be discussed in the A-level section of the course.

Exercise 11.1

Given the list of policy objectives mentioned above, which do you consider to warrant the highest priority for a government?

Summary

- Macroeconomic performance can be measured in relation to several indicators, each of which may be seen as a target for macroeconomic policy.
- The achievement of stability in prices (low inflation) has been a prime target in recent years.
- Governments may also wish to achieve a high rate of employment (low unemployment) and to achieve equilibrium on the balance of payments.
- In addition, there may be a wish to promote economic growth, to conserve the environment and to achieve an equitable distribution of income in society.

11.2 Instruments of macroeconomic policy

There are three broad types of macroeconomic policy that are available to a government wishing to improve the economy's performance in relation to these macroeconomic objectives. These are fiscal policy, monetary policy and supply-side policy.

Fiscal policy

The term **fiscal policy** covers a range of policy measures that affect government expenditures and revenues. Remember that government expenditure is a component of aggregate demand, so measures that affect government expenditure would be expected to have an impact on aggregate demand. If an economy is in recession, then an expansion of aggregate demand may help to encourage firms to increase their production in order to meet the increase in demand, thus helping to move the economy out of recession. Similarly, the government may influence aggregate demand by reducing taxes, thus encouraging individual firms and households to increase their expenditure.

> ### Key term
>
> Fiscal policy: decisions made by the government on its expenditure, taxation and borrowing.

Figure 11.2 illustrates how this could work. If aggregate demand shifts from AD_0 to AD_1, this has the effect of increasing equilibrium real output from Y_0 to Y_1. However, notice that this may also affect prices. Indeed, if aggregate demand expands when the economy is already at full employment (in the vertical section of the AS curve) equilibrium real output would not change, and the only effect would be to increase the overall price level.

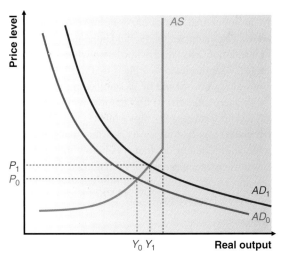

Figure 11.2 An increase in aggregate demand

Monetary policy

The term **monetary policy** covers policies that seek to influence the economy by using interest rates or money supply. As financial markets have developed, it has become increasingly difficult to control money supply, so the main instrument of monetary policy is interest rates.

> ### Key term
>
> Monetary policy: decisions made by the government regarding monetary variables such as the money supply or interest rates.

Through the interest rate, monetary policy affects aggregate demand. At higher interest rates, firms undertake less expenditure on investment, and households undertake less consumption spending. This is partly because when the interest rate is relatively high, the cost of borrowing becomes high, and firms and people are discouraged from borrowing for expenditure purposes.

Supply-side policy

The term **supply-side policy** refers to a range of measures that are intended to influence aggregate supply. These may operate directly on aggregate supply, or on influencing firms' and households' confidence in the future path of the economy, with the intention of affecting their behaviour.

> ### Key term
>
> Supply-side policy: a range of measures intended to have an impact on aggregate supply – and specifically the potential capacity of the economy to produce.

Examples of supply-side measures include encouraging investment in physical and human capital. For example, creating a stable macroeconomic environment may encourage firms to invest; raising levels of education and training increases the productivity of workers. Similarly, overall productivity can be raised by making markets more flexible and by promoting competition, so that firms have an incentive to reduce costs and produce more.

11.3 Inflation

The discussion in Chapter 8 suggested that persistent inflation can arise only through persistent excessive growth in the money stock. Aggregate demand and supply analysis can be used to analyse the situation.

For an economy that is in macroeconomic equilibrium, there are two ways in which prices can begin to increase. First, there could be a leftward shift in the aggregate supply curve. Second, there could be a rightward shift in aggregate demand.

A shift in aggregate supply

Figure 11.3 shows the effects of a supply-side shock on the macroeconomy. For example, suppose there is an increase in the price of oil that raises costs for producers in an economy. Firms will wish to supply less output at any given price, and the aggregate supply schedule shifts to the left. The economy moves to a new equilibrium position, with lower real output and a higher price level.

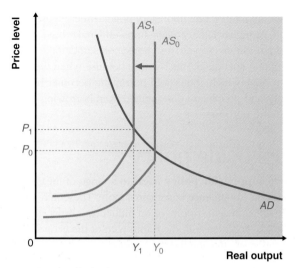

Figure 11.3 A supply shock

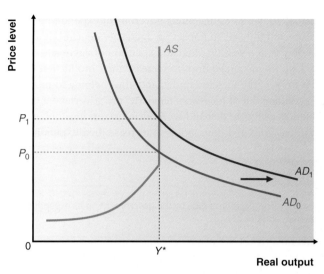

Figure 11.4 A shift in aggregate demand

Notice what has happened here – the economy has moved from one equilibrium position to another. However, there is no further tendency for things to continue to change. There has been a once-off increase in the general price level, but on reaching the new equilibrium, the price rise does not continue. In other words, this supply shift has not led to persistent inflation. Indeed, in the quantity theory equation ($MV = PY$), Y has fallen and P has increased, but nothing has happened to influence M or V. In this sense, it cannot be argued that a supply shift leads to inflation, ceteris paribus.

The oil-price shock of 1973/74 was a prime example of a shock in aggregate supply that affected countries all around the world. As real output fell, many governments intervened to try to combat the onset of recession and rising unemployment. In many cases, they did this by trying to stimulate aggregate demand – for instance, by increasing government expenditure, which is one of the components of aggregate demand, in other words, by using fiscal policy. However, it was not the supply shift that resulted in inflation, but governments' response to it in the form of a shift in aggregate demand.

A shift in aggregate demand

Figure 11.4 shows a shift to the right in the aggregate demand curve. When the economy starts in equilibrium at full employment, as in this case, the only result of the shift in aggregate demand is an increase in the price level. Furthermore, if the shift was indeed caused by an increase in government expenditure, financed by an increase in money supply, and if the government persists in this policy in the hope of stimulating an increase in real output, the result will be that AD continues to shift to the right. Prices continue to increase, but real output remains unaffected. In this scenario the end result is inflation, and not just a move to a new macroeconomic equilibrium.

Implications for policy

If it is the case that the root cause of inflation is that money supply is rising more rapidly than real output, then the policy seems clear – namely, the government should prevent money supply from continuing to increase. This is exactly what was argued by an influential school of economists known as the **Monetarists**. For example, the Nobel Laureate Milton Friedman argued that inflation was 'always and everywhere a monetary phenomenon'. The monetarists argued that the key aim of macroeconomic policy should be to stabilise money supply and to allow the macroeconomy to find its own way to equilibrium – and that it would settle at full employment. Others (in particular, the **Keynesians**) argued that it was possible that the economy would settle at an equilibrium that was below full employment, and that a more active approach to managing the economy was necessary. These arguments will be explored further in the A-level section of the course.

Key terms

Monetarists: a group of economists who believed that the macroeconomy always adjusts rapidly to the full-employment level of output. They also argue that monetary policy should be the prime instrument for stabilising the economy.

Keynesians: a group of economists who believed that the macroeconomy could settle in an equilibrium that was below the full employment level.

Deflation

In many countries inflation has become seen as the norm, so people expect prices always to be rising. However, there are periods in some countries where the overall price level falls over time. This is known as **deflation**.

Key term

Deflation: a period in which the overall price level is falling.

Some economists (for example, those in the Keynesian school) argue that deflation is harmful to the economy, because if people expect prices to fall they may decide to defer their spending plans in anticipation of getting better deals in the future. This results in a decrease in aggregate demand, and creates a downward spiral in economic activity.

Such periods have been rare in recent years. Even during the financial crisis that began in the late 2000s, few countries experienced falling prices, and many used a policy known as quantitative easing to bolster aggregate demand when interest rates fell to very low levels. This is essentially a form of monetary policy that results in an increase in money supply.

Policy evaluation

Monetary policy is seen as the most effective way in which a government can influence inflationary or deflationary pressure in an economy through influencing interest rates, and thus aggregate demand. Fiscal policy could also be used, but tends to have stronger but less predictable effects on real output and employment or on prices. During the financial crisis of the late 2000s, many countries faced a complex combination of rapidly rising levels of public debt, falling output and employment and continuing inflation. The policy response was mixed. Interest rates were already very low, and for the UK and the eurozone they were so low that they could not be reduced any further in order to stimulate aggregate demand. At the same time, to use fiscal policy to expand demand would potentially add further to public debt. Some governments thus responded by using monetary policy in the form of expanding money supply to combat the recession, whilst reducing government expenditure in order to control public debt.

Supply-side policy is not designed for stabilisation or to influence inflation in the short run, as it is primarily aimed at long-run economic growth.

Summary

- Inflation can be initiated on the demand or supply side of the economy.
- The quantity theory of money suggests that inflation can only become persistent if the money stock is increasing more rapidly than real output.
- The Monetarist school of economists argued that inflation was a monetary phenomenon, and that policy should focus on stabilising money supply.
- The Keynesians argued that the economy could settle below full-employment equilibrium, so that more active management was needed.

11.4 Inflation and the balance of payments

In the macroeconomy, there are complex interrelationships and trade-offs between inflation, unemployment, the balance of payments and the exchange rate. An understanding of these relationships is important in analysing macroeconomic policy.

A key relationship is that between inflation and the balance of payment – and the exchange rate also enters the story. Suppose an economy enters a period of inflation, as described in the previous section. The government tries to stimulate aggregate demand, but in so doing inflation sets in. If the inflation rate in a country is higher than in its trading partners, then the competitiveness of domestic goods will be affected. This puts pressure either on the current account of the balance of payments or on the exchange rate.

Fixed exchange rates

If the country is operating a fixed exchange rate system, then if domestic inflation is higher than inflation abroad, the downward pressure on the exchange rate will mean that the government has to take steps to maintain the value of the currency. If such a policy is to be sustainable in the long run, the authorities will need to take steps to affect the demand and supply of the currency such that the fixed rate to which the authorities are committed becomes the equilibrium rate. Otherwise, the disequilibrium in the foreign exchange market will persist, and continuous action will be needed to maintain the exchange rate. With finite stocks of foreign exchange, this is not possible.

This may mean taking measures to contract the economy. This would entail **expenditure dampening** (expenditure reducing) – that is, reducing domestic demand such that there is a fall in the demand for imports, thus shifting the supply curve for the domestic currency. In addition, if the domestic rate of inflation can be brought down relative to that of trading partners, then there will also be some **expenditure switching** if some foreign consumers switch to buying home-produced goods, thus stimulating exports and shifting the demand for the currency.

An alternative approach might be to use **exchange controls**. In other words, the authorities may regulate the amount of foreign exchange that is available for domestic residents who want to purchase goods, services or assets from abroad. Such controls were part of the package of measures that Malaysia introduced to cope with the Asian financial crisis in 1998. At this time, speculators were targeting the ringgit, so controlling capital movements was one way of protecting the currency. However, this approach also entails holding the exchange market in a state of disequilibrium, so it cannot not be sustained indefinitely, particularly in a world that has become increasingly interconnected through the process of globalisation. This makes it more difficult for a country to isolate itself from international markets. For a highly open country like Malaysia, it is especially difficult.

Key terms

Expenditure dampening: a reduction in domestic demand for imports so that the supply curve for the domestic economy shifts.

Expenditure switching: a situation in which the demand for exports of a country increases because some foreign consumers switch to buying from that country, thus shifting the demand for the domestic currency.

Exchange controls: a policy under which the authorities regulate the amount of foreign currency available for domestic residents to import goods, services or assets from abroad.

Floating exchange rates

If the government is operating a floating exchange rate system, the currency will depreciate in response to the relatively high level of domestic inflation, or the deficit on the current account of the balance of payments will need to be covered by a surplus on the financial account.

If the currency depreciates, then the result is to restore the competitiveness of domestic goods. This is known as the purchasing power parity theory of exchange rates, which argues that the exchange rate will always adjust to maintain the real competitiveness of domestic goods. However, if the original pressure on prices arose from excess aggregate demand, the depreciation can worsen the situation. In other words, if the elasticity of supply of exports is low, then an increase in the demand for exports caused by the depreciation adds to the pressure on prices, and the economy finds itself in an inflationary spiral. The authorities may then be forced to intervene to contract the economy.

The other way in which the balance of payments may be maintained is if a deficit on the current account of the balance of payments is balanced by a surplus on the financial account. Such a surplus may require an increase in domestic interest rates, which also has the effect of reducing aggregate demand, as both firms and consumers are likely to reduce expenditure if the interest rate (the cost of borrowing) increases.

Either way, it would seem that high domestic inflation relative to the rest of the world is unsustainable in the long run. It is also clear that the design of macroeconomic policy is a complex balancing act, in which decision-makers must monitor the economy's performance across a range of different targets. This is because of the **trade-offs** that exist between the various policy targets. In other words, policies that may improve performance in relation to one target may have adverse effects on other targets.

Evaluation of policy

The extent to which a government can use fiscal, monetary or supply-side policy to tackle a disequilibrium on the current account

of the balance of payments depends on whether a fixed or a floating exchange rate is in force. Under a fixed exchange rate regime, the priority for policy is to maintain the exchange rate and fiscal policy is needed to control aggregate demand. In other words, if there is a deficit on the current account, fiscal policy is used to reduce aggregate demand in order to eliminate the deficit. Monetary policy cannot be used for this purpose because increasing interest rates in order to reduce aggregate demand attracts inflows of financial capital that require further adjustment to maintain the exchange rate. Under floating exchange rates, the overall balance of payments comes into balance through the adjustment of the exchange rate, so policy intervention is not needed, unless the authorities are concerned if a large deficit on the current account is being offset by a large surplus on the financial account. Such a surplus would mean that the current account deficit is being covered by the sale of assets abroad, which may not be sustainable in the long run. Supply-side policy that increases the long-run capacity of the economy to produce can lead to an improvement in the international competitiveness of the economy, and thus lead to an improvement in the current account of the balance of payments. However, these benefits will only be seen in the long run.

Key term

Policy trade-off: the situation that arises when a policy that improves performance in relation to one policy target damages performance in relation to another.

Exercise 11.2

Given the following list of policy objectives, discuss the possible conflicts that may arise between them, and how these might be resolved:

a low inflation
b low unemployment
c high economic growth
d a low deficit on the current account of the balance of payments
e maintenance of a high environmental quality
f equity in the distribution of income

Summary

- The design of macroeconomic policy is a complex balancing act because of trade-offs between policy targets.
- If an economy experiences high inflation relative to other countries, this can lead to disequilibrium in the balance of payments or in the exchange market.
- This can then have knock-on effects for full employment.
- Whether the economy is operating on fixed or on floating exchange rates, the competitiveness of domestic goods in international markets must be taken into account in setting macroeconomic policy.

Examination questions

1 a Explain what is meant by a current account deficit. [8]

b Discuss the effectiveness and desirability of imposing tariffs to correct a current account deficit. [12]

Cambridge AS and A Level Economics 9708, Paper 2, Q4, June 2008

2 a Explain how a rapid rate of inflation in a country will affect its floating exchange rate. [8]

b Discuss whether a government should operate a fixed exchange rate system. [12]

Cambridge AS and A Level Economics 9708, Paper 21, Q4, November 2009

3 a Explain the difference between expenditure-switching and expenditure-dampening policies as a means of correcting a balance of payments disequilibrium. [8]

b Outline the current account position of your country or another economy you have studied. Discuss its ability to improve its performance on the current account. [12]

Cambridge AS and A Level Economics 9708, Paper 2, Q4, June 2007

12 Economic efficiency and market failure

In studying AS Economics, you became familiar with the use of the demand and supply model and the way in which prices act as signals in guiding resource allocation. It is time to take this analysis further and adopt a wider view of the process of resource allocation within society. An important question is whether markets can be relied upon to guide this process, or whether there are times when they will fail. In other words, if prices are allowed to guide resource allocation, will the result be beneficial for society as a whole, and will this lead to efficiency? This chapter begins to address this by reminding you of how prices can act as market signals to guide resource allocation, and by exploring what is meant by efficiency in economics. In this discussion, some new tools will be needed in order to identify what constitutes an efficient allocation of resources.

Learning outcomes

After studying this chapter, you should:
- be aware of how the price mechanism works to allocate resources
- understand the concepts of productive and allocative efficiency
- be familiar with the way in which resources are allocated in a free market economy
- appreciate the situations in which markets may fail to allocate resources effectively
- be familiar with the notion of Pareto optimality.

12.1 Resource allocation and efficiency

Prices and resource allocation

The AS section of the book set out the way in which prices act as signals to consumers and producers, and thus enable equilibrium to be reached in a market. In this chapter, this analysis is extended to consider how the price mechanism can work in a society made up of many markets, and whether the outcome produces an allocation of resources that is beneficial for a society.

Chapter 5 established some of the framework for this discussion by introducing the notions of consumer and producer surplus, and by looking at the effect on a market if firms are free to enter or exit from a market.

The notions of consumer surplus and producer surplus are important because they can be used to evaluate the total benefit that consumers and producers receive from consuming and producing a good. When consumers all pay the same price for a good in a market, then the area of consumer surplus can be interpreted as the total welfare that consumers receive from consuming that good. Similarly, the producer surplus is interpreted as the surplus earned by firms over and above the minimum return that would have kept them in the market.

The underlying assumption that is made in this context is that consumers aim to maximise their surplus, and firms aim to maximise profits. In other words, both consumers and firms are assumed to be motivated by self-interest, and the key question is whether this will lead to a good outcome for society as a whole.

Efficiency

In tackling the fundamental economic problem of scarcity, a society needs to find a way of using its limited resources as effectively as possible. In normal parlance it might be natural to refer to this as a quest for *efficiency*. From an economist's point of view there are two key aspects of efficiency, both of which are important in evaluating whether markets in an economy are working effectively.

Chapter 1 introduced one of these aspects in relation to the production possibility curve (*PPC*). Figure 12.1 shows a country's production possibility curve. One of the choices to be made in allocating resources in this country is between producing agricultural or manufactured goods.

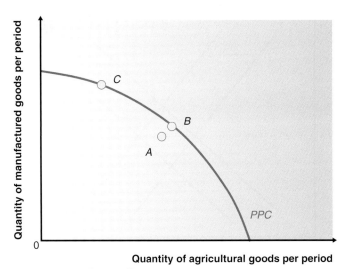

Quantity of manufactured goods per period

Quantity of agricultural goods per period

Figure 12.1 Productive efficiency

In Chapter 1 it was seen that at a production point such as *A*, the economy would not be using its resources fully, since by moving to a point *on* the *PPC* it would be possible to produce more of both types of good. For example, if production took place at point *B*, then more of both agricultural and manufactured goods could be produced, so that society would be better off than at *A*.

A similar claim could be made for any point along the *PPC*: it is more efficient to be at a point *on* the frontier than at some point *within* it. However, if you compare point *B* with point *C*, you will notice that the economy produces more manufactured goods at *C* than at *B* – but only at the expense of producing fewer agricultural goods.

This draws attention to the trade-off between the production of the two sorts of goods. It is difficult to judge whether society is better off at *B* or at *C* without knowing more about the preferences of consumers.

This discussion highlights the two aspects of efficiency. On the one hand, there is the question of whether society is operating on the *PPC*, and thus using its resources effectively. On the other hand, there is the question of whether society is producing the balance of goods that consumers wish to consume. These two aspects of efficiency are known as *productive efficiency* and *allocative efficiency*, and are discussed in more detail below.

An efficient point for a society would be one in which no redistribution of resources could make any individual better off without making some other individual worse off. This is known as the *Pareto criterion*, after the nineteenth-century economist Vilfredo Pareto, who first introduced the concept.

Notice, however, that *any* point along the *PPC* is a **Pareto optimum**: with a different distribution of income among individuals in a society, a different overall equilibrium will be reached.

Key term

Pareto optimum: an allocation of resources is said to be a Pareto optimum if no reallocation of resources can make an individual better off without making some other individual worse off.

Efficiency in a market

Aspects of efficiency can be explored further by considering an individual market. First, however, it is necessary to identify the conditions under which productive and allocative efficiency can be attained.

Productive efficiency

The production process entails combining a range of inputs of factors of production in order to produce output. Firms may find that there are benefits from large-scale production, so that efficiency may improve as firms expand production.

One way of measuring **productive efficiency** is in terms of the **average total cost** of production. This is simply the total cost of production divided by the quantity of output produced. Productive efficiency can then be defined in terms of the minimum average cost at which output can be produced, noting that average cost is likely to vary at different scales of output. **Economies of scale** occur when an increase in the scale of production leads to production at lower long-run average cost.

Key terms

Productive efficiency: attained when a firm operates at minimum average total cost, choosing an appropriate combination of inputs (cost efficiency) and producing the maximum output possible from those inputs (technical efficiency).

Average total cost: total cost divided by the quantity produced.

Economies of scale: occur for a firm when an increase in the scale of production leads to production at lower long-run average cost.

There are two aspects to productive efficiency. One entails making the best possible use of the inputs of factors of production: in other words, it is about producing as much output as possible from a given set of inputs. This is sometimes known as **technical efficiency**. However, there is also the question of whether the *best* set of inputs has been chosen. For example, there may be techniques of production that use mainly capital and not much labour, and alternative techniques that are more labour intensive. The firm's choice between these techniques will depend crucially on the relative prices of capital and labour. This is sometimes known as **cost efficiency**.

Key terms

Technical efficiency: attaining the maximum possible output from a given set of inputs.

Cost efficiency: the appropriate combination of inputs of factors of production, given the relative prices of those factors.

To attain productive efficiency, both technical efficiency and cost efficiency need to be achieved. In other words, productive efficiency is attained when a firm chooses the appropriate combination of inputs (cost efficiency) and produces the maximum output possible from those inputs (technical efficiency).

It is worth noting that the choice of technique of production may depend crucially upon the level of output that the firm wishes to produce. The balance of factors of production may well change according to the scale of activity. If the firm is producing very small amounts of output, it may well choose a different combination of capital and labour than if it were planning mass production on a large scale.

Thus, the firm's decision process is a three-stage procedure. First, the firm needs to decide how much output it wants to produce. Second, it has to choose an appropriate combination of factors of production, given that intended scale of production. Third, it needs to produce as much output as possible, given those inputs. Once the intended scale of output has been decided, the firm has to minimise its costs of production. These decisions are part of the response to the question of *how* output should be produced. Remember also the concept of *marginal cost*, which refers to the cost faced by a firm in changing the output level by a small amount. This becomes an important part of the discussion.

Allocative efficiency

Allocative efficiency is about whether an economy allocates its resources in such a way as to produce a balance of goods and services that matches consumer preferences. In a complex modern economy, it is clearly difficult to identify such an ideal result. How can an appropriate balance of goods and services be identified?

Key term

Allocative efficiency: achieved when society is producing an appropriate bundle of goods relative to consumer preferences.

Take the market for an individual product, such as the market for laptop computers that was considered in Chapter 5. It was then argued that in the long run, the market could be expected to arrive at an equilibrium price and quantity at which there was no incentive for firms either to enter the market or to exit from it. Figure 12.2 will remind you of the market situation.

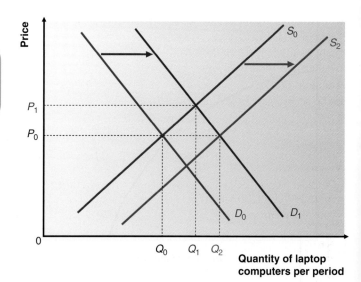

Figure 12.2 The market for laptop computers revisited

The sequence of events in the diagram shows that, from an initial equilibrium with price at P_0 and quantity traded at Q_0, there was an increase in demand, with the demand curve shifting to D_1. In response, existing firms expanded their supply, moving up the supply curve. However, the lure of the producer surplus (abnormal profits) that was being made by these firms then attracted more firms into the market, such that the supply curve shifted to S_2, a process that brought the price back down to the original level of P_0.

Now think about that price from the point of view of a firm. P_0 is at a level where there is no further incentive to attract new firms, but no firm wishes to leave the market. In other words, no surplus is being made on that marginal unit, and the marginal firm is just breaking even on it. The price in this context would seem to be just covering the marginal cost of production.

However, it was also argued that from the consumers' point of view any point along the demand curve could be regarded as the marginal benefit received from consuming a good or service.

Where is all this leading? Putting together the arguments, it would seem that market forces can carry a market to a position in which, from the firms' point of view, the price is equal to marginal cost, and from the consumers' point of view, the price is equal to marginal benefit.

This is an important result. Suppose that the marginal benefit from consuming a good were higher than the marginal cost to society of producing it. It could then be argued that society would be better off producing more of the good because, by increasing production, more could be added to benefits than to costs. Equally, if the marginal cost were above the marginal benefit from consuming a good, society would be producing too much of the good and would benefit from producing less. The best possible position is thus where marginal benefit is equal to marginal cost – in other words, where *price is set equal to marginal cost*.

If all markets in an economy operated in this way, resources would be used so effectively that no reallocation of resources could generate an overall improvement. Allocative efficiency would be attained. The key question is whether the market mechanism will work sufficiently well to ensure that this happens – or whether it will fail. In other words, are there conditions that could arise in a market, in which price would not be set at marginal cost?

Key term

Dynamic efficiency: a view of efficiency that takes into account the effect of innovation and technical progress on productive and allocative efficiency in the long run.

The notion of dynamic efficiency stemmed from the work of Joseph Schumpeter, who argued that a preoccupation with static efficiency (efficiency in the short run) may sacrifice opportunities for greater efficiency in the long run. In other words, there may be a trade-off between achieving efficiency today and improving efficiency tomorrow.

Exercise 12.1

Consider Figure 12.3, which shows a production possibility curve (*PPC*) for an economy that produces consumer goods and investment goods.

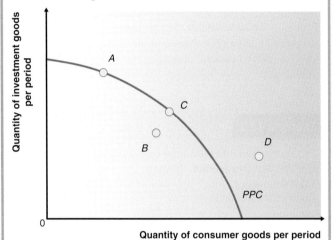

Figure 12.3 A production possibility curve

Identify each of the following (*hint*: in some cases more than one answer is possible):

a a point of productive inefficiency
b a point that is Pareto-superior to B
c a point of productive efficiency
d a point of allocative efficiency
e an unattainable point (*hint:* think about what would need to happen for society to reach such a point)

Summary

- A society needs to find a way of using its limited resources as efficiently as possible.
- Productive efficiency occurs when firms have chosen appropriate combinations of factors of production and produce the maximum output possible from those inputs.
- Allocative efficiency occurs when firms produce an appropriate bundle of goods and services, given consumer preferences.
- An allocation of resources is said to be a Pareto optimum if no reallocation of resources can make an individual better off without making some other individual worse off.
- An individual market exhibits aspects of allocative efficiency when the marginal benefit received by society from consuming a good or service matches the marginal cost of producing it – that is, when price is equal to marginal cost.
- Dynamic efficiency recognises that there may be a trade-off between efficiency in the short run and in the long run.

12.2 The working of a market economy

Dynamic efficiency

The discussion of efficiency so far has been conducted in terms of how to make the best use of existing resources, producing an appropriate mix of goods and services and using factor inputs as efficiently as possible given existing knowledge and technology. This is good as far as it goes, but it does represent a relatively static view of efficiency.

Dynamic efficiency goes one step further, recognising that the state of knowledge and technology changes over time. For example, investment in research and development today means that production can be carried out more efficiently at some future date. Furthermore, the development of new products may also mean that a different mix of goods and services may serve consumers better in the long term.

The previous section showed that the price mechanism allows a society to allocate its resources effectively if firms respond to changes in prices. Consumers express changes in their preferences by their decisions to buy (or not to buy) at the going price, which leads to a change in the equilibrium price. Firms thus respond to changes in consumer demand, given the incentive of profitability, which is related to price. In the short run, existing firms adjust their output levels along the supply curve. In the long run, firms enter into markets (or exit from them) in response to the relative profitability of the various economic activities that take place in the economy. But how does this work out in practice in a 'real-life' economy?

One way of viewing this system is through the notion of opportunity cost, introduced in Chapter 1. For example, in choosing to be active in the market for video recordings, a firm faces an opportunity cost. If it uses its resources to produce cheap mobile phones, it is *not* using those resources to produce smartphones. There may come a point at which the cost of producing cheap mobile phones becomes too high, if the profitability of smartphones is so much higher than that for cheap mobile phones, because of changes in the pattern of consumer demand. When the firm finds that it is not covering its opportunity costs, it will transfer production from the cheap mobile phone market to the smartphone market. Notice that this discussion is built on the assumption that firms are free to enter a market, or to exit from it.

This sort of system of resource allocation is often referred to as **capitalism**. The key characteristic of capitalism is that individuals own the means of production, and can pursue whatever activities they choose – subject, of course, to the legal framework within which they operate.

The government's role in a free capitalist economy is relatively limited, but nonetheless important. A basic framework of *property rights* is essential, together with a basic legal framework. However, the state does not intervene directly in the production process. Secure property rights are significant, as this assures the incentives for the owners of capital.

Within such a system, consumers try to maximise the satisfaction they gain from consuming a range of products, and firms seek to maximise their profits by responding to consumer demand through the medium of price signals.

As has been shown, this is a potentially effective way of allocating resources. In the eighteenth century Adam Smith discussed this mechanism, arguing that when consumers and firms respond to incentives in this way, resources are allocated effectively through the operation of an **invisible hand**, which guides firms to produce the goods and services that consumers wish to consume. Although individuals pursue their self-interest, the market mechanism ensures that their actions will bring about a good result for society overall. A solution to the coordination problem is thus found through the free operation of markets. Such market adjustments provide a solution to Samuelson's three fundamental economic questions of what? how? and for whom?

However, Adam Smith also sounded a word of warning. He felt that there were too many factors that interfered with the free market system, such as over-protectionism and restrictions on trade. At the same time, he was not utterly convinced that a free market economy would be wholly effective, noting also that firms might at times collude to prevent the free operation of the market mechanism:

> ❝People of the same trade seldom meet together, even for merriment and diversion, but the conversation ends in a conspiracy against the public, or in some contrivance to raise prices ...❞
>
> Adam Smith, *The Wealth of Nations*, Vol. I

However, even where individual consumers and firms pursue their own self-interest, their decisions can nonetheless result in efficiency being achieved in the way that resources are allocated.

In practice, most economies operate as mixed economies. Prices are used to allocate resources, but with some government intervention.

Exercise 12.2

Discuss the extent to which the country in which you live operates as a free market economy. This requires you to think about the ways in which the government intervenes in the allocation of resources.

Summary

- The price mechanism allows society to arrive at an efficient allocation of resources.
- Adam Smith saw a free market system operating through an invisible hand, which guides firms in producing the goods and services that consumers wish to consume.
- Most economies operate as mixed economies, in which there is some intervention by government to influence resource allocation.

Key terms

Capitalism: a system of production in which there is private ownership of productive resources, and individuals are free to pursue their objectives with minimal interference from government.

Invisible hand: a term used by Adam Smith to describe the way in which resources are allocated in a market economy.

13 Externalities and cost–benefit analysis

If markets are to be effective in guiding the allocation of resources in society, a precondition is that market prices are able to reflect the full costs and benefits associated with market transactions. However, there are many situations in which this is not so, and there are costs or benefits that are external to the workings of the market mechanism. This chapter examines the circumstances in which this may happen, and provides a justification for government intervention to improve the workings of the market.

Learning outcomes

After studying this chapter, you should:

- recognise situations in which the free-market mechanism may fail to take account of costs or benefits that are associated with market transactions
- be familiar with situations in which there may be a divergence between private and social costs or benefits, such that price is not set equal to marginal cost
- be able to use diagrams to analyse positive and negative externalities in either production or consumption
- appreciate reasons why government may need to intervene in markets in which externalities are present
- be familiar with a wide range of examples of externalities
- recognise ways in which external costs or benefits may be valued
- understand how decisions can be made using cost–benefit analysis.

13.1 Market failure

There may be situations that arise in which the market fails to bring about the best outcome in terms of resource allocation. This is known as **market failure**.

> **Key term**
>
> **Market failure**: a situation in which the free market mechanism does not lead to an optimal allocation of resources – for example, where there is a divergence between marginal social benefit and marginal social cost.

Chapter 1 introduced the notion of public goods, where the free-rider problem would make it unlikely that the free market would supply the appropriate amount. The notions of merit and demerit goods were also discussed. These are examples of market failure, because the free market does not provide the optimal quantities of these goods.

Information failures

If markets are to be effective in guiding resource allocation, it is important that economic decision-makers receive full and accurate information about market conditions. Consumers need information about the prices at which they can buy and the quality of the products for sale. Producers need to be able to observe how consumers react to prices. Information is thus of crucial significance if markets are to work. However, there are some markets in which not all traders have access to good information, or in which some traders have more or better access to it than others. This is known as a situation of **asymmetric information**, and can be a source of market failure.

> **Key term**
>
> **Asymmetric information**: a situation in which some participants in a market have better information about market conditions than others.

Healthcare

One example of asymmetric information is in healthcare. Suppose you go to your dentist for a check-up. He tells you that you have a filling that needs to be replaced, although you have had no pain or problems with it. In this situation the seller in a market has much better information about the product than the buyer. You as the buyer have no idea whether or not the recommended treatment is needed, and without going to another dentist for a second opinion you have no way of finding out. You might think this is an unsatisfactory situation, as it seems to give a lot of power to the seller relative to the consumer. The situation is even worse where the dentist does not even publish the prices for treatment until after it has been carried out!

The same argument applies in the case of other areas of healthcare, where doctors have better information than their patients about the sort of treatment that is needed.

Exercise 13.1

Ethel, an old-age pensioner, is sitting quietly at home when the doorbell rings. At the door is a stranger called Frank, who tells her that he has noticed that her roof is in desperate need of repair, and if she does not get something done about it very soon, there will be problems in the next rainstorm. Fortunately, he can help – for a price. Discuss whether there is a market failure in this situation, and what Ethel (or others) can do about it.

Education

The market for education is similar. Teachers or government inspectors may know more about the subjects and topics that students need to study than the students do themselves. This is partly because teachers are able to take a longer view and can see education provision in a broader perspective. Students taking economics at university may have to take a course in mathematics and statistics in their first year, and some will always complain that they have come to study economics, not maths. It is only later that they come to realise that competence in maths is crucial these days for the economics that they will study later in their course.

Not everyone in the education market has access to the same information

How could this problem be tackled? The answer would seem to be obvious – if the problem arises from an information failure, then the answer should be to improve the information flow, in this case to students. This might be achieved by providing a convincing explanation of why the curriculum has been designed in a particular way. It may also be necessary to provide incentives for students to study particular unpopular subjects, perhaps by making success a requirement for progression to the next stage of the course. By understanding the economic cause of a problem, it is possible to devise a strategy that should go some way towards removing the market failure.

Second-hand cars

One of the most famous examples of asymmetric information relates to the second-hand (or 'pre-owned', by the latest terminology) car market. This is because the first paper that drew attention to the problem of asymmetric information, by Nobel laureate George Akerlof, focused on this market.

Akerlof argued that there are two types of car. Some cars are good runners and are totally reliable, whereas some are continually breaking down and needing parts and servicing; the latter are known as 'lemons' in the USA (allegedly from fruit machines, where lemons offer the lowest prize). The problem in the second-hand car market arises because the owners of cars (potential sellers) have better information about their cars than the potential buyers. In other words, when a car owner decides to sell a car, he or she knows whether it is a lemon or a good-quality car – but a buyer cannot tell.

In this sort of market, car dealers can adopt one of two possible strategies. One is to offer a high price and buy up all the cars in the market, knowing that the lemons will be sold on at a loss. The problem is that, if the lemons make up a large proportion of the cars in the market, this could generate overall losses for the dealers. The alternative is to offer a low price, and just buy up all the lemons to sell for scrap. In this situation, the market for good-quality used cars is effectively destroyed – an extreme form of market failure!

Again, the solution may be to tackle the problem at its root, by finding a way to provide information. In the case of second-hand cars, some dealers may offer warranties as a way of improving the flow of information about the quality of cars for sale.

Exercise 13.2

The *Guardian* newspaper in the UK reported on 27 August 2004 that the pharmaceutical company GlaxoSmithKline had been forced to publish details of a clinical trial of one of its leading antidepressant drugs following a lawsuit that had accused the company of concealing evidence that the drug could be harmful to children. Discuss the extent to which this situation may have led to a market failure because of information problems.

Firm dominance in a market

Another form of market failure may occur when a firm or firms hold such a strong position in a market that they can take advantage of the situation at the expense of others – either their consumers or their suppliers. For example, a firm may be able to charge a higher price for its product because of the lack of effective competition in the market. This will be discussed further in Chapters 16 and 17.

Market failure also occurs when some element of costs or benefits is not reflected in market prices. These are known as *externalities*, which are discussed in the next section.

Exercise 13.3

Identify the form of market failure associated with each of the following.

a The use of hard drugs.
b The provision of a police officer.
c Vaccination against measles.
d A situation in which a firm cannot easily monitor how hard an employee is working.
e A firm with such a dominant position in a market that it is able to raise the price of its product.

Summary

- Information deficiency can lead to market failure in other situations: for example, where some participants in a market have better information about some aspect(s) of the market than others.
- Examples of this include healthcare, education and second-hand cars.

13.2 What is an externality?

Externality is one of those ugly words invented by economists, which says exactly what it means. It simply describes a cost or a benefit that is external to the market mechanism.

Key term

Externality: a cost or a benefit that is external to a market transaction, and is thus not reflected in market prices.

An externality will lead to a form of market failure because, if the cost or benefit is not reflected in market prices, it cannot be taken into consideration by all parties to a transaction. In other words, there may be costs or benefits resulting from a transaction that are borne (or enjoyed) by some third party not directly involved in that transaction. This in turn implies that decisions will not be aligned with the best interests of society.

For example, if there is an element of costs that is not borne by producers, it is likely that 'too much' of the good will be produced. Where there are benefits that are not included, it is likely that too little will be produced. Later in the chapter, it will be shown that this is exactly what does happen. Externalities can affect either demand or supply in a market: that is to say, they may arise either in **consumption** or in **production**.

Key terms

Consumption externality: an externality that impacts on the consumption side of a market, which may be either positive or negative.
Production externality: an externality that impacts on the production side of a market, which may be either positive or negative.

In approaching this topic, begin by tackling Exercise 13.4, which offers an example of each type of externality.

Exercise 13.4

Each of the following situations describes a type of externality. Does it affect production or consumption?
a A factory situated in the centre of a town, and close to a residential district, emits toxic fumes through a chimney during its production process. As a result, residents living nearby have to wash their clothes more frequently, and incur higher medical bills as a result of breathing in the fumes.
b Residents living along a main road festoon their houses with lavish lights and decorations during major festivals, helping passers-by to capture the festive spirit.

Toxic fumes

Example **a** in Exercise 13.4 is a negative production externality. The factory emits toxic fumes that impose costs on the residents (third parties) living nearby, who incur high washing and medical bills. The households face costs as a result of the production activities of the firm, so the firm does not face the full costs of its activity.

Thus, the **private costs** faced by the producer are lower than the social costs: that is, the costs faced by society as a whole. The producer will take decisions based only on its private costs, ignoring the **external costs** it imposes on society. From society's point of view, **social costs** are the sum of private and external costs.

Key terms

Private cost: a cost incurred by an individual (firm or consumer) as part of its production or other economic activities.

External cost: a cost that is associated with an individual's (a firm or household's) production or other economic activities, which is borne by a third party.

Social cost: the sum of private and external costs.

Figure 13.1 illustrates this situation under the assumption that firms operate in a competitive market (i.e. there is not a monopoly). Here, *D* (*MSB*) represents the demand curve, which was characterised in Chapter 5 as representing the marginal social benefit derived from consuming a good. In other words, the demand curve represents consumers' willingness to pay for the good, and thus reflects their marginal valuation of the product.

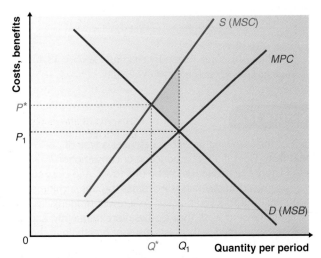

Figure 13.1 A negative production externality

Producers face marginal private costs given by the line *MPC*, but in fact impose higher costs than this on society. Thus *S* represents the supply curve that includes these additional costs imposed on society. This may be regarded as being the marginal social cost (*MSC*) of the firms' production.

If the market is unregulated by the government, firms will choose how much to supply on the basis of the marginal (private) cost they face, shown by *MPC* in Figure 13.1. The market equilibrium will thus be at quantity traded Q_1, where firms just break even on the marginal unit sold; price will be set at P_1.

This is not a good outcome for society, as it is clear that there is a divergence between the price in the market and the 'true' marginal cost – in other words, a divergence between marginal social benefit and marginal social cost. It is this

divergence that is at the heart of the market failure. The last unit of this good sold imposes higher costs on society than the marginal benefit derived from consuming it. Too much is being produced.

In fact, the optimum position is at Q^*, where marginal social benefit is equal to marginal social cost. This will be reached if the price is set equal to (social) marginal cost at P^*. Less of the good will be consumed, but also less pollution will be created, and society will be better off than at Q_1.

The extent of the welfare loss that society suffers can be identified: it is shown by the shaded triangle in Figure 13.1. Each unit of output that is produced above Q^* imposes a cost equal to the vertical distance between *MSC* and *MPC*. The shaded area thus represents the difference between marginal social cost and marginal benefit over the range of output between the optimum output and the free-market level of output.

Festive lights and decorations

Example **b** in Exercise 13.4 is an example of a positive consumption externality. Residents of this street decorate their homes in order to share the festival spirit with passers-by. The benefit they gain from the decorations (the **private benefit**) spills over and adds to the enjoyment of others (providing **external benefit**). In other words, the social benefits from the residents' decision to provide festive decorations go beyond the private enjoyment that they receive. The **social benefit** is equal to the sum of private and external benefits.

Key terms

Private benefit: a benefit incurred by an individual (firm or consumer) as part of its production or other economic activities.

External benefit: a benefit that is associated with an individual's (a firm or household's) production or other economic activities, which is borne by a third party.

Social benefit: the sum of private and external benefits.

Figure 13.2 illustrates this situation. *MPB* represents the marginal private benefits gained by residents from the festive decorations; but *MSB* represents the full marginal social benefit that the community gains, which is higher than the *MPB*. Residents will provide decorations up to the point Q_2, where their marginal private benefit is just balanced by the marginal cost of the decorations. However, if the full social benefits received are taken into account, Q^* would be the optimum point: the residents do not provide enough décor for the community to reach the optimum. The shaded triangle in Figure 13.2 shows the welfare loss: that is, the amount of social benefit forgone if the outcome is at Q_2 instead of Q^*.

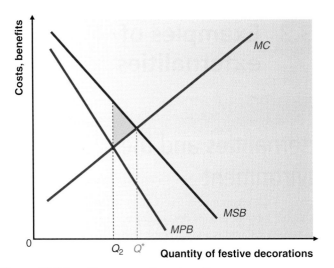

Figure 13.2 A positive consumption externality

Positive and normative revisited

Example **b** may be seen as a reminder of the distinction between positive and normative analysis, which was introduced in Chapter 1. Economists would agree that Figure 13.2 shows the effects of a beneficial consumption externality. However, probably not everyone would agree that the lavish festive decorations are providing such benefits. This is where a *normative judgement* comes into play. It could equally be argued that the lavish decorations are unsightly and inappropriate, or that they constitute a distraction for drivers and are therefore likely to cause accidents. After all, not everyone enjoys the garish.

Exercise 13.4 (continued)

Discussion has centred around two examples of externalities: a production externality that had negative effects, and a consumption externality that was beneficial to society. In fact, there are two other possibilities. Do the following affect production or consumption, and are they positive or negative?

c A factory that produces chemicals, which is located on the banks of a river, installs a new water purification plant that improves the quality of water discharged into the river. A fish farm located downstream finds that its productivity increases, and that it has to spend less on filtering the water.

d Fatima enjoys playing her music at high volume late at night, in spite of the fact that she lives in a flat with inadequate sound insulation. The neighbours prefer peace and quiet, but cannot escape the noise of Fatima's music.

Water purification

Example **c** in Exercise 13.4 is a production externality that has *positive* effects. The action taken by the chemical firm to purify its waste water has beneficial effects on the fish farm, which finds that its costs have

been reduced without it having taken any action whatsoever. Indeed, it finds that it has to spend less on filtering the water.

Figure 13.3 shows the position facing the chemicals firm. It faces relatively high marginal private costs given by *MPC*. However, its actions have reduced the costs faced by the fish farm, so the 'social' cost of the firm's production activities is lower than its private cost. Thus, in this case marginal social cost, shown by *MSC* in the figure, is lower than marginal private cost. The firm will produce up to the point where *MPC* equals marginal social benefit: that is, at Q_3.

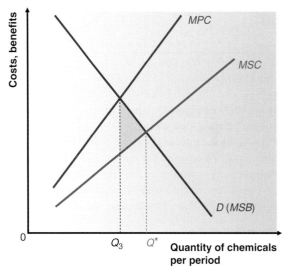

Figure 13.3 A positive production externality

In this market position, notice that the marginal benefit that society receives from consuming the product is higher than the marginal social cost of producing it, so too little of the product is being consumed for society's good. Society would be better off at Q^*, where marginal social benefit is equal to marginal social cost.

Again, the shaded triangle in Figure 13.3 represents the extent of the inefficiency: it is given by the excess of marginal social benefit over marginal social cost, over the range of output between the market outcome and society's optimum position.

Loud music

Example **d** in Exercise 13.4 is a *negative* consumption externality. Fatima gains benefit from listening to her music at high volume, but the neighbours also hear her music and suffer as a result. Their private benefit is reduced by having to hear the music when all they want is peace and quiet.

Figure 13.4 illustrates this.

The situation can be interpreted in terms of the benefits that accrue as a result of Fatima's consumption of loud music. She gains benefit as shown by the line *MPB*, which represents marginal private benefit. However, the social benefit is lower than this if the vexation suffered by the neighbours is taken into

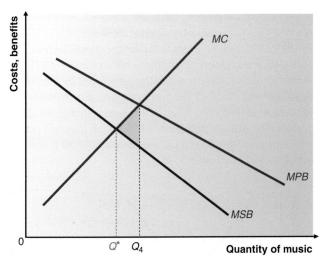

Figure 13.4 A negative consumption externality

account, so *MSB* in Figure 13.4 represents the marginal social benefits from Fatima's loud music.

Fatima will listen to music up to the point where her marginal private benefit is just equal to the marginal cost of playing it, at Q_4. However, the optimal position that takes the neighbours into consideration is where marginal social benefit is equal to marginal cost – at Q^*. Thus, Fatima plays too much music for the good of society.

Exercise 13.5

Discuss examples of some externalities that you meet in everyday situations, and classify them as affecting either production or consumption.

Externalities occur in a wide variety of market situations, and constitute an important source of market failure. This means that externalities may hinder the achievement of good resource allocation from society's perspective. The final section of this chapter explores some ways in which attempts have been made to measure the social costs imposed by externalities. First, however, a number of other externalities that appear in various parts of the economy will be examined.

Summary

- Markets can operate effectively only if all relevant costs and benefits are taken into account in decision-making.
- Some costs and benefits are external to the market mechanism, and are thus neglected, causing a distortion in resource allocation.
- Such external costs and benefits are known as 'externalities'.
- Externalities may occur in either production or consumption, thereby affecting either demand or supply.
- Externalities may be either positive or negative, but either way resources will not be optimally allocated if they are present.

13.3 Examples of externalities

Externalities and the environment

Concern for the environment has been growing in recent years, with 'green' lobbyist groups demanding attention, sometimes through demonstrations and protests. There are so many different facets to this question that it is sometimes difficult to isolate the core issues. Externalities lie at the heart of much of the debate.

Some of the issues are international in nature, such as the debate over global warming. At the heart of this concern is the way in which emissions of greenhouse gases are said to be warming up the planet. Sea levels are rising and major climate change seems imminent.

One reason why this question is especially difficult to tackle is that actions taken by one country can have effects on other countries. Scientists argue that the problem is caused mainly by pollution created by transport and industry, especially in the richer countries of the world. However, poorer countries suffer the consequences as well, especially countries such as Bangladesh, where much of the land is low lying and prone to severe flooding – indeed, two-thirds of the country was under water during the floods of 2004.

In principle, this is very similar to example **a** in Exercise 13.4: it is an example of a negative production externality, in which the nations causing most of the damage face only part of the costs caused by their lifestyles and production processes. The inevitable result in an unregulated market is that too much pollution is produced.

When externalities cross international borders in this way, the problem can be tackled only through international cooperation. For example, at the Kyoto World Climate Summit held in Japan in 1997, almost every developed nation agreed to cut greenhouse gas emissions by 6% by 2010. (The USA, the largest emitter of carbon dioxide, withdrew from the agreement in early 2001, fearing the consequences of such a restriction on the US economy.)

Global warming is not the only example of international externality effects. Scandinavian countries have suffered from acid rain caused by pollution in other European countries, including the UK. Forest fires left to burn in Indonesia have caused air pollution in neighbouring Singapore.

Another environmental issue concerns rivers. Some of the big rivers of the world, such as the Nile in Africa, pass through several countries on their way to the sea. For Egypt, through which the river runs at the end of its journey, the Nile is crucial for the livelihood of the economy. If countries further upstream were to increase their usage of the river, perhaps through new irrigation projects, this could have disastrous effects on Egypt. Again, the actions of one set of economic agents would be having damaging effects on others, and these effects would not be reflected in market prices, in the sense that the upstream countries would not have to face the full cost of their actions.

Part of the problem here can be traced back to the difficulty of enforcing property rights. If the countries imposing the costs could be forced to make appropriate payment for their actions, this would help to bring the costs back within the market mechanism. Such a process is known in economics as 'internalising the externality', and will be examined later in this chapter.

Concern has also been expressed about the loss of *biodiversity*, a word that is shorthand for 'biological diversity'. The issue here is that when a section of rainforest is cleared to plant soya, or for timber, it is possible that species of plants, insects or animals whose existence is not even known at present may be wiped out. Many modern medicines are based on chemicals that occur naturally in the wild. By eradicating species before they have been discovered, possible scientific advances will be forgone. Notice that when it comes to measuring the value of what is being destroyed, biodiversity offers particular challenges – namely, the problem of putting a value on something that might not even be there!

Externalities and transport

Cities in many parts of the world, such as Singapore and London, have been attempting to tackle traffic congestion. When traffic on the roads reaches a certain volume, congestion imposes heavy costs on road users. This is another example of an externality.

Figure 13.5 illustrates the situation.

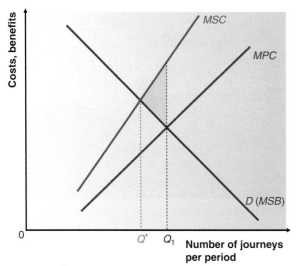

Figure 13.5 Traffic congestion

Suppose that D (MSB) represents the demand curve for car journeys along a particular stretch of road. When deciding whether or not to undertake a journey, drivers will balance the marginal benefit gained from making the journey against the marginal cost that they face. This is given by MPC – the marginal private cost of undertaking journeys. When the road is congested, a motorist who decides to undertake the journey adds to the congestion, and slows the traffic. The MPC curve incorporates the cost to the motorist of joining a congested road, and the chosen number of journeys will be at Q_1.

However, in adding to the congestion the motorist not only suffers the costs of congestion, but also imposes some marginal increase in costs on all other users of the road, as everyone suffers from the slower journeys resulting from the extra congestion. Thus, the marginal social costs (MSC) of undertaking journeys are higher than the cost faced by any individual motorist. MSC is therefore higher than MPC. Society would be better off with lower congestion: that is, with the number of journeys undertaken being limited to Q^*, where marginal social benefit equals marginal social cost.

Externalities and health

Healthcare is a sector in which there is often public provision, or at least some state intervention in support of the health services. However, in many countries public provision of healthcare is augmented with private healthcare, and the use of private health insurance schemes is on the increase. Again, externalities can help to explain why there should be a need for government to intervene.

Consider the case of vaccination against a disease such as measles. Suppose an individual is considering whether or not to be vaccinated. Being vaccinated reduces the probability of that individual contracting the disease, so there are palpable potential benefits. However, these benefits must be balanced against the costs. There may be a direct charge for the vaccine; some individuals may have a phobia against needles; or they may be concerned about possible side-effects. Individuals will opt to be vaccinated only if the marginal expected benefit to them is at least as large as the marginal cost.

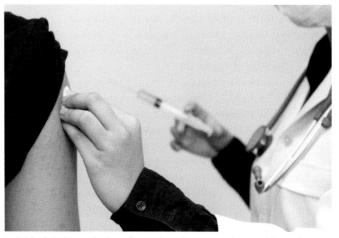

Individuals balance the benefits against the costs before deciding whether to have the measles vaccination

From society's point of view, however, there are potential benefits that individuals will not take into account. After all, if they do contract measles, there is a chance of their passing it on to others. Indeed, if lots of people decide not to be vaccinated, there is the possibility of a widespread epidemic, which would be costly and damaging to many.

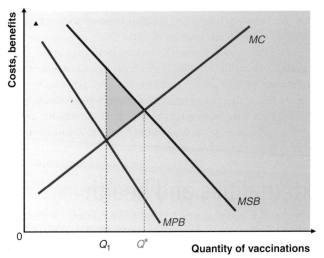

Figure 13.6 Vaccination

Figure 13.6 illustrates this point.

The previous paragraph argues that the social benefits to society of having people vaccinated against measles exceed the private benefits that will be perceived by individuals, so that marginal social benefits exceed marginal private benefits. Private individuals will choose to balance marginal private benefit against marginal private cost at Q_1, whereas society would prefer more people to be vaccinated at Q^*. This parallels the discussion of a positive consumption externality.

Externalities and education

As you are reading this textbook, it is reasonably safe to assume that you are following a course in economics. You have decided to demand education. This is yet another area in which externalities may be important.

When you decided to take A-levels (including economics), there were probably a number of factors that influenced your decision. Perhaps you intend to demand even more education in the future, by proceeding to study at university. Part of your decision process probably takes into account the fact that education improves your future earnings potential. Your expected lifetime earnings depend in part upon the level of educational qualifications that you attain. Research has shown that, on average, graduates earn more during their lifetimes than non-graduates. This is partly because there is a productivity effect: by becoming educated, you cultivate a range of skills that in later life will make you more

productive, and this helps to explain why you can expect higher lifetime earnings than someone who chooses not to demand education.

What does society get out of this? Evidence suggests that, not only does education improve productivity, but a *group* of educated workers cooperating with each other becomes even more productive. This is an externality effect, as it depends upon interaction between educated workers – but each individual perceives only the individual benefit, and not the benefits of cooperation.

In other words, when you decide to undertake education, you do so on the basis of the expected private benefits that you hope to gain from education. However, you do not take into account the additional benefits through cooperation that society will reap. So here is another example of a positive consumption externality.

Externalities and tourism

As international transport has become easier and cheaper, more people are wanting to travel to new and different destinations. For less developed countries, this offers an opportunity to earn much-needed foreign exchange.

There has been some criticism of this. The building of luxury hotels in the midst of the poverty that characterises many less developed countries is said to have damaging effects on the local population by emphasising differences in living standards.

Luxury hotels in midst of poverty in Gujarat, India

However, constructing the infrastructure that tourists need may have beneficial effects on the domestic economy. Improved roads and communication systems can benefit local businesses. This effect can be interpreted as an externality, in the sense that the local firms will face lower costs as a result of the facilities provided for the tourist sector.

Summary

- Externalities arise in many aspects of economic life.
- Environmental issues are especially prone to externality effects, as market prices do not always incorporate environmental issues, especially where property rights are not assigned.
- Congestion on the roads can be seen as a form of externality.
- Externalities also arise in the areas of healthcare provision and education, where individuals do not always perceive the full social benefits that arise.

13.4 Social cost–benefit analysis

The importance of externalities in regard to environmental and other issues means that it is especially important to be aware of externalities when taking decisions that are likely to affect the environment. This is especially important for large-scale projects that can have far-reaching effects on the economy, such as the construction of a new dam or a major road-building project. If good decisions are to be taken, it is crucial to be able to measure the external costs and benefits that are associated with those decisions.

This suggests that in taking such decisions, it is important to be able to weigh up the costs and benefits of a scheme. If it turns out that the benefits exceed the costs, it might be thought appropriate to go ahead. However, in valuing the costs and the benefits, it is clearly important to include some estimate for the externalities involved in order that the decision can be based on all relevant factors. In other words, it is important to take a 'long and wide view' and not to focus too narrowly on purely financial costs and benefits.

A further complication is that with many such schemes the costs and benefits will be spread out over a long period of time, and it is important to come to a reasonable balance between the interests of present and future generations.

Social cost–benefit analysis is a procedure for bringing together the information needed to make appropriate decisions on such large-scale schemes. This entails a sequence of key steps.

Key term

Social cost–benefit analysis: a process of evaluating the worth of a project by comparing its costs and benefits, including both direct and social costs and benefits – including externality effects.

1 Identify relevant costs and benefits

The first step is to identify all relevant costs and benefits. This needs to cover all of the direct costs of the project. These can probably be identified relatively easily, and include the production costs, labour costs and so on.

The indirect costs also need to be identified, and this is where externality effects need to be considered. For example, in constructing a dam across a river, there are the visible direct costs that are inevitably entailed in such a large engineering project. But there are also the indirect costs – i.e. the *opportunity costs*. How many people and businesses will be uprooted by the project, and how much land that could have been used for agriculture will be flooded as a result of the new dam? Similarly, in a road-building scheme, it is important to think in terms not only of the costs of construction, but also of the opportunity cost – how else could the land being used for the road have been used? How will the increase in traffic affect the quality of life enjoyed by local residents? For example, they may suffer from noise from the traffic using the road, or from the traffic fumes. Similarly, direct and indirect benefits need to be identified. The dam may bring benefits in terms of hydro-electric power, or irrigation for crops. A new road may increase the efficiency of transportation, and reduce costs for firms.

2 Valuation

If the costs and benefits are to be compared, they all need to be given a monetary valuation. It is likely that some of them will be items that have a market price attached to them. For these, valuation is not a problem. However, for externalities, or for other indirect costs and benefits without a market valuation, it is necessary to establish a **shadow price** – an estimate of the monetary value of each item. Notice that this can be quite difficult, as some of the external costs may be elusive, especially if the impact is on the quality of life, rather than on measureable production loss.

3 Discounting the future

It is also important to recognise that costs and benefits that will flow from the project at some point in the future need to be expressed in terms of their value in the present. From today's perspective, a benefit that is immediate is more valuable than one that will only become relevant in 20 years' time. In order to incorporate this notion into the calculations, we need to **discount** the future at an appropriate rate, and calculate the **net present value** of the future stream of costs and benefits associated with the project under consideration. Notice that a government taking decisions on behalf of future generations may choose a higher discount rate than consumers who prefer to enjoy benefits in the present. Equally, a government that is feeling vulnerable may prefer to provide benefits in the present to persuade the electorate, rather than taking decisions that will not bear fruit until the distant future. In other words, there may be a political backdrop to take into account.

Key terms

Shadow price: an estimate of the monetary value of an item that does not carry a market price.

Discount: a process whereby the future valuation of a cost or benefit is reduced (discounted) in order to provide an estimate of its present value.

Net present value: the estimated value in the current time period of the discounted future net benefit of a project.

The decision-making process

If it is possible to identify all the private and external costs of a project, to place a monetary valuation on each of them and to choose an appropriate discount rate, then there is a framework for taking decisions about a project. The bottom line is whether the total social benefits expected to arise from a project outweigh the social costs.

This may sound straightforward, but it is important to remember all the assumptions on which such decisions would be based. In particular, the valuations made of the various elements of benefits and costs may be considered to be at least partially subjective, and different members of society may take different views of what is an appropriate discount rate. However, this does not mean that social cost–benefit analysis is unhelpful. For example, a government may be choosing between a range of different development projects. By using consistent assumptions in valuation and discount rates across the projects, it may be possible to produce a coherent *ranking* of alternative projects, and thus identify the project that would produce the highest benefit–cost ratio.

Exercise 13.6

Suppose there is a proposal to construct a new industrial estate close to where you live. Identify the costs and benefits of the scheme, including direct costs and benefits and not forgetting externalities. Discuss how you could bring these components together to analyse the overall net benefit of the project.

Summary

- A number of approaches have been proposed to measure externalities. Measurement may enable a social cost–benefit analysis to be made of projects involving a substantial externality element.
- The first step is to identify all direct and indirect (private and external) benefits and costs of a project.
- Each component must then be valued.
- An appropriate discount rate needs to be applied to those benefits and costs that will arise in the future.
- The project with the highest ratio of benefits to costs is likely to be the one that is most beneficial for society.

Examination questions

1 The government in Namibia stated that electricity prices should cover cost and should also be based on the principle of allocative efficiency. Discuss whether this approach to pricing can be supported in theory. [25]

Cambridge AS and A Level Economics 9708, Paper 4, Q2, June 2008

2 Economists talk about the need for resources to be used efficiently. Explain what they mean by this and discuss whether it is possible in practice to achieve such efficiency. [25]

Cambridge AS and A Level Economics 9708, Paper 43, Q7, November 2011

3 a Explain the market failure which arises from the characteristics of public goods. [8]

b Discuss whether the use of cost–benefit analysis helps to improve economic decision-making. [12]

Cambridge AS and A Level Economics 9708, Paper 2, Q3, November 2008

4 The diamond market

The world diamond market was badly hit by the start of the global economic slowdown in 2008. Mines were shut in Southern Africa and Canada, diamond cutters and polishers lost their jobs in India and retail jewellers went out of business in the US. One small piece of good news for the diamond industry was the decision of New York's government not to introduce a planned 5% luxury tax on jewellery and watches priced over $20000 in its 2009–2010 budget.

Figure 1 shows the monthly price indices for three sizes of diamond (0.5, 3.0 and 4.0 carats) from October 2006 to December 2008.

Diamond mining has a controversial history. Mines are expensive to operate and have been associated with low pay for workers and appalling working conditions. In Africa diamonds have financed civil wars. In Canada's North West Territories mining has been held responsible for damage to the habitat of wildlife.

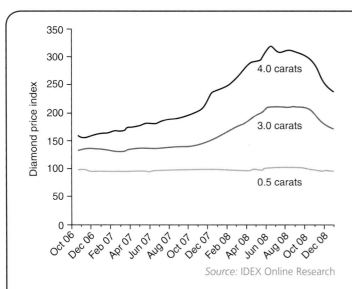

Source: IDEX Online Research

Figure 1 Diamond price indices, October 2006–December 2008
(base month for each index July 2004 = 100)

a Compare the price behaviour of the three sizes of diamond between July 2004 and December 2008. [3]

b Explain **two** possible influences on the demand for diamonds. [4]

c Show, with the help of a diagram, how the introduction of the 5% luxury tax would have affected the supply of diamonds. [4]

d Using an example from the data, explain the meaning of external cost. [3]

e Discuss how well diamonds might serve as money if people lose confidence in paper currency. [6]

Cambridge AS and A Level Economics 9708, Paper 21, Q1, November 2011

14 Marginal utility and consumer choice

Chapter 2 explained the nature of demand as part of the basis for the demand and supply model. This chapter extends that analysis by introducing the notion of marginal utility and using this to add to your understanding of the demand curve. The consumer's budget line is introduced, and there is some discussion of how a consumer's reaction to a change in the price of a good can be broken down into two separate effects – the income effect and the substitution effect.

Learning outcomes

After studying this chapter, you should:
- be familiar with the concepts of total and marginal utility
- understand the law of diminishing marginal utility and what this reveals about the nature of the demand curve
- be aware of importance of the equi-marginal principle
- be familiar with the limitations of marginal utility theory
- understand the nature of a consumer's budget line
- understand the notion of an individual's indifference curve
- be able to identify a consumer's choice point to maximise utility
- be familiar with the income and substitution effects of a price change.

14.1 Marginal utility theory

Suppose you could measure the satisfaction that you derive from consuming a good? For example, consider the case of chocolate bars. Consuming a chocolate bar gives you a certain amount of satisfaction – which economists often refer to as **utility** in this context. Imagine that it is possible to put a numerical value on this utility, and for the sake of argument that the utility you get from consuming a chocolate bar is 30 'utils', this being the unit in which utility is measured.

Economists refer to the utility of a good, in this case, how much satisfaction you receive from consuming a chocolate bar

Having consumed the chocolate bar, you are now offered a second, which you also consume, this time receiving 26 utils of utility. You probably get less utility from the second bar simply because you have already had some chocolate – and the more chocolate bars you eat, the less utility you are likely to get from the additional bar. Notice here that the valuation of the utility refers to the additional satisfaction that is gained from the second bar. This is therefore known as the **marginal utility** from consuming an additional chocolate bar. Indeed, there will come a time when you have eaten so much chocolate that you cannot face eating any more, as you know you would be ill. Table 14.1 shows the marginal utility that Majida gains from consuming chocolate bars.

Key terms

Utility: the satisfaction received from consuming a good or service.
Marginal utility: the additional utility gained from consuming an extra unit of a good or service.

Table 14.1 Utility from chocolate

Number of bars	Marginal utility (utils)
1	30
2	26
3	21
4	15
5	8
6	0

In this example, the sixth chocolate bar gives no satisfaction to Majida, who has already had enough chocolate for the day.

This idea that the more of a good you consume, the less additional pleasure you get from the extra unit of it is known as the **law of diminishing marginal utility**. It is a 'law' because it has been found to be universally true. If you keep consuming more of something, you get less additional satisfaction from extra units. Figure 14.1 plots the marginal utility values on a graph. The law of diminishing marginal utility ensures that the *MU* curve is downward sloping.

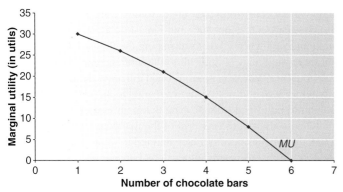

Figure 14.1 A marginal utility curve

Key term

Law of diminishing marginal utility: states that the more units of a good that are consumed, the lower the utility from consuming those additional units.

If it were really possible to measure satisfaction in this way, it would also be possible to calculate the total utility that Majida receives from consuming chocolate bars. For instance, if she consumes two bars, she gets 30 + 26 = 56 utils. If she has a third bar, her *total utility* would be 77 utils.

The relationship between 'total' and 'marginal' appears in many areas of economic analysis, and it is good to be clear about it. The 'marginal' value is calculated as the change in the 'total'.

Exercise 14.1

Table 14.2 shows the total utility that Nazim obtains from consuming a good. Calculate the marginal utility at each level.

Table 14.2 Nazim's total utility from good X

Units of X	Total utility (utils)
1	10
2	19
3	27
4	34
5	40
6	45
7	49

Draw the *MU* curve on a diagram.

Summary

- Marginal utility represents the additional satisfaction that a consumer receives from consuming an additional unit of a good.
- Marginal utility diminishes the more of a good is consumed.

14.2 Marginal utility and demand

If marginal utility were measured in terms of money, then the *MU* curve would become a person's demand curve. Consider Figure 14.2. The quantity of the good Q^* provides this individual with marginal utility of MU^*. If the price of the good were higher than MU^*, then the individual would not buy Q^* of the good, as the price exceeds his valuation. On the other hand, if price were to be set lower than MU^*, then the individual would be prepared to buy more than Q^*, as the marginal utility would be higher than the asking price. Another way of putting this is to say that the consumer will purchase the good up to the point where the price is equal to the marginal utility gained from consuming the good. Of course, a similar argument applies at each point along the *MU* curve, so this is indeed the individual's demand curve when utility is measured in money terms.

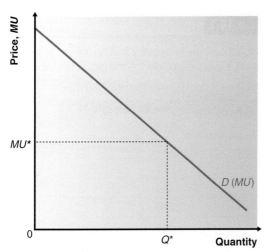

Figure 14.2 An individual's demand curve

The previous discussion of the demand curve emphasised that the curve shows the relationship between the quantity demanded of a good and its price, ceteris paribus. In other words, it focused on the relationship between demand and price, holding other influences on demand constant. This argument also applies in this case. Changes in the price of other goods, in consumer incomes or in preferences would all affect the position of the demand (*MU*) curve.

This highlights the fact that decisions about the consumption of one good are interconnected with decisions being made about other goods. If a consumer chooses to consume more of one good, that means there is less income available to be spent on other goods. Furthermore, a decision to consume more of one good will affect the consumption of complementary and substitute goods. So rather than focusing on a consumer's decisions about the demand for a single good, it is also necessary to consider the demand for a bundle of goods and services, and how a consumer can arrive at a joint decision.

The equi-marginal principle

To keep things simple, consider an individual choosing a combination of two goods, X and Y. The individual gains utility from each good, and sets out to maximise the utility received from consumption of both. The quantity chosen of one good affects the demand for the other, given a limited budget to spend on the items. Therefore, it is not a simple question of setting marginal utility equal to price, as the decision on one good affects the position of the *MU* curve for the other good because of the linkage through the budget constraint.

It turns out that the best a consumer can do is to consume the two goods at the point where the ratio of the marginal utilities of the two goods is equal to the ratio of their prices. In other words, this is where:

$$\frac{MU_X}{MU_Y} = \frac{P_X}{P_Y}$$

This is known as the **equi-marginal principle**. It describes the conditions under which a consumer will maximise his or her utility. In principle, this can be extended to the case where consumers are choosing between many goods and services.

Key term

Equi-marginal principle: a consumer does best in utility terms by consuming at the point where the ratio of marginal utilities from two goods is equal to the ratio of their prices.

Limitations of marginal utility theory

The marginal utility approach provides insights into consumer behaviour, but it has its limitations. First, utility is not something that can be measured; there is no objective way of valuing utility, which will vary from individual to individual. In other words, because each consumer is different and has different preferences, it is impossible to compare utility between individuals. One person may gain different utility from $1 than another, and there is no way of comparing their utility values. This does not mean that the analysis is unhelpful – but it must be recognised that there are limitations when it comes to putting the theory into practice. For example, it may be difficult to think of aggregating across individual consumers in order to build a market demand curve for a good. However, it will be shown that there are some important insights to be gained from pushing this analysis a bit further.

It is also difficult to conceive of the marginal utility approach when the analysis needs to be extended to multiple goods and services, so that the many interactions between the demand for one good and the demand for another need to be taken into account. One way of making some sense of this would be to consider the consumer's choice as being between the utility gained from one good and the utility gained from all other goods considered together. However, let us assume that a consumer is choosing between two goods.

The budget line

Suppose that Abdul has $1.20 to spend, and wants to split his purchases between apples (which are 20c each) and cola (which is 40c per bottle). He can choose to spend the whole amount on apples, or on cola – or can buy some of each. Given these prices, he could buy six apples or three bottles of cola. The possibilities are shown as the **budget line** in Figure 14.3. This connects the combinations of apples and cola that Abdul could purchase. For example, he could buy four apples and one bottle of cola, as marked on the figure. One way of interpreting the budget line is as the boundary showing the combinations of apples and cola that Abdul can afford – he could not choose to consume beyond the budget line.

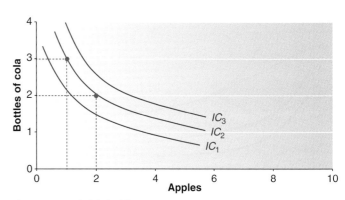

Figure 14.4 Abdul's indifference curves

Abdul's choice

Abdul cannot choose to be on just any of the curves, as he is constrained by his budget line. However, if the budget line is superimposed on the map of indifference curves, his choice can be identified. This can be seen in Figure 14.5. The highest indifference curve that Abdul can reach given his budget line (*BL*) is IC_2. The budget line just touches the indifference curve at one point, where Abdul consumes two bottles of cola and two apples. At any other point along the budget line or below it, he would receive lower utility than this. The tangency point at A is his choice point.

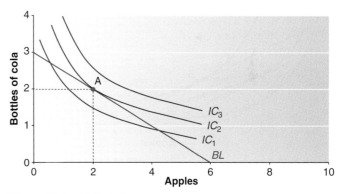

Figure 14.5 Abdul's choice

The effect of a change in budget

Suppose that Abdul receives an increase in his income, so that his budget for spending on these goods increases: for example, suppose he found an extra 80c in his pocket so he now had $2 to spend on these goods. Given that the prices of the goods remains as before, his budget line moves out, but keeps the same slope as before. This is shown in Figure 14.6, where the budget line moves from BL_0 to BL_1. As a result, Abdul can now reach a higher indifference curve by moving from point A to point B. He now consumes three bottles of cola and four apples. In this example, Abdul increases his consumption of both goods as income rises, indicating that they are both *normal goods*.

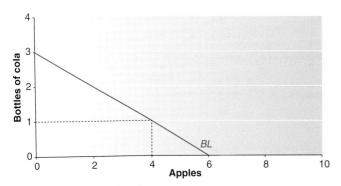

Key term

> **Budget line**: shows the boundary of an individual's consumption set, given the amount available to spend and the prices of the goods.

Figure 14.3 Abdul's budget line

The indifference curve

In order to analyse Abdul's choice between apples and cola, some way is needed to show his preferences on the diagram. This can be done using **indifference curves**. An indifference curve shows the various combinations of apples and cola that give Abdul equal satisfaction – that is, equal utility. These are downward-sloping, because Abdul can trade off the satisfaction received from one of the goods against that from the other. In other words, if he consumes fewer apples, he needs to consume more cola in order to maintain equal utility.

Key term

> **Indifference curve**: shows the combinations of two goods that give equal utility to a consumer.

Figure 14.4 shows three such curves. Consider the curve IC_2. This shows that Abdul would receive equal utility from consuming two bottles of cola and two apples as he would from three bottles of cola and one apple. Similarly, any point along this curve would be equally satisfactory to Abdul (if he could consume fractions of bottles or apples). The same argument applies to the other curves shown in the diagram, but because we assume that Abdul would prefer more to less, he would maximise utility by reaching the highest possible curve that he can reach. In other words he would prefer to be on IC_2 than on IC_1, but IC_3 would be better than both.

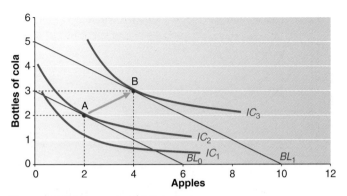

Figure 14.6 A change in Abdul's budget

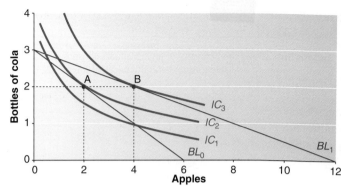

Figure 14.8 A fall in the price of apples

This need not be the case. The indifference curves could be such that the change in income causes Abdul to consume less of one of the goods. In other words, one of the goods could be an *inferior good*. These concepts were introduced in Chapter 2. Figure 14.7 illustrates this on the assumption that Abdul can consume fractions of bottles of cola and apples. In this example, Abdul responds to the change in income by consuming more apples, but less cola.

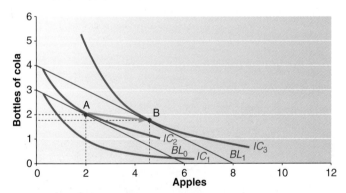

Figure 14.7 A change in Abdul's budget when cola is an inferior good

A fall in the price of apples

If there is a fall in the price of apples, Abdul's budget line is again affected. Figure 14.8 shows what happens to his budget line if the price of apples halves. He can now consume either three bottles of cola (if he spends his entire budget on cola), or 12 apples. With this set of indifference curves, his choice changes from point A to point B, and he continues to consume two bottles of cola, but now chooses four apples.

Notice that a fall in the price of apples has two separate effects on Abdul. On the one hand, there has been a change in the *relative* price of apples and cola, so Abdul will tend to substitute his consumption from the more expensive to the cheaper item (i.e. he will tend to switch from consuming cola to consuming apples). However, there is also a second effect, which is that the fall in the price of apples means that Abdul has higher real income, in the sense that his budget line is shifted out, and his choice set has expanded. These effects were introduced briefly in Chapter 2.

It is possible to identify these two effects. Consider Figure 14.9. This time, suppose that there is an increase in the price of apples, shifting the budget line from BL_0 to BL_1. Abdul's initial choice point is at A, and the increase in the price of apples means that he can no longer reach this point, and thus ends up at B. Given the new relative prices, the shadow budget line BL^* shows the level of income that would have left Abdul at his original utility level – that is, this would have allowed him to reach IC_2. The impact of the price change is thus partly a substitution effect along the indifference curve from A to C, and partly an income effect from C to B.

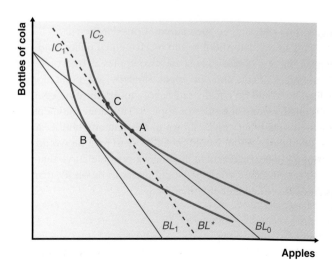

Figure 14.9 Income and substitution effects of a price change

Notice that in this example, both apples and cola are normal goods, and the **substitution and income effect** work in the same direction. In other words, when the price of apples increases, both income and substitution effects reduce the consumption of apples.

Figure 14.10 shows that when apples are an inferior good, the substitution and income effects work in opposite directions. Abdul's tendency to substitute cola for apples (from A to C) is partly offset by the income effect from C to B: as income falls, Abdul tends to consume more apples.

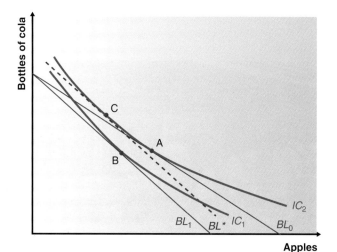

Figure 14.10 Income and substitution effects of a price change when apples are an inferior good

Key terms

Income effect of a price change: reflects the way that a change in the price of a good affects purchasing power (real income).

Substitution effect of a price change: reflects the way that a change in the price of a good affects relative prices.

Do consumers always act rationally?

Marginal utility theory rests on the crucial assumption that consumers act rationally in taking decisions about their spending and consumption by setting out to maximise their utility. Recent advances in **behavioural economics** suggest that this is not always the case.

This branch of economic analysis recognises that the psychology of human decision making is more complex than the simple desire to maximise utility. People do not always focus on purely economic influences, but may act on impulse, or in response to their feelings. This can lead them to take decisions about their spending that cannot be explained only by utility maximisation. For example, they may make charitable donations or may purchase more of some goods than would be dictated by rational economic behaviour, perhaps because there were seen to be special offers available.

Key term

Behavioural economics: a branch of economics that builds on the psychology of human behaviour in decision making.

Increasingly, behavioural economists are using experimental situations to discover more about how people react in situations of risk and how their spending behaviour is influenced by impulse and in response to stimuli. This analysis is potentially valuable to firms: if they can understand what induces people to behave in certain ways, they may be able to influence their spending.

Exercise 14.2

Suppose that Jennifer is allocating her available budget between two goods. Using a diagram, explain the impact of an increase in the price of one of the goods, distinguishing between the income and substitution effects.

Summary

- Diminishing marginal utility helps to explain why demand curves are downward sloping.
- The equi-marginal principle shows that an individual's utility is maximised where the ratio of the marginal utilities of two goods is equal to the ratio of their prices.
- The budget line shows the combination of goods that an individual can consume given the amount available to spend and the prices of the goods.
- An indifference curve maps the preferences of a consumer between two goods.
- Utility from consuming two goods is maximised where an indifference curve is at a tangent to the budget line.
- The effects of a price change can be divided into an income effect and a substitution effect.

15 Firms and how they operate

Firms play a central role in the operation of markets. This chapter introduces the theory of the firm by examining some of the key concepts that are needed for this important part of economic analysis. The discussion will explore the relationship between costs and production, and how firms may act to maximise profit.

Learning outcomes

After studying this chapter, you should:

- be aware of the reason for the birth of firms, and the desire for their growth
- be familiar with short- and long-run cost curves and their characteristics
- understand the significance of economies of scale in the context of the growth of firms
- understand the profit maximisation motive and its implications for firms' behaviour.

15.1 The nature of firms

What is a firm?

One way of answering this question is to say that firms exist in order to organise production: they bring together various factors of production, and organise the production process in order to produce output.

There are various forms that the organisation of a firm can take. Perhaps the simplest is that of *sole proprietor*, in which the owner of the firm also runs the firm. Examples are an independent shop, hairdresser or taxi driver, where the owner is liable for the debts of the enterprise, but also gets to keep any profits.

The owner of an independent shop in Mauritius is liable for the debts but is able to keep the profits

In some professions, firms are operated on a *partnership* basis. Examples here are doctors', dentists' and solicitors' practices. Profits are shared between the partners, as are debts, according to the contract drawn up between them. Some non-professional enterprises, such as some builders and hardware stores, also operate in this way.

Private joint-stock companies are owned by shareholders, each of whom has contributed funds to the business by buying shares. However, each shareholder's responsibility for the debts of the company is limited to the amount he or she paid for the shares. Profits are distributed to shareholders as dividends. The shares in a private company of this kind are not traded on the stock exchange, and the firms tend to be controlled by the shareholders themselves. Many local businesses are operated on this basis. Private limited companies have limited liability for the firm's debts, as mentioned above. Many family firms also operate in this way, with the families maintaining control through their ownership of shares.

Firms that are owned by shareholders, but are listed on the stock exchange are *public joint-stock companies*. Again, the liability of the shareholders is limited to the amount they have paid for their shares. Such companies are required to publish their annual accounts and also to publish an annual report to their shareholders. Day-to-day decision-making is normally delegated to a board of directors (who are not major shareholders), appointed at the annual general meeting (AGM) of the shareholders.

Firm size

An important decision facing any firm is to choose its scale of operation. If you look around the economy, you will see that the size of firms varies enormously, from small one-person operations up to mega-sized multinational corporations. Such firms may need to continue to grow in order to compete with other large-scale competitors in global markets. There may be many reasons why firms wish to expand their operations. This chapter will begin to explain why this is so, and show how the decision about how much output to produce depends upon what a firm is trying to achieve, and on the market environment in which it is operating.

Later in the chapter you will see that the way in which a firm is organised may influence the way in which decisions are taken on key economic issues – indeed, it may affect the whole motivation of a firm in decision-taking. However, for now all such forms of organisation will be referred to simply as 'firms'.

The nature of the activity being undertaken by the firm and its scale of operation will help to determine its most efficient form of organisation. For firms to operate successfully, they must minimise the transaction costs of undertaking business.

Exercise 15.1

Identify firms that are operating in your town or city. Which of them would you classify as being relatively small-scale enterprises, and which operate on a more national basis?

Summary

- A firm is an organisation that exists to bring together factors of production in order to produce goods or services.
- Firms range, in the complexity of their organisation, from sole proprietors to public limited companies.
- Firms vary in size, from one-person concerns to large multinational corporations operating in global markets.

15.2 Costs and revenue for firms

Costs of production

To understand why firms wish to grow, it is important to examine the costs of production that they face. This section focuses on the relationship between costs and the level of output produced by a

firm. Diagrams will be used to illustrate this relationship using a series of cost curves that apply in various circumstances.

For simplicity, it is assumed that the firm under consideration produces a single product. Of course, in reality this does not apply to all firms. There are many large conglomerate firms that produce a range of different products. However, this complicates the analysis unnecessarily, so the focus here is on a firm that produces a single product.

In order to undertake production, the firm uses productive resources known as factors of production. These include *human resources* (labour, entrepreneurship and management), *natural resources* (land, raw materials, energy) and *produced resources* (physical capital). These factors of production are organised by the firm in order to produce output. For example, in the leisure sector, your local gym uses capital in the form of exercise equipment, and labour in the form of the training staff and receptionist. In transport, a taxi firm uses capital in the form of the cars, and labour – the drivers and phone operators.

Notice that these factors have some differing characteristics that affect the analysis of firms' behaviour. In the short run, the firm faces limited flexibility. Varying the quantity of labour input that the firm uses may be relatively straightforward – it can increase the use of overtime, or hire more workers, fairly quickly. However, varying the amount of capital the firm has at its disposal may take longer. For example, it takes time to commission a new piece of machinery, or to build a new sports centre – or a Channel Tunnel! Hence labour is regarded as a flexible factor and capital as a fixed factor. The definitions of the **short run** and **long run** are based on this assumption.

Key terms

Short run: the period over which a firm is free to vary its input of one factor of production (labour) but faces fixed inputs of the other factors.

Long run: the period over which the firm is able to vary the inputs of all its factors of production.

The production function

As the firm changes its volume of production, it needs to vary the inputs of its factors of production. Thus, the total amount of output produced in a given period depends upon the inputs of labour, capital and other inputs used in the production process. Of course, there are many different ways of combining these inputs, some combinations being more efficient than others. The **production function** summarises the technically most efficient combinations for any given output level. It specifies how the level of output produced by a firm depends upon the quantities of the factors of production that are utilised.

The nature of technology in an industry will determine the way in which output varies with the quantity of inputs. However, one thing is certain. If the firm increases the amount of inputs of the variable factor (labour) while holding constant the input of the other factors, it will gradually derive less additional output per unit of labour for each further increase. This is known as the **law of diminishing returns** (or the *law of variable proportions*), and is one of the few 'laws' in economics. It is a short-run concept, as it relies on the assumption that capital and other factor inputs are fixed.

> ### Key terms
>
> **Production function**: relationship that embodies information about technically efficient ways of combining labour and other factors of production to produce output.
>
> **Law of diminishing returns**: law stating that if a firm increases its inputs of one factor of production while holding inputs of other factors fixed, eventually the firm will get diminishing marginal returns from the variable factor.

It can readily be seen why this should be the case. Suppose a firm has ten computer operators working in a travel agency, using ten computers. The 11th worker may add some extra output, as the workers may be able to 'hot-desk' and take their coffee breaks at different times. The 12th worker may also add some extra output, perhaps by keeping the printers stocked with paper. However, if the firm keeps adding staff without increasing the number of computers, each extra worker will be adding less additional output to the office. Indeed, the 20th worker may add nothing at all, being unable to get access to a computer.

Figure 15.1 illustrates the short-run relationship between labour input and total physical product (TPP_L), with capital held constant. The shape of the TPP_L curve reflects the law of diminishing returns: as labour input increases, the amount of additional output produced gets smaller. An increase in the amount of capital available will raise the amount of output produced for any given labour input, so the TPP_L will shift upwards, as shown in Figure 15.2.

The production function thus carries information about the physical relationship between the inputs of the factors of production and the physical quantity of output. With this information and knowledge of the prices that the firm must pay for its inputs of the factors of production, it is possible to map out the way in which costs will change with the level of output.

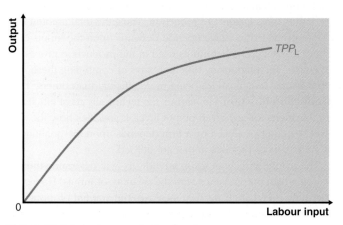

Figure 15.1 A short-run production function

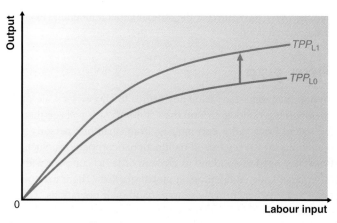

Figure 15.2 The effect of an increase in capital

We can view the firm's decision process as a three-stage procedure. First, the firm needs to decide how much output it wants to produce. Second, it chooses an appropriate combination of factors of production given that intended scale of production. Third, it attempts to produce as much output as possible given those inputs. Another way of expressing this is that, having chosen the intended scale of output, the firm tries to minimise its costs of production.

Total, marginal and average costs

In talking about costs, economists distinguish between total, marginal and average costs. **Total cost** is the sum of all costs that are incurred in order to produce a given level of output. Total cost will always increase as the firm increases its level of production, as this will require more inputs of factors of production, materials and so on. **Average cost** is simply the cost per unit of output – it is total cost divided by the level of output produced.

> ### Key terms
>
> **Total cost**: the sum of all costs that are incurred in producing a given level of output.
>
> **Average cost**: total cost divided by the quantity produced, sometimes known as unit cost or average total cost.

Equally important as these measures is the concept of marginal cost. Economists rely heavily on the idea that firms, consumers and other economic actors can make good decisions by thinking in terms of the margin. This is known as the **marginal principle**. For example, a firm may examine whether a small change in its behaviour makes matters better or worse. In this context, marginal cost is important. It is defined as the change in total cost associated with a small change in output. In other words, it is the additional cost incurred by the firm if it increases output by one unit.

Marginal principle: the idea that firms (and other economic agents) may take decisions by considering the effect of small changes from an existing situation.

Costs in the short run

Because the firm cannot vary some of its inputs in the short run, some costs may be regarded as fixed, and some as variable. In this short run, some fixed costs are **sunk costs**: that is, they are costs that the firm cannot avoid paying even if it chooses to produce no output at all. Short-run total costs (*STC*) are the sum of **fixed** and **variable costs**:

total costs = total fixed costs (*TFC*) + total variable costs (*TVC*)

Total costs will increase as the firm increases the volume of production because more of the variable input is needed to increase output. The way in which the costs will vary depends on the nature of the production function, and on whether the prices of labour or other factor inputs alter as output increases.

Sunk costs: costs incurred by a firm that cannot be recovered if the firm ceases trading.
Fixed costs: costs that do not vary with the level of output.
Variable costs: costs that do vary with the level of output.

A common assumption made by economists is that in the short run, at very low levels of output, total costs will rise more slowly than output, but that as diminishing returns set in, total costs will accelerate, as shown in Figure 15.3.

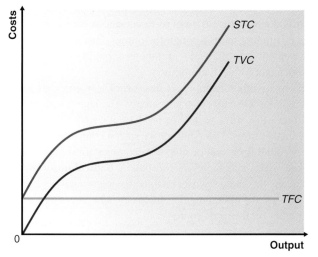

Figure 15.3 Costs in the short run

Short-run average and marginal curves are plotted in Figure 15.4, which shows how they relate to each other. First, notice that short-run average total costs (*SATC*) are shown as a U-shaped

curve. This is the form often assumed in economic analysis. *SATC* is the sum of average fixed and variable costs (*SAFC* and *SAVC*, respectively). Average fixed costs slope downwards throughout – this is because fixed costs do not vary with the level of output, so as output increases, *SAFC* must always get smaller, as the fixed costs are spread over more and more units of output. However, *SAVC* is also a U-shape, and it is this that gives the U-shape to *SATC*.

A very important aspect of Figure 15.4 is that the short-run marginal cost curve (*SMC*) cuts both *SAVC* and *SATC* at their minimum points. This is always the case. If you think about this for a moment, you will realise that it makes good sense. If you are adding on something that is greater than the average, the average must always increase. For a firm, when the marginal cost of producing an additional unit of a good is higher than the average cost of doing so, the average cost must rise. If the marginal cost is the same as the average cost, then average cost will not change. This is quite simply an arithmetic property of the average and the marginal, and always holds true. So when you draw the average and marginal cost curves for a firm, the marginal cost curve will always cut average cost at the minimum point of average cost. Another way of viewing marginal cost is as the slope or gradient of the total cost curve.

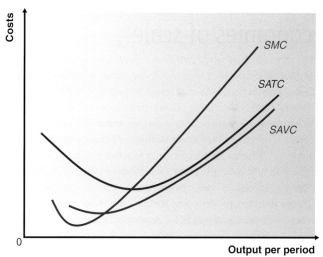

Figure 15.4 The firm's short-run cost curves

Remember that the short-run cost curves show the relationship between the volume of production and costs under the assumption that the quantity of capital and other inputs are fixed, so that in order to change output the firm has to vary the amount of labour. The position of the cost curves thus depends on the quantity of capital. In other words, there is a short-run average total cost curve for each given level of other inputs.

Costs in the long run

In the long run, a firm is able to vary capital and labour (and other factor inputs). It is thus likely to choose the level of capital that is appropriate for the level of output that it expects to

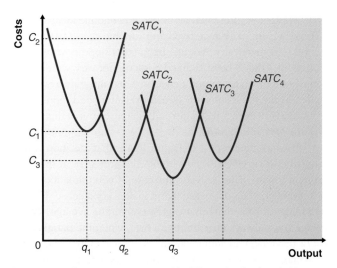

Figure 15.5 Short-run cost curves with different levels of capital input

produce. Figure 15.5 shows a selection of short-run average total cost curves corresponding to different expected output levels, and thus different levels of capital. With the set of *SATC* curves in Figure 15.5, the long-run average cost curve also takes on a U-shape.

Economies of scale

One of the reasons why firms find it beneficial to be large is the existence of economies of scale. These occur when a firm finds that it is more efficient in cost terms to produce on a larger scale.

It is not difficult to imagine industries in which economies of scale are likely to arise. For example, recall the notion of the division of labour, which you encountered during the AS part of the course. When a firm expands, it reaches a certain scale of production at which it becomes worthwhile to take advantage of division of labour. Workers begin to specialise in certain stages of the production process, and their productivity increases. Because this is only possible for relatively large-scale production, this is an example of economies of scale. It is the size of the firm (in terms of its output level) that enables it to produce more efficiently – that is, at lower average cost.

Although the division of labour is one source of economies of scale, it is by no means the only source, and there are several explanations of cost benefits from producing on a large scale. Some of these are industry-specific, and thus some sectors of the economy exhibit more significant economies of scale than others – it is in these activities that the larger firms tend to be found. There are no hairdressing salons that come into the top ten largest firms, but there are plenty of oil companies.

Technology

One source of economies of scale is in the technology of production. There are many activities in which the technology is such that large-scale production is more efficient.

One source of technical economies of scale arises from the physical properties of the universe. There is a physical relationship between the volume and surface area of an object, whereby the storage capacity of an object increases proportionately more than its surface area. Consider the volume of a cube. If the cube is 2 metres each way, its surface area is $6 \times 2 \times 2 = 24$ square metres, while its volume is $2 \times 2 \times 2 = 8$ cubic metres. If the dimension of the cube is 3 metres, the surface area is 54 square metres (more than double the surface area of the smaller cube) but the volume is 27 cubic metres (more than three times the volume of the smaller cube). Thus the larger the cube, the lower the average cost of storage. A similar relationship applies to other shapes of storage containers, whether they are barrels or ships.

What this means in practice is that a large ship can transport proportionately more than a small ship, or that large storage tanks hold more liquid relative to the surface area of the tank than small tanks. Hence there may be benefits in operating on a large scale.

Furthermore, some capital equipment is designed for large-scale production, and would only be viable for a firm operating at a high volume of production. Agricultural machinery designed for large plantations cannot be used in small fields; a production line for car production would not be viable for small levels of output. In other words, there may be *indivisibilities* in the production process.

In addition to indivisibilities, there are many economic activities in which there are high overhead expenditures. Such components of a firm's costs do not vary directly with the scale of production. For example, having built a factory, the cost of that factory is the same regardless of the amount of output that is produced in it. Expenditure on research and development could be seen as such an overhead, which may be viable only when a firm reaches a certain size.

Notice that there are some economic activities in which these overhead costs are highly significant. For example, think about the Channel Tunnel that links England with France. The construction (overhead) costs were enormous compared to the costs of running trains through the tunnel. Thus the overhead cost element is substantial – and the economies of scale will also be significant for such an industry.

There are other examples of this sort of cost structure, such as railway networks and electricity supply. The largest firm in such a market will always be able to produce at a lower average cost than smaller firms. This could prove such a competitive advantage that no other firms will be able to become established in that market, which may therefore constitute a **natural monopoly**. Intuitively, this makes sense. Imagine having several underground railway systems operating in a single city, all competing against each other on the same routes!

Management and marketing

A second source of economies of scale pertains to the management of firms. One of the key factors of production is managerial input. A certain number of managers are required to oversee the production process. As the firm expands, there is a range of volumes of output over which the management team does not need to grow as rapidly as the overall volume of the firm, as a large firm can be managed more efficiently. Notice that there are likely to be limits to this process. At some point, the organisation begins to get so large and complex that management finds it more difficult to manage. At this point **diseconomies of scale** are likely to cut in – in other words, average costs may begin to rise with an increase in output at some volume of production.

> ### Key terms
>
> **Natural monopoly**: arises in an industry where there are such substantial economies of scale that only one firm is viable.
>
> **Diseconomies of scale**: occur for a firm when an increase in the scale of production leads to higher long-run average costs.

Similarly, the cost of marketing a product may not rise as rapidly as the volume of production, leading to further scale economies. One interpretation of this is that we might see marketing expenses as a component of fixed costs – or at least as having a substantial fixed cost element.

Finance and procurement

Large firms may have advantages in a number of other areas. For example, a large firm with a strong reputation may be able to raise finance for further expansion on more favourable terms than a small firm. This, of course, reinforces the market position of the largest firms in a sector and makes it more difficult for relative newcomers to become established.

Once a firm has grown to the point where it is operating on a relatively large scale, it will also be purchasing its inputs in relatively large volumes. In particular, this relates to raw materials, energy and transport services. When buying in bulk in this way, firms may be able to negotiate good deals with their suppliers, and thus again reduce average cost as output increases.

It may even be the case that some of the firm's suppliers will find it beneficial to locate in proximity to the firm's factory, which would reduce costs even more.

External economies of scale

The factors listed so far that may lead to economies of scale arise from the internal expansion of a firm. If the firm is in an industry that is itself expanding, there may also be external economies of scale.

Some of the most successful firms of recent years have been in activities that require high levels of technology and skills. The computer industry is one example of an economic activity that has expanded rapidly. As the sector expands, a pool of skilled labour is

built up that all the firms can draw upon. The very success of the sector encourages people to acquire the skills needed to enter it, colleges may begin to find it viable to provide courses, and so on. Each individual firm benefits in this way from the overall expansion of the sector. The greater availability of skilled workers reduces the amount that individual firms need to spend on training.

Computer engineering is by no means the only example of this. Formula 1 development teams, pharmaceutical companies and others similarly enjoy external economies of scale.

Economies of scope

There are various ways in which firms expand their scale of operations. Some do so within a relatively focused market, but others are multi-product firms that produce a range of different products, sometimes in quite different markets.

For example, look at Nestlé. You may immediately think of instant coffee, and indeed Nestlé produces 200 different brands of instant coffee worldwide. However, Nestlé also produces baby milk powder, mineral water, ice cream and pet food, and has diversified into hotels and restaurants – not to mention locally popular items such as lemon cheesecake-flavoured Kit Kats (a strong seller in Japan).

Such conglomerate companies can benefit from **economies of scope**, whereby there may be benefits of size across a range of different products. These economies may arise because there are activities that can be shared across the product range. For example, a company may not need a finance or accounting section for each different product, or human resource or marketing departments. There is thus scope for economies to be made as the firm expands.

> ### Key term
>
> **Economies of scope**: economies arising when average cost falls as a firm increases output across a range of different products.

> ### Exercise 15.2
>
> Which of the following reflects a movement along a long-run average cost curve, and which would cause a shift of a long-run average cost curve?
>
> a A firm becomes established in a market, learning the best ways of utilising its factors of production.
>
> b A firm observes that average cost falls as it expands its scale of production.
>
> c The larger a firm becomes, the more difficult it becomes to manage, causing average cost to rise.
>
> d A firm operating in the financial sector installs new, faster computers, enabling its average cost to fall for any given level of service that it provides.

Returns to scale

In Figure 15.6, if the firm expands its output up to q^*, long-run average cost falls. Up to q^* of output is the range over which there are economies of scale. To the right of q^*, however, long-run average cost rises as output continues to be increased, and the firm experiences diseconomies of scale. The output q^* itself is at the intermediate state of **constant returns to scale**.

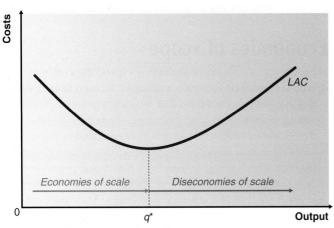

Figure 15.6 The long-run average cost curve

Key term

Constant returns to scale: found when long-run average cost remains constant with an increase in output – in other words, when output and costs rise at the same rate.

It is important not to confuse the notion of returns to scale with the idea introduced earlier of diminishing marginal returns to a factor. The two concepts arise in different circumstances. The law of diminishing returns to a factor applies in the short run, when a firm increases its inputs of one factor of production while facing fixed amounts of other factors. It is thus solely a short-run phenomenon. Diseconomies of scale (sometimes known as *decreasing returns to scale*) can occur in the long run, and the term refers to how output changes as a firm varies the quantities of all factors.

If the firm is operating at the lowest possible level of long-run average costs, it is in a position of productive efficiency. For example, in Figure 15.6 the point q^* may be regarded as the optimum level of output, in the sense that it minimises average cost per unit of output.

Revenue

In the AS part of the course (see Chapter 4), you saw how the total revenue received by a firm varies along the demand curve, according to the price elasticity of demand. In the same way that there is a relationship between total, average and marginal cost, there is also a relationship between **total revenue**, **average revenue** and **marginal revenue**.

Exercise 15.3

A firm faces long-run total cost conditions as shown in Table 15.1.

Table 15.1 Output and long-run costs

Output (000 units per week)	Total cost (£000)
0	0
1	32
2	48
3	82
4	140
5	228
6	352

a Calculate long-run average cost and long-run marginal cost for each level of output.
b Plot long-run average cost and long-run marginal cost curves on a graph. (*Hint:* don't forget to plot *LMC* at points that are halfway between the corresponding output levels.)
c Identify the output level at which long-run average cost is at a minimum.
d Identify the output level at which *LAC* = *LMC*.
e Within what range of output does this firm enjoy economies of scale?
f Within what range of output does the firm experience diseconomies of scale?
g If you could measure the nature of returns to scale, what would characterise the point where *LAC* is at a minimum?

Key terms

Total revenue: the revenue received by a firm from its sales of a good or service; it is the quantity sold, multiplied by the price.

Marginal revenue: the additional revenue received by the firm if it sells an additional unit of output.

Average revenue: the average revenue received by the firm per unit of output; it is total revenue divided by the quantity sold.

Figure 15.7 reminds you of the relationship between total revenue and the *PED*. The marginal revenue (*MR*) curve has also been added to the figure, and has a fixed relationship with the average revenue (*AR*) curve. This is for similar mathematical reasons as the relationship between marginal and average costs explained earlier in this chapter. *MR* shares the intercept point on the vertical axis (at point *A* on Figure 15.7), and has exactly twice the slope of *AR*. Whenever you have to draw this figure, remember that *MR* and *AR* have this relationship, meeting at *A*, and with the distance *BC* being the same as the distance *CD*. *MR* is zero (meets the horizontal axis) at the maximum point of the total revenue curve.

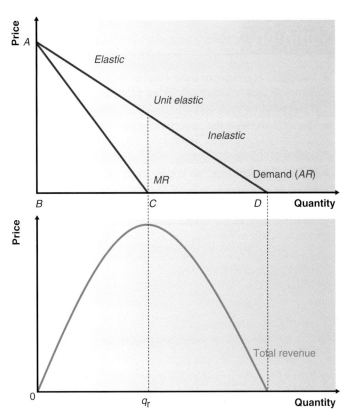

Figure 15.7 Elasticity and total revenue

15.3 Profit maximisation

The opening section of this chapter stated that firms exist to organise production by bringing together the factors of production in order to produce output. This begs the question of what motivates them to produce particular *levels* of output, and at what price.

Traditional economic analysis has tended to start from the premise that firms set out with the objective of *maximising profits*. In analysing this, economists define profits as the difference between the total revenue received by a firm and the total costs that it incurs in production:

$$\text{profits} = \text{total revenue} - \text{total cost}$$

Total revenue here is seen in terms of the quantity of the product that is sold multiplied by the price. Total cost includes the fixed and variable costs that have already been discussed. However, one important item of costs should be highlighted before going any further.

Consider the case of a sole proprietor – a small local business such as a gym or a taxi firm. It seems reasonable to assume that such a firm will set out to maximise its profits. However, from the entrepreneur's perspective there is an opportunity cost of being in business, which may be seen in terms of the earnings that the proprietor could make in an alternative occupation. This required rate of return is regarded as a fixed cost, and is included in the total cost of production.

The same procedure applies to cost curves for other sorts of firm. In other words, when economists refer to costs, they include the rate of return that a firm needs to make it stay in a particular market in the long run. Accountants dislike this, as 'opportunity cost' cannot be identified as an explicit item in the accounts. This part of costs is known as **normal profit**.

Profits made by a firm above that level are known as **supernormal profits**, **abnormal profits** or **economic profits**.

Summary

- A firm may face inflexibility in the short run, with some factors being fixed in quantity and only some being variable.
- The short run is defined in this context as the period over which a firm is free to vary some factors, but not others.
- The long run is defined as the period over which the firm is able to vary the input of all of its factors of production.
- The production function shows how output can be efficiently produced through the input of factors of production.
- The law of diminishing returns states that, if a firm increases the input of a variable factor while holding input of the fixed factor constant, eventually the firm will get diminishing marginal returns from the variable factor.
- Short-run costs can be separated into fixed, sunk and variable costs.
- There is a clear and immutable relationship between total, average and marginal costs.
- For a U-shaped average cost curve, marginal cost always cuts the minimum point of average cost.
- The total revenue received by a firm varies with the price elasticity of demand.
- There is a clear relationship between total, average and marginal revenue.

Key terms

Normal profit: the rate of return that a firm needs in order to remain in business – it is the opportunity cost of being in a market.

Abnormal, **supernormal** or **economic profits**: profits above normal profits.

In the short run, a firm may choose to remain in a market even if it is not covering its opportunity costs, provided its revenues are covering its variable costs. Since the firm has already incurred fixed costs, if it can cover its variable costs in the short run, it will be better off remaining in business and paying off part of the fixed costs than exiting the market and losing all of its fixed costs. Thus, the level of average variable costs represents the shut-down price, below which the firm will exit from the market in the short run. In situations where firms in a market are making abnormal profits, it is likely that other firms will be attracted to enter the market. The absence or existence of abnormal profits will thus be important in influencing the way in which a market may evolve over time.

How does a firm choose its output level if it wishes to maximise profits? An application of the marginal principle shows how. Suppose a firm realises that its marginal revenue is higher than its marginal cost of production. What does this mean for profits? If it were to sell an additional unit of its output, it would gain more in revenue than it would incur additional cost, so its profits would increase. Similarly, if it found that its marginal revenue was less than marginal cost, it would be making a loss on the marginal unit of output, and profits would increase if the firm sold less. This leads to the conclusion that profits will be maximised at the level of output at which marginal revenue (MR) is equal to marginal cost (MC). Indeed, $MR = MC$ is a general rule that tells a firm how to maximise profits in any market situation.

Summary

- Traditional economic analysis assumes that firms set out to maximise profits, where profits are defined as the excess of total revenue over total cost.
- This analysis treats the opportunity cost of a firm's resources as a part of fixed costs. The opportunity cost is known as normal profit.
- Profits above this level are known as abnormal profits.
- A firm maximises profits by choosing a level of output such that marginal revenue is equal to marginal cost.

16 Perfect competition and monopoly

The previous chapter discussed the way in which firms may be expected to operate. Further analysis shows that the behaviour of firms is strongly influenced by the market environment in which they find themselves. It is therefore now time to look at market structure more closely in order to evaluate the way that markets work, and the significance of this for resource allocation. The fact that firms try to maximise profits is not in itself bad for society. However, the structure of a market has a strong influence on how well the market performs. 'Structure' here is seen in relation to a number of dimensions, but in particular to the number of firms operating in a market and the way in which they interact. This chapter considers two extreme forms of market structure: perfect competition and monopoly.

Learning outcomes

After studying this chapter, you should:

- be familiar with the assumptions of the model of perfect competition
- understand how a firm chooses profit-maximising output under perfect competition
- appreciate how a perfectly competitive market reaches long-run equilibrium
- understand how the characteristics of long-run equilibrium affect the performance of the market in terms of productive and allocative efficiency
- be familiar with the assumptions of the model of monopoly
- understand how the monopoly firm chooses the level of output and sets its price
- understand why a monopoly can arise in a market
- understand how the characteristics of the monopoly equilibrium affect the performance of the market in terms of productive and allocative efficiency.

16.1 Market structure

Firms cannot take decisions without some awareness of the market in which they are operating. In some markets, firms find themselves to be such a small player that they cannot influence the price at which they sell. In others, a firm may find itself to be the only firm, which clearly gives it much more discretion in devising a price and output strategy. There may also be many intermediate situations where the firm has some control over price, but needs to be aware of rival firms in the market.

Economists have devised a range of models that allow such different **market structures** to be analysed. Before looking carefully at the most important types of market structure, the key characteristics of alternative market structures will be introduced. The main models are summarised in Table 16.1. In many ways, we can regard these as a spectrum of markets with different characteristics.

> **Key term**
>
> **Market structure**: the market environment in which a firm operates.

Table 16.1 Types of market structure

	Perfect competition	Monopolistic competition	Oligopoly	Monopoly
Number of firms	Many	Many	Few	One
Freedom of entry	Not restricted	Not restricted	Some barriers	High barriers to entry
Firm's influence over price	None	Some	Some	Price maker, subject to the demand curve
Nature of product	Homogeneous	Differentiated	Varied	No close substitutes
Examples	Cauliflowers, onions	Fast-food outlets, travel agents	Cars, mobile phones	PC operating systems, local water supply

Perfect competition

At one extreme is perfect competition. This is a market in which each individual firm is a price taker. This means that there is no individual firm that is large enough to be able to influence the price, which is set by the market as a whole. This situation would arise where there are many firms operating in a market, producing a product that is much the same whichever firm produces it. You might think of a market for a particular sort of vegetable, for example. One cauliflower is very much like another, and it would not be possible for a particular cauliflower-grower to set a premium price for its product.

Such markets are also typified by freedom of entry and exit. In other words, it is relatively easy for new firms to enter the market, or for existing firms to leave it to produce something else. The market price in such a market will be driven down to that at which the typical firm in the market just makes enough profit to stay in business. If firms make more than this, other firms will be attracted in, and thus abnormal profits will be competed away. If some firms in the market do not make sufficient profit to want to remain in the market, they will exit, allowing price to drift up until again the typical firm just makes enough to stay in business.

Monopoly

At the other extreme of the spectrum of market structures is monopoly. This is a market where there is only one firm in operation. Such a firm has some influence over price, and can choose a combination of price and output in order to maximise its profits. The monopolist is not entirely free to set any price that it wants, as it must remain aware of the demand curve for its product. Nonetheless, it has the freedom to choose a point along its demand curve.

Bill Gates is the former chief executive and chairman of Microsoft

The nature of a monopolist's product is that it has no close substitutes – either actual or potential – so it faces no competition. An example might be Microsoft, which for a long time held a global monopoly for operating systems for personal computers (PCs). At the time of the famous trial in 1998, Microsoft was said to supply operating systems for about 95% of the world's PCs.

Another condition of a monopoly market is that there are barriers to the entry of new firms. This means that the firm is able to set its price such as to make profits that are above the minimum needed to keep the firm in business, without attracting new rivals into the market.

Monopolistic competition

Between the two extreme forms of market structure are many intermediate situations in which firms may have some influence over their selling price, but still have to take account of the fact that there are other firms in the market. One such market is known as monopolistic competition. This is a market in which there are many firms operating, each producing similar but not identical products, so that there is some scope for influencing price, perhaps because of brand loyalty. However, firms in such a market are likely to be relatively small. Such firms may find it profitable to make sure that their own product is differentiated from other goods, and may advertise in order to convince potential customers that this is the case. For example, small-scale local restaurants may offer different styles of cooking.

Oligopoly

Another intermediate form of market structure is oligopoly, which literally means 'few sellers'. This is a market in which there are just a few firms that supply the market. Each firm will take decisions in close awareness of how other firms in the market may react to their actions. In some cases, the firms may try to collude – to work together in order to behave as if they were a monopolist – thus making higher profits. In other cases, they may be intense rivals, which will tend to result in abnormal profits being competed away. The question of whether firms in an oligopoly collude or compete has a substantial impact on how the overall market performs in terms of resource allocation, and whether consumers will be disadvantaged as a result of the actions of the firms in the market.

Barriers to entry

It has been argued that if firms in a market are able to make abnormal profits, this will act as an inducement for new firms to try to gain entry into that market in order to share in those profits. A barrier to entry is a characteristic of a market that prevents new firms from joining the market. The existence of such barriers is thus of great importance in influencing the market structure that will evolve.

For example, if a firm holds a patent on a particular good, this means that no other firm is permitted by law to produce the product, and the patent-holding firm thus has a monopoly. The firm may then be able to set a price such as to make abnormal profits without fear of rival firms competing away those profits. On the other hand, if there are no barriers to entry in a market, then if the existing firms set price to make abnormal profits, new firms will join the market, and the increase in market supply will push price down until no abnormal profits are being made.

Summary

- The decisions made by firms must be taken in the context of the market environment in which they operate.
- Under conditions of perfect competition, each firm must accept the market price as given, but can choose how much output to produce in order to maximise profits.
- In a monopoly market, where there is only one producer, the firm can choose output and price (subject to the demand curve).
- Monopolistic competition combines some features of perfect competition and some characteristics of monopoly. Firms have some influence over price and will produce a differentiated product in order to maintain this influence.
- Oligopoly exists where a market is occupied by just a few firms. In some cases, these few firms may work together to maximise their joint profits; in other cases, they may seek to outmanoeuvre each other.

16.2 Perfect competition

Assumptions

At one end of the spectrum of market structures is **perfect competition**. This model has a special place in economic analysis because, if all its assumptions were fulfilled, and if all markets operated according to its precepts (including the markets for leisure goods and services, and for transportation services), the best allocation of resources would be ensured for society as a whole. Although it may be argued that this ideal is not often achieved, perfect competition nonetheless provides a yardstick by which all other forms of market structure can be evaluated. The assumptions of this model are as follows:
- Firms aim to maximise profits.
- There are many participants (both buyers and sellers).
- The product is homogeneous.
- There are no barriers to entry to or exit from the market.
- There is perfect knowledge of market conditions.

Key term

Perfect competition: a form of market structure that produces allocative and productive efficiency in long-run equilibrium.

Profit maximisation

The first assumption is that firms act to maximise their profits. You might think that firms acting in their own self-interest are unlikely to do consumers any favours. However, it transpires that this does not interfere with the operation of the market. Indeed, it is the pursuit of self-interest by firms and consumers that ensures that the market works effectively.

Many participants

This is an important assumption of the model: that there are so many buyers and so many sellers that no individual trader is able to influence the market price. The market price is thus determined by the operation of the market.

On the sellers' side of the market, this assumption is tantamount to saying that there are limited economies of scale in the industry. If the minimum efficient scale (that is, the level of output at which a firm's long-run average costs reach their minimum) is small relative to market demand, then no firm is likely to become so large that it will gain influence in the market.

A homogeneous product

This assumption means that buyers of the good see all products in the market as being identical, and will not favour one firm's product over another. If there were brand loyalty, such that one firm was more popular than others, then that firm would be able to charge a premium on its price. By ruling out this possibility the previous assumption is reinforced, and no individual seller is able to influence the selling price of the product.

No barriers to entry or exit

By this assumption, firms are able to join the market if they perceive it to be a profitable step, and they can exit from the market without hindrance. This assumption is important when it comes to considering the long-run equilibrium towards which the market will tend.

Perfect knowledge

It is assumed that all participants in the market have perfect information about trading conditions in the market. In particular, buyers always know the prices that firms are charging, and thus can buy the good at the cheapest possible price. Firms that try to charge a price above the market price will get no takers. At the same time, traders are aware of the product quality.

Perfect competition in the short run
The firm under perfect competition

With the above assumptions, it is possible to analyse how a firm will operate in the market. An important implication of these assumptions is that no individual trader can influence the price of the product. In particular, this means that the firm is a **price taker**, and has to accept whatever price is set in the market as a whole.

> ### Key term
>
> **Price taker**: a firm that must accept whatever price is set in the market as a whole.

As a price taker, the firm faces a perfectly elastic demand curve for its product, as is shown in Figure 16.1. In this figure P_1 is the price set in the market, and the firm cannot sell at any other price. If it tries to set a price above P_1 it will sell nothing, as buyers are fully aware of the market price and will not buy at a higher price, especially as they know that there is no quality difference between the products produced by different firms in the market. What this also implies is that the firm can sell as much output as it likes at that going price – which means there is no incentive for any firm to set a price below P_1. Thus, all firms charge the same price, P_1.

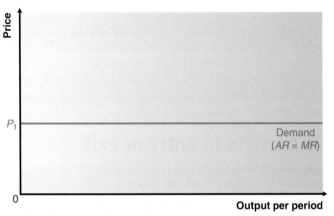

Figure 16.1 The firm's demand curve

The firm's short-run supply decision

If the firm can sell as much as it likes at the market price, how does it decide how much to produce?

The previous chapter explained that to maximise profits a firm needs to set output at such a level that marginal revenue is equal to marginal cost. Figure 16.2 illustrates this rule by adding the short-run cost curves to the demand curve. (Remember that SMC cuts $SAVC$ and $SATC$ at their minimum points.) As the demand curve is horizontal, the firm faces constant average and marginal revenue and will choose output at q_1, where $MR = SMC$.

If the market price were to change, the firm would react by changing output, but always choosing to supply output at the level at which $MR = SMC$. This suggests that the short-run marginal cost curve represents the firm's short-run supply curve:

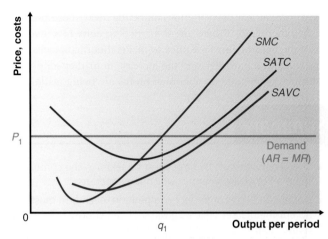

Figure 16.2 The firm's short-run supply decision

in other words, it shows the quantity of output that the firm would supply at any given price.

However, there is one important proviso to this statement. If the price falls below short-run average variable cost, the firm's best decision will be to exit from the market, as it will be better off just incurring its fixed costs. So the firm's **short-run supply curve** is the SMC curve above the point where it cuts $SAVC$ (at its minimum point).

> ### Key term
>
> **Short-run supply curve**: for a firm operating under perfect competition, the curve given by its short-run marginal cost curve above the price at which $SMC = SAVC$; for the industry, the short-run supply curve is the horizontal sum of the supply curves of the individual firms in the industry.

Industry equilibrium in the short run

One crucial question not yet examined is how the market price comes to be determined. To answer this, it is necessary to consider the industry as a whole. In this case there is a conventional downward-sloping demand curve. This is formed according to preferences of consumers in the market and is shown in Figure 16.3.

On the supply side, it has been shown that the individual firm's supply curve is its marginal cost curve above $SAVC$. If you add up the supply curves of each firm operating in the market, the result is the industry supply curve, shown in Figure 16.3 as Supply = ΣSMC (where 'Σ' means 'sum of'). The price will then adjust to P_1 at the intersection of demand and supply. The firms in the industry between them will supply Q_1 output, and the market will be in equilibrium.

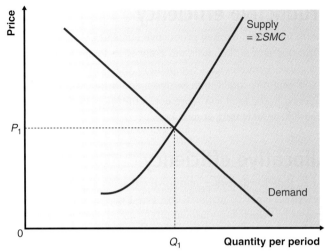

Figure 16.3 A perfectly competitive industry in short-run equilibrium

The firm in short-run equilibrium revisited

As this seems to be a well-balanced situation, with price adjusting to equate market demand and supply, the only question is why it is described as just a *short-run equilibrium*. The clue to this is to be found back with the individual firm.

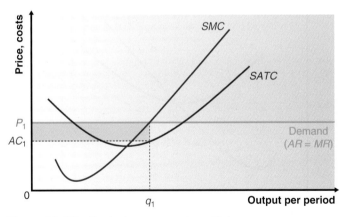

Figure 16.4 The firm in short-run supply equilibrium

Figure 16.4 illustrates the position facing an individual firm in the market. As before, the firm maximises profits by accepting the price P_1 as set in the market and producing up to the point where $MR = SMC$, which is at q_1. However, now the firm's average revenue (which is equal to price) is greater than its average cost (which is given by AC_1 at this level of output). The firm is thus making supernormal profits at this price. (Remember that 'normal profits' are included in average cost.) The total amount of supernormal profits being made is shown as the shaded area on the graph. Notice that average revenue minus average costs equals profit per unit, so multiplying this by the quantity sold determines total profit.

This is where the assumption about freedom of entry becomes important. If firms in this market are making profits above opportunity cost, the market is generating more profits than other markets in the economy. This will prove attractive to other firms, which will seek to enter the market – and the assumption is that there are no barriers to prevent them from doing so.

This process of entry will continue for as long as firms are making supernormal profits. However, as more firms join the market, the position of the industry supply curve, which is the sum of the supply curves of an ever-larger number of individual firms, will be affected. As the industry supply curve shifts to the right, the market price will fall. At some point the price will have fallen to such an extent that firms are no longer making supernormal profits, and the market will then stabilise.

If the price were to fall even further, some firms would choose to exit from the market, and the process would go into reverse. Therefore price can be expected to stabilise such that the typical firm in the industry is just making normal profits.

Perfect competition in long-run equilibrium

Figure 16.5 shows the situation for a typical firm and for the industry as a whole once long-run equilibrium has been reached and firms no longer have any incentive to enter or exit the market. The market is in equilibrium, with demand equal to supply at the going price. The typical firm sets marginal revenue equal to marginal cost to maximise profits, and just makes normal profits.

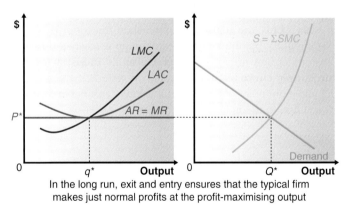

In the long run, exit and entry ensures that the typical firm makes just normal profits at the profit-maximising output

Figure 16.5 Long-run equilibrium under perfect competition

The long-run supply curve

Comparative static analysis can be used to explore this equilibrium a little more deeply. Suppose there is an increase in the demand for this product. Perhaps, for some reason, everyone becomes convinced that the product is really health promoting, so demand increases at any given price. This disturbs the market equilibrium, and the question then is whether (and how) equilibrium can be restored.

Figure 16.6 reproduces the long-run equilibrium that was shown in Figure 16.5. Thus, in the initial position market price is at P^*, the typical firm is in long-run equilibrium, producing q^*, and the industry is producing Q^*. Demand was initially at D_0, but with the increased popularity of the product it has shifted to D_1. In the short run this pushes the market price up to P_1 for the industry because, as market price increases, existing firms have the incentive to supply more output: that is, they move along their short-run supply curves. So in the short run a typical firm starts to produce q_1 output. The combined supply of the firms then increases to Q_1.

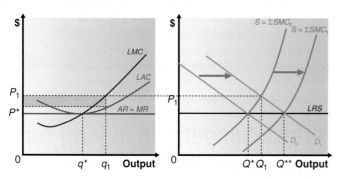

Figure 16.6 Adjusting to an increase in demand under perfect competition

However, at the higher price the firms start making supernormal profits (shown by the shaded area in Figure 16.6), so in time more firms will be attracted into the market, pushing the short-run industry supply curve to the right. This process will continue until there is no further incentive for new firms to enter the market – which occurs when the price has returned to P^*, but with increased industry output at Q^{**}. In other words, the adjustment in the short run is borne by existing firms, but the long-run equilibrium is reached through the entry of new firms. This suggests that the **industry long-run supply curve** (LRS) is horizontal at price P^*, which is the minimum point of the long-run average cost curve for the typical firm in the industry.

> **Key term**
>
> **Industry long-run supply curve**: under perfect competition, a curve that is horizontal at the price which is the minimum point of the long-run average cost curve for the typical firm in the industry.

Efficiency under perfect competition

Having reviewed the characteristics of long-run equilibrium in a perfectly competitive market, you may wonder what is so good about such a market in terms of productive and allocative efficiency.

Productive efficiency

For an individual market, productive efficiency is reached when a firm operates at the minimum point of its long-run average cost curve. Under perfect competition, this is indeed a feature of the long-run equilibrium position. So, productive efficiency is achieved in the long run – but not in the short run, when a firm need not be operating at minimum average cost.

Allocative efficiency

For an individual market, allocative efficiency is achieved when price is set equal to marginal cost (see Chapter 12). Again, the process by which supernormal profits are competed away, through the entry of new firms into the market, ensures that price is equal to marginal cost within a perfectly competitive market in long-run equilibrium. So allocative efficiency is also achieved. Indeed, firms set price equal to marginal cost even in the short run, so allocative efficiency is a feature of perfect competition in both the short run and the long run.

> **Exercise 16.1**
>
> Figure 16.7 shows the short-run cost curves for a firm that is operating in a perfectly competitive market.
>
>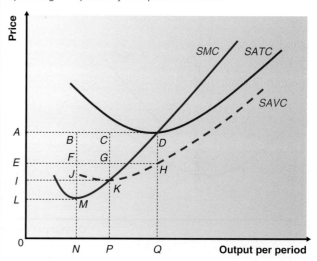
>
> **Figure 16.7** A firm operating under short-run perfect competition
>
> **a** At what price would the firm just make 'normal' profits?
> **b** What area would represent total fixed cost at this price?
> **c** What is the shutdown price for the firm?
> **d** Within what range of prices would the firm choose to operate at a loss in the short run?
> **e** Identify the firm's short-run supply curve.
> **f** Within what range of prices would the firm be able to make short-run supernormal profits?
> **g** What conditions must hold for supernormal profits to be competed to zero in the long run?

Exercise 16.2

Starting from a diagram like Figure 16.6, track the response of a perfectly competitive market to a decrease in market demand for a good – in other words, explain how the market adjusts to a leftward shift of the demand curve.

Evaluation of perfect competition

A criticism sometimes levelled at the model of perfect competition is that it is merely a theoretical ideal, based on a sequence of assumptions that rarely holds in the real world. Perhaps you have some sympathy with that view.

It could be argued that the model does hold for some agricultural markets. One study in the USA estimated that the elasticity of demand for an individual farmer producing sweetcorn was −31 353, which is pretty close to being perfectly elastic.

The elasticity of demand for a farmer producing sweetcorn in the USA was very close to being perfectly elastic

However, to argue that the model is useless because it is unrealistic is to miss a very important point. By allowing a glimpse of what the ideal market would look like, at least in terms of resource allocation, the model provides a measure against which alternative market structures can be compared. Furthermore, economic analysis can be used to investigate the effects of relaxing the assumptions of the model, which can be another valuable exercise. For example, it is possible to examine how the market is affected if firms can differentiate their products, or if traders in the market are acting with incomplete information.

So, although there may be relatively few markets that display all the characteristics of perfect competition, that does not destroy the usefulness of the model in economic theory. It will continue to be a reference point when examining alternative models of market structure.

Summary

- The model of perfect competition describes an extreme form of market structure. It rests on a sequence of assumptions.
- Its key characteristics include the assumption that no individual trader can influence the market price of the good or service being traded, and that there is freedom of entry and exit.
- In such circumstances each firm faces a perfectly elastic demand curve for its product, and can sell as much as it likes at the going market price.
- A profit-maximising firm chooses to produce the level of output at which marginal revenue (*MR*) equals marginal cost (*MC*).
- The firm's short-run marginal cost curve, above its short-run average variable cost curve, represents its short-run supply curve.
- The industry's short-run supply curve is the horizontal summation of the supply curves of all firms in the market.
- Firms may make supernormal profits in the short run, but because there is freedom of entry these profits will be competed away in the long run by new firms joining the market.
- The long-run industry supply curve is horizontal, with price adjusting to the minimum level of the typical firm's long-run average cost curve.
- Under perfect competition in long-run equilibrium, both productive efficiency and allocative efficiency are achieved.

16.3 Monopoly

At the opposite end of the spectrum of market structures is **monopoly**, which strictly speaking is a market with a single seller of a good. However, there is a bit more to it than that, and economic analysis of monopoly rests on some important assumptions. In the real world, the Competition and Markets Authority, the official body in the UK with responsibility for monitoring monopoly markets, is empowered to investigate mergers which could restrict competition. Similar bodies operate in other countries around the world. In a situation where a single firm dominates a market, it may be able to act as if it were the only firm – a dominant monopoly. Some discussion of the theory of how monopoly markets operate is necessary in order to understand why such monitoring is required. First, consider a pure monopoly market, in which there is a single seller.

Key term

Monopoly: a form of market structure in which there is only one seller of a good.

Assumptions

The assumptions of the monopoly model are as follows:

- There is a single seller of a good.
- There are no substitutes for the good, either actual or potential.
- There are barriers to entry into the market.

It is also assumed that the firm aims to maximise profits. These assumptions all have their counterparts in the assumptions of perfect competition, and in one sense this model can be described as being at the opposite end of the market structure spectrum.

If there is a single seller of a good, and if there are no substitutes for the good, the monopoly firm is thereby insulated from competition. Furthermore, any barriers to entry into the market will ensure that the firm can sustain its market position into the future. The assumption that there are no potential substitutes for the good reinforces the situation. (Chapter 18 explores what happens if this assumption does not hold.)

A monopoly in equilibrium

The first point to note is that a monopoly firm faces the market demand curve directly. Thus, unlike in perfect competition, the demand curve slopes downwards. For the monopolist, the demand curve may be regarded as showing average revenue (notice that for a firm charging the same price for all units sold, price is the same as average revenue). Unlike a firm under perfect competition, therefore, the monopolist has some influence over price, and can make decisions regarding price as well as output. This is not to say that the monopolist has complete freedom to set the price, as the firm is still constrained by market demand. However, the firm is a price maker and can choose a location along the demand curve.

Chapter 15 recalled the nature of the relationship between total revenue and the own-price elasticity of demand (*PED*) along a straight-line demand curve. The key graphs are reproduced here as Figure 16.8. The analysis pointed out that the price elasticity of demand is elastic above the mid-point of the demand curve and inelastic in the lower half, with total revenue increasing with a price fall when demand is elastic, and falling with a price fall when demand is inelastic.

As with the firm under perfect competition, a monopolist aiming to maximise profits will choose to produce at the level of

output at which marginal revenue equals marginal cost. This is at Q_m in Figure 16.9. Having selected output, the monopolist will then set the price at the highest level at which all output will be sold – in Figure 16.9 this is P_m.

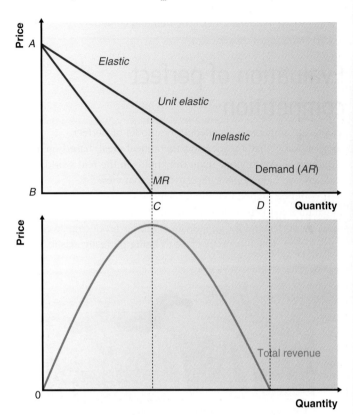

Figure 16.8 Elasticity and total revenue

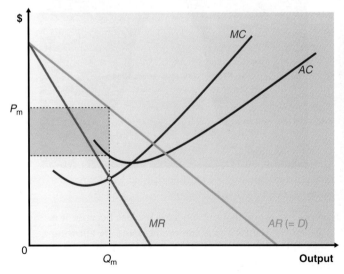

Figure 16.9 Profit maximisation and monopoly

This choice allows the monopolist to make supernormal profits, which can be identified as the shaded area in the figure. As before, this area is average revenue minus average cost, which gives profit per unit, multiplied by the quantity.

It is at this point that barriers to entry become important. Other firms may see that the monopoly firm is making healthy supernormal profits, but the existence of barriers to entry will prevent those profits from being competed away, as would happen in a perfectly competitive market.

It is important to notice that the monopolist cannot be guaranteed always to make such substantial profits as are shown in Figure 16.9. The size of the profits depends upon the relative position of the market demand curve and the cost curves. If the cost curves in the diagram were higher, the monopoly profits would be much smaller, as the distance between average revenue and average costs would be less. It is even possible that the cost curves will be so high as to force the firm to incur losses, in which case it would be expected to shut down.

Exercise 16.3

Table 16.2 shows the demand faced by a monopolist at various prices.

Table 16.2 A monopolist's demand schedule

Demand (000s per week)	Price (£)
0	80
1	70
2	60
3	50
4	40
5	30
6	20
7	10

a Calculate total revenue and marginal revenue for each level of demand.
b Plot the demand curve (AR) and marginal revenue on a graph.
c Plot total revenue on a separate graph.
d Identify the level of demand at which total revenue is at a maximum.
e At what level of demand is marginal revenue equal to zero?
f At what level of demand is there unit price elasticity of demand?
g If the monopolist maximises profits, will the chosen level of output be higher or lower than the revenue-maximising level?
h What does this imply for the price elasticity of demand when the monopolist maximises profits?

Exercise 16.4

Draw a diagram to analyse the profit-maximising level of output and price for a monopolist, and analyse the effect of an increase in demand.

How do monopolies arise?

Monopolies may arise in a market for a number of reasons. In a few instances, a monopoly is created by the authorities. For example, for 150 years the UK Post Office held a licence giving it a monopoly on delivering letters. From the beginning of 2006, the service was fully liberalised. The Post Office monopoly covered a wide range of services, but its coverage was gradually eroded over the years, and it was finally privatised in 2013. Nonetheless, it remains an example of one way in which a monopoly can be created.

The patent system offers a rather different form of protection for a firm. The patent system was designed to provide an incentive for firms to innovate through the development of new techniques and products. By prohibiting other firms from copying the product for a period of time, a firm is given a temporary monopoly.

In some cases the technology of the industry may create a monopoly situation. In a market characterised by substantial economies of scale, there may not be room for more than one firm in the market. This could happen where there are substantial fixed costs of production but low marginal costs: for example, in establishing an underground railway in a city, a firm faces very high fixed costs in building the network of track and stations and buying the rolling stock. However, once it is in operation, the marginal cost of carrying an additional passenger is very low.

Figure 16.10 illustrates this point. The firm in this market enjoys economies of scale right up to the limit of market demand. The largest firm operating in the market can always produce at a lower cost than any potential entrant, so will always be able to price such firms out of the market. Here the economies of scale act as an effective barrier to the entry of new firms and the market is a natural monopoly. A profit-maximising monopoly would thus set $MR = MC$, produce at quantity Q_m and charge a price P_m.

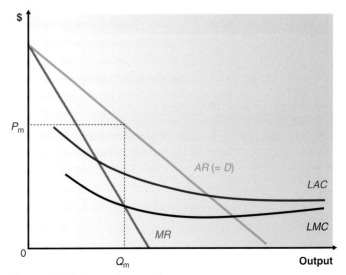

Figure 16.10 A natural monopoly

Such a market poses particular problems regarding allocative efficiency. Notice in the figure that marginal cost is below average cost over the entire range of output. If the firm were to charge a price equal to marginal cost, it would inevitably make a loss, so such a pricing rule would not be viable.

There are markets in which firms have risen to become monopolies by their actions in the market. Such a market structure is sometimes known as a competitive monopoly. Firms may get into a monopoly position through effective marketing, through a process of merger and acquisition, or by establishing a new product as a widely accepted standard.

In the first Microsoft trial in 1998, it was claimed that Microsoft had gained 95% of the world market for operating systems for PC computers. The firm claimed that this is because it was simply very good at what it does. However, part of the reason why it was on trial was that other interested parties alleged that Microsoft was guilty of unfair market tactics and predatory behaviour.

Exercise 16.5

In 2000, AOL merged with Time Warner, bringing together an internet service provider with an extensive network and a firm in the entertainment business.

AOL Time Warner

One product that such a merged company might produce is a digitised music performance that could be distributed through the internet. Think about the sorts of costs entailed in producing and delivering such a product, and categorise them as fixed or variable costs. What does this imply for the economies of scale faced by the merged company?

Monopoly and efficiency

The characteristics of the monopoly market can be evaluated in relation to productive and allocative efficiency (see Figure 16.9).

Productive efficiency

A firm is said to be productively efficient if it produces at the minimum point of long-run average cost. It is clear from the figure that this is extremely unlikely for a monopoly. The firm will produce at the minimum point of long-run average cost only if it so happens that the marginal revenue curve passes through this exact point – and this would happen only by coincidence.

Allocative efficiency

For an individual firm, allocative efficiency is achieved when price is set equal to marginal cost. It is clear from Figure 16.9 that this will not be the case for a profit-maximising monopoly firm. The firm chooses output where MR equals MC; however, given that MR is below AR (i.e. price), price will always be set above marginal cost.

Summary

- A monopoly market is one in which there is a single seller of a good.
- The model of monopoly used in economic analysis also assumes that there are no substitutes for the goods or services produced by the monopolist, and that there are barriers to the entry of new firms.
- The monopoly firm faces the market demand curve, and is able to choose a point along that demand curve in order to maximise profits.
- Such a firm may be able to make supernormal profits, and sustain them in the long run because of barriers to entry and the lack of substitutes.
- A monopoly may arise because of patent protection or from the nature of economies of scale in the industry (a 'natural monopoly').
- A profit-maximising monopolist does not achieve allocative efficiency, and is unlikely to achieve productive efficiency in the sense of producing at the minimum point of the long-run average cost curve.

17 Monopolistic competition and oligopoly

The previous chapter introduced the models of perfect competition and monopoly, and described them as being at the extreme ends of a spectrum of forms of market structure. In between those two extremes are other forms of market structure, which have some but not all of the characteristics of either perfect competition or monopoly. It is in this sense that there is a spectrum of structures. Attention in this chapter is focused on some of these intermediate forms of market structure, including a discussion of the sorts of pricing strategy that firms may adopt, and how they decide which to go for. This chapter also discusses ways in which firms may try to prevent new firms from joining a market, in terms of both pricing and non-price strategies. The theory of contestable markets completes the discussion.

Learning outcomes

After studying this chapter, you should:
- be familiar with the range of market situations that exists between the extremes of perfect competition and monopoly
- understand the meaning of product differentiation and its role in the model of monopolistic competition
- understand the notion of oligopoly and be familiar with approaches to modelling firm behaviour in an oligopoly market
- understand the benefits that firms may gain from forming a cartel – and the tensions that may result
- understand the significance of concentration in a market and how to measure it
- be aware of the relationship between firm size and concentration
- understand what is meant by market dominance
- be familiar with factors that may give rise to natural and strategic barriers to entry
- be aware of some of the effects on a market if competition is limited.

17.1 Monopolistic competition

If you consider the characteristics of the markets that you frequent on a regular basis, you will find that few of them display all of the characteristics associated with perfect competition. However, there may be some that show a few of these features. In particular, you will find some markets in which there appears to be intense competition among many buyers, but in which the products for sale are not identical. For example, think about restaurants. In many cities, you will find a wide range of restaurants, cafés and coffee bars that compete with each other for business, but do so by offering slightly different products: this is called **product differentiation**.

The theory of **monopolistic competition** was devised by Edward Chamberlin, writing in the USA in the 1930s, and his name is often attached to the model, although Joan Robinson published her book on imperfect competition in the UK at the same time. The motivation for the analysis was to explain how markets worked when they were operating neither as monopolies nor under perfect competition.

> ### Key terms
>
> **Product differentiation**: a strategy adopted by firms that marks their product as being different from their competitors'.
> **Monopolistic competition**: a market that shares some characteristics of monopoly and some of perfect competition.

The model describes a market in which there are many firms producing similar, but not identical products: for example, package holidays, hairdressers and fast-food outlets. In the case of fast-food outlets, the high streets of many cities are characterised by large numbers of different types of takeaway – burgers, curries, noodles, fried chicken and so on.

The monopolistic competition model describes the fast-food market in many cities, such as Hong Kong

Model characteristics

Three important characteristics of the model of monopolistic competition distinguish this sort of market from others.

Product differentiation

First, firms produce differentiated products and face downward-sloping demand curves. In other words, each firm competes with the others by making its product slightly different. This allows the firms to build up brand loyalty among their regular customers, which gives them some influence over price. It is likely that firms will engage in advertising in order to maintain such brand loyalty, and heavy advertising is a common characteristic of a market operating under monopolistic competition.

Because other firms are producing similar goods, there are substitutes for each firm's product, which means that demand is relatively price elastic (although this does not mean that it is never inelastic). However, it is certainly not perfectly price elastic, as was the case with perfect competition. These features – that the product is not homogeneous and demand is not perfectly price elastic – represent significant differences from the model of perfect competition.

Freedom of entry

Second, there are no barriers to entry into the market. Firms are able to join the market if they observe that existing firms are making supernormal profits. New entrants will be looking for

some way to differentiate their product slightly from the others – perhaps the next fast-food restaurant will be Nepalese or Peruvian.

This characteristic distinguishes the market from the monopoly model, as does the existence of fairly close substitutes.

Low concentration

Third, the concentration ratio in the industry tends to be relatively low, as there are many firms operating in the market. For this reason, a price change by one of the firms will have negligible effects on the demand for its rivals' products.

This characteristic means that the market is also different from an oligopoly market, where there are a few firms that interact strategically with each other.

Overview

Taking these three characteristics together, it can be seen that a market of monopolistic competition has some of the characteristics of perfect competition and some features of monopoly; hence its name.

Short-run equilibrium

Figure 17.1 represents short-run equilibrium under monopolistic competition. D_s is the demand curve and MR_s is the corresponding marginal revenue curve. AC and MC are the average and marginal cost curves for a representative firm in the industry. If the firm is aiming to maximise profits, it will choose the level of output such that $MR_s = MC$. This occurs at output q_s, and the firm will then choose the price that clears the market at p_s.

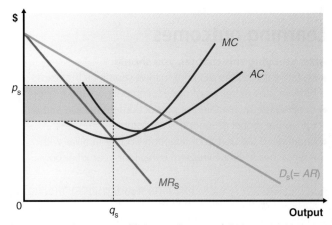

Figure 17.1 Short-run equilibrium under monopolistic competition

This closely resembles the standard monopoly diagram that was introduced in Chapter 16. As with monopoly, a firm under monopolistic competition faces a downward-sloping demand curve, as already noted. The difference is that now it is assumed that there is free entry into the market under monopolistic competition, so that Figure 17.1 represents equilibrium only in the short run. This is because the firm shown in the figure is making supernormal profits, shown by the shaded area (which is $AR - AC$ multiplied by output).

The importance of free entry

This is where the assumption of free entry into the market becomes important. In Figure 17.1 the supernormal profits being made by the representative firm will attract new firms into the market. The new firms will produce differentiated products, and this will affect the demand curve for the representative firm's product. In particular, the new firms will attract some customers away from this firm, so that its demand curve will tend to shift to the left. Its shape may also change as there are now more substitutes for the original product.

Long-run equilibrium

This process will continue as long as firms in the market continue to make profits that attract new firms into the activity. It may be accelerated if firms are persuaded to spend money on advertising in an attempt to defend their market shares. The advertising may help to keep the demand curve downward sloping, but it will also affect the position of the average cost curve, by pushing up average cost at all levels of output.

Figure 17.2 shows the final position for the market. The typical firm is now operating in such a way that it maximises profits (by setting output such that $MR = MC$); at the same time, the average cost curve (AC) at this level of output is at a tangent to the demand curve. This means that $AC = AR$, and the firm is just making normal profit (i.e. is just covering opportunity cost). There is thus no further incentive for more firms to join the market. In Figure 17.2 this occurs when output is at q_1 and price is set at p_1.

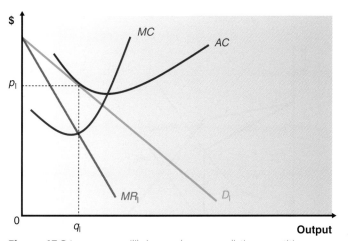

Figure 17.2 Long-run equilibrium under monopolistic competition

Evaluation

One way of evaluating the market outcome under this model is to examine the consequences for productive and allocative efficiency. It is clear from Figure 17.2 that neither of these conditions will be met. The representative firm does not reach the minimum point on the long-run average cost curve, and so does not attain productive efficiency; furthermore, the price charged is above marginal cost, so allocative efficiency is not achieved.

If the typical firm in the market is not fully exploiting the possible economies of scale that exist, it could be argued that product differentiation is damaging society's total welfare, in the sense that product differentiation allows firms to keep their demand curves downward sloping. In other words, too many different products are being produced. However, this argument could be countered by pointing out that consumers may enjoy having more freedom of choice. The very fact that they are prepared to pay a premium price for their chosen brand indicates that they have some preference for it.

Another crucial difference between monopolistic competition and perfect competition is that under monopolistic competition firms would like to sell more of their product at the going price, whereas under perfect competition they can sell as much as they like at the going price. This is because price under monopolistic competition is set above marginal cost. The use of advertising to attract more customers and to maintain consumer perception of product differences may be considered a problem with this market. It could be argued that excessive use of advertising to maintain product differentiation is wasteful, as it leads to higher average cost curves than needed. On the other hand, the need to compete in this way may result in less X-inefficiency than under a complacent monopolist.

Exercise 17.1

Figure 17.3 shows a firm under monopolistic competition.

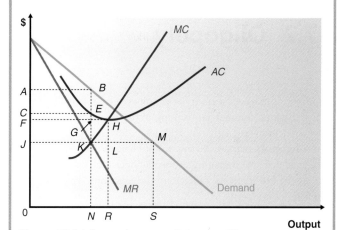

Figure 17.3 A firm under monopolistic competition

a Identify the profit-maximising level of output.
b At what price would the firm sell its product?
c What supernormal profits (if any) would be made by the firm?
d Is this a short-run or a long-run equilibrium? Explain your answer.
e Describe the subsequent adjustment that might take place in the market (if any).
f At what level of output would productive efficiency be achieved? (Assume that AC represents long-run average cost for this part of the question.)

Summary

- The theory of monopolistic competition has its origins in the 1930s, when economists such as Edward Chamberlin and Joan Robinson were writing about markets that did not conform to the models of perfect competition and monopoly.
- The model describes a market where there are many firms producing similar, but not identical products.
- By differentiating their product from those of other firms, it is possible for firms to maintain some influence over price.
- To do this, firms engage in advertising to build brand loyalty.
- There are no barriers to entry into the market, and concentration ratios are low.
- Firms may be able to make supernormal profits in the short run.
- In response, new entrants join the market, shifting the demand curves of existing firms and affecting their shape.
- The process continues until supernormal profits have been competed away, and the typical firm has its average cost curve at a tangent to its demand curve.
- Neither productive nor allocative efficiency is achieved in long-run equilibrium.
- Consumers may benefit from the increased range of choice on offer in the market.

17.2 Oligopoly

A number of markets seem to be dominated by relatively few firms – think of commercial banking in the UK, cinemas or the newspaper industry. A market with just a few sellers is known as an **oligopoly** market. An important characteristic of such markets is that when making economic decisions each firm must take account of its rivals' behaviour and reactions. The firms are therefore interdependent.

Key term

Oligopoly: a market with a few sellers, in which each firm must take account of the behaviour and likely behaviour of rival firms in the industry.

An important characteristic of oligopoly is that each firm has to act strategically, both in reacting to rival firms' decisions and in trying to anticipate their future actions and reactions.

There are many different ways in which a firm may take such strategic decisions, and this means that there are many ways in which an oligopoly market can be modelled, depending on how the firms are behaving. This chapter reviews just a few such models.

Oligopolies may come about for many reasons, but perhaps the most convincing concerns economies of scale. An oligopoly is likely to develop in a market where there are some economies of scale – economies that are not substantial enough to require a natural monopoly, but which are large enough to make it difficult for too many firms to operate at minimum efficient scale.

Within an oligopoly market, firms may adopt rivalrous behaviour or they may choose to cooperate with each other. The two attitudes have implications for how markets operate. Cooperation will tend to take the market towards the monopoly end of the spectrum, whereas non-cooperation will take it towards the competitive end. In either scenario, it is likely that the market outcome will be somewhere between the two extremes.

The kinked demand curve model

One model of oligopoly revolves around how a firm perceives its demand curve. This is called the kinked demand curve model, and was developed by Paul Sweezy in the USA in the 1930s.

The model relates to an oligopoly in which firms try to anticipate the reactions of rivals to their actions. One problem that arises is that a firm cannot readily observe its demand curve with any degree of certainty, so it must form expectations about how consumers will react to a price change.

Figure 17.4 shows how this works. Suppose the price is currently set at P^*; the firm is selling Q^* and is trying to decide whether to alter the price. The problem is that it knows for sure about only one point on the demand curve: that is, when the price is P^*, the firm sells Q^*.

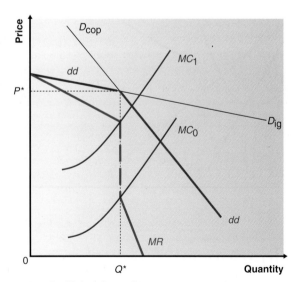

Figure 17.4 The kinked demand curve

However, the firm is aware that the degree of sensitivity to its price change will depend upon whether or not the other firms in the market will follow its lead. In other words, if its rivals ignore the firm's price change, there will be more sensitivity to this change than if they all follow suit.

Figure 17.4 shows the two extreme possibilities for the demand curve which the firm perceives that it faces. If other firms ignore its action, D_{ig} will be the relevant demand curve, which is relatively elastic. On the other hand, if the other firms copy the firm's moves, D_{cop} will be the relevant demand curve.

The question then is: under what conditions will the other firms copy the price change, and when will they not? The firm may imagine that if it raises its price, there is little likelihood that its rivals will copy. After all, this is a non-threatening move that gives market share to the other firms. So for a price increase, D_{ig} is the relevant section.

On the other hand, a price reduction is likely to be seen by the rivals as a threatening move, and they are likely to copy in order to preserve their market positions. For a price decrease, then, D_{cop} is relevant.

Putting these together, the firm perceives that it faces a kinked demand curve (dd). Furthermore, if the marginal revenue curve is added to the picture, it is seen to have a discontinuity at the kink. It thus transpires that Q^* is the profit-maximising level of output under a wide range of cost conditions from MC_0 to MC_1; so, even in the face of a change in marginal costs, the firm will not alter its behaviour.

Thus, the model predicts that if the firm perceives its demand curve to be of this shape, it has a strong incentive to do nothing, even in the face of changes in costs. However, it all depends upon the firm's perceptions. If there is a general increase in costs that affects all producers, this may affect the firm's perception of rival reaction, and thus encourage it to raise price. If other firms are reading the market in the same way, they are likely to follow suit. Notice that this model does not explain how the price reaches P^* in the first place.

Game theory

A more recent development in the economic theory of the firm has been in the application of **game theory**. This began as a branch of mathematics, but it became apparent that it had wide applications in explaining the behaviour of firms in an oligopoly.

> ### Key term
>
> **Game theory**: a method of modelling the strategic interaction between firms in an oligopoly.

Game theory itself has a long history, with some writers tracing it back to correspondence between Pascal and Fermat in the mid-seventeenth century. Early applications in economics were by Antoine Augustin Cournot in 1838, Francis Edgeworth in 1881 and J. Bertrand in 1883, but the key publication was the book by John von Neumann and Oskar Morgenstern, *Theory of Games and Economic Behaviour*, in 1944. Other famous names in game theory include John Nash (played by Russell Crowe in the film *A Beautiful Mind*), John Harsanyi and Reinhard Selton, who shared the 1994 Nobel prize for their work in this area.

Almost certainly, the most famous game is the **prisoners' dilemma**, introduced in a lecture by Albert Tucker (who taught John Nash at Princeton) in 1950. This simple example of game theory turns out to have a multitude of helpful applications in economics.

> ### Key term
>
> **Prisoners' dilemma**: an example of game theory with a range of applications in oligopoly theory.

Two prisoners, Al Fresco and Des Jardins, are being interrogated about a major crime, and the police know that at least one of the prisoners is guilty. The two are kept in separate cells and cannot communicate with each other. The police have enough evidence to convict them of a minor offence, but not enough to convict them of the major one.

Each prisoner is offered a deal. If he turns state's evidence and provides evidence to convict the other prisoner, he will get off – unless the other prisoner also confesses. If both refuse to deal, they will just be charged with the minor offence. Table 17.1 summarises the sentences that each will receive in the various circumstances.

Table 17.1 The prisoners' dilemma: possible outcomes (years in jail)

		Des			
		Confess		Refuse	
Al	Confess	10	10	0	15
	Refuse	15	0	5	5

In each case, Al's sentence (in years) is shown in red and Des's in blue. In terms of the entries in the table, if both Al and Des refuse to deal, they will be convicted of the minor offence, and each will go down for 5 years. However, if Al confesses and Des refuses to deal, Al will get off completely free, and Des will take the full rap of 15 years. If Des confesses and Al refuses, the reverse happens. However, if both confess, they will each get 10 years.

Think about this situation from Al's point of view, remembering that the prisoners cannot communicate, so Al does not know what Des will choose to do and vice versa. You can see from Table 17.1 that, whatever Des chooses to do, Al will be better off confessing. If Des confesses, Al is better off confessing also, going down for 10 years instead of 15; if Des refuses, Al is still better off confessing, going free instead of getting a 5-year term. John Nash referred to such a situation as a **dominant strategy**.

> ### Key term
>
> **Dominant strategy**: a situation in game theory where a player's best strategy is independent of those chosen by others.

The dilemma is, of course, symmetric, so for Des too the dominant strategy is to confess. The inevitable result is that, if both prisoners are selfish, they will both confess – and both will then get 10 years in jail. If they had both refused to deal, they would both have been better off; but this is too risky a strategy for either of them to adopt. A refusal to deal might have led to 15 years in jail.

What has this to do with economics? Think about the market for DIY products. Suppose there are two firms (Diamond Tools and Better Spades) operating in a duopoly market (i.e. a market with only two firms). Each firm has a choice of producing 'high' output or 'low' output. The profit made by one firm depends upon two things: its own output and the output of the other firm.

Table 17.2 shows the range of possible outcomes for a particular time period. Consider Diamond Tools: if it chooses 'low' when Better Spades also chooses 'low', it will make $2 million profit (and so will Better Spades); but if Diamond Tools chooses 'low' when Better Spades chooses 'high', Diamond Tools will make zero profits and Better Spades will make $3 million.

Table 17.2 Diamond Tools and Better Spades: possible outcomes (profits in $m)

		Better spades			
		High		Low	
Diamond Tools	High	1	1	3	0
	Low	0	3	2	2

The situation that maximises joint profits is for both firms to produce low; but suppose you were taking decisions for Diamond Tools – what would you choose?

If Better Spades produces 'low', you will maximise profits by producing 'high', whereas if Better Spades produces 'high', you will still maximise profits by producing high! So Diamond Tools has a dominant strategy to produce high – it is the profit-maximising action whatever Better Spades does, even though it means that joint profits will be lower.

Given that the table is symmetric, Better Spades faces the same decision process, and also has a dominant strategy to choose high, so they always end up in the northwest corner of the table, even though southeast would be better for each of them. Furthermore, after they have made their choices and seen what the other has chosen, each firm feels justified by its actions, and thinks that it took the right decision, given the rival's move. This is known as a **Nash equilibrium**, which has the characteristic that neither firm needs to amend its behaviour in any future period. This model can be used to investigate a wide range of decisions that firms need to take strategically.

Key term

Nash equilibrium: a situation occurring within a game when each player's chosen strategy maximises payoffs given the other player's choice, so no player has an incentive to alter behaviour.

Exercise 17.2

Suppose there are two cinemas, X and Y, operating in a town; you are taking decisions for Firm X. You cannot communicate with the other firm; both firms are considering only the next period. Each firm is choosing whether to set price 'high' or 'low'. Your expectation is that the payoffs (in terms of profits) to the two firms are as shown in Table 17.3 (Firm X in red, Firm Y in blue).

Table 17.3 Cinemas X and Y: possible outcomes

		Firm Y			
		High price		Low	
Firm X	High price	0	10	1	15
	Low price	15	1	4	4

a If Firm Y sets price high, what strategy maximises profits for Firm X?
b If Firm Y sets price low, what strategy maximises profits for Firm X?
c So what strategy will Firm X adopt?
d What is the market outcome?
e What outcome would maximise the firms' joint profit?
f How might this outcome be achieved?
g Would the outcome be different if the game were played over repeated periods?

Cooperative games and cartels

Look back at the prisoners' dilemma game in Table 17.2. It is clear that the requirement that the firms are unable to communicate with each other is a serious impediment from the firms' point of view. If both firms could agree to produce 'low', they would maximise their joint profits, but they will not risk this strategy if they cannot communicate.

If they could join together in a **cartel**, the two firms could come to an agreement to adopt the low–low strategy. However, if they were to agree to this, each firm would have a strong incentive to cheat because, if each now knew that the other firm was going to produce low, they would also know that they could produce high and dominate the market – at least, given the payoffs in the table.

Key term

Cartel: an agreement between firms on price and output with the intention of maximising their joint profits.

This is a common feature of cartels. Collusion can bring high joint profits, but there is always the temptation for each of the member firms to cheat and try to sneak some additional market share at the expense of the other firms in the cartel.

There is another downside to the formation of a cartel. In most countries around the world (with one or two exceptions, such as Hong Kong) they are illegal. For example, in the UK the operation of a cartel is illegal under the UK Competition Act, under which the Office of Fair Trading is empowered to fine firms up to 10% of their turnover for each year the cartel is found to have been in operation.

This means that overt collusion is rare. The most famous example is not between firms but between nations, in the form of the Organisation of Petroleum Exporting Countries (OPEC), which over a long period of time has operated a cartel to control the price of oil.

Some conditions may favour the formation of cartels – or at least, some form of collusion between firms. The most important of these is the ability of each of the firms involved to monitor the actions of the other firms, and so ensure that they are keeping to the agreement.

Collusion in practice

Although cartels are illegal, the potential gains from collusion may tempt firms to find ways of working together. In some cases, firms have joined together in rather loose strategic alliances, in which they may work together on part of their business, perhaps in undertaking joint research and development or technology swaps.

For example, in 2000 General Motors (GM) and Fiat took an equity stake in each other's companies, with GM wanting to expand in Europe and needing to find out more about the technology of making smaller cars. Such alliances have not always been a success, and in the GM–Fiat case, GM and Fiat separated in 2005.

The airline market is another sector where strategic alliances have been important, with the Star Alliance, the One World Alliance and SkyTeam carving up the long-haul routes between them. Such alliances offer benefits to passengers, who can get access to a wider range of destinations and business-class lounges and frequent-flier rewards, and to the airlines, which can economise on airport facilities by pooling their resources. However, the net effect is to reduce competition, and the regulators have interfered with some suggested alliances, such as that between British Airways and American Airlines in 2001, which was investigated by regulators on both sides of the Atlantic. The conditions under which the alliance would have been permitted were such that British Airways withdrew the proposal. This proposed alliance resurfaced in August 2008, when the European Commission opened a new anti-trust investigation into a revenue-sharing deal announced between British Airways, American Airlines and Iberia.

Passengers benefit from strategic alliances between airlines

Alternatively, firms may look for **tacit collusion**, in which the firms in a market observe each other's behaviour very closely and refrain from competing on price, even if they do not actually communicate with each other. Such collusion may emerge gradually over time in a market, as the firms become accustomed to market conditions and to each other's behaviour.

Key term

Tacit collusion: a situation occurring when firms refrain from competing on price, but without communication or formal agreement between them.

One way in which this may happen is through some form of price leadership. If one firm is a dominant producer in a market, then it may take the lead in setting the price, with the other firms following its example. It has been suggested that the OPEC cartel operated according to this model in some periods, with Saudi Arabia acting as the dominant country.

An alternative is *barometric price leadership*, in which one firm tries out a price increase and then waits to see whether other firms follow. If they do, a new higher price has been reached without the need for overt discussions between the firms. On the other hand, if the other firms do not feel the time is right for the change, they will keep their prices steady and the first firm will drop back into line or else lose market share. The initiating firm need not be the same one in each round. It has been argued that the domestic air travel market in the USA has operated in this way on some internal routes. The practice is facilitated by the ease with which prices can be checked via computerised ticketing systems, so that each firm knows what the other firms are doing.

The frequency of anti-cartel cases brought by regulators in recent years suggests that firms continue to be tempted by the gains from collusion. The operation of a cartel is now a criminal act in the UK, as it has been in the USA for some time.

Summary

- An oligopoly is a market with a few sellers, each of which takes strategic decisions based on likely rival actions and reactions.
- As there are many ways in which firms may interact, there is no single way of modelling an oligopoly market.
- One model is the kinked demand curve model, which argues that firms' perceptions of the demand curve for their products are based on their views about whether or not rival firms will react to their own actions.
- This suggests that price is likely to remain stable over a wide range of market conditions.
- Game theory is a more recent and more flexible way of modelling interactions between firms.
- The prisoners' dilemma can demonstrate the potential benefits of collusion, but also shows that in some market situations each firm may have a dominant strategy to move the market away from the joint profit-maximising position.
- If firms could join together in a cartel, they could indeed maximise their joint profits – but there would still be a temptation for firms to cheat, and try to steal market share. Such action would break up the cartel, and move the market away from the joint profit-maximising position.
- However, cartels are illegal in most societies.
- Firms may thus look for covert ways of colluding in a market: for example, through some form of price leadership.

Exercise 17.3

For each of the following markets, identify the model that would most closely describe it (e.g. perfect competition, monopoly, monopolistic competition or oligopoly).

a A large number of firms selling branded varieties of toothpaste.
b A sole supplier of postal services.
c A large number of farmers producing cauliflowers, sold at a common price.
d A situation in which a few large banks supply most of the market for retail banking services.
e A sole supplier of rail transport.

17.3 Market concentration

The discussion above has shown that the models of perfect competition and monopoly produce very different outcomes for productive and allocative efficiency. Perfect competition produces a 'good' allocation of resources, but monopoly results in a deadweight loss. In the real-world economy it is not quite so simple. In particular, not every market is readily classified as following either of these extreme models. Indeed, you might think that the majority of markets do not correspond to either of the models, but instead display a mixture of characteristics.

An important question is whether markets such as oligopoly behave more like a competitive market or more like a monopoly. This chapter has shown that there are many different ways in which markets with just a few firms operating can be modelled, because there are many ways in which the firms may interact.

It is helpful to have some way of gauging how close a particular market is to being a monopoly. One way of doing this is to examine the degree of concentration in the market. Later it will be seen that this is not all that is required to determine how efficiently a market will operate; but it is a start.

Concentration is normally measured by reference to the **concentration ratio**, which measures the market share of the largest firms in an industry. For example, the three-firm concentration ratio measures the market share of the largest three firms in the market; the five-firm concentration ratio calculates the share of the top five firms, and so on. Concentration can also be viewed in terms of employment, reflected in the proportion of workers in any industry that are employed in the largest firms.

Key term

n-firm concentration ratio: a measure of the market share of the largest *n* firms in an industry.

Consider the following example. Table 17.4 gives average circulation figures for firms that publish national newspapers in the UK. In the final column these are converted into market shares. Where one firm produces more than one newspaper, their circulations have been combined (e.g. News International publishes both the *Sun* and *The Times*).

Table 17.4 Concentration in the UK newspaper industry, July 2008

Firm	Average circulation	Market share (%)
News International Newspapers Ltd	3 470 711	36.3
Associated Newspapers Ltd	2 077 545	21.7
Trinity Mirror plc	1 318 168	13.8
Express Newspapers Ltd	1 292 330	13.5
Telegraph Group Ltd	799 021	8.4
Guardian Newspapers Ltd	292 909	3.1
Independent Newspapers (UK) Ltd	178 576	1.9
Financial Times Ltd	130 695	1.4

Source: www.abc.org.uk

The three-firm concentration ratio is calculated as the sum of the market shares of the biggest three firms: that is, 36.3 + 21.7 + 13.8 = 71.8%.

Concentration ratios may be calculated on the basis of either shares in output or shares in employment. In the above example, the calculation was on the basis of output (daily circulation). The two measures may give different results because the largest firms in an industry may be more capital-intensive in their production methods, which means that their share of employment in an industry will be smaller than their share of output. For the purposes of examining market structure, however, it is more helpful to base the analysis of market share on output.

This might seem an intuitively simple measure, but it is too simple to enable an evaluation of a market. For a start, it is important to define the market appropriately; for instance, in the above example are the *Financial Times* and the *Sun* really part of the same market?

There may be other difficulties too. Table 17.5 gives some hypothetical market shares for two markets. The five-firm concentration ratio is calculated as the sum of the market shares of the largest five firms. For markets A and B, the result is the same. In both cases the market is perceived to be highly concentrated, at 75%. However, the nature of likely interactions between the firms in these two markets is very different because the large relative size of Firm 1 in Market A is likely to give it substantially more market power than any of the largest five firms in Market B. Nonetheless, the concentration ratio is useful for giving a first impression of how the market is likely to function.

Table 17.5 Market shares (% of output)

Largest firms in rank order	Market A	Market B
Firm 1	68	15
Firm 2	3	15
Firm 3	2	15
Firm 4	1	15
Firm 5	1	15

Scale and market concentration

An important issue that arises as firms become larger concerns the number of firms that a market can support. Suppose that economies of scale are available right up to the limit of market demand, as in Figure 17.5. If more than one firm were to try to supply this market, each producing at minimum average cost, there would be substantial excess supply, and the situation would not be viable.

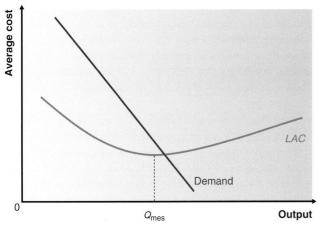

Figure 17.5 How many firms can a market support?

In this situation, the largest firm in the market will come to dominate, as it will be able to produce at lower average costs than any potential competitor. This will be reinforced if there are significant learning-by-doing effects, which will further entrench the largest firm as the market leader. Such a market is likely to become a natural monopoly.

Such substantial economies of scale are not available in all sectors. It will depend upon the nature of technology and all the other factors that can give rise to economies of scale. In some activities there may be little scope at all for economies of scale. For example, there are no great fixed costs in setting up a restaurant or a hairdressing salon – at least, compared with those involved in setting up a steel plant or an underground railway. The level of output at which minimum average cost is reached for such activities may thus be relatively small compared with market demand, so there may be room for many firms in the market. This helps to explain the proliferation of bars, takeaway restaurants and hairdressing salons.

There may also be an intermediate position, where the economies of scale are not sufficient to bring about a monopoly situation, but only relatively few firms can operate efficiently.

How does this affect the way in which a market works? Is there any reason to believe that a monopoly or oligopoly will work against society's best interests? If market share is concentrated among a small number of firms, does this inevitably mean that consumers will suffer?

The answer to these questions depends upon the behaviour of firms within the market. There may be an incentive for a monopoly firm to use its market power to increase its profits. It can do this by restricting the amount of output that it releases on to the market, and by raising the price to consumers. In Chapter 16 it was shown that a monopoly has the incentive to act in this way, since by lowering output and raising price it can increase its overall profits. From the consumer's point of view, the result is a loss of consumer surplus.

If there is an incentive for a single firm to act in this way, there is a similar incentive for firms in an oligopoly to do the same, as they can increase their joint profits – with the same effects on consumers. However, the oligopoly case is more complicated, as there is always the possibility that individual firms will try to increase their own share of the market at the expense of others in the oligopoly.

Market dominance

A key issue is whether firms actually have the market power to exploit consumers in this way. Do firms have market dominance that can be exploited to bring higher profits? In other words, to what extent do firms have the freedom to set prices at their preferred levels, and to what extent do they have to take into account the actions of other firms or face other constraints?

Even monopoly firms have to accept the constraint of the demand curve. They are not free to set a price at any level they choose, otherwise consumers would simply not buy the product.

The question is more one of whether firms are free to choose where to position themselves on their demand curve, rather than having to accept the market equilibrium price.

The fact that most countries have legislation in place to protect consumers from this sort of exploitation by firms recognises that firms might have market power and also have an incentive to use it. In the UK this monitoring is in the hands of the Competition and Markets Authority. For these purposes, a firm is said to have a dominant position if its market share exceeds 40%. The existence of such bodies helps to act as a restraint on anti-competitive practices by firms.

There may also be natural constraints that limit the extent to which a firm is able to achieve a position of dominance in a market. An important consideration is whether a firm (or firms) in a market needs to be aware of the possibility of new firms joining the market. Remember that in Chapter 16 a perfectly competitive market was seen to tend towards a long-run equilibrium. In response to an increase in consumer demand, a key part of the adjustment involved the entry of new firms, which would be attracted into the market when the incumbent firms were seen to be making abnormal profits. This had the effect of competing away those profits until the incentive for entry was removed. Can firms in a market prevent this from happening?

Barriers to entry

Another way of thinking about this is to examine what might constitute a **barrier to entry** of new firms into a market. If such barriers are present, the existing firm or firms may be able to continue to make higher profits.

> ### Key term
>
> **Barrier to entry**: a characteristic of a market that prevents new firms from readily joining the market.

Economies of scale

One source of entry barriers is the existence of economies of scale. If the largest firm has a significant cost advantage over later entrants, it can adopt a pricing strategy that makes it very difficult for new firms to become established.

This advantage of the existing firm is likely to be reinforced by a learning-by-doing effect, by which a firm becomes more proficient as it gathers experience of operating in a particular industry. This could produce an even stronger cost advantage that would need to be overcome by new entrants.

Ownership of raw materials

Suppose that the production of a commodity requires the input of a certain raw material, and that a firm in the market controls the supply of that raw material. You can readily see that this

would be a substantial barrier to the entry of new firms. A key commodity in the fashion industry is that of diamonds. Until recently, De Beers controlled the world's supply of uncut diamonds, and there was no way that new firms could enter the market because of the agreements that De Beers had with mining companies and governments in those parts of the world where diamonds are mined. This monopoly lasted for many years and only began to break down in the early years of the twenty-first century.

Diamonds are a key commodity in the fashion industry

The patent system

The patent system exists to provide protection for firms developing new products or processes. The rationale for this is that, unless firms know that they will have ownership over innovative ideas, they will have no incentive to be innovative. The patent system ensures that, at least for a time, firms can be assured of gaining some benefit from their innovations. For the duration of the patent, they will be protected from competition. This therefore constitutes a legal barrier to the entry of new firms.

Advertising and publicity

Advertising can be regarded as a component of fixed costs, because expenditure on it does not vary directly with the volume of output. If the firms in an industry typically spend heavily on advertising, it will be more difficult for new firms to become established, as they too will need to advertise widely in order to attract customers.

Similarly, firms may spend heavily on achieving a well-known brand image that will ensure customer loyalty. Hence they may invest a lot in the design and packaging of their merchandise.

Notice that such costs are also sunk costs, and cannot be recovered if the new firm fails to gain a foothold. It has sometimes been suggested that the cost of excessive advertising should be included in calculations of the social cost of monopoly.

Research and development

A characteristic of some industries is the heavy expenditure undertaken on research and development (R&D). A prominent example is the pharmaceutical industry, which spends large amounts on researching new drugs – and new cosmetics.

This is another component of fixed costs, as it does not vary with the volume of production. Again, new firms wanting to break into the market know that they will need to invest heavily in R&D if they are going to keep up with the new and better drugs and cosmetics always coming on to the market.

Strategic and innocent barriers to entry

In the case of economies of scale, it could be argued that the advantage of the largest firm in the industry is a purely natural barrier to entry that arises from the market position of the firm.

In other cases, it may be that firms can consciously erect barriers in order to make entry into the market more difficult for potential new firms. In other words, firms may make strategic moves to protect their market position behind entry barriers.

One example of this might be the advertising undertaken by firms. Some firms have become (and remain) well known by dint of heavy advertising expenditures. In some cases these expenditures have very little impact on market shares, and merely serve to maintain the status quo. However, for potential entrants they make life very difficult. Any new firm coming into the market has to try to match the advertising levels of existing firms in order to gain a viable market share. Effectively, existing firms have increased the fixed costs of being in the market, making entry more difficult to achieve. For example, when the soft drink Sunny Delight was launched in the early part of the twenty-first century, it had to undertake a large-scale television advertising campaign to try to break into a market dominated by Coca-Cola and PepsiCo.

An alternative method is for an existing firm to operate with spare capacity, making it clear to potential entrants that entry will trigger a price war. The surplus capacity adds credibility to this threat, as the existing firm is seen to be able to increase output – and thus force down price – very quickly.

Exercise 17.4

For each of the following, explain under what circumstances the action of the firm constitutes a barrier to entry and discuss whether there is a strategic element to it, or whether it might be regarded as a 'natural' or 'innocent' barrier.

a A firm takes advantage of economies of scale to reduce its average costs of production.
b A firm holds a patent on the sale of a product.
c A firm engages in widespread advertising of its product.
d A firm installs surplus capacity relative to normal production levels.
e A firm produces a range of very similar products under different brand names.
f A firm chooses not to set price at the profit-maximising level.
g A firm spends extensively on research and development in order to produce a better product.

Summary

- It is important to be able to evaluate the degree of concentration in a market.
- While not a perfect measure, the concentration ratio is one way of doing this, by calculating the market share of the largest firms.
- Cost conditions in a market may affect the number of firms that can operate profitably.
- Firms that attain market dominance may be able to harness market power at the expense of consumers, reducing output and raising price.
- This is especially the case where the existing firm or firms are protected by barriers to entry.
- When firms do use such market power, there is a deadweight loss to society that reflects allocative inefficiency.

18 The objectives of firms and their pricing strategies

Although firms may aim to maximise profits, as in the traditional model, this may not always be the case. This chapter examines alternative objectives that firms may adopt, and explores why this might be. It also considers alternative pricing strategies that may be adopted by firms, including situations in which firms may be able to charge different prices to different groups of customers, a process known as price discrimination. The important notion of contestable markets is also explained.

Learning outcomes

After studying this chapter, you should:

- be aware of the need for firms to grow if they wish to compete in global markets
- be familiar with alternative motivations of firms and how these affect decision-making
- be aware of the principal-agent issue, and its influence on the motivations of firms
- be aware of the relative merits of perfect competition and monopoly in terms of market performance
- understand the conditions under which price discrimination is possible and how this affects consumers and producers
- be aware of possible pricing rules that can be adopted by firms
- understand the notion of cost-plus pricing and how this may relate to profit maximisation
- be familiar with the idea of predatory pricing
- understand the notion of contestable markets and its implications for firms' behaviour
- be familiar with entry deterrence strategies.

Of course, not all firms become giants, and many small firms operate profitably and effectively. In part, this may reflect the nature of the markets in which small firms thrive. The service sector in particular provides opportunity for small firms to operate effectively, perhaps because of the absence of economies of scale, or because there are niche products where small firms have a competitive advantage over larger enterprises. After all, small firms may be more flexible and responsive to customer needs, and able to provide a high quality personal service. Small firms tend to emerge in times of high unemployment, when jobs are scarce and self-employment becomes an attractive option for some individuals, as it can offer high job satisfaction.

There are drawbacks with being small as a firm. Obtaining finance for investment may be more difficult, and a small firm may find it more difficult to survive when times are hard. In some markets, competing with larger firms may pose problems.

Firms may wish to increase their size in order to gain market power within the industry in which they are operating. A firm that can gain market share, and perhaps become dominant in the market, may be able to exercise some control over the price of its product, and thereby influence the market. However, firms may wish to grow for other reasons, which will be explained later in the chapter.

The headquarters of Google in California, USA

18.1 The growth of firms

A feature of the economic environment in recent years has been the increasing size of firms. Some, such as Microsoft, Wal-Mart and Google, have become giants. Why is this happening?

Organic growth

Some firms grow simply by being successful. For example, a successful marketing campaign may increase a firm's market share, and provide it with a flow of profits that can be reinvested to expand the firm even more. Some firms may choose to borrow in order to finance their growth, perhaps by issuing shares (equity).

Such *organic growth* may encounter limits. A firm may find that its product market is saturated, so that it can grow further only at the expense of other firms in the market. If its competitors are able to maintain their own market shares, the firm may need to diversify its production activities by finding new markets for its existing product, or perhaps offering new products.

There are many examples of such activity. Tesco, the leading UK supermarket, has launched itself into new markets by opening branches overseas, and has also introduced a range of new products, including financial services, to its existing customers. Microsoft has famously used this strategy, by selling first its internet browser and later its media player as part of its Windows operating system, in an attempt to persuade existing customers to buy its new products.

Diversification may be a dangerous strategy: moving into a market in which the firm is inexperienced and where existing rival firms already know the business may pose quite a challenge. In such circumstances, much may depend on the quality of the management team.

Mergers and acquisitions

Instead of growing organically – that is, based on the firm's own resources – many firms choose to grow by merging with, or acquiring, other firms. The distinction here is that an *acquisition* (or takeover) may be hostile, whereas a *merger* may be the coming together of equals, with each firm committed to forming a single entity.

Growth in this way has a number of advantages: for example, it may overcome the management problem and allow some rationalisation to take place. On the other hand, firms tend to develop their own culture, or way of doing things, and some mergers have foundered because of an incompatibility of corporate cultures.

Mergers (or acquisitions) can be of three different types. A **horizontal merger** is a merger between firms operating in the same industry and at the same stage of the production process: for example, the merger of two car assembly firms. The car industry has been characterised by such mergers, including the takeover of Rover by BMW in 1994 and the merger of Daimler-Benz with Chrysler in 1998. The merger of Hewlett-Packard with Compaq is another example of a horizontal merger.

A horizontal merger can affect the degree of market concentration because after the merger takes place there are fewer independent firms operating in the market. This may increase the market power held by the new firm.

A car assembly plant merging with a tyre producer, on the other hand, is an example of a **vertical merger**. A real-life example of this was the merger in 2000 of AOL with Time-Warner.

A car assembly plant merging with a tyre producer is an example of a vertical merger

Vertical mergers may be either upstream or downstream. If a car company merges with a component supplier, that is known as *backward integration*, as it involves merging with a firm that is involved in an earlier part of the production process. *Forward integration* entails merging in the other direction, as for example if the car assembly plant decided to merge with a large distributor.

Vertical integration may allow rationalisation of the process of production. Car producers often work on a just-in-time basis, ordering components for the production line only as they are required. This creates a potential vulnerability because if the supply of components fails then production has to stop. If a firm's component supplier is part of the firm rather than an independent operator, this may improve the reliability of, and confidence in, the just-in-time process, and in consequence may make life more difficult for rival firms. However, vertical mergers have different implications for concentration and market power.

The third type of merger involves the merging of two firms that are operating in quite different markets or industries. For example, companies like Unilever or Nestlé operate in a wide range of different markets, partly as a result of acquisitions.

One argument in favour of **conglomerate mergers** is that they reduce the risks faced by firms. Many markets follow fluctuations that are in line with the business cycle but are not always fully synchronised. By operating in a number of markets that are on different cycles, the firm can even out its activity overall. However, it is not necessarily an efficient way of doing business, as the different activities undertaken may require different skills and specialisms. In recent years, conglomerate mergers seem to have become less popular.

Key terms

Horizontal merger: a merger between two firms at the same stage of production in the same industry.

Vertical merger: a merger between two firms in the same industry, but at different stages of the production process.

Conglomerate merger: a merger between two different firms operating in different markets.

Not all mergers turn out to be successful, and there may be circumstances in which merged firms choose to 'demerge' and split. A common factor that can lead to this happening is where firms from different countries merge, only to find that their corporate cultures are incompatible. This can even happen with firms from the same country, where management styles in the individual companies do not fit well together. In other situations, it may be that synergies achieved between the production activities of the firms are not as strong as expected. Demergers can turn out to be costly and acrimonious.

Exercise 18.1

Categorise each of the following as a horizontal, vertical or conglomerate merger.

a The merger of a firm operating an instant coffee factory with a coffee plantation.
b The merger of a brewer and a bakery.
c The merger of a brewer and a crisp manufacturer.
d The merger of a soft drinks manufacturer with a chain of fast-food outlets.
e The merger of an internet service provider with a film studio.
f A merger between two firms producing tyres for cars.

Summary

- Firms tend to grow over time, either through organic growth or through mergers and acquisitions.
- Firms may wish to grow to gain market share or market power.
- Mergers can be horizontal, vertical or conglomerate.

18.2 Alternative motivations of firms

Most of the discussion so far has rested on the assumption that firms set out to maximise profits. When we consider a relatively small, owner-managed firm, this may be a reasonable assumption – but it is clear that many firms do not fall into this category. Firms may not always appear to be only concerned with profit – indeed, many firms have taken up the notion of *corporate social responsibility*, in which they set out to contribute to the communities in which they are located.

There may be explanations for this.

For many larger firms – especially public limited companies – the owners may not be involved in running the business. This gives rise to the **principal–agent (or agency) problem**. In a public limited company, the shareholders delegate the day-to-day decisions concerning the operation of the firm to managers who act on their behalf. In this case the shareholders are the principals, and the managers are the agents who run things for them. In other words, there is a divorce of ownership from control.

Key term

Principal–agent problem: a situation in which people (principals) cannot be sure that those who act on their behalf (agents) will act in their best interests, as a result of asymmetric information.

If the agents are in full sympathy with the objectives of the owners, there is no problem and the managers will take exactly the decisions that the owners would like. Problems arise when there is conflict between the aims of the owners and those of the managers.

One simple explanation of why this problem arises is that the managers like a quiet life, and therefore do not push for the absolute profit-maximising position, but do just enough to keep the shareholders off their backs. Herbert Simon referred to this as '**satisficing**' behaviour, where managers aim to produce satisfactory profits rather than maximum profits.

Another possibility is that managers become negligent because they are not fully accountable. One manifestation of this may be organisational slack: costs will not be minimised, as the firm is not operating as efficiently as it could. This is an example of what is called **X-inefficiency**. For example, in Figure 18.1 *LAC* is the long-run average cost curve showing the most efficient cost positions for the firm at any output level. With X-inefficiency, a firm could end up producing output q_1 at average cost AC_1. Thus, in the presence of X-inefficiency the firm will be operating above its long-run average cost curve.

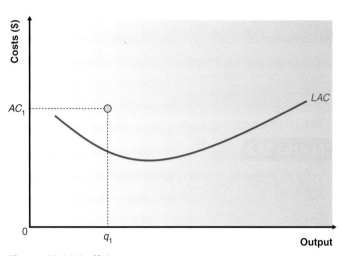

Figure 18.1 X-inefficiency

Key terms

Satisficing: behaviour under which the managers of firms aim to produce satisfactory results for the firm – for example, in terms of profits – rather than trying to maximise them.

X-inefficiency: occurs when a firm is not operating at minimum cost, perhaps because of organisational slack.

Some writers have argued that the managers may be pursuing other objectives. For example, some managers may enjoy being involved in the running of a large business, and may prefer to see the firm gaining market share – perhaps beyond the profit-maximising level. Others may like to see their status rewarded and so will want to divert part of the profits into managerial perks – large offices, company cars and so on. Or they may feel that having a large staff working for them increases their prestige inside the company. These sorts of activity tend to reduce the profitability of firms.

Revenue maximisation

The industrial economist William Baumol argued that managers may set out with the objective of maximising revenue. One reason is that in some firms managerial salaries are related to turnover rather than profits. The effects of this can be seen by looking back at Figure 15.7 on page 123. You can see that total revenue is maximised at the peak of the TR curve (where $MR = 0$), at q_r. A revenue-maximising firm will produce more output than a profit-maximising one, and will need to charge a lower price in order to sell the extra output. This should be apparent from the fact that profits are maximised where $MR = MC$, which must be at a positive level of MR – and thus to the left of q_r in Figure 15.7.

Baumol pointed out that the shareholders might not be too pleased about this. The way the firm behaves then depends upon the degree of accountability that the agents (managers) have to the principals (shareholders). For example, the shareholders may have sufficient power over their agents to be able to insist on some minimum level of profits. The result may then be a compromise solution.

Sales maximisation

In some cases, managers may focus more on the volume of sales than on the resulting revenues. This could lead to output being set even higher, to the point at which total revenue only just covers total cost. Remember that total cost includes normal profit – the opportunity cost of the resources tied up in the firm. The firm would have to close down if it did not cover this opportunity cost.

Again, the extent to which the managers will be able to pursue this objective without endangering their positions with the shareholders depends on how accountable the managers are to the shareholders. Remember that the managers are likely to have much better information about the market conditions and the internal functioning of the firm than the shareholders, who view the firm only remotely. This may be to the managers' advantage.

Summary

- For many larger firms, where day-to-day control is delegated to managers, a principal–agent problem may arise if there is conflict between the objectives of the owners (principals) and those of the managers (agents).
- This may lead to satisficing behaviour and to X-inefficiency.
- William Baumol suggested that managers may set out to maximise revenue rather than profits; others have suggested that sales or the growth of the firm may be the managers' objectives.

18.3 Perfect competition and monopoly compared

It is important to understand why this debate about how firms behave is so important for society. Some insight to this can be gained by comparing the outcomes from a perfectly competitive market with those of a monopoly.

Chapter 16 set out the models of perfect competition and monopoly. Each has different implications for resource allocation. A monopoly, by its behaviour, distorts resource allocation, and by comparing a monopoly market with a perfectly competitive market, it is possible to identify the extent of the distortion. To do this, the situation can be simplified by setting aside the possibility of economies of scale. This is perhaps an artificial assumption to make, but it could be relaxed.

Suppose that there is an industry with no economies of scale, which can be operated either as a perfectly competitive market with many small firms, or as a monopoly firm running a large number of small plants.

Figure 18.2 shows the market demand curve ($D = AR$) and the long-run supply curve under perfect competition (LRS). If the market is operating under perfect competition, the long-run equilibrium will produce a price of P_{pc} and the firms in the industry will together supply Q_{pc} output. Consumer surplus (the surplus that consumers gain from consuming this product) is given by the area $AP_{pc}E$. This is a measure of the welfare that society receives from consuming the good, as was explained in Chapter 5.

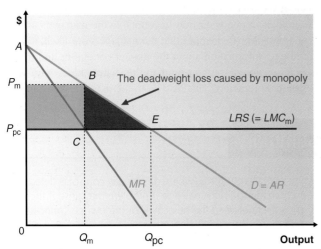

Figure 18.2 Comparing perfect competition and monopoly

Now suppose that the industry is taken over by a profit-maximising monopolist. The firm can close down some of the plants to vary its output over the long run, and the LRS can be regarded as the monopolist's long-run marginal cost curve. As the monopoly firm faces the market demand curve directly, it will also face the MR curve shown, so will maximise profits at quantity Q_m and charge a price P_m.

Thus, the effect of this change in market structure is that the profit-maximising monopolist produces less output than a perfectly competitive industry and charges a higher price.

It is also apparent that consumer surplus is now very different, as in the new situation it is limited to the area AP_mB. Looking more carefully at Figure 18.2, you can see that the loss of consumer surplus has occurred for two reasons. First, the monopoly firm is now making profits shown by the blue shaded area P_mBCP_{pc}. This is a redistribution of welfare from consumers to the firm, but as the monopolist is also a member of society, this does not affect overall welfare. However, there is also a loss, which represents a loss to society resulting from the monopolisation of the industry. This is measured by the area of the red triangle BCE. This is known as the **deadweight loss** that society incurs as a result of the restriction to competition. Notice that a small number of firms in collusion with each other may have similar effects to a monopoly.

Key term

Deadweight loss: loss of consumer surplus that arises when a monopoly restricts output and raises price.

Exercise 18.2

Figure 18.3 shows a market in which there are only two firms operating.

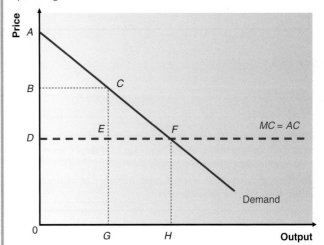

Figure 18.3 Anti-competitive behaviour

a The two firms competing in the market produce at constant marginal cost OD, which means that average cost is also constant and equal to marginal cost. Competing intensively, the price is driven down to a level at which no surplus above marginal cost is made. Identify the price charged, the quantity traded and consumer surplus.

b Suppose the two firms decide to collude to raise price to a level OB. Identify the quantity traded and the consumer surplus.

c You should have found that consumer surplus is much smaller in the second situation than in the first. What has happened to the areas that were formerly part of consumer surplus?

This deadweight loss is a measure of the welfare loss imposed on society in a monopoly situation. However, there are two key aspects of efficiency, as was shown in Chapter 12. The loss in *allocative efficiency* shown in Figure 18.2 may be partly offset by improved *productive efficiency*: for example, because a monopoly is able to take advantage of economies of scale that would be sacrificed if it were to be split into many small firms, none of which would be able to reach the minimum average cost level of output.

The existence of the deadweight loss provides the rationale for intervention by the UK's Competition and Markets Authority, which have the responsibility for protecting consumer interests and attempting to promote competition.

Summary

- A comparison of perfect competition with monopoly reveals that a profit-maximising monopoly firm operating under the same cost conditions as a perfectly competitive industry will produce less output, charge a higher price and impose a deadweight loss on society.
- Real-world markets do not often conform to the models of perfect competition or monopoly, which are extreme forms of market structure.

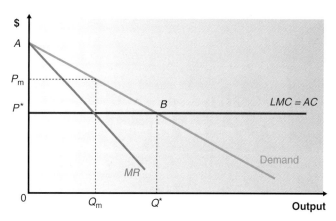

Figure 18.4 Perfect price discrimination

18.4 Pricing strategies and contestable markets

The alternative motivations followed by firms can result in a range of pricing strategies adopted depending on opportunities and market conditions.

Price discrimination

A profit-maximising monopoly firm will set a price that is above marginal cost, producing a level of output that is below the level required for allocative efficiency. However, there is a special case in which a monopolist could produce the level of output that is efficient in resource allocation terms.

Consider Figure 18.4. Suppose this market is operated by a monopolist that faces the constant marginal cost curve LMC. (This is to simplify the analysis.) The previous section showed that under perfect competition the market outcome would be a price P^* and quantity Q^*. What would induce the monopolist to produce at Q^*?

One of the assumptions made throughout the analysis so far is that all consumers in a market get to pay the same price for the product. This leads to the notion of consumer surplus, which was introduced in Chapter 5. In Figure 18.4, if the market were operating under perfect competition and all consumers were paying the same price, consumer surplus would be given by the area AP^*B. If the market were operated by a monopolist, also charging the same price to all buyers, then profits would be maximised where $MC = MR$: that is, at quantity Q_m and price P_m.

But suppose this assumption is now relaxed; suppose that the monopolist is able to charge a different price to each individual consumer. A monopolist is then able to charge each consumer a price that is equal to his or her willingness to pay for the good. In other words, the demand curve effectively becomes the marginal revenue curve, as it represents the amount that the monopolist will receive for each unit of the good. It will then maximise profits at point B in Figure 18.4, where MR (i.e. AR) is equal to LMC. The difference between this situation and that under perfect competition is that the area AP^*B is no longer consumer surplus, but producer surplus: that is, the monopolist's profits. The monopolist has hijacked the whole of the original consumer surplus as its profits.

From society's point of view, total welfare is the same as it is under perfect competition (but more than under monopoly without discrimination). However, now there has been a redistribution, from consumers to the monopoly – and presumably to the shareholders of the firm. This situation is known as **perfect price discrimination** or **first-degree price discrimination**.

Key term

Perfect/first-degree price discrimination: a situation arising in a market whereby a monopoly firm is able to charge each consumer a different price.

Perfect price discrimination is fairly rare in the real world, although it might be said to exist in the world of art or fashion, where customers may commission a painting, sculpture or item of designer jewellery and the price is a matter of negotiation between the buyer and supplier.

The Fort St George Museum in Chennai, India. Perfect price discrimination exists in the art world

However, there are situations in which partial price discrimination is possible. For example, students or old-age pensioners may get discounted bus fares, the young and/or old may get cheaper access to sporting events or theatres, etc. In these instances, individual consumers are paying different prices for what is in fact the same product.

Conditions for price discrimination

There are three conditions under which a firm may be able to price discriminate:
- The firm must have market power.
- The firm must have information about consumers and their willingness to pay – and there must be identifiable differences between consumers (or groups of consumers).
- The consumers must have limited ability to resell the product.

Market power

Clearly, price discrimination is not possible in a perfectly competitive market, where no seller has the power to charge other than the going market price. So price discrimination can take place only where firms have some ability to vary the price.

Information

From the firm's point of view, it needs to be able to identify different groups of consumers with different willingness to pay. What makes price discrimination profitable for firms is that different consumers display different sensitivities to price: that is, they have different price elasticities of demand.

Ability to resell

If consumers could resell the product easily, then price discrimination would not be possible, as consumers would

engage in **arbitrage**. In other words, the group of consumers who qualified for the low price could buy up the product and then turn a profit by reselling to consumers in the other segment(s) of the market. This would mean that the firm would no longer be able to sell at the high price, and would no longer try to discriminate in pricing.

> **Key term**
>
> **Arbitrage**: a process by which prices in two market segments will be equalised by a process of purchase and resale by market participants.

In the case of student discounts and old-age concessions, the firm can identify particular groups of consumers; and such 'products' as bus journeys and dental treatment cannot be resold. But why should a firm undertake this practice?

The simple answer is that, by undertaking price discrimination, the firm is able to increase its profits by switching sales from a market with relatively low marginal revenue to a market where it is higher.

An extreme form of price discrimination was used by NAPP Pharmaceutical Holdings in the UK, as a result of which the firm was fined £3.2 million by the Office of Fair Trading (OFT). NAPP sold sustained-release morphine tablets and capsules in the UK. These are drugs administered to patients with incurable cancer. NAPP realised that the market was segmented. The drugs were sold partly to the National Health Service (NHS) for use in hospitals, but were also prescribed by GPs. As these patients were terminally ill, they tended to spend a relatively short time in hospital before being sent home. NAPP realised that GPs tended to prescribe the same drugs as the patients had received in hospital. It therefore reduced its price to hospitals by 90%, thereby forcing all competitors out of the market and gaining a monopoly in that market segment. It was then able to increase the price of these drugs prescribed through GPs, and so maximise profits. The OFT investigated the firm, fined it and instructed it to stop its actions, thus saving the NHS £2 million per year.

> **Exercise 18.3**
>
> In which of the following products might price discrimination be possible? Explain your answers.
>
> **a** hairdressing
> **b** peak and off-peak rail travel
> **c** apples
> **d** air tickets
> **e** newspapers
> **f** plastic surgery
> **g** soft drinks

Pricing rules

In the analysis of market structure, it was assumed that firms set out to maximise profits. However, they may set out to achieve other objectives. The price of a firm's product is a key strategic variable that must be manipulated in order to attain whatever objective the firm wishes to achieve.

Figure 18.5 illustrates the variety of pricing rules that are possible. The figure shows a firm operating under a form of market structure that is not perfect competition – because the firm faces a downward-sloping demand curve for its product shown by $AR (= D)$.

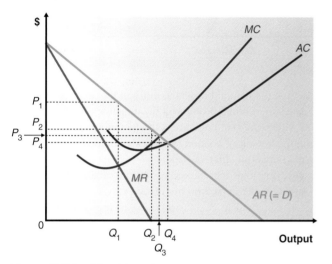

Figure 18.5 Possible pricing rules

Profit maximisation

If the firm chooses to maximise profits, it will choose output such that marginal revenue is equal to marginal cost, and will then set the price to clear the market. In terms of the figure, it will set output at Q_1 and price at P_1.

Revenue maximisation

As mentioned in Section 18.2, the economist William Baumol argued that, if there is a divorce of ownership from control in the organisation of a firm, whereby the shareholders have delegated day-to-day decision making to managers (a principal–agent situation), the managers may find themselves with some freedom to pursue other objectives, such as revenue maximisation. A revenue maximiser in Figure 18.5 would choose to produce at the output level at which marginal revenue is zero. This occurs at Q_2 in the figure, with the price set at P_2.

Sales maximisation

If instead managers set out to maximise the volume of sales subject to covering opportunity cost, they will choose to set output

at a level such that price equals average cost, which will clear the market. In Figure 18.5 this happens at Q_4 (with price at P_4).

Allocative efficiency

It has been argued that allocative efficiency in an individual market occurs at the point where price is equal to marginal cost. In Figure 18.5 this is at Q_3 (with price P_3). However, from the firm's perspective there is no obvious reason why this should become an objective of the firm, as it confers no particular advantage.

Exercise 18.4

For each of the following situations, identify the pricing rule most appropriate to achieve the firm's objectives, and comment on the implications that this has for efficiency.

a A firm producing DVD recorders tries to achieve as high a market share as possible, measured in value terms.
b A local gymnasium tries to make as high a surplus over costs as can be achieved.
c A national newspaper sets out to maximise circulation (subject to covering its costs), knowing that this will affect advertising revenues.
d A farmer producing onions finds that it cannot influence the price of its product.

Predatory pricing

Perhaps the most common context in which price wars have broken out is where an existing firm or firms have reacted to defend the market against the entry of new firms.

One example occurred in 1996, in the early years of easyJet, the low-cost air carrier, which was then trying to become established. When easyJet started flying the London–Amsterdam route, charging its now well-known low prices, the incumbent firm (KLM) reacted very aggressively, driving its price down to a level just below that of easyJet. The response from easyJet was to launch legal action against KLM, claiming it was using unfair market tactics.

So-called **predatory pricing** is illegal under English, Dutch and EU law. It should be noted that, in order to declare an action illegal, it is necessary to define that action very carefully – otherwise it will not be possible to prove the case in the courts. In the case of predatory pricing, the legal definition is based on economic analysis.

Key term

Predatory pricing: an anti-competitive strategy in which a firm sets price below average variable cost in an attempt to force a rival or rivals out of the market and achieve market dominance.

Remember that if a firm fails to cover average variable costs, its strategy should be to close down immediately, as it would be better off doing so. The courts have backed this theory, and state that a pricing strategy should be interpreted as being predatory if the price is set below average variable costs, as the only motive for remaining in business while making such losses must be to drive competitors out of business and achieve market dominance. This is known as the Areeda–Turner principle (after the case in which it was first argued in the USA).

On the face of it, consumers have much to gain from such strategies through the resulting lower prices. However, a predator that is successful in driving out the opposition is likely to recoup its losses by putting prices back up to profit-maximising levels thereafter, so the benefit to consumers is short lived.

Having said that, the low-cost airlines survived the attempts of the established airlines to hold on to their market shares. Indeed, in the post-9/11 period, which was a tough one for the airlines for obvious reasons, the low-cost airlines flourished while the more conventional established airlines went through a very difficult period indeed.

In some cases, the very threat of predatory pricing may be sufficient to deter entry by new firms, if the threat is a credible one. In other words, the existing firms need to convince potential entrants that they, the existing firms, will find it in their best interests to fight a price war, otherwise the entrants will not believe the threat. The existing firms could do this by making it known that they have surplus capacity, so that they would be able to increase output very quickly in order to drive down the price.

Whether entry will be deterred by such means may depend in part on the characteristics of the potential entrant. After all, a new firm may reckon that, if the existing firm finds it worth sacrificing profits in the short run, the rewards of dominating the market must be worth fighting for. It may therefore decide to sacrifice short-term profit in order to enter the market – especially if it is diversifying from other markets and has resources at its disposal. The winner will then be the firm that can last the longest; but, clearly, this is potentially very damaging for all concerned.

Exercise 18.5

Discuss the extent to which consumers benefit from a price war.

Limit pricing

An associated but less extreme strategy is limit pricing. This assumes that the incumbent firm has some sort of cost advantage over potential entrants, for example economies of scale.

Figure 18.6 shows a firm facing a downward-sloping demand curve, and thus having some influence over the price of its product. If the firm is maximising profits, it is setting output at Q_0 and price at P_0. As average revenue is comfortably above average cost at this price, the firm is making healthy supernormal profits.

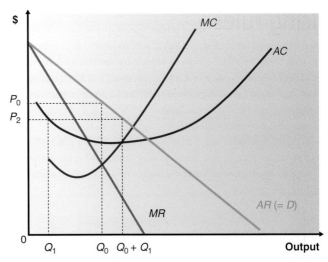

Figure 18.6 Limit pricing

Suppose that the natural barriers to entry in this industry are weak. The supernormal profits will be attractive to potential entrants. Given the cost conditions, the incumbent firm is enjoying the benefit of economies of scale, although producing below the minimum efficient scale.

If a new firm joins the market, producing on a relatively small scale, say at Q_1, the impact on the market can be analysed as follows. The immediate effect is on price, as now the amount $Q_0 + Q_1$ is being produced, pushing price down to P_2. The new firm (producing Q_1) is just covering average cost, so is making normal profits and feeling justified in having joined the market. The original firm is still making supernormal profits, but at a lower level than before. The entry of the new firm has competed away part of the original firm's supernormal profits.

One way in which the firm could have guarded against entry is by charging a lower price than P_0 to begin with. For example, if it had set output at $Q_0 + Q_1$ and price at P_2, then a new entrant joining the market would have pushed the price down to a level below P_2, and without the benefit of economies of scale would have made losses and exited the market. In any case, if the existing firm has been in the market for some time it will have gone through a process of learning by doing, and therefore will have a lower average cost curve than the potential entrant. This makes it more likely that limit pricing can be used.

Thus, by setting a price below the profit-maximising level, the original firm is able to maintain its market position in the longer run. This could be a reason for avoiding making too high a level of supernormal profits in the short run, in order to make profits in the longer term.

Notice that such a strategy need not be carried out by a monopolist, but could also occur in an oligopoly, where existing firms may jointly seek to protect their market against potential entry.

Contestable markets

It has been argued that in some markets, in order to prevent the entry of new firms, the existing firm would have to charge such a low price that it would be unable to reap any supernormal profits at all.

This theory was developed by William Baumol and is known as the theory of **contestable markets**. It was in recognition of this theory that the monopoly model in Chapter 16 included the assumption that there must be no substitutes for the good, *either actual or potential*.

Key term

Contestable market: a market in which the existing firm makes only normal profit, as it cannot set a price higher than average cost without attracting entry, owing to the absence of barriers to entry and sunk costs.

For a market to be contestable, it must have no barriers to entry or exit and no sunk costs. Sunk costs refer to costs that a firm incurs in setting up a business and which cannot be recovered if the firm exits the market. Furthermore, new firms in the market must have no competitive disadvantage compared with the incumbent firm(s): in other words, they must have access to the same technology, and there must be no significant learning-by-doing effects. Entry and exit must be rapid.

Under these conditions, the incumbent firm cannot set a price that is higher than average cost because, as soon as it does, it will open up the possibility of hit-and-run entry by new firms, which can enter the market and compete away the supernormal profits.

Consider Figure 18.7, which shows a monopoly firm in a market. The argument is that, if the monopolist charges the profit-maximising price, then in a contestable market the firm will be vulnerable to hit-and-run entry – a firm could come into the market, take some of the supernormal profits and then exit again. The only way the monopolist can avoid this happening is to set price equal to average cost, so that there are no supernormal profits to act as an incentive for entry.

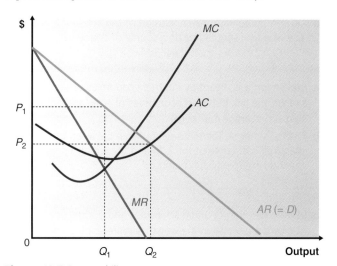

Figure 18.7 Contestability

On the face of it, the conditions for contestability sound pretty stringent. In particular, the firm in Figure 18.7 enjoys some economies of scale, so you would think that some sunk costs had been incurred.

However, suppose a firm has a monopoly on a domestic air route between two destinations. An airline with surplus capacity (i.e. a spare aircraft sitting in a hangar) could enter this route and exit again without incurring sunk costs in response to profits being made by the incumbent firm. This is an example of how contestability may limit the ability of the incumbent firm to use its market power.

Notice in this example that, although the firm only makes normal profits, neither productive nor allocative efficiency is achieved.

A moot point is whether the threat of entry will in fact persuade firms that they cannot set a price above average cost. Perhaps the firms can risk making some profit above normal profits and then respond to entry very aggressively if and when it happens. After all, it is difficult to think of an example in which there are absolutely no sunk costs. Almost any business is going to have to advertise in order to find customers, and such advertising expenditure cannot be recovered. Pricing is not the only strategy that firms adopt in order to deter entry by new firms.

Summary

- In some markets a monopolist may be able to engage in price discrimination by selling its product at different prices to different consumers or groups of consumers.
- This enables the firm to increase its profits by absorbing some or all of the consumer surplus.
- Under first-degree price discrimination, the firm is able to charge a different price to each customer and absorb all consumer surplus.
- The firm can practise price discrimination only where it has market power, where consumers have differing elasticities of demand for the product, and where consumers have limited ability to resell the product.
- There are many pricing rules that a firm may choose to adopt, depending on the objectives it wishes to achieve.
- Although price wars are expected to be damaging for the firms involved, they do break out from time to time.
- This may occur when firms wish to increase their market shares, or when existing firms wish to deter the entry of new firms into the market.
- Predatory pricing is an extreme strategy that forces all firms to endure losses. It is normally invoked in an attempt to eliminate a competitor, and is illegal in many countries.
- Limit pricing occurs when a firm or firms choose to set the price below the profit-maximising level in order to prevent entry. The limit price is the highest price that an existing firm can set without allowing entry.
- In contestable markets, the incumbent firm or firms may be able to make only normal profit.
- Contestability requires that there are no barriers to entry or exit and no sunk costs – and that the incumbent firm(s) have no cost advantage over hit-and-run entrants.

Examination questions

1 BG is a rapidly growing energy company with operations in 25 countries engaged in the exploration, production and distribution of natural gas and oil. This requires complex chains of physical infrastructure, major investment funds and detailed commercial agreements with different countries.

a Explain why economies of scale might be significant in an industry such as gas supply. [12]

b Discuss whether companies that supply energy are likely to operate in contestable markets. [13]

Cambridge AS and A Level Economics 9708, Paper 41, Q3, November 2009

2 In many cities worldwide, newspaper publishers compete with each other. Some types of newspapers are sold, but publishers also produce others that are distributed free of charge. Many people and companies pay to advertise in the free newspapers.

a Explain the different ways that economists classify profits and consider whether it is possible to make a profit from a newspaper that is distributed free. [12]

b Discuss how a firm might compete in a market. [13]

Cambridge AS and A Level Economics 9708, Paper 4, Q2, June 2009

3 In 2007 the cost of a single ticket on London trains bought at the time of travel was £4. The same ticket bought in advance was £2.50 if used up to 19.00 hrs and £2 after 19.00 hrs. Children could travel free at any time, and those over 60 could travel free after 09.00 hrs.

a Explain what is meant by price discrimination and analyse what evidence there is of price discrimination in the above statement. [12]

b Discuss how the output and pricing policy adopted by a firm might differ depending on the market structure in which it operates. [13]

Cambridge AS and A Level Economics 9708, Paper 41, Q3, June 2010

4 The success of supermarkets

In some countries supermarkets dominate food shopping. In the UK 75% of the food bought for home use comes from supermarkets. A third of that comes from one supermarket, Tesco. Tesco makes billions of pounds profit, one third of which goes to the government in taxes. It employs 110 000 people in the UK and many more in developing countries.

In the past, UK shoppers queued to buy expensive food from many small shops with limited choice and restricted opening times. Now, in supermarkets, they have the benefit of a wide choice, reasonable prices, international dishes, organic produce, fair trade items, clear labels of the contents of the products and, because of intense competition between the supermarkets, some open 24 hours.

However, the media complain that supermarkets are not competitive but monopolies. They say their profits are too high, they have caused small shops to close and forced suppliers in developing countries to accept low prices and to pay low wages.

It must be remembered that supermarkets grew because they gave the customer what they wanted and aimed at certain types of shoppers. One supermarket, which started as a small shop, insisted on selling only high quality products while another offered customers low prices.

Supermarkets also adapted to changing market trends. One began to supply products with its own brand name which were sold more cheaply because there were no advertising costs. A further brilliant idea in expanding their business was the introduction of a store loyalty card. Shoppers with a loyalty card are given discounts, which encourages them to continue to shop in the same supermarket.

The most successful supermarkets expanded their businesses by buying large sites to build huge stores. (They are criticised for such building, especially if it destroys parts of the countryside or environment.) They expanded into non-food products to fill these stores, making it possible for consumers to buy many household items from clothes to kitchen utensils to electrical goods in the same shop. Supermarkets have also recently introduced on-line shopping and home deliveries.

Many small shops have closed. There are bound to be casualties in retailing. How can the blame for that be the fault of the supermarket? Their size should not be a concern. It is, after all, the consumer who decides where to shop and what to buy.

Source: adapted from article by Judi Bevan, Royal Society of Arts Journal

a How has the type of market structure in food retailing in the UK changed? [3]

b To what extent does the article support the view that the consumer is sovereign in food retailing? [4]

c Explain what the various objectives of a firm might be. [5]

d Do you agree with the conclusion of the article that the size of a firm should not be a source of concern? [8]

Cambridge AS and A Level Economics 9708, Paper 41, Q1, November 2010

5 a Explain what is meant by internal economies of scale, and analyse the link between economies of scale and a firm's long-run average cost curve. [12]

b Discuss whether there is a relationship between the marginal cost curve of the firm and the supply curve of the industry to which it belongs. [13]

Cambridge AS and A Level Economics 9708, Paper 41, Q3, November 2010

6 a Discuss whether demand schedules and budget line diagrams are similar in the way they represent the effect of
i a rise in the price of a good
ii a rise in a consumer's income. [12]

b Analyse what is meant by the equi-marginal principle of consumer demand and whether itcan be linked to the derivation of a market demand curve. [13]

Cambridge AS and A Level Economics 9708, Paper 43, Q3, June 2011

19 Market imperfections and microeconomic policy

In earlier chapters, a number of situations have been identified in which markets may not produce the best outcomes for society in terms of resource allocation. These situations may arise because of the nature of some goods (public, merit or demerit goods, for example). In some cases, it may be that the problem stems from the presence of costs or benefits that are not captured by the pricing mechanism (externalities), or it may be that it is the structure of the market that causes problems (monopoly or other forms of imperfect competition). Indeed, it is also the case that government intervention itself may introduce market distortions. This chapter examines policies that may be introduced to achieve efficient resource allocation and correct market failure. It will also discuss microeconomic policy designed to influence the distribution of income and wealth in society. In addition, the possibility of government failure will be outlined.

Learning outcomes

After studying this chapter, you should:

- be aware of the significance of market failure in its various forms
- be familiar with policies designed to address market failure, including merit and demerit goods and externalities
- understand how monopolistic elements in a market can lead to imperfections in resource allocation
- appreciate the difficulties of dealing with natural monopoly situations
- be aware that regulation of an industry does not necessarily address issues of inefficiency
- be familiar with the economic underpinnings and the operation of competition policy
- be aware of the rationale for governments to redistribute income and wealth, and the polices that can be used for this purpose
- be able to evaluate the strengths and weaknesses of government interventions.

19.1 Market failure

Consequences of market failure

Market failure is a situation in which the free-market mechanism fails to produce the best allocation of resources for society as a whole. For example, in the presence of a negative production externality such as pollution (discussed in Chapter 13), marginal social costs exceed marginal private costs, leading firms to act in such a way as to produce 'too much pollution'. This divergence between social and marginal costs means that resources fail to be allocated in the best possible way. There are some other ways in which marginal social and private costs or benefits may diverge – for instance, in the case of public, merit or demerit goods. Such a divergence can also take place when some economic agents have better information than others, or can wield some form of market power.

Why does it matter? From the point of view of society, this analysis of market failure suggests that resources could be better used, thus making members of society better off. The authorities may therefore wish to intervene, if they can find a way of correcting the market failure. However, the authorities must also be aware that intervention can itself distort the way in which resources are allocated, so any policy needs to be carefully designed, and try to anticipate the indirect consequences.

Policies to address market failure

In seeking to design microeconomic policy to tackle market failure, the vital first step is to understand the source of market failure, as it is important that any policy targets the root cause of the problem. For example, if the market failure arises from information problems, it would seem natural to address this by providing information.

Merit and demerit goods

Consider an example of a merit good. Such a good exists where the decision-maker believes that there is a divergence between the marginal benefit that actually accrues from its consumption.

Figure 19.1 shows how this situation can be analysed.

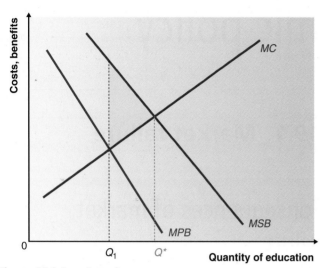

Figure 19.1 A merit good

The example used here is education. In many countries around the world, everyone is required to attend school up to a certain number of years. Part of this requirement may be attributed to a merit good argument. It can be argued that education provides benefits to society in excess of those that are perceived by individuals. In other words, society believes that individuals will derive a benefit from education that they will not realise until after they have acquired that education. Thus, a government may decree that everyone must consume education up to the age of 16, whether they want to or not and whether they have the means to do so or not. This is a merit good argument. In Figure 19.1 marginal social benefit (MSB) is shown as being higher than marginal private benefit (MPB). Thus, society would like to provide Q^* education, where $MSB = MC$ (marginal social cost), but individuals would choose to consume only Q_1 education, where $MPB = MC$, because they do not expect the future benefits to be as high as the government does.

In this case there may be other issues affecting the market for education. For example, there could also be positive externality effects if educated workers were better able to cooperate with each other. There may be a further argument that individuals may fail to demand sufficient education because of information failure: in other words, they may not perceive the full benefits that will arise from education. The situation may be aggravated if parents have the responsibility of financing their children's education, because they are taking decisions *on behalf of* their children. In the case of tertiary education, there is no guarantee that parents will agree with their children about the benefits of a university education – it could go either way.

Another important issue that arises in the context of education concerns equity in access to higher education. Research has

shown that graduates tend to enjoy higher lifetime earnings than non-graduates. However, if some groups have better access to credit markets than others, then those groups may be more able to take advantage of a university education. Specifically, it has been argued that people from low-income households may be discouraged from taking up university places because of failure in credit markets. In other words, the difficulty of raising funds in the present to pay for a university education may prevent people from gaining the longer-term benefits of having received a university education – hence the launching of student loan schemes, which should help to address this particular form of market failure.

In some societies it has been suggested that the merits of education are better perceived by some groups in society than others. Thus in some developing countries, individuals in relatively well-off households demand high levels of education, as they realise the long-run benefits that they can receive in terms of higher earnings – and, perhaps, political influence. In contrast, low-income households in remote rural areas may not see the value of education. As a result, drop-out from secondary – and even primary – education tends to be high. This has been especially noticeable in some countries in sub-Saharan Africa. This is clearly a merit good argument that may need to be addressed by government, perhaps by making primary education compulsory or free – or both.

Other examples of merit goods are museums, libraries and art galleries. These are goods that are provided or subsidised because someone somewhere thinks that communities should have more of them. Economists are wary of playing the merit good card too often, as it entails such a high normative element. It is also difficult sometimes to disentangle merit good arguments from externality effects.

Similar analysis can be supplied in the case of a demerit good. Figure 19.2 shows the market for an opiate drug. Marginal private benefits (MPB) are shown as being much higher than marginal social benefits (MSB), so that in a free market too much of this drug is consumed. Society would like to be at Q^*, but ends up at Q_1. In this particular market, the government may see the marginal social benefit from consuming this drug to be so low (e.g. at MSB^* in the figure) that consumption should be driven to zero.

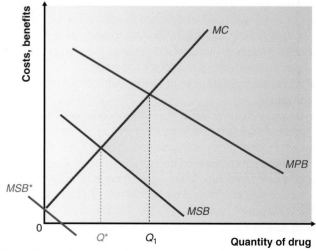

Figure 19.2 A demerit good

Again, this could be interpreted as partly an information problem, in the sense that individual consumers may not perceive the dangers of addiction and thus may overvalue this drug. In addition, addiction would have the effect of making an individual's demand for the good highly inelastic in the long run. However, it is paternalistic of the government to intervene directly for this reason, although it might wish to correct other externalities – for instance, those imposed on others when addicts steal to fund their habit.

An alternative approach is to try to remove the information failure; some governments have adopted this approach in seeking to educate people about the dangers of tobacco smoking.

The market for tobacco is characterised in Figure 19.3. Demand (*MPB*) represents the marginal private benefit that consumers gain from smoking tobacco. However, the government believes that consumers underestimate the damaging effects of smoking, so that the true benefits are given by *MSB* (marginal social benefit). Given the marginal cost (supply) curve, in an unregulated market consumers will choose to smoke up to Q_1 tobacco. The optimum for society, however, is at Q^*.

One way of tackling this problem is through taxation. If the government imposes a tax shown by the red line in Figure 19.3, this effectively shifts the supply curve to the market, as shown in the figure. This raises the price in the market, so consumers are persuaded to reduce their consumption to the optimal level at Q^*. Notice that because the demand curve (*MPB*) is quite steep (relatively inelastic), a substantial tax is needed in order to reach Q^*. Empirical evidence suggests that the demand for tobacco is relatively inelastic – and therefore tobacco taxes need to comprise a large portion of the price of a packet of cigarettes if they are to have an impact on smoking. This analysis will be extended later in the chapter.

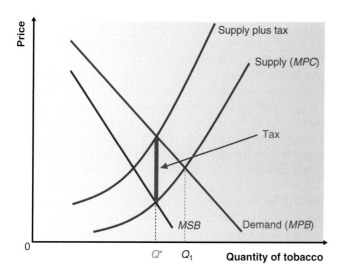

Figure 19.3 Taxing tobacco

Conversely, if the government wishes to encourage the consumption of a merit good, it may do so through subsidies.

Thus, the museum service is subsidised, and the ballet and opera have enjoyed subsidies in the past. Figure 19.4 shows how such a subsidy might be used to affect the quantity of museum services provided. Demand (*MPB*) again shows the demand for museum services from the public, which is below the marginal social benefit (*MSB*) that the authorities perceive to be the true value of museum services. Thus the free-market equilibrium position is at Q_1, although the government believes that Q^* is the socially optimum position. By providing a subsidy, the supply curve is shifted to the right, and consumers will choose to demand the optimum quantity at the subsidised price P_2.

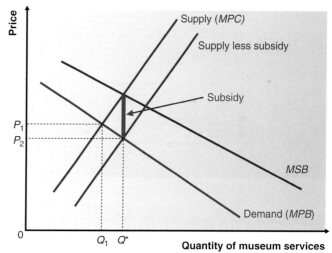

Figure 19.4 Subsidising museums

Externalities

Externalities arise in situations where there are items of cost or benefit associated with transactions, and these are not reflected in market prices. In these circumstances a free market will not lead to an optimum allocation of resources. One approach to dealing with such market situations is to bring those externalities into the market mechanism – a process known as **internalising an externality**. For example, in the case of pollution this principle would entail forcing the polluting firms to face the full social cost of their production activities. This is sometimes known as the *polluter pays* principle.

> **Key term**
>
> **Internalising an externality:** an attempt to deal with an externality by bringing an external cost or benefit into the price system.

Pollution

Figure 19.5 illustrates a negative production externality: pollution. Suppose that firms in the market for chemicals use a production process that emits toxic fumes, thereby imposing costs on society that the firms themselves do not face. In other words, the marginal private costs faced by these firms are less than the marginal social costs that are inflicted on society. As explained earlier in the chapter, firms in this market will choose to produce up to point Q_1 and charge a price of P_1 to consumers. At this point, marginal social benefit is below the marginal cost of producing the chemicals, so it can be claimed that 'too much' of the product is being produced – that society would be better off if production were at Q^*, with a price charged of P^*.

Pollution is a negative production externality

Note that this optimum position is not characterised by *zero* pollution. In other words, from society's point of view it pays to abate pollution only *up to* the level where the marginal benefit of reducing pollution is matched by the marginal cost of doing so. Reducing pollution to zero would be too costly.

How can society reach the optimum output of chemicals at Q^*? In line with the principle that the polluter should pay, one approach would be to impose a tax on firms such that polluters face the full cost of their actions. In Figure 19.5, if firms were required to pay a tax equivalent to the vertical distance between marginal private cost (*MPC*) and marginal social cost (*MSC*), they would choose to produce at Q^*, paying a tax equal to the green line on the figure.

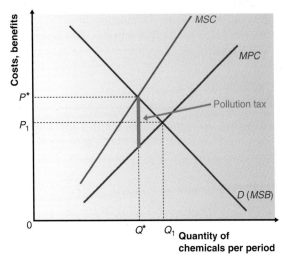

Figure 19.5 Pollution

An alternative way of looking at this question is via a diagram showing the marginal benefit and marginal cost of emissions reduction. In Figure 19.6, *MB* represents the marginal social benefits from reducing emissions of some pollutant and MC is the marginal costs of reducing emissions. The optimum amount of reduction is found where marginal benefit equals marginal cost, at e^*. Up to this point, the marginal benefit to society of reducing emissions exceeds the marginal cost of the reduction, so it is in the interest of society to reduce pollution. However, beyond that point the marginal cost of reducing the amount of pollution exceeds the benefits that accrue, so society will be worse off. Setting a tax equal to t^* in Figure 19.6 will induce firms to undertake the appropriate amount of emission reduction.

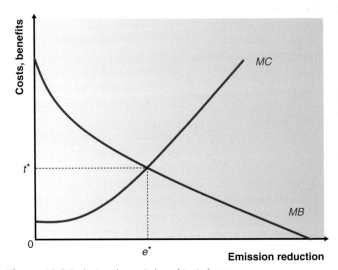

Figure 19.6 Reducing the emission of toxic fumes

This is not the only way of reaching the objective, however. Figure 19.6 suggests that there is another possibility – namely, to impose environmental standards, and to prohibit emissions beyond e^*. This amounts to controlling quantity rather than price; and, if the government has full information about marginal costs and marginal benefits, the two policies will produce the equivalent result.

Either of the approaches outlined above will be effective – *if* the authorities have full information about the marginal costs and benefits. But how likely is this? There are many problems with this proviso. The measurement of both marginal benefits and marginal costs is fraught with difficulties.

The marginal social benefits of reducing pollution cannot be measured with great precision, for many reasons. It may be argued that there are significant gains to be made in terms of improved health and lower death rates if pollution can be reduced, but quantifying this is not straightforward. Even if it were possible to evaluate the saving in resources that would need to be devoted to future medical care resulting from the pollution, there are other considerations: quantification of the direct improvements to quality of life; whether or not to take international effects into account when formulating domestic policy; and the appropriate discount rate for evaluating benefits that will be received in the future. Moreover, the environmentalist and the industrialist may well arrive at different evaluations of the benefits of pollution control, reflecting their different viewpoints.

The measurement of costs may also be problematic. For example, it is likely that there will be differences in efficiency between firms. Those using modern technology may face lower costs than those using relatively old capital equipment. Do the authorities try to set a tax that is specific to each firm to take such differences into account? If they do not, but instead set a flat-rate tax, then the incentives may be inappropriate. This would mean that a firm using modern technology would face the same tax as one using old capital. The firm using new capital would then tend to produce too little output relative to those using older, less efficient capital.

Tradable pollution permits

Another approach is to use a *tradable pollution permit system*, under which the government issues or sells permits to firms, allowing them to pollute up to a certain limit. These permits are then tradable, so that firms that are relatively 'clean' in their production methods and do not need to use their full allocation of permits can sell their polluting rights to other firms, whose production methods produce greater levels of pollution.

One important advantage of such a scheme lies in the incentives for firms. Firms that pollute because of their relatively inefficient production methods will find they are at a disadvantage because they face higher costs. Rather than continuing to purchase permits, they will find that they have an incentive to produce less pollution – which, of course, is what the policy is intended to achieve. In this way, the permit system uses the market to address the externality problem – in contrast to direct regulation of environmental standards, which tries to solve pollution by overriding the market.

A second advantage is that the overall level of pollution can be controlled by this system, as the authorities control the total amount of permits that are issued. After all, the objective of the policy is to control the overall level of pollution, and a mixture of 'clean' and 'dirty' firms may produce the same amount of total emissions as uniformly 'slightly unclean' firms.

However, the permit system may not be without its problems. In particular, there is the question of enforcement. For the system to be effective, sanctions must be in place for firms that pollute beyond the permitted level, and there must be an operational and cost-effective method for the authorities to check the level of emissions.

Furthermore, it may not be a straightforward exercise for the authorities to decide upon the appropriate number of permits to issue in order to produce the desired reduction in emission levels. Some alternative regulatory systems share this problem, as it is not easy to measure the extent to which marginal private and social costs diverge.

One possible criticism that is unique to a permit form of regulation is that the very different levels of pollution produced by different firms may seem inequitable – as if those firms that can afford to buy permits can pollute as much as they like. On the other hand, it might be argued that those most likely to suffer from this are the polluting firms, whose public image is likely to be tarnished if they acquire a reputation as heavy polluters. This possibility might strengthen the incentives of such firms to clean up their production. Taking the strengths and weaknesses of this approach together, it seems that on balance such a system could be effective in regulating pollution.

Global warming

Global warming is widely seen to require urgent and concerted action at a worldwide level. The Kyoto summit of 1997 laid the foundations for action, with many of the developed nations agreeing to take action to reduce emissions of carbon dioxide and other 'greenhouse' gases that are seen to be causing climate change. Although the USA withdrew from the agreement in early 2001, apparently concerned that the US economy might be harmed, in November of that year 178 other countries did reach agreement on how to enforce the Kyoto Accord. The absence of US cooperation is potentially significant, however, as the USA is the world's largest emitter of carbon dioxide, responsible for about a quarter of the world's greenhouse gas emissions.

At the heart of the Kyoto Accord was the decision of countries to reduce their greenhouse gas emissions by an agreed percentage by 2010. The method chosen to achieve these targets was based on a tradable pollution permit system. This was seen to be especially demanding for countries such as Japan, whose industry is already relatively energy-efficient. Japan was thus concerned that there should be sufficient permits available for purchase. More explicitly, it was concerned that sloppy compliance by Russia would limit the amount of permits on offer. The issues of monitoring and compliance are thus seen as critical.

The NIMBY syndrome

One problem that arises in trying to deal with externalities is that you cannot please all of the people all of the time. For example, it may well be that it is in society's overall interests to relocate unsightly facilities – it may even be that everyone would agree about this; but such facilities have to be located somewhere, and someone is almost bound to object because they are the ones to suffer. This is the **NIMBY (not in my back yard)** syndrome.

Key term

NIMBY (not in my back yard): a syndrome under which people are happy to support the construction of an unsightly or unsocial facility, so long as it is not in their neighbourhood (back yard).

For example, many people would agree that it is desirable for the long-run sustainability of the economy that cleaner forms of energy are developed. One possibility is to build wind farms. People may well be happy for these to be constructed – *as long as* they do not happen to be living near them. This may not be the best example, however, as the effectiveness of wind farms is by no means proven, and there is a strong movement against their use on these grounds.

Exercise 19.1

You discover that your local authority has chosen to locate a new landfill site for waste disposal close to your home. What costs and benefits for society would result? Would these differ from your private costs and benefits? Would you object?

Property rights

The existence of a system of secure property rights is essential as an underpinning for the economy. The legal system exists in part to enforce property rights, and to provide the set of rules under which markets operate. When property rights fail, there is a failure of markets.

One of the reasons underlying the existence of some externalities is that there is a failing in the system of property rights. For example, think about the situation in which a factory is emitting toxic fumes into a residential district. One way of viewing this is that the firm is interfering with local residents' clean air. If those residents could be given property rights over clean air, they could require the firm to compensate them for the costs it is inflicting. However, the problem is that, with such a wide range of people being affected to varying degrees (according to prevailing winds and how close they live to the factory), it is impossible in practical terms to use the assignment of property rights to internalise the pollution externality. This is because the problem of coordination requires high transaction costs in order for property rights to be individually enforced. Therefore, the government effectively takes over the property rights on behalf of the residents, and acts as a collective enforcer.

Nobel Prize winner Ronald Coase argued that externality effects could be internalised in conditions where property rights could be enforced, and where the transaction costs of doing so were not too large.

Summary

- Free markets do not always lead to the best possible allocation of resources: there may be market failure.
- Governments may wish to intervene to try to correct market failure and thus bring about a better outcome for society as a whole.
- In seeking to counter the harmful effects of externalities, governments look for ways of internalising the externality, by bringing external costs and benefits within the market mechanism.
- For example, the 'polluter pays' principle argues that the best way of dealing with a pollution externality is to force the polluter to face the full costs of its actions.
- Attempts have been made to tackle pollution through taxation, the regulation of environmental standards and the use of pollution permits.
- In some cases the allocation of property rights can be effective in curbing the effects of externalities – so long as the transaction costs of implementing it are not too high.

19.2 Imperfect competition

Chapter 16 discussed the model of perfect competition, and argued that the entry and exit of firms ensures that a market will evolve towards a situation in which price is equal to marginal cost. In the absence of production externalities, marginal cost here can be interpreted as marginal social costs – it is the cost to society of producing the marginal unit of this good. If the demand curve is interpreted as representing marginal social benefit, then this is tantamount to saying that under long-run perfectly competitive equilibrium, marginal social cost is equal to marginal social benefit – and there is no market failure present.

However, this rests on the assumption that the market is perfectly competitive. Firms are fairly passive actors under perfect competition, responding perhaps rather tamely to changes in consumer preferences. The real world is not necessarily like that, and in many markets, firms have more power over their actions than has so far been suggested.

In the extreme, there are markets in which production is dominated by a single firm. In 1998 Microsoft was taken to court in the USA, accused of abusing its dominant position. At the time, Microsoft was said to control 95% of the market for operating systems for PC computers – and not just in the USA: this was 95% of the *world* market. When a firm achieves such dominance, there is no guarantee that it will not try to exploit its position at the expense of consumers.

The very fact that there was a court case against Microsoft bears witness to the need to protect consumers against dominant firms. In the UK, the Competition and Markets Authority took on responsibility for competition policy in April 2014, with a brief to promote competition, both within and outside the UK, for the benefit of consumers. This body brought together the Competition Commission and certain consumer functions of the Office of Fair Trading. Other countries around the world have similar agencies whose aim is to protect consumers. For example, the Competition Commission of Pakistan was established in 2007; New Zealand has its Commerce Commission; Mauritius similarly has its Competition Commission. Malaysia has the Malaysia Competition Commission (MyCC), with the stated aim to 'protect the competitive process for the benefit of businesses, consumers and the economy' (*www.mycc.gov.my*).

This is one example of how imperfect competition can lead to a distortion in the allocation of resources. Firms with a dominant position in a market may be able to drive prices to a level that is above marginal cost; consumers then lose out in terms of allocative efficiency. How is the market affected if the extent of competition in it is limited? By restricting output and raising price, firms are able to increase their profits, effectively increasing the market price to a level above the marginal cost of production. This implies that there is a loss of allocative efficiency in this situation. From society's point of view, too little of the product is being produced. To the extent that the monopolist is a member of society, the increase in producer surplus might be regarded as a redistribution from consumers to producers. However, more crucial is the fact that there is a loss of consumer surplus that is not recoverable.

Regulation of monopoly and mergers

The effectiveness of the market system in allocating resources requires prices to act as signals to producers about consumer demand. Firms will be attracted into activities where consumer demand is buoyant and profitability is high, and will tend to exit from activities in which demand is falling and profitability is low.

This process relies on the existence of healthy competition between firms, and on freedom of entry to and exit from markets. In the absence of these conditions, resources may not be best allocated according to the pattern of consumer demand. For example, if there are barriers to entering a market, the existing firms in the market may have the power to restrict output and raise the price, producing less of the product than is desirable for society. As explained in Chapter 18, such barriers to entry may arise from features such as economies of scale or the patent system. In some situations, existing firms may take strategic action to deter entry.

This is one area of the economy in which governments often choose to intervene to protect consumers. As mentioned above,

this may operate through the establishment of an official body such as a Competition Commission. Such bodies have the power to investigate markets that appear to be overly concentrated or in which competition appears weak. They can also take action to encourage competition in markets. This is known as **competition policy**.

> ### Key term
>
> Competition policy: a set of measures designed to promote competition within markets to encourage efficiency and protect consumer interests.

One of the knotty problems that arises here is that if firms benefit from economies of scale, it may be more productively efficient to allow large firms to develop than to fragment the industry into lots of small firms in the name of encouraging competition. Thus, the authorities have to find a way of balancing the potential costs of losing allocative efficiency against the potential benefits of productive efficiency.

In seeking to evaluate the situation in a market, the competition authorities face a series of challenges. Apart from anything else, market conditions are always changing, so it becomes difficult to observe how firms are behaving. For example, the prices of foreign holidays could rise for many reasons other than the abuse of market power by tour operators or other firms in the market. Such price rises could be because of increases in the price of oil, affecting transport costs. They could equally be the result of changes in the foreign exchange rate, or many other factors affecting the market. The authorities thus need to be careful in coming to a decision. They may need to investigate a variety of market conditions before judging a firm's behaviour. A key issue may be the extent to which the market is contestable. In other words, a judgment needs to be made as to the extent to which a firm faces potential competition, which may restrict the amount of market power that it can wield.

Merger and acquisition activity has led to the creation of some giant firms in recent years, and one responsibility of the competition authorities is to monitor such activity, which may be seen to have an effect on concentration in markets. An example is the way that the UK's Competition and Markets Authority blocked a proposed takeover of Manchester United Football Club by BSkyB on the grounds that this would not be beneficial for consumers.

Economic analysis and competition policy

Chapter 18 undertook a comparison of perfect competition and monopoly, and it is this analysis that lies at the heart of competition policy. Figure 19.7 should remind you of the discussion.

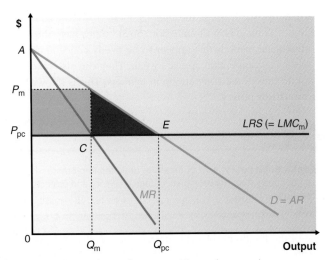

Figure 19.7 Comparing perfect competition and monopoly

Here it is assumed there is an industry that can operate either under perfect competition, with a large number of small firms, or as a multi-plant monopolist. For simplicity, it is also assumed that there is no cost difference between the two forms of market structure, so that the long-run supply schedule (*LRS*) under perfect competition is perceived by the monopolist as its long-run marginal cost curve. In other words, in long-run equilibrium the monopoly varies output by varying the number of plants it is operating.

Under perfect competition, output would be set at Q_{pc} and market price would be P_{pc}. However, a monopolist will choose to restrict output to Q_m and raise the price to P_m. Consumer surplus will be reduced by this process, partly by a transfer of the blue rectangle to the monopoly as profits, and partly by the red triangle of deadweight loss. It is this deadweight loss that imposes a cost on society that competition policy is intended to alleviate.

Indeed, this analysis led to a belief in what became known in the economics literature as the *structure–conduct–performance paradigm*. At the core of this belief, illustrated in Figure 19.8, is the simple idea that the structure of a market, in terms of the number of firms, determines how firms in the market conduct themselves, which in turn determines how well the market performs in achieving productive and allocative efficiency.

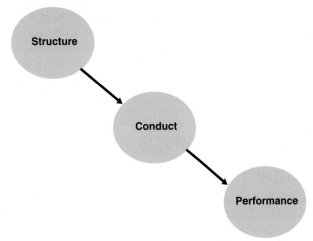

Figure 19.8 The structure–conduct–performance paradigm

Thus, under perfect competition firms cannot influence price, and all firms act competitively to maximise profits, thereby producing good overall performance of the market in allocating resources. On the other hand, under monopoly the single firm finds that it can extract consumer surplus by using its market power, and as a result the market performs less well.

This point of view leads to a distrust of monopoly – or, indeed, of any market structure in which firms might be seen to be conducting themselves in an anti-competitive manner. Moreover, it is the structure of the market itself that leads to this anti-competitive behaviour.

If this line of reasoning is accepted, then monopoly is always bad, and mergers that lead to higher concentration in a market will always lead to allocative inefficiency in the market's performance. Thus, legislation in the USA tends to presume that a monopoly will work against the interests of society. However, there are some important issues to consider before pinning too much faith on this assumption.

Cost conditions

The first issue concerns the assumption that cost conditions will be the same under perfect competition as under monopoly. This simplifies the analysis, but there are many reasons to expect economies of scale in a number of economic activities. If this assumption is correct, then a monopoly firm will face lower cost conditions than would apply under perfect competition.

In Figure 19.9, *LRS* represents the long-run supply schedule if an industry is operating under perfect competition. The perfectly competitive equilibrium would be at output level Q_{pc} with the price at P_{pc}. However, suppose that a monopolist had a strong cost advantage, and was able to produce at constant long-run marginal cost LMC_m. It would then maximise profit by choosing the output Q_m, where MR_m is equal to LMC_m, and would sell at a price P_m. In this situation the monopolist could actually produce more output at a lower price than a firm operating under perfect competition.

Notice that in the monopoly situation the market does not achieve allocative efficiency, because with these cost conditions setting price equal to marginal cost would require the firm to produce Q^* output. However, this loss of allocative efficiency is offset by the improvements in productive efficiency that are achieved by the monopoly firm.

It could be argued that the monopolist should be regulated, and forced to produce at Q^*. However, what incentives would this establish for the firm? If a monopolist knows that whenever it makes supernormal profits the regulator will step in and take them away, it will have no incentive to operate efficiently. Indeed, Joseph Schumpeter argued that monopoly profits were an incentive for innovation, and would benefit society, because only with monopoly profits would firms be able to engage in research and development (R&D). In other words, it is only when firms are relatively large, and when they are able to make supernormal profits, that they are able to devote resources to R&D. Small firms operating in a perfectly competitive market do not have the resources or the incentive to be innovative.

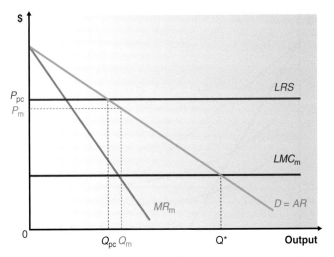

Figure 19.9 Suppose that monopoly offers much better cost conditions?

Figure 19.10 illustrates a less extreme case. As before, equilibrium under perfect competition produces output at Q_{pc} and price at P_{pc}. The monopoly alternative faces lower long-run marginal cost, although with a less marked difference than before: here the firm produces Q_m output in order to maximise profits, and sets price at P_m.

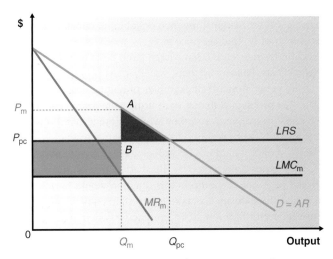

Figure 19.10 Cost conditions again – a less extreme example

Analysis of this situation reveals that there is a deadweight loss given by the red triangle; this reflects the allocative inefficiency of monopoly. However, there is also a gain in productive efficiency represented by the green rectangle. This is part of monopoly profits, but under perfect competition it was part of production costs. In other words, production under the monopoly is less wasteful in its use of resources.

Is society better off under monopoly or under perfect competition? In order to evaluate the effect on total welfare, it is necessary to balance the loss of allocative efficiency (the red triangle) against the gain in productive efficiency (the green rectangle). In Figure 19.10 it would seem that the rectangle is larger than the triangle, so society overall is better off with the monopoly. Of course, there is also the distribution of income to take into account – the

area $P_m ABP_{pc}$ would be part of consumer surplus under perfect competition, but under monopoly becomes part of the firm's profits.

Contestability

A second important issue concerns contestability, which was introduced in Chapter 18. If barriers to entry into the market are weak, and if the sunk costs of entry and exit are low, the monopoly firm will need to temper its actions to avoid potential entry.

Thus, in judging a market situation, the degree of contestability is important. If the market is perfectly contestable, then the monopoly firm cannot set a price that is above average cost without allowing hit-and-run entry. In this case, the regulator does not need to intervene. Even without perfect contestability, the firm may need to set a price that is not so high as to induce entry. In other words, it may choose not to produce at the profit-maximising level of output, and to set a price below that level.

Concentration and collusion

The structure–conduct–performance argument suggests that it is not only monopolies that should be the subject of competition policy, but any market in which firms have some influence over price. In other words, oligopolies also need careful attention, because of the danger that they will collude, and act *as if* they were a joint monopoly. After all, it was argued that where a market has just a small number of sellers there may be a temptation to collude, either in a cartel or tacitly. For this reason, government authorities may be wary of markets in which concentration ratios are simply high, even if not 100%.

For this reason, it is important to examine whether a concentrated market is *always* and *necessarily* an anti-competitive market. This is tantamount to asking whether structure necessarily determines conduct. A high concentration ratio may mean that there are a small number of firms of more or less equal size, or it could mean that there is one large firm and a number of smaller competitors. In the latter case you might expect the dominant firm to have sufficient market power to control price.

With a small number of equally sized firms it is by no means certain that they will agree to collude. They may be very conscious of their respective market shares, and so act in an aggressively competitive way in order to defend them. This may be especially true where the market is not expanding, so that a firm can grow only at the expense of the other firms. Such a market could well display intense competition, causing it to drift towards the competitive end of the scale. This would suggest that the authorities should not presume guilt in a merger investigation, since the pattern of market shares may prove significant in determining the firms' conduct, and hence the performance of the market.

Globalisation

Another significant issue is that a firm that comes to dominate a domestic market may still face competition in the broader global market. This may be especially significant within the European single market.

In this regard, there has been a longstanding debate about how a domestic government should behave towards its large firms. Some economists believe that the government should allow such firms to dominate the domestic market in order that they can become 'national champions' in the global market. This has been especially apparent in the airline industry, where some national airlines are heavily subsidised by their national governments in order to allow them to compete internationally. Others have argued that if a large firm faces competition within the domestic market, this should help to encourage its productive efficiency, enabling it to become more capable of coping with international competition.

Exercise 19.2

Discuss whether a concentrated market is necessarily anti-competitive.

Summary

- Competition policy refers to a range of measures designed to promote competition in markets and to protect consumers in order to enhance the efficiency of markets in resource allocation.
- One view is that market structure determines the conduct of firms within a market, and this conduct then determines the performance of the market in terms of allocative efficiency.
- A profit-maximising monopolist will produce less output at a higher price than a perfectly competitive market, causing allocative inefficiency.
- However, there may be situations in which the monopolist can enjoy economies of scale, and thereby gain in productive efficiency.
- In the presence of contestability, a monopolist may not be able to charge a price above average cost without encouraging hit-and-run entry.
- In a concentrated market, the pattern of market shares may influence the intensity of competition between firms.
- A firm that is a monopoly in its own country may be exposed to competition in the international markets in which it operates.

19.3 Natural monopoly and privatisation

Chapter 16 noted the case of the natural monopoly, and hinted that this poses particular problems with regard to allocative efficiency. Figure 19.11 involves an industry with substantial economies of scale relative to market demand – indeed, the minimum efficient

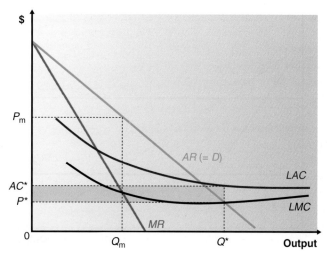

Figure 19.11 A natural monopoly

scale is beyond the market demand curve. (In other words, long-run average cost is still falling beyond market demand.)

This market is almost bound to end up as a monopoly, because the largest firm is always able to dominate the market and undercut smaller competitors, as it has a natural cost leadership position. If the monopoly chooses to maximise profits, it will set marginal revenue equal to marginal cost, choose output Q_m and set price at P_m.

Such industries tend to have large fixed costs relative to marginal costs. Railway systems, water or gas supply and electricity generation are all examples of natural monopolies.

The key problem is that, if such firms were forced to set a price equal to marginal cost, they would make a loss. If the firm in Figure 19.11 were required to set price equal to marginal cost, i.e. at P^*, then it would not be viable: average cost would be AC^*, with losses represented by the shaded area on the diagram.

In the past, one response to this situation would have been to nationalise the industry (i.e. take it into state ownership), since no private-sector firm would be prepared to operate at a loss, and the government would not allow firms running such natural monopolies to act as profit-maximising monopolists making supernormal profits.

In order to prevent the losses from becoming too substantial, many utilities such as gas and electricity supply adopted a pricing system known as a *two-part tariff system*, under which all consumers paid a monthly charge for being connected to the supply, and on top of that a variable amount based on usage. In terms of Figure 19.11, the connection charge would cover the difference between AC^* and P^*, spread across all consumers, and the variable charge would reflect marginal cost.

However, as time went by this sort of system came to be heavily criticised. In particular, it was argued that the managers of the nationalised industries were insufficiently accountable. This could be regarded as an extreme form of the principal–agent problem, in which the consumers (the principals) had very little control over the actions of the managers (their agents), a situation leading to widespread X-inefficiency and waste.

In the 1980s such criticism led to widespread privatisation in the UK (i.e. the transfer of nationalised industries into private ownership), one central argument being that now at least the managers would have to be accountable to their shareholders, which would encourage an increase in efficiency. However, this did not remove the original problem: that they were natural monopolies. So privatisation was accompanied by the imposition of a regulatory system to ensure that the newly privatised firms did not abuse their monopoly situations.

Wherever possible, privatisation was also accompanied by measures to encourage competition, which was seen as an even better way to ensure efficiency improvements. This proved to be more feasible in some industries than in others, because of the nature of economies of scale – there is little to be gained by requiring that there must be several firms in a market where the economies of scale can be reaped only by one large firm. However, the changing technology in some of the industries did allow some competition to be encouraged, especially in telecommunications.

Where it was not possible, or feasible, to encourage competition, regulation was seen as the solution. Attention of the regulatory bodies focused on price, and the key control method was to allow price increases each year at a rate that was a set amount below changes in the retail price index (RPI). This became known as the (RPI − X) rule, and was widely used, the idea being that it would force companies to look for productivity gains to eliminate the X-inefficiency that had built up. The X refers to the amount of productivity gain that the regulator believes can be achieved, expressed in terms of the change in average costs. For example, if the regulator believed that it was possible to achieve productivity gains of 5% per year, and if the RPI was increasing at a rate of 10% per year, then the maximum price increase that would be allowed in a year would be 10% − 5% = 5%.

There are problems inherent in this approach. For example, how does the regulator set X? This is problematic in a situation where the company has better information about costs than the regulator – another instance of the problems caused by the existence of asymmetric information. There is also the possibility that the firm will achieve its productivity gains by reducing the quality of the product, or by neglecting long-term investment for the future and allowing maintenance standards to lapse.

It is also important to realise that as time goes by, if the (RPI − X) system is effective, the X-inefficiency will be gradually squeezed out, and the X will have to be reduced as it becomes ever more difficult to achieve productivity gains.

In some cases **regulatory capture** is a further problem. This occurs when the regulator becomes so closely involved with the firm it is supposed to be regulating that it begins to champion its cause rather than imposing tough rules where they are needed.

Key term

Regulatory capture: a situation in which the regulator of an industry comes to represent its interests rather than regulating it.

An alternative method of regulation would be to place a limit on the rate of return the firm is permitted to make, thereby preventing it from making supernormal profits. This too may affect the incentive mechanism: the firm may not feel the need to be as efficient as possible, or may fritter away some of the profits in managerial perks to avoid declaring too high a rate of return.

Exercise 19.3

Find out what official agencies are responsible for competition policy in the country in which you study. How effective do you think they have been in promoting competition amongst firms in the economy?

Summary

- Natural monopolies pose particular problems for policy, as setting price equal to marginal cost forces such firms to make a loss.
- In the past, many such industries were run by the state as nationalised industries.
- However, this led to widespread X-inefficiency.
- In the UK, many of these industries were privatised after 1979.
- Regulation was put into place to ensure that the newly privatised firms did not abuse their market positions.
- Prices were controlled through the application of the (RPI − X) rule.
- In some cases regulatory capture was a problem, whereby the regulators became too close to their industries.

19.4 Inequality in income and wealth

All societies are characterised by some inequality – and some poverty. Although the two are related, they are not the same. Indeed, poverty might be regarded as one aspect of inequality.

If there is a wide gap between the richest and poorest households, it is important to evaluate just how poor are those poorest households, and whether they should be regarded as being 'in poverty'. This requires a definition of poverty.

One approach is to define a basket of goods and services that is regarded as being the minimum required to support human life. Households that are seen to have income that falls short of allowing them to purchase that basic bundle of goods would be regarded as being in **absolute poverty**. Worldwide, people are regarded as being in extreme poverty if their income is below $1.25 per person per day. For example, in Pakistan, 22.6% of the population fall into this category, compared with 41.6% in India.

22.6% of the population of Pakistan fall into the absolute poverty category

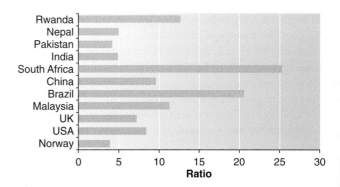

Note: Countries are in descending order of GDP per capita in PPP$.
Source: Human Development Report

Figure 19.12 Quintile income ratio

Poverty can also be defined in relative terms. If a household has insufficient income for the members of the household to participate in the normal social life of the country, then they are said to be in **relative poverty**. This is also defined in terms of a poverty line. In the UK, the line is defined as 50% of the median adjusted household disposable income (the median is the income of the middle-ranked household).

Key terms

Absolute poverty: the situation of a household whose income is insufficient to purchase the minimum bundle of goods and services needed to sustain human life.

Relative poverty: the situation in which household income falls below 50% of median-adjusted household income.

The percentage falling below the poverty line is not a totally reliable measure, as it is also important to know how far below the poverty line households are falling. Thus the income gap (the distance between household income and the poverty line) is useful for measuring the intensity of poverty as well as its incidence.

Inequality is a broader concept, as it relates to the overall distribution of income and wealth within society. Measuring inequality provides a substantial challenge, as it requires data on income at the household level across the country. One measure is to look at the ratio of the richest 20% of households to the poorest 20%, which is known as the *quintile income ratio*. Figure 19.12 shows this ratio for a selection of countries. In this group, Pakistan shows the least inequality, with the richest 20% of the population receiving 4.7 times as much as the poorest 20%. At the other extreme is South Africa, where the richest 20% receive more than 20 times as much income as the poorest 20%.

There is widespread agreement that governments should take responsibility for ensuring an acceptable distribution of income and wealth in society, and should also be responsible for alleviating poverty. The focus in this chapter will be on income redistribution.

The Lorenz curve

Although the usual types of graph are not well suited to presenting such data visually, there is a method of presenting the data visually via the **Lorenz curve**. Some Lorenz curves are shown in Figure 19.13.

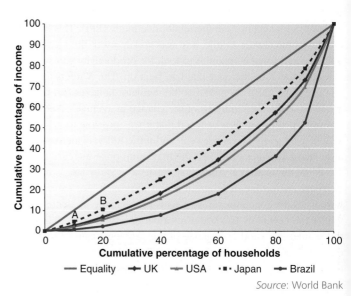

Source: World Bank

Figure 19.13 Lorenz curves

Key term

Lorenz curve: a graphical way of depicting the distribution of income within a country.

Lorenz curves are constructed as follows. First the households in a country are ranked in order of income. Then the shares of different income groups in total income are calculated. For example, consider Japan in Figure 19.13. The poorest 10% ('decile') of households receive 4.8% of total household incomes, and this is plotted as point **A** on the figure. The poorest 20% ('quintile') of households receive 10.6% of total income (point **B**), and so on. Plotting such points across the whole income distribution provides the Lorenz curve.

Suppose that income were perfectly equally distributed between households. In other words, suppose the poorest 10% of households received exactly 10% of income, the poorest 20% received 20% and so on. The Lorenz curve would then be a straight line going diagonally across the figure.

To interpret the country curves, the closer a country's Lorenz curve is to the diagonal equality line, the more equal is the distribution. You can see from the figure that Japan comes closest to the equality line. The UK and the US curves are closer together, but there seems to be slightly more inequality in the USA, as its Lorenz curve is further from the equality line. Brazil has also been included on the figure, as an example of a society in which there is substantial inequality.

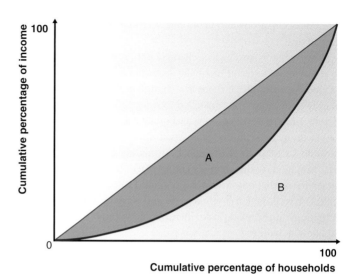

Figure 19.14 The Gini index and the Lorenz curve

This is often expressed as a percentage (but sometimes as a proportion). The closer the Gini index is to 100, the further the Lorenz curve is from equality, and thus the more unequal is the income distribution. The Gini index values for the countries in Figure 19.13 are shown in Table 19.2.

Table 19.2 The Gini index

Country	Gini index
USA	40.8
UK	36.1
Japan	24.9
Brazil	60.0

Key term

Gini index: a measure of the degree of inequality in a society.

Exercise 19.4

Use the data provided in Table 19.1 to calculate the ratios of top decile income to bottom decile income, and of top quintile income to bottom quintile income. Then draw Lorenz curves for the two countries, and compare the inequalities shown for Belarus and South Africa with each other and with the countries already discussed.

Table 19.1 Income distribution in South Africa and Belarus

	Percentage share of income or consumption	
	South Africa	**Belarus**
Lowest decile	1.1	5.1
Lowest quintile	2.9	11.4
Second quintile	5.5	15.2
Third quintile	9.2	18.2
Fourth quintile	17.7	21.9
Highest quintile	64.8	33.3
Highest decile	45.9	20.0

Source: *World Bank*

Causes of inequality and poverty

Inequality arises through a variety of factors, some relating to the operation of the labour market, some reflecting patterns in the ownership of assets, and some arising from the actions of governments.

Labour market explanations

Chapter 20 will set out a number of ways in which the labour market is expected to give rise to inequalities in earnings. This arises from demand and supply conditions in labour markets, which respond to changes in the pattern of consumer demand for goods and services, and changes in international comparative advantage between countries. Furthermore, differences between

The Gini index

The Lorenz curve is fine for comparing income distribution in just a few countries. However, it would also be helpful to have an index that could summarise the relationship in a numerical way. The **Gini index** does just this. It is a way of trying to quantify the equality of income distribution in a country, and is obtained by calculating the ratio of the area between the equality line and the country's Lorenz curve (area *A* in Figure 19.14) to the whole area under the equality line (area *A* + *B* in Figure 19.14).

different occupations and economic sectors reinforce income inequalities.

However, a by-product of changes in the structure of the economy may be rising inequality between certain groups in society. For example, if there is a change in the structure of employment away from unskilled jobs towards occupations that require a higher level of skills and qualifications, then this could lead to an increase in inequality, with those workers who lack the skills to adapt to changing labour market conditions being disadvantaged by the changes taking place. In other words, if the premium that employers are prepared to pay in order to hire skilled or well-qualified workers rises as a result of changing technology in the workplace, then people without those skills are likely to suffer.

The decline in the power of the trade unions may have contributed to the situation, as low-paid workers may find that their unions are less likely to be able to offer employment protection. It has been argued that this is a good thing if it increases the flexibility of the labour market. However, again a balance is needed between worker protection and having free and flexible markets.

Ownership of assets

Perhaps the most obvious way in which the ownership of assets influences inequality and its changes through time is through inheritance. When wealth accumulates in a family over time, and is then passed down to succeeding generations, this generates a source of inequality that does not arise from the current state of the economy or the operations of markets.

It is important to be aware that income and wealth are not the same. Income is a 'flow' that households receive each period, whereas wealth is a 'stock', being the accumulation of assets that a household owns. Wealth tends to be considerably less evenly distributed than income. In the UK in the mid-2000s, the wealthiest 10% of households in the UK were estimated to own 44% of the identified wealth.

Notice, however, that although wealth and income are not the same thing, inequality in wealth can also lead to inequality in income, as wealth (the ownership of assets) leads to an income flow, from rents and profits.

Demographic change

A feature of many countries in recent years has been a change in the age structure of the population. Improved medical drugs and treatments have meant that people are living longer, and this has combined with low fertility rates to bring about an increase in the proportion of the population who are in the older age groups. This has put pressure on the provision of pensions, and increased the vulnerability of this group in society. State pensions have been funded primarily by the contributions of those in work, but if the number of people of working age falls as a proportion of the whole population, then this funding stream comes under pressure.

Many countries have seen a change in the age structure of the population

19.5 The effectiveness of government intervention

There are several ways in which government intervention influences the distribution of income in a society, although not all of these interventions are expressly intended to do so. Most prominent is the range of transfer payments and taxation that has been implemented. The extent to which such measures are effective varies between countries. In some developing economies, the lack of resources and the institutional structure may impede the effectiveness of measures – for example, if the government lacks the infrastructure needed to collect taxes effectively.

Benefits

There are two forms of benefit that households can receive to help equalise the income distribution. First, there are various types of cash benefit, designed to protect families whose income in certain circumstances would otherwise be very low. Second, there are benefits in kind, such as health and education. These accrue to individual households depending on the number of members of the household and their age and gender. Such benefits were discussed in Chapter 6.

Taxation

Direct taxes (taxes levied directly on incomes) tend to be progressive. In other words, higher income groups pay tax at a higher rate. In 2010/11, people earning more than £1 million in the year on average paid 44.4% of the income as tax, whereas those in the £15,000–19,999 income range paid 11.3% in tax.

In the UK the main direct taxes are income tax, corporation tax (paid by firms on profits), capital gains tax (paid by individuals who sell assets at a profit), inheritance tax and petroleum revenue tax (paid by firms operating in the North Sea). There is also the council tax, collected by local authorities. Many countries have a similar range of direct taxes in place.

With a tax such as income tax, its progressive nature is reflected in the way the tax rate increases as an individual moves into a higher income range. In other words, the **marginal tax rate** increases as income increases. The **progressive** nature of the tax ensures that it does indeed help to reduce inequality in income distribution — although its effects are less than those of the cash benefits discussed earlier.

The effect of **indirect taxes**, on the other hand, can sometimes be **regressive**: in other words, indirect taxes may impinge more heavily on lower-income households. Indirect taxes are taxes that are paid on items of expenditure, rather than on income.

Key terms

Direct tax: a tax levied directly on income.

Marginal tax rate: tax on additional income, defined as the change in tax payments due divided by the change in taxable income.

Progressive tax: a tax in which the marginal tax rate rises with income, i.e. a tax bearing most heavily on the relatively well-off members of society.

Indirect tax: a tax on expenditure, e.g. VAT.

Regressive tax: a tax bearing more heavily on the relatively poorer members of society.

One reason for using indirect taxes such as a sales tax is to raise funds for the government in order to finance the expenditure that they undertake. You might think that raising money in this way to provide goods and services that would otherwise not be provided would be a benefit to society. But there is a downside to this action, even if all the funds raised by a sales tax are spent wisely. In addition to allowing governments to raise revenue, a sales tax can be used to try to correct a market failure.

Why should some of these taxes be regressive? Take the tobacco tax. In the first place, the number of smokers is higher among lower-income groups than among the relatively rich – research has shown that only about 10% of people in professional groups now smoke compared with nearly 40% of those in unskilled manual groups. Second, expenditure on tobacco tends to take a lower proportion of income of the rich compared with that of the poor, even for those in the former group who do smoke. Thus, the tobacco tax falls more heavily on lower-income groups than on the better-off. It is estimated that for households in the bottom quintile of the income distribution in 2008/09, indirect taxes accounted for 28.2% of disposable income, compared with 12.8% for households in the top quintile.

Extension: welfare loss of a sales tax

An important question is how a sales tax will affect total welfare in society. Consider Figure 19.15, which shows the market for DVDs. Suppose that the government imposes a specific tax on DVDs. This would have the effect of taking market equilibrium from the free-market position at P^* with quantity traded at Q^* to a new position, with price now at P_t and quantity traded at Q_t. Remember that the price rises by less than the amount of the tax, implying that the incidence of the tax falls partly on buyers and partly on sellers. In Figure 19.15 consumers pay more of the tax (the area P^*P_tBE) than the producers (who pay FP^*EG). The effect on society's overall welfare will now be examined.

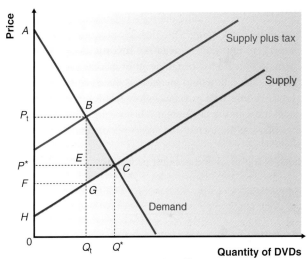

Figure 19.15 A sales tax and economic welfare

Remember that the total welfare that society receives from consuming a product is the sum of consumer and producer surplus. The situation before and after the sales tax is as follows. Before the tax, consumer surplus is given by the area AP^*C and producer surplus is given by the triangle P^*CH. How about afterwards? Consumer surplus is now the smaller triangle AP_tB, and producer surplus is FGH. The area P_tBGF is the revenue raised by the government from the tax, which should be included in total welfare on the assumption that the government uses this wisely. The total amount of welfare is now $ABGH$. If you compare these total welfare areas before and after the tax, you will realise that they differ by the area BCG. This triangle represents a deadweight loss that arises from the imposition of the tax. It is sometimes referred to as the **excess burden** of the tax.

Key term

Excess burden of a sales tax: the deadweight loss to society following the imposition of a sales tax.

So, even where the government intervenes to raise funding for its expenditure – and spends wisely – a distortion is introduced to resource allocation, and society must bear a loss of welfare.

The poverty trap

Problems can arise when a system of means-tested benefits co-exists with a progressive income tax structure. Consider the incentives facing a person who is receiving welfare benefits because of unemployment or low pay. Such an individual may find that there is no incentive to take a job or to work more hours because the gain in terms of earnings would be lower than the loss of benefits payments or the increase in tax liability. This is known as the **poverty trap**.

This creates a dilemma for the authorities, who would like to provide protection for the poor, but also want to offer incentives for people to work. Finding the right balance between these two things can be challenging. One possible solution that had been proposed is to introduce a **negative income tax**. Under such a system, people with a certain level of income would pay no tax, and the tax rate would increase as their income grew above that level. People with incomes below that level would receive payment through the tax system. This would remove the poverty trap by phasing the increase in tax as people earned more income. However, no such system has yet been implemented because of logistical and political problems.

Key terms

Poverty trap: a situation in which an individual has no incentive to take a job or to work longer hours because the loss of benefits and/or increase in tax payments outweighs the gain from increased earnings.

Negative income tax: a system whereby support for people on low incomes is provided through the tax system rather than by the direct payment of benefits.

Prohibition

Another example of how government intervention may have unintended effects is when action is taken to prohibit the consumption of a demerit good. Consider the case of a hard drug. It can be argued that there are substantial social disbenefits arising from the consumption of hard drugs, and that addicts and potential addicts are in no position to make informed decisions about their consumption of them. One response to such a situation is to consider making the drug illegal – that is, to impose **prohibition**.

Key term

Prohibition: an attempt to prevent the consumption of a demerit good by declaring it illegal.

Figure 19.16 shows how the market for a hard drug might look. You may wonder why the demand curve takes on this shape. The argument is that there are two types of drug user. There are the recreational users, who will take the drug if it is available at a reasonable price, but who are not addicts. In addition, there is a hard core of habitual users who are addicts, whose demand for the drug is highly inelastic. Thus, at low prices demand is relatively elastic because of the presence of the recreational users, who are relatively price-sensitive. At higher prices the recreational users drop away, and demand from the addicts is highly price-inelastic. Suppose that the supply in free market equilibrium is given by S_0; the equilibrium will be with price P_0 and quantity traded Q_0. If the drug is made illegal, this will affect supply. Some dealers will leave the market to trade in something else, and the police will succeed in confiscating a certain proportion of the drugs in the market. However, they are unlikely to be totally successful, so supply could move to, say, S_1.

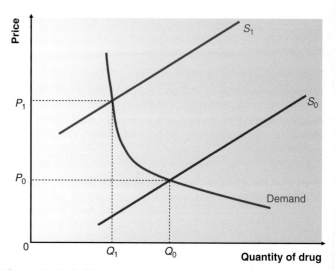

Figure 19.16 Prohibition

In the new market situation, price rises substantially to P_1, and quantity traded falls to Q_1. However, what has happened is that the recreational users have dropped out of the market, leaving a hard core of addicts who will pay any price for the drug, and who may resort to muggings and robberies in order to finance their habit. This behaviour clearly imposes a new sort of externality on society. And the more successful the police are in confiscating supplies, the higher the price will be driven. There may thus be disadvantages in using prohibition as a way of discouraging consumption of a demerit good.

Achieving a balance of taxation between direct and indirect taxes is an important aspect of the government's redistributive policy. A switch in the balance from direct to indirect taxes will tend to increase inequality in a society. It is also important to be aware that taxation may have intergenerational effects. High taxation today in order to fund expenditure on today's generation may leave future generations struggling for resources. This is related to the notion of sustainable development. On the other hand, high taxation today in order to provide improved living conditions for future generations may increase poverty in the current generation. There is thus a need to maintain a careful balance across the generations, which requires the government to be able to take a long-term view. In this context, having a stable political environment is significant, as without such stability, governments may be tempted to take a short-run view.

Equity and efficiency

There may be times when there is a trade-off between efficiency and equity in policy design. A policy designed to promote allocative efficiency may not work to offer sufficient protection to the poor. A tax on tobacco intended to correct a market failure may fall disproportionately on low-income groups within society. Here again, balance is needed to ensure that policy offers sufficient protection for the poor without compromising the efficiency with which markets are able to work in allocating resources.

Price stabilisation

For many developing countries that rely on exporting primary products, the instability of commodity prices may be damaging, as this makes it difficult to forecast export revenues from one year to the next. Governments may look for policies that can help to stabilise prices, and thus revenues. One possibility is to launch a buffer stock scheme, under which the scheme buys the commodity when supply is buoyant and prices are low, and sells it when supply is low, and prices are correspondingly high. This has the effect of stabilising the price within the domestic economy. However, such schemes are costly to operate. The storage costs can be high, and if an attempt is made to stabilise the price at too high a level, stocks will accumulate, adding further to storage costs in the long run.

In some less-developed countries, governments have tried to appease urban populations by holding prices of key staple food items low. This can cause a market failure by harming the incentives for farmers to improve production.

Incentives and nudge theory

One of the key insights of economics concerns the importance of incentives in influencing the behaviour of economic agents. This is crucial for the design of microeconomic policy, and governments need to understand how people respond to different types of incentives.

The use of indirect taxes to correct market failure rests on the assumption that people respond to prices, so that an increase in the price of a good will tend to lead to a reduction in demand

Chapter 14 introduced the ideas emerging from behavioural economics. This branch of economic analysis blends ideas from psychology with microeconomic analysis, and suggests that people do not always act rationally as traditional economic analysis tends to assume. One aspect of this is that people may not always react solely to price signals in their decision making. They may make decisions based on habit or buy goods on impulse. Indeed, they may take decisions based on humanitarian motives, or through a sense of loyalty.

From a government perspective, this analysis may offer new ways of inducing people to take decisions that are beneficial for society. This is sometimes known as **nudge theory**, under which governments may be able to nudge people towards taking decisions and adopting behaviour that the authorities want to encourage.

Key term

Nudge theory: a notion based on behavioural economics suggesting that people can be nudged towards behaviour that is beneficial for society.

One example of this is where shops are encouraged to display healthy foods in more prominent positions to encourage impulse buying. The idea has also been used to develop campaigns that encourage social behaviour – for example, signs that say 'Take your litter home – other people do'. This tries to persuade people that it is their responsibility to behave in certain ways.

Exercise 19.5

Discuss how you would design a policy or campaign to encourage social behaviour by people living near you.

Government failure

Some roles are critical for a government to perform if a mixed economy is to function effectively. A vital role is the provision by the government of an environment in which markets can operate effectively. There must be stability in the political system if firms and consumers are to take decisions with confidence about the future. And there must be a secure system of property rights, without which markets could not be expected to work.

In addition, there are sources of market failure that require intervention. This does not necessarily mean that governments need to substitute markets with direct action. However, it does mean that they need to be more active in markets that cannot operate effectively, while at the same time performing an enabling role to encourage markets to work well whenever this is feasible. However, in some circumstances, **government failure** can arise. This refers to a situation in which government intervention introduces new market distortions, thus offsetting the intended effects.

Key term

Government failure: a misallocation of resources arising from government intervention.

Such intervention entails costs. There are costs of administering, and costs of monitoring the policy to ensure that it is working as intended. This includes the need to look out for the unintended distorting effects that some policies can have on resource allocation in a society. It is therefore important to check that the marginal costs of implementing and monitoring policies do not exceed their marginal benefits.

Summary

- The government can influence the distribution of income by benefit payments and direct taxes.
- Income tax is progressive when higher income households pay higher rates of tax.
- Indirect taxes are often regressive because of the patterns of consumer spending.
- The financial account measures transactions in financial assets, including investment flows.
- There may sometimes be a trade-off between equity and efficiency in the effects of microeconomic policy interventions.
- Incentives are important in influencing the behaviour of economic agents.
- Some government interventions may have unintended consequences, resulting in a situation known as government failure.

20 The labour market

The economic analysis of labour markets sheds light on a range of topical issues. How are wages determined? Differences in wages between people in different occupations and with different skills can be contentious. For example, why should footballers or pop stars earn such high wages compared with nurses or firefighters? This chapter begins by looking at the labour market as an application of demand and supply analysis. The chapter also explores the role of trade unions and the government in wage determination.

Learning outcomes

After studying this chapter, you should:
- understand that the demand for labour is a derived demand
- be aware of the relationship between labour input and total and marginal physical product
- understand the concept of marginal revenue product
- be familiar with how a profit-maximising firm chooses the quantity of labour input to use in production
- be aware of the factors that influence the elasticity of demand for labour
- understand the decision of an individual worker as regards labour supply
- be aware of the choice made by the individual worker between work and leisure
- understand the reasons for earnings differentials between people working in different occupations and with different skills
- understand ways in which labour markets may be imperfect
- be aware of the operation of a labour market in which there is a monopsony buyer of labour
- be aware of ways in which governments may cause imperfections in labour markets through their interventions
- understand how unemployment may arise in a market
- understand the role of trade unions in the economy
- understand the effects of trade union activity on the labour market.

20.1 Demand for labour

Firms are involved in production. They organise the factors of production in order to produce output. Labour is one of the key factors of production used by firms in this process, but notice that labour is valued not for its own sake, but for the output that it produces. In other words, the fundamental reason for firms to demand labour is for the revenue that can be obtained from selling the output that is produced by using labour. The demand for labour is thus a **derived demand**, and understanding this is crucial for an analysis of the labour market.

To illustrate this, consider a firm that manufactures cricket bats. The firm hires labourers to operate the machinery that is used in production. However, the firm does not hire a labourer because he or she is a nice person. The firm aims to make profit by selling the cricket bats produced, and the labourer is needed because of the labour services that he or she provides. This notion of derived demand underpins the analysis of labour markets.

Key terms

Derived demand: demand for a good not for its own sake, but for what it produces – for example, labour is demanded for the output that it produces.

Total physical product of labour (TPP_L): in the short run, the total amount of output produced at different levels of labour input with capital held fixed.

Marginal physical product of labour (MPP_L): the additional quantity of output produced by an additional unit of labour input.

Chapter 16 introduced the notion of the short-run production function, showing the relationship between the quantity of labour input used and the quantity of output produced. Figure 20.1 should remind you of this. Here TPP_L is the **total physical product of labour**. As this is a short-run production function, capital cannot be varied: remember, this is how the short run is defined in this context.

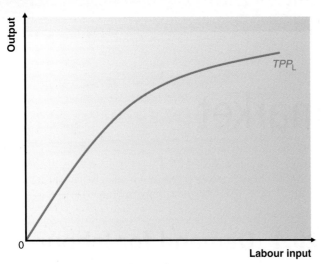

Figure 20.1 A short-run production function

The curve is drawn to show diminishing returns to labour. In other words, as labour input increases, the amount of additional output that is produced diminishes. This is because capital becomes relatively scarcer as the amount of labour increases without a corresponding increase in capital.

In examining the demand for labour, it is helpful to work with the **marginal physical product of labour**, which is the amount of additional output produced if the firm increases its labour input by 1 unit (e.g. adding 1 more person-hour), holding capital constant. This is in fact given by the slope of TPP_L. An example is shown in Figure 20.2. When labour input is relatively low, such as at L_0, the additional output produced by an extra unit of labour is relatively high, at q_0, since the extra unit of labour has plenty of capital with which to work. However, as more labour is added, the marginal physical product falls, so at L_1 labour the marginal physical product is only q_1.

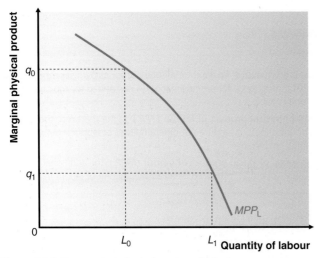

Figure 20.2 The marginal physical product of labour

What matters to the firm is the revenue that it will receive from selling the additional output produced. In considering the profit-maximising amount of labour to employ, therefore, the firm

needs to consider the marginal physical product multiplied by the marginal revenue received from selling the extra output, which is known as the **marginal revenue product of labour (MRP_L)**.

Key term

Marginal revenue product of labour (MRP_L): the additional revenue received by a firm as it increases output by using an additional unit of labour input, i.e. the marginal physical product of labour multiplied by the marginal revenue received by the firm.

If the firm is operating in a perfectly competitive market, then marginal revenue and price are the same and MRP_L is MPP_L multiplied by the price. However, if the firm faces a downward-sloping demand curve, it has to reduce the price of its product in order to sell the additional output. Marginal revenue is then lower than price, as the firm must lower the price on all of the output that it sells, not just on the last unit sold.

Consider a firm operating under perfect competition, and setting out to maximise profits. Figure 20.3 shows the marginal revenue product curve. The question to consider is how the firm chooses how much labour input to use. This decision is based partly on knowledge of the MRP_L, but it also depends on the cost of labour.

The main cost of using labour is the wages paid to the workers. There may be other costs – hiring costs and so on – but these can be set aside for the moment. Assuming that the labour market is perfectly competitive, so that the firm cannot influence the market wage and can obtain as much labour as it wants at the going wage rate, the wage can be regarded as the **marginal cost of labour (MC_L)**.

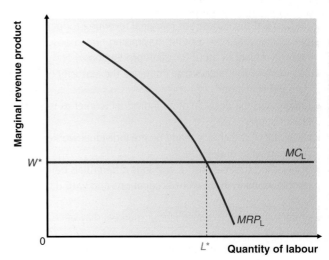

Figure 20.3 The labour decision of a profit-maximising firm in a competitive market

If the marginal revenue received by the firm from selling the extra output produced by extra labour (i.e. the MRP_L) is higher than the wage, then hiring more labour will add to profits. On the other hand, if the MRP_L is lower than the wage, then the firm is already hiring too much labour. Thus, it pays the firm to hire labour up to the point where the MRP_L is just equal to the wage. On Figure 20.3, if the wage is W^*, the firm is maximising profits at L^*. The MRP_L curve thus represents the firm's demand for labour curve. This approach is known as **marginal productivity theory**.

Key terms

Marginal cost of labour (MC_L): the additional cost to a firm of an additional unit of labour input.

Marginal productivity theory: an approach based on the assumption that the demand for labour depends upon the marginal revenue product of labour.

This profit-maximising condition can be written as:

wage = marginal revenue × marginal physical product of labour

which is the same as:

$$\text{marginal revenue} = \frac{\text{wage}}{MPP_L} \text{ [= marginal cost]}$$

Remember that capital input is fixed for the firm in the short run, so the wage divided by the MPP_L is the firm's cost per unit of output at the margin. This shows that the profit-maximising condition is the same as that derived for a profit-maximising firm in Chapter 16: in other words, profit is maximised where marginal revenue equals marginal cost. This is just another way of looking at the firm's decision.

Exercise 20.1

Table 20.1 shows how the total physical product of labour varies with labour input for a firm operating in competitive product and labour markets. The price of the product is $5 and the wage rate is $30.

Table 20.1 A profit-maximising firm

Labour input per period	Output (goods per period)
0	0
1	7
2	15
3	22
4	27
5	29

a Calculate the marginal physical product of labour at each level of labour input.
b Calculate the marginal revenue product of labour at each level of labour input.
c Plot the MRP_L on a graph and identify the profit-maximising level of labour input.
d Suppose that the firm faces fixed costs of $10. Calculate total revenue and total costs at each level of labour input, and check the profit-maximising level.

Factors affecting the position of the demand for labour curve

There are a number of factors that determine the position of a firm's labour demand curve. First, anything that affects the marginal physical product of labour will also affect the MRP_L. For example, if a new technological advance raises the productivity of labour, it will also affect the position of the MRP_L. In Figure 20.4 you can see how the demand for labour would change if there were an increase in the marginal productivity of labour as a result of new technology. Initially demand is at MRP_{L0}, but the increased technology pushes the curve to MRP_{L1}. If the wage remains at W^*, the quantity of labour hired by the firm increases from L_0 to L_1. Similarly, in the long run, if a firm expands the size of its capital stock, this will also affect the demand for labour.

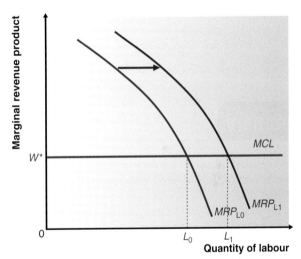

Figure 20.4 The effect of improved technology

As MRP_L is given by MPP_L multiplied by marginal revenue, any change in marginal revenue will also affect labour demand. In a perfectly competitive product market, this means that any change in the price of the product will also affect labour demand. For example, suppose there is a fall in demand for a firm's product, so that the equilibrium price falls. This will have a knock-on effect on the firm's demand for labour, as illustrated in Figure 20.5. Initially, the firm was demanding L_0 labour at the wage rate W^*, but the fall in demand for the product leads to a fall in marginal revenue product (even though the physical productivity of labour has not changed), from MRP_{L0} to MRP_{L1}. Only L_1 labour is now demanded at the wage rate W^*. This serves as a reminder that the demand for labour is a derived demand that is intimately bound up with the demand for the firm's product.

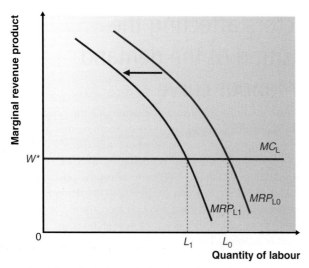

Figure 20.5 The effect of a fall in the demand for a firm's product on the demand for labour

A number of possible reasons could underlie a change in the price of a firm's product – it could reflect changes in the price of other goods, changes in consumer incomes or changes in consumer preferences. All of these indirectly affect the demand for labour.

Summary

- The demand for labour is a derived demand, as the firm wants labour not for its own sake, but for the output that it produces.
- In the short run, a firm faces diminishing returns to increases in labour input if capital is held constant.
- The marginal physical product of labour is the amount of output produced if the firm employs an additional unit of labour, keeping capital input fixed.
- The marginal revenue product of labour is the marginal physical product multiplied by marginal revenue.
- With perfect competition in the product market, marginal revenue and price are the same, but if the firm needs to reduce its price in order to sell additional units of output, then marginal revenue is smaller than price.
- A profit-maximising firm chooses labour input such that the marginal cost of labour is equal to the marginal revenue product of labour. This is equivalent to setting marginal revenue equal to marginal cost.
- The firm has a downward-sloping demand curve for labour, given by the marginal revenue product curve.
- The position of the firm's labour demand curve depends on those factors that influence the marginal physical product, such as technology and efficiency, but also on the price of the firm's product.

20.2 Elasticity of the demand for labour

In addition to the factors affecting the position of the demand for labour curve, it is also important to examine its shape. In particular, what factors affect the firm's elasticity of demand for labour with respect to changes in the wage rate? In other words, how sensitive is a firm's demand for labour to a change in the wage rate (the cost of labour)?

In studying AS economics, you will have been introduced to the influences on the price elasticity of demand, and identified the most important as being the availability of substitutes, the relative size of expenditure on a good in the overall budget and the time period over which the elasticity is measured (see Chapter 4). In looking at the elasticity of demand for labour, similar influences can be seen at work.

One significant influence on the elasticity of demand for labour is the extent to which other factors of production, such as capital, can be substituted for labour in the production process. If capital or some other factor can be readily substituted for labour, then an increase in the wage rate (ceteris paribus) will induce the firm to reduce its demand for labour by relatively more than if there were no substitute for labour. The extent to which labour and capital are substitutable varies between economic activities, depending on the technology of production, as there may be some sectors in which it is relatively easy for labour and capital to be substituted, and others in which it is quite difficult.

Second, the share of labour costs in the firm's total costs is important in determining the elasticity of demand for labour. In many service activities, labour is a highly significant share of total costs, so firms tend to be sensitive to changes in the cost of labour. However, in some capital-intensive manufacturing activity, labour may comprise a much smaller share of total production costs.

Third, as was argued above, capital will tend to be inflexible in the short run. Therefore, if a firm faces an increase in wages, it may have little flexibility in substituting towards capital in the short run, so the demand for labour may be relatively inelastic. However, in the longer term, the firm will be able to adjust the factors of production towards a different overall balance. Therefore, the elasticity of demand for labour is likely to be higher in the long run than in the short run.

These three influences closely parallel the analysis of what affects the price elasticity of demand. However, as the demand for labour is a derived demand, there is an additional influence that must be taken into account: the price elasticity of demand for the product. The more price elastic is demand for the product, the more sensitive will the firm be to a change in the wage rate, as high elasticity of demand for the product limits the extent to which an increase in wage costs can be passed on to consumers in the form of higher prices.

In order to derive an industry demand curve for labour, it is necessary to add up the quantities of labour that firms in that industry would want to demand at any wage rate, given the price of the product. As individual firms' demand curves are downward sloping, the industry demand curve will also slope downwards. In other words, more labour will be demanded at a lower wage rate, as shown in Figure 20.6.

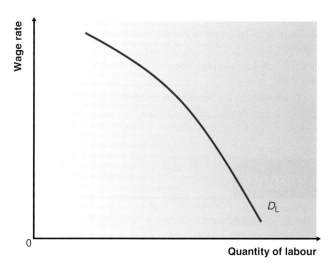

Figure 20.6 An industry demand for labour curve

Exercise 20.2

Using diagrams, explain how each of the following will affect a firm's demand for labour:

a A fall in the selling price of the firm's product.
b Adoption of working practices that improve labour productivity.
c An increase in the wage (in a situation where the firm must accept the wage as market determined).
d An increase in the demand for the firm's product.

Summary

- The elasticity of demand for labour depends upon the degree to which capital may be substituted for labour in the production process.
- The share of labour in a firm's total costs will also affect the elasticity of demand for labour.
- Labour demand will tend to be more elastic in the long run than in the short run, as the firm needs time to adjust its production process following a change in market conditions.
- As the demand for labour is a derived demand, the elasticity of labour demand will also depend on the price elasticity of demand for the firm's product.

20.3 Labour supply

So far, labour supply has been considered only as it is perceived by a firm, and the assumption has been that the firm is in a perfectly competitive market for labour, and cannot influence the 'price' of labour. Hence the firm sees the labour supply curve as being perfectly elastic, as drawn in Figure 20.3, where labour supply was described as MC_L.

However, for the industry as a whole, labour supply is unlikely to be flat. Intuitively, you might expect to see an upward-sloping labour supply curve. The reason for this is that more people will tend to offer themselves for work when the wage is relatively high. But this is only part of the background to the industry labour supply curve.

An increase in the wage rate paid to workers in an industry will have two effects. On the one hand, it will tend to attract more workers into that industry, thereby increasing labour supply. However, the change may also affect the supply decisions of workers already in that industry, and for existing workers an increase in the wage rate may have ambiguous effects.

Individual labour supply

Consider an individual worker who is deciding how many hours of labour to supply. Every choice comes with an opportunity cost, so if a worker chooses to take more leisure time, he or she is choosing to forgo income-earning opportunities. In other words, the wage rate can be seen as the opportunity cost of leisure. It is the income that the worker has to sacrifice in order to enjoy leisure time.

Now think about the likely effects of an increase in the wage rate. Such an increase raises the opportunity cost of leisure. This in turn has two effects. First, as leisure time is now more costly, there will be a substitution effect against leisure. In other words, workers will be motivated to work longer hours.

However, as the higher wage brings the worker a higher level of real income, a second effect comes into play, encouraging the consumption of more goods and services – including leisure, if it is assumed that leisure is a normal good.

Notice that these two effects work against each other. The substitution effect encourages workers to offer more labour at a higher wage because of the effect of the change in the opportunity cost of leisure. However, the real income effect encourages the worker to demand more leisure as a result of the increase in income. The net effect could go either way.

It might be argued that at relatively low wages the substitution effect will tend to be the stronger. However, as the wage continues to rise, the income effect may gradually become stronger, so that at some wage level the worker will choose to supply less labour and will demand more leisure. The individual labour supply curve will then be backward bending, as shown in Figure 20.7, where an increase in the wage rate above W^* induces the individual to supply fewer hours of work in order to enjoy more leisure time.

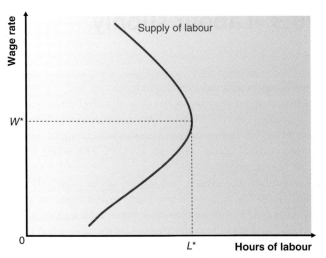

Figure 20.7 A backward-bending individual labour supply curve

It is important to realise that decisions about labour supply may also be influenced by job satisfaction. A worker who finds his or her work to be satisfying may be prepared to accept a lower wage than a worker who really hates every minute spent at work. Indeed, firms may provide other **non-pecuniary benefits** – in other words, firms may provide benefits that are not fully reflected in wages. These are sometimes known as *fringe benefits*. This might include a subsidised canteen or other social facilities. It could also include in-work training, pension schemes or job security. If this is the case, then in choosing one job over another, workers may consider not only the wage rate, but the overall package offered by employers. In other words, by providing non-pecuniary benefits, firms may effectively shift the position of their labour supply curves, as workers will be prepared to supply more labour at any given wage rate. It may also be seen as a way in which firms can encourage loyalty, and thus hold on to workers when the job market is tight.

In-work training is one of the fringe benefits that may influence a worker's decision to change jobs

Key term

Non-pecuniary benefits: benefits offered to workers by firms that are not financial in nature.

Industry labour supply

At industry level, the labour supply curve can be expected to be upward sloping. Although individual workers may display backward-bending supply curves, when workers in a market are aggregated, higher wages will induce people to join the market, either from outside the workforce altogether or from other industries where wages have not risen.

Summary

- For an individual worker, a choice needs to be made between income earned from working and leisure.
- The wage rate can be seen as the opportunity cost of leisure.
- An increase in the wage rate will encourage workers to substitute work for leisure through the substitution effect.
- There is also an income effect, which may mean that workers will demand more leisure at higher income levels.
- If the income effect dominates the substitution effect, then the individual labour supply curve may become backward bending.
- However, when aggregated to the industry level, higher wages will encourage more people into the industry, so the industry supply curve is not expected to be backward bending.

20.4 Labour market equilibrium

Bringing demand and supply curves together for an industry shows how the equilibrium wage is determined. Figure 20.8 shows a downward-sloping labour demand curve (D_L) based on marginal productivity theory, and an upward-sloping labour supply curve (S_L). Equilibrium is found at the intersection of demand and supply. If the wage is lower than W^* employers will not be able to fill all their vacancies, and will have to offer a higher wage to attract more workers. If the wage is higher than W^* there will be an excess supply of labour, and the wage will drift down until W^* is reached and equilibrium obtained.

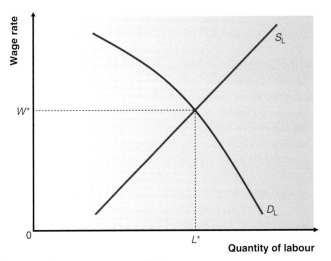

Figure 20.8 Labour market equilibrium

Comparative static analysis can be used to examine the effects of changes in market conditions. For instance, a change in the factors that determine the position of the labour demand curve will induce a movement of labour demand and an adjustment in the equilibrium wage. Suppose there is an increase in the demand for the firm's product. This will lead to a rightward shift in the demand for labour, say from D_{L0} to D_{L1} in Figure 20.9. This in turn will lead to a new market equilibrium, with the wage rising from W_0 to W_1.

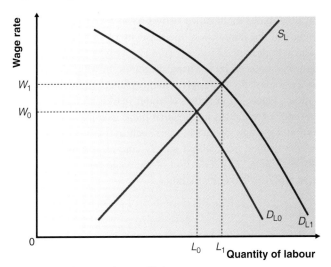

Figure 20.9 Labour market equilibrium

This may not be the final equilibrium position, however. If the higher wages in this market now encourage workers to switch from other industries in which wages have not risen, this will lead to a longer-term shift to the right of the labour supply curve. In a free market, the shift will continue until wage differentials are no longer sufficient to encourage workers to transfer.

Exercise 20.3

Sketch a diagram to analyse the effects on labour market equilibrium if there is a fall in the selling price of a firm's product.

Summary

- Labour market equilibrium is found at the intersection of labour demand and labour supply.
- This determines the equilibrium wage rate for an industry.
- Comparative static analysis can be used to analyse the effects of changes in market conditions.
- Changes in relative wages between sectors may induce movement of workers between industries.

20.5 Labour markets

So far, the focus has been on the demand and supply of labour, seen sometimes through the eyes of a firm, sometimes through the eyes of a worker and sometimes by looking at an industry labour market. It is important to realise that these are separate levels of analysis. In particular, there is no single labour market in an economy, any more than there is a single market for goods. In reality, there is a complex network of labour markets for people with different skills and for people in different occupations, and there are overlapping markets for labour corresponding to different product markets.

Transfer earnings and economic rent
Transfer earnings

Many factors of production have some flexibility about them, in the sense that they can be employed in a variety of alternative uses. A worker may be able to work in different occupations and industries; computers can be put to use in a wide range of activities. The decision to use a factor of production for one particular job rather than another carries an opportunity cost, which can be seen in terms of the next best alternative activity in which that factor could have been employed.

For example, consider a woman who chooses to work as a waitress because the pay is better than she could obtain as a shop assistant. By making this choice, she forgoes the opportunity to work at the department store. The opportunity cost is seen in terms of this forgone alternative. If the department store were to raise its rates of pay in order to attract more staff, there would come a point where the waitress might reconsider her decision and decide to be a shop assistant after all, as the opportunity cost of being a waitress has risen.

The threshold at which this decision is taken leads to the definition of transfer earnings. **Transfer earnings** are defined in terms of the minimum payment that is required in order to keep a factor of production in its present use.

Key term

Transfer earnings: the minimum payment required to keep a factor of production in its present use.

Economic rent

In a labour market, transfer earnings can be thought of as the minimum payment that will keep the marginal worker in his or her present occupation or sector. This payment will vary from worker to worker; moreover, where there is a market in which all workers receive the same pay for the same job, there will be some workers who receive a wage in excess of their transfer earnings. This excess of payment to a factor over and above what is required to keep it in its present use is known as **economic rent**.

Key term

Economic rent: a payment received by a factor of production over and above what would be needed to keep it in its present use.

The total payments to a factor can thus be divided between these two – part of the payment is transfer earnings, and the remainder is economic rent.

Probably the best way of explaining how a worker's earnings can be divided between transfer earnings and economic rent is through an appropriate diagram. Figure 20.10 illustrates the two concepts. In the labour market as drawn, firms' demand for labour is a downward-sloping function of the wage rate. Workers' supply of labour also depends on the wage rate, with workers being prepared to supply more labour to the labour market at higher wages. Equilibrium is the point at which demand equals supply, with wage rate W^* and quantity of labour L^*.

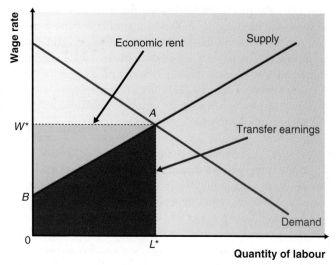

Figure 20.10 Transfer earnings and economic rent

Think about the nature of the labour supply curve. It reveals how much labour the workers are prepared to supply at any given wage rate. At the equilibrium wage rate W^*, there is a

worker who is supplying labour at the margin. If the wage rate were to fall even slightly below W^*, the worker would withdraw from this labour market, perhaps to take alternative employment in another sector or occupation. In other words, the wage rate can be regarded as the transfer earnings of the marginal worker. A similar argument can be made about any point along the labour supply curve.

This means that the area under the supply curve up to the equilibrium point can be interpreted as the transfer earnings of workers in this labour market. In Figure 20.10 this is given by the area $OBAL^*$.

Total earnings are given by the wage rate multiplied by the quantity of labour supplied (here, area OW^*AL^*). Economic rent is thus that part of total earnings that is not transfer earnings. In Figure 20.10 this is the triangle BW^*A. The rationale is that this area represents the total excess that workers receive by being paid a wage (W^*) that is above the minimum required to keep them employed in this market.

If you think about it, you will see that this is similar to the notion of producer surplus, which is the difference between the price received by firms for a good or service and the price at which the firms would have been prepared to supply that good or service.

The balance between transfer earnings and economic rent

What determines the balance between the two aspects of total earnings? In this connection, the elasticity of supply of labour is of critical importance.

This can be seen by studying diagrams showing varying degrees of elasticity of supply. First, consider two extreme situations. Figure 20.11 shows a labour market in which supply is perfectly elastic. This implies that there is limitless supply of labour at the wage rate W. In this situation there is no economic rent to be gained from labour supply, and all earnings are transfer earnings. Any reduction of the wage below W will mean that all workers leave the market.

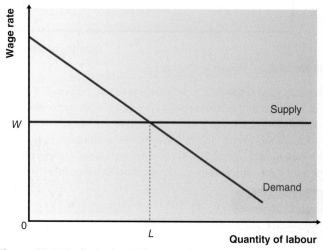

Figure 20.11 Perfectly elastic labour supply

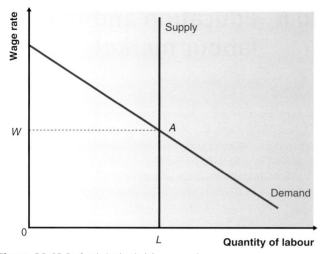

Figure 20.12 Perfectly inelastic labour supply

Now consider Figure 20.12. Here labour supply is perfectly inelastic. There is a fixed amount of labour being supplied to the market and, whatever the wage rate, that amount of labour remains the same. Another way of looking at this is that there is no minimum payment needed to keep labour in its present use. Now the entire earnings of the factor are made up by economic rent (i.e. the area 0*WAL*).

This illustrates how important the elasticity of labour supply is in determining the balance between transfer earnings and economic rent. The more inelastic supply is, the higher the proportion of total earnings that is made up of economic rent.

Surgeons and butchers: the importance of supply

Consider an example of differential earnings – say, surgeons and butchers. First think about the surgeons. Surgeons are in relatively inelastic supply, at least in the short run. The education required to become a surgeon is long and demanding, and is

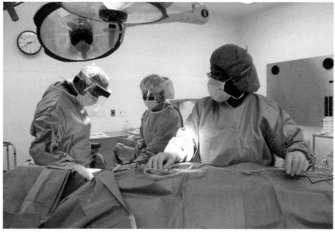

You need certain skills and abilities to become a surgeon

certainly essential for entry into the occupation. Furthermore, not everyone is cut out to become a surgeon, as this is a field that requires certain innate abilities and talents. This implies that the supply of surgeons is limited and does not vary a great deal with the wage rate. If this is the case, then the earnings of surgeons are largely made up of economic rent.

The situation may be reinforced by the fact that, once an individual has trained as a surgeon, there may be few alternative occupations to which, if disgruntled, he or she could transfer. There is a natural limit to how many surgeons there are, and to their willingness to exit from the market.

How about butchers? The training programme for butchers is less arduous than for surgeons, and a wider range of people are suitable for employment in this occupation. Labour supply for butchers is thus likely to be more elastic than for surgeons, and so economic rent will be relatively less important than in the previous case. If butchers were to receive high enough wages, more people would be attracted to the trade and wage rates would eventually fall.

In addition, there are other occupations into which butchers can transfer if they want to find another job: they might look to other sections of the catering sector, for example. This reinforces the relatively high elasticity of supply.

The importance of demand

Economic rent has been seen to be more important for surgeons than for butchers, but is this the whole story? The discussion so far has centred entirely on the supply side of the market. But demand is also important.

Indeed, it is the position of the demand curve when interacting with supply that determines the equilibrium wage rate in a labour market. It may well be that the supply of workers skilled in underwater basket weaving is strictly limited; but if there is no demand for underwater basket weavers then there is no scope for that skill to earn high economic rents. In the above example, it is the relatively strong demand for surgeons relative to their limited supply that leads to a relatively high equilibrium wage in the market.

Evaluation

This analysis can be applied to answer some questions that often appear about the labour market. In particular, why should the top footballers and pop stars be paid such high salaries, whereas valued professions such as nurses and firefighters are paid much less?

A footballer such as Wayne Rooney is valued because of the talent that he displays on the pitch, and because of his ability to bring in the crowds who want to see him play. This makes him a good revenue earner for his club, and reflects his high marginal productivity. In addition, his skills are rare – some would say unique. Wayne Rooney is thus in extremely limited supply. This combination of high marginal productivity and limited supply leads to a high equilibrium wage rate.

Wayne Rooney playing for Manchester United

For nurses and firefighters, society may value them highly in one sense – that they carry out a vital, and sometimes dangerous, occupation. However, they are not valued in the sense of displaying high marginal productivity. Furthermore, the supply is by no means as limited as in the case of top-class professional footballers. These factors taken together help to explain why there are such large differences in salaries between occupations. This is one example of how marginal productivity theory helps to explain features of the real world that non-economists often find puzzling.

Summary

- In a modern economy, there is a complex network of labour markets for workers with different skills, working in different occupations and industries.
- The total payments to a factor of production can be separated into transfer earnings and economic rent.
- Transfer earnings represent the minimum payment needed to keep a factor of production in its present use.
- Economic rent is a payment received by a factor of production over and above what would be needed to keep it in its present use.
- The balance between transfer earnings and economic rent depends critically on the elasticity of supply of a particular kind of labour.
- The position of the demand curve is also important.

20.6 Education and the labour market

The above discussion has highlighted the importance of education and training in influencing wage differentials between occupational groups. Education and training might be regarded as a form of barrier to entry into a labour market, affecting the elasticity of supply of labour. Because of differences in innate talents and abilities – not to mention personal inclinations – wage differentials can persist even in the long run in certain occupations. However, economists expect there to be some long-run equilibrium level of differential that reflects the preference and natural talent aspects of various occupations.

Changes in the pattern of consumer demand for goods over time will lead to changes in those equilibrium differentials. For example, during the computer revolution, when firms were increasing their use of computers at work and households were increasing their use of home computers, there was a need for more computer programmers to create the software that people wanted, and a need for more computer engineers to fix the computers when they crashed. This meant that the wage differential for these workers increased. This in turn led to a proliferation of courses on offer to train or retrain people in these skills. Then, as the supply of such workers began to increase, so the wage differential narrowed.

This is what economists would expect to observe if the labour market is working effectively, with wages acting as signals to workers about what skills are in demand. It is part of the way in which a market system guides the allocation of resources.

Individual educational choices

In specific cases, such as that of the computer programmers, you can see how individuals may respond to market signals. Word gets around that computer programmers are in high demand, and individual workers and job-seekers respond to that. However, not all education is geared so specifically towards such specific gaps in the market. How do individuals take decisions about education?

Such a decision can be regarded as an example of cost–benefit analysis. In trying to decide whether or not to undertake further education, an individual needs to balance the costs of such education against its benefits. One important consideration is that the costs tend to come in the short run, but the benefits only in the long run. Much of the discussion of student university tuition fees centres on this issue. Should students incur high debts now in the expectation of future higher earnings? Work through Exercise 20.4 to take this further.

Exercise 20.4

Suppose you are considering undertaking a university education. Compile a list of the benefits and the costs that you expect to encounter if you choose to do so. Discuss how you would go about balancing the benefits and costs, remembering that the timing of these needs to be taken into account.

In Exercise 20.4 you will have identified a range of benefits and costs. On the costs side are the direct costs in terms of tuition fees and living expenses, and there are also opportunity costs – the fact that you will have to delay the time when you start earning an income. But there are benefits to set against these costs, which may include the enjoyment you get from undertaking further study and the fact that university can be a great experience – that is, it can be a consumption good as well as an investment good. And, almost certainly, you have considered the fact that you can expect higher future earnings as a university graduate than as a non-graduate.

In spite of evidence that lifetime earnings can be boosted by education, people may still demand too little education for the best interest of society. This may be because there are externality effects associated with education. Although education has been shown to improve productivity, it has also been found that groups of educated workers are able to cooperate and work together so that collectively they are even more productive than they are as individuals. From this point of view, an individual worker may not perceive the full social benefit of higher education.

Figure 20.13 is a reminder of this argument. If marginal social benefit (MSB) is higher than marginal private benefit (MPB), there is a tendency for individuals to demand too little education, choosing to acquire Q_1 education rather than the amount Q^*, which is the best for society. This argument may be used to suggest that government should encourage people to undertake more education.

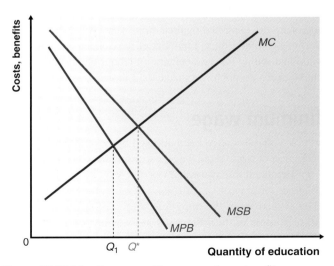

Figure 20.13 Education as a positive consumption externality

Summary

- Wage differentials may act as signals to guide potential workers in their demand for training and retraining.
- People demand education partly for the effect it will have on their future earnings potential.
- Externality effects may mean that people choose to demand less education than is desirable for society as a whole.

20.7 Market failure in labour markets

There are many ways in which labour markets may fail to achieve the most desirable results for society at large. Such market failure can occur on either the demand or the supply side of the market. On the demand side, it may be that employers – as the buyers of labour – have market power that can be exploited at the expense of the workers. Alternatively, it may be that some employers act against the interests of some groups of workers relative to others through some form of discrimination in their hiring practices or wage-setting behaviour. On the supply side, there may be restrictions on the supply of some types of labour, or it may be that trade unions find themselves able to bid wages up to a level that is above the free-market equilibrium.

On another level, the very existence of unemployment might be interpreted as indicating disequilibrium in the labour market – although there may also be reasons to expect there always to be some unemployment in a modern economy. Finally, there are some forms of government intervention that may have unintended effects on labour markets.

Monopsony

So far, the discussion of the labour market has assumed that firms are operating in a perfectly competitive market situation. However, suppose that one firm is the sole user of a particular type of labour, or is the dominant firm in a city or region. Such a firm may be able to exercise market power. A market like this is known as a **monopsony**.

Key term

Monopsony: a market in which there is a single buyer of a good, service or factor of production.

When a firm is competing for labour with other firms in the market, it has to accept the equilibrium wage that arises from the intersection of demand and supply – as in Figure 20.8. However, a firm that is a monopsonist faces the market supply curve of labour directly, rather than simply accepting the equilibrium market wage. It views this supply curve as its *average cost of labour* because it shows the average wage rate that it would need to offer to obtain any given quantity of labour input.

Figure 20.14 shows a monopsonist's demand curve for labour, which is the marginal revenue product curve (MRP_L), and its supply curve of labour, seen by the firm as its average cost curve of labour (AC_L). If the firm were competing with other firms for labour, equilibrium would be where supply equals demand, which would be with the firm using L^* labour at a wage rate W^*.

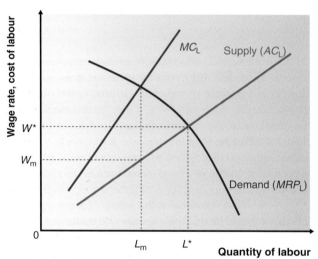

Figure 20.14 A monopsony buyer of labour

From the perspective of the monopsonist firm facing the supply curve directly, if at any point it wants to hire more labour, it has to offer a higher wage to encourage more workers to join the market – after all, that is what the AC_L curve tells it. However, the firm would then have to pay that higher wage to all its workers, so the marginal cost of hiring the extra worker is not just the wage paid to that worker, but the increased wage paid to all the other workers as well. So the marginal cost of labour curve (MC_L) can be added to the diagram.

If the monopsonist firm wants to maximise profit, it will hire labour up to the point where the marginal cost of labour is equal to the marginal revenue product of labour. Therefore it will use labour up to the level L_m, which is where $MC_L = MRP_L$. In order to entice workers to supply this amount of labour, the firm need pay only the wage W_m. (Remember that AC_L is the supply curve of labour.) You can see, therefore, that a profit-maximising monopsonist will use less labour, and pay a lower wage, than a firm operating under competitive conditions. From society's perspective, this entails a cost.

Exercise 20.5

Figure 20.15 shows a firm in a monopsonistic labour market.

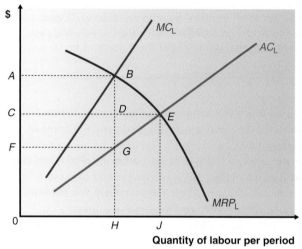

Figure 20.15 A monopsonistic labour market

a What would the wage rate be if this market were perfectly competitive, and how much labour would be employed?
b What wage would the firm, as a monopsony, offer to its workers and how much labour would it employ?
c Which area represents the employer's wage bill?
d What surplus does this generate for the firm?

Effects of government intervention

Labour markets can be a source of politically sensitive issues. Unemployment is often seen as a key indicator of the performance of the economy and a prime cause of poverty in society. There has been an increasing concern in recent years with issues of health and safety and with ensuring that workers are not exploited by their employers. This has induced governments to introduce a number of measures to provide the institutional setting for the operation of labour markets. However, such measures do not always have their intended effects.

Minimum wage

One policy that has often been adopted by governments is the introduction of a minimum wage, according to which employers are not permitted to pay a wage below a level set by the legislation.

The objectives of the minimum wage policy are threefold. First, it is intended to protect workers against exploitation by bad employers. Second, it aims to improve incentives to work by ensuring that 'work pays', thereby tackling the problem of voluntary unemployment. Third, it aims to alleviate poverty by raising the living standards of the poorest groups in society.

Such policies have been contentious, with critics claiming that they meet none of these objectives. It has been argued that the minority of bad employees can still find ways of exploiting their workers: for example, by paying them on a piecework rate so that there is no set wage per hour. Another criticism is that the policy is too indiscriminate to tackle poverty, and that a more sharply focused policy is needed for this purpose. But perhaps most contentious of all is the argument that, far from providing a supply-side solution to unemployment, a minimum wage causes an increase in unemployment because of its effects on the demand for labour.

First, consider a firm operating under conditions of perfect competition, so that it has to accept the wage that is set in the overall market of which it is a part. In Figure 20.16 the firm's demand curve is represented by its marginal revenue product curve (MRP_L), and in a free market it must accept the equilibrium wage W^*. It thus uses labour up to l^*.

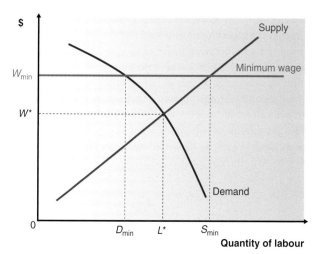

Figure 20.17 The effect of a minimum wage in a perfectly competitive labour market

When the government sets the minimum wage at W_{min}, all firms react by reducing their demand for labour at the higher wage. Their combined demand is now D_{min}, but the supply of labour is S_{min}. The difference between these ($S_{min} - D_{min}$) is unemployment. Furthermore, it is involuntary unemployment – these workers would like to work at the going wage rate, but cannot find a job.

Notice that there are two effects at work. Some workers who were formerly employed have lost their jobs – there are $L^* - D_{min}$ of these. In addition, however, the incentive to work is now improved (this was part of the policy objective, remember?), so there are now an additional $S_{min} - L^*$ workers wanting to take employment at the going wage rate. Thus, unemployment has increased for two reasons.

However, it is not always the case that the introduction of a minimum wage leads to an increase in unemployment. For example, in the market depicted in Figure 20.18 the minimum wage has been set below the equilibrium level, so will have no effect on firms in the market, which will continue to pay W^* and employ L^* workers. At the time of the introduction of the National Minimum Wage in the UK, McDonald's argued that it was in fact already paying a wage above the minimum rate set.

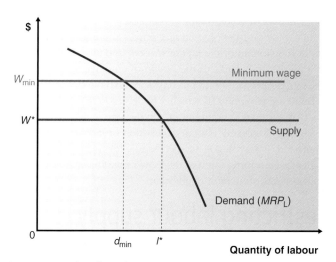

Figure 20.16 The effect of a minimum wage on a firm in a competitive labour market

If the government now steps in and imposes a minimum wage, so that the firm cannot set a wage below W_{min}, it will reduce its labour usage to d_{min}, since it will not be profitable to employ labour beyond this point.

This effect will be similar for all the other firms in the market, and the results of this can be seen in Figure 20.17. Now the demand curve is the combined demand of all the firms in the market, and the supply curve of labour is shown as upward sloping, as it is the market supply curve. In free-market equilibrium the combined demand of firms in the market is L^*, and W^* emerges as the equilibrium wage rate.

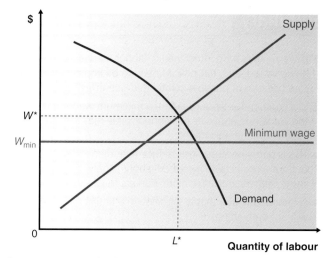

Figure 20.18 A non-binding minimum wage in a competitive labour market

This is not the only situation in which a minimum wage would not lead to unemployment. Suppose that the labour market in question has a monopsony buyer of labour. The firm's situation is shown in Figure 20.19. In the absence of a minimum wage, the firm sets its marginal cost of labour equal to its marginal revenue product, hiring L_0 labour at a wage W_0. A minimum wage introduced at the level W_{min} means that the firm now hires labour up to the point where the wage is equal to the marginal revenue product and, as drawn in Figure 20.19, this takes the market back to the competitive outcome.

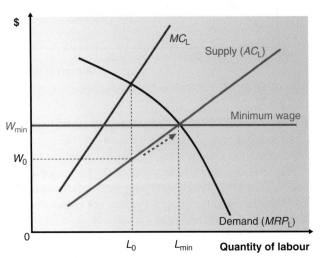

Figure 20.19 A minimum wage with a monopsony buyer of labour

Notice that the authorities would have to be very knowledgeable to set the minimum wage at exactly the right level to produce this outcome. However, any wage between W_0 and W_{min} will encourage the firm to increase its employment to some extent, as the policy reduces its market power. Of course, setting the minimum wage above the competitive equilibrium level will again lead to some unemployment. Thus, it is critical to set the wage at the right level if the policy is to succeed in its objectives.

Summary

- Governments have intervened in labour markets to protect low-paid workers, but policies need to be implemented with care because of possible unintended side-effects.
- In a competitive labour market, a minimum wage that raises the wage rate above its equilibrium value may lead to an increase in unemployment.
- This is partly because firms reduce their demand for labour, but it also reflects an increased labour supply, as the higher wage is an incentive for more workers to join the market.
- A minimum wage that is set below the equilibrium wage will not be binding.
- A minimum wage established in a monopsony market may have the effect of raising employment.

20.8 Trade unions

Trade unions are associations of workers that negotiate with employers on pay and working conditions. Guilds of craftsmen existed in Europe in the Middle Ages, but the formation of workers' trade unions did not become legal in the UK until 1824. In the period following the Second World War, about 40% of the labour force in the UK were members of a trade union. This percentage increased during the 1970s, peaking at about 50%, but since 1980 there has been a steady decline to below 30%.

Key term

Trade union: an organisation of workers that negotiates with employers on behalf of its members.

Trade unions have three major objectives: wage bargaining, the improvement of working conditions, and security of employment for their members. In exploring the effect of the unions on a labour market, it is important to establish whether the unions are in a position to exploit market power and interfere with the proper functioning of the labour market, and also whether they are a necessary balance to the power of employers and thus necessary to protect workers from being exploited.

There are two ways in which a trade union may seek to affect labour market equilibrium. On the one hand, it may limit the supply of workers into an occupation or industry. On the other hand, it may negotiate successfully for higher wages for its members. It turns out that these two possible strategies have similar effects on market equilibrium.

Restricting labour supply

Figure 20.20 shows the situation facing a firm, with a demand curve for labour based on marginal productivity theory. The average going wage in the economy is given by W^*, so if the

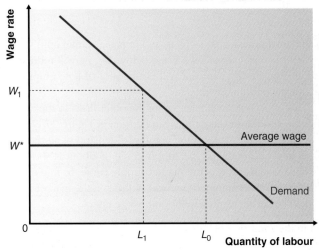

Figure 20.20 A trade union restricts the supply of labour

firm can obtain workers at that wage, it is prepared to employ up to L_0 labour.

However, if the firm faces a trade union that is limiting the amount of labour available to just L_1, then the union will be able to push the wage up to W_1. This might happen where there is a closed shop: in other words, where a firm can employ only those workers who are members of the union. A closed shop allows the union to control how many workers are registered members, and therefore eligible to work in the occupation.

In this situation the union is effectively trading off higher wages for its members against a lower level of employment. The union members who are in work are better off – but those who would have been prepared to work at the lower wage of W^* either are unemployed or have to look elsewhere for jobs. If they are unemployed, this imposes a cost on society. If they are working in a second-choice occupation or industry, this may also impose a social cost, in the sense that they may not be working to their full potential.

The extent of the trade-off depends crucially on the elasticity of demand for labour, as you can see in Figure 20.21. When the demand for labour is relatively more elastic, as shown by D_{L0}, the wage paid by the firm increases to W_0, whereas with the relatively more inelastic demand for labour D_{L1} the wage increases by much more, to W_1.

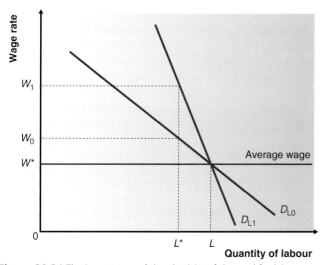

Figure 20.21 The importance of the elasticity of demand for labour

This makes good intuitive sense. The elasticity of demand would be low in situations where a firm could not readily substitute capital for labour, where labour formed a small share of total costs, and where the price elasticity of demand for the firm's product was relatively inelastic. If the firm cannot readily substitute capital for labour, the union has a relatively strong bargaining position. If labour costs are a small part of total costs, the firm may be ready to concede a wage increase, as it will have limited overall impact. If the demand for the product is price inelastic, the firm may be able to pass the wage increase on in the form of a higher price for the product without losing large volumes of sales. Thus, these factors improve the union's ability to negotiate a good deal with the employer.

Negotiating wages

A trade union's foremost function can be regarded as negotiating higher wages for its members. Figure 20.22 depicts this situation. In the absence of union negotiation, the equilibrium for the firm is where demand and supply intersect, so the firm hires L_e labour at a wage of W_e.

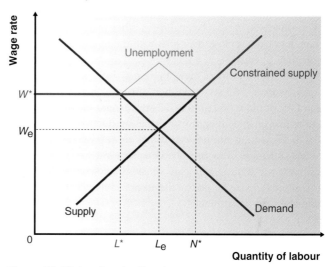

Figure 20.22 A trade union fixes the wage

If the trade union negotiates a wage of W^*, such that the firm cannot hire any labour below that level, this alters the labour supply curve, as shown by the kinked red line. The firm now employs only L^* labour at this wage. So, again, the effect is that the union negotiations result in a trade-off between the amount of labour hired and the wage rate. When the wage is at W^*, unemployment is shown on Figure 20.22 as $N^* - L^*$.

The elasticity of demand for labour again affects the outcome, as shown in Figure 20.23. This time, with the relatively more inelastic demand curve D_{L1}, the effect on the quantity of labour employed (falling from L_e to L^{**}) is much less than when demand is relatively more elastic (falling from L_e to L^*).

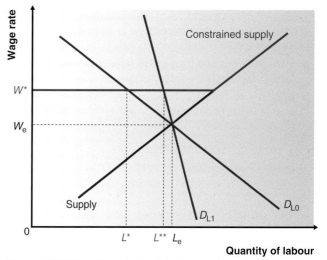

Figure 20.23 The effect of elasticity of demand for labour when the union fixes the wage

From the point of view of allocative efficiency, the problem is that trade union intervention in the market may prevent wages from acting as reliable signals to workers and firms, and therefore may lead to a sub-optimal allocation of resources.

Job security

One possible effect of trade union involvement in a firm is that workers will have more job security: in other words, they may become less likely to lose their jobs with the union there to protect their interests.

From the firm's point of view, there may be a positive side to this. If workers feel secure in their jobs, they may be more productive, or more prepared to accept changes in working practices that enable an improvement in productivity.

For this reason, it can be argued that in some situations the presence of a trade union may be beneficial in terms of a firm's efficiency. Indeed, the union may sometimes take over functions that would otherwise be part of the responsibility of the firm's human resource department.

Labour market flexibility

One of the most telling criticisms of trade unions is that they have affected the degree of flexibility of the labour market. The most obvious manifestation of this is that their actions limit the entry of workers into a market.

This may happen in any firm, where existing workers have better access to information about how the firm is operating, or about forthcoming job vacancies, and so can make sure that their own positions can be safeguarded against newcomers. This is sometimes known as the **insider–outsider phenomenon**. Its

effect is strengthened and institutionalised by the presence of a trade union, or by professional bodies.

Key term

Insider–outsider phenomenon: where existing workers can protect their position against newcomers because they have inside information about how the firm operates.

This and other barriers to entry erected by a trade union can limit the effectiveness and flexibility of labour markets by making it more difficult for firms to adapt to changing market conditions.

Summary

- Trade unions exist to negotiate for their members on pay, working conditions and job security.
- If trade unions restrict labour supply, or negotiate wages that are above the market equilibrium, the net effect is a trade-off between wages and employment.
- Those who remain in work receive higher pay, but at the expense of other workers who either have become unemployed or work in second-choice occupations or industries.
- However, by improving job security, unions may make workers more prepared to accept changes in working practices that lead to productivity gains.
- Barriers to the entry and exit of workers may reduce firms' flexibility to adapt to changing market conditions.

Examination questions

1 In some countries the power of trade unions has decreased. In other countries, trade unions have organised major strikes, resulting in employees refusing to work.

   a Is the existence of a trade union likely to be the main factor that affects the supply of labour? [10]

   b Discuss how the theory of wage determination through market forces might need to be altered when trade unions exist in an industry. [15]

   Cambridge AS and A Level Economics 9708, Paper 4, Q4, June 2008

2 Large firms necessarily become monopolistic. Monopolies adopt practices that are undesirable. Therefore, large firms should be regulated by governments. Discuss whether there is any truth in this argument. [25]

   Cambridge AS and A Level Economics 9708, Paper 4, Q3, June 2008

3 There has been much discussion recently about the effect of climate change and the efficient use of economic resources. Discuss whether the efficient allocation of resources can be achieved only if governments are involved in the process. [25]

   Cambridge AS and A Level Economics 9708, Paper 41, Q2, November 2009

4 The use of cars causes market failure. To achieve an efficient use of resources it would be better if governments intervened to affect both the production and the use of cars. Explain the meaning of the terms 'market failure' and 'the efficient use of resources' and analyse whether economic theory can be used to support this argument. [25]

Cambridge AS and A Level Economics 9708, Paper 43, Q2, June 2011

5 Discuss what might cause inequalities in wage rates in an economy. [25]

Cambridge AS and A Level Economics 9708, Paper 4, Q3, June 2009

6 a In a perfectly competitive labour market, is the demand for a worker's services the main factor influencing the wage rate of that worker? [12]

  b Analyse how the wage rate paid might change if labour and product markets move from being perfectly competitive to being imperfectly competitive. [13]

Cambridge AS and A Level Economics 9708, Paper 43, Q4, November 2011

21 National income and economic growth

There are many ways of judging the overall performance of an economy, but perhaps most fundamental is the question of the quantity of resources available to the country's residents, how the quantity of resources compares to those available in other countries, and whether those resources are growing over time. This is because the availability of resources affects the standard of living that can be enjoyed by the residents. This chapter looks at how the quantity of resources can be measured and at some of the problems that arise in undertaking international comparisons of the standard of living. There is discussion of the government budget, the national debt and the need for sustainability. The chapter explores economic growth, which is key to the improvement of well-being, and sets out some of the limitations of a strategy that aims to maximise the growth of GDP or GNI.

Learning outcomes

After studying this chapter, you should:
- be familiar with the notions of gross domestic product and other measures of national income
- be aware of the strengths and weaknesses of using GDP as a measure of the standard of living, especially in the context of international comparisons
- be familiar with alternative ways of comparing living standards across countries
- be familiar with the notion of the government budget
- be aware of the problems associated with deficit financing
- understand the meaning of economic growth and productivity
- be familiar with factors that can affect the rate of economic growth, particularly the role of investment
- be aware of differences in growth rates between countries and of the explanations that have been advanced to explain them
- be able to evaluate the importance to a society of economic growth and the costs that such growth may impose
- understand the meaning and significance of sustainable growth.

21.1 Measuring national income

The standard of living that can be achieved by the residents of a country will be strongly influenced by the quantity of resources available – although, of course, the way in which those resources are divided amongst the country's residents will also be important.

In terms of measurement, it would thus be helpful to be able to count up the total quantity of resources in an economy, and to explore how they are divided between the country's residents. This is easier said than done. A typical economy produces a wide range of different goods and services during a given time period. This might include rice, onions, cars, electronic goods, curry, banking services and so on. The quantities of these are all likely to be counted in different units of measurement, so adding them together is problematic.

What can be done is to measure the value of these various commodities in money terms – and this is the approach that governments use. One problem that arises with this is that the unit of measurement (money) changes in value because prices change over time. This was discussed in Chapter 9, where the distinction was drawn between real and nominal values.

The total amount of goods and services produced in an economy during a time period is known as the gross domestic product (GDP). This is one of the most important economic indicators used in judging the performance of an economy. If GDP is measured using current prices, the resulting value is in **nominal** terms, whereas **real GDP**, measured at constant prices, provides an indicator that has been adjusted for the effects of changing prices.

Key terms

Nominal GDP: GDP measured at current prices.

Real GDP: GDP measured at constant prices (the prices prevailing in a base year), such that inflation has been taken into account.

Three ways of measuring GDP

When it comes to undertaking the measurement of GDP, three alternative approaches can be taken. One possibility is to add up the total expenditure undertaken in the economy during a period – this would include the various items purchased by households, the expenditure by firms on capital equipment, spending by government and net export spending. Notice that although foreigners may purchase domestic goods, domestic residents also spend money on imported goods – which is why it is *net* export spending that is included when calculating total expenditure. A second possibility is to measure the total amount of income received by people in the country in the form of wages, salaries, profits, rent, etc. Finally, it is possible to add up the total amount of output produced by firms in the economy. This needs to be calculated in terms of the value added by each firm to avoid doublecounting. In principle, these three measures should produce the same result.

In practice, when these measurements are undertaken the three answers are never quite the same, as it is impossible to measure with complete accuracy. The published data for GDP are therefore calculated as the average of these three measures, each of which gives information about different aspects of a society's total resources.

The expenditure estimate describes how those resources are being used, so that it can be seen what proportion of society's resources is being used for consumption and what for investment, etc.

The income estimate reports on the way in which households earn their income. In other words, it tells something about the balance between rewards to labour (e.g. wages and salaries), capital (profits), land (rents), enterprise (self-employment) and so on.

The output estimate focuses on the structure of the economy. One way in which countries differ is in the balance between primary production such as agriculture, secondary activity such as manufacturing, and tertiary activity such as services. Service activity has increased in importance in many economies in recent years: for example, financial services have in particular emerged as a strong part of the UK's comparative advantage.

Figure 21.1 traces real GDP in Pakistan since 1962, measured in US$ billions. In some ways this is an unhelpful way of presenting the data, as the trend component of the series is so strong. In other words, real GDP has been increasing steadily throughout the period. There are one or two periods in which there was a movement away from the trend, but these are relatively rare and not easy to analyse. This reflects the nature of economic variables such as GDP, where the fluctuations around trend are small relative to the trend, but can seem substantial when the economy is experiencing them.

The ratio of nominal to real GDP is a price index, known as the **GDP deflator**. This is defined as:

$$\text{price index} = \frac{\text{GDP at current prices}}{\text{GDP at constant prices}} \times 100$$

This provides another measure of the average level of prices in the economy.

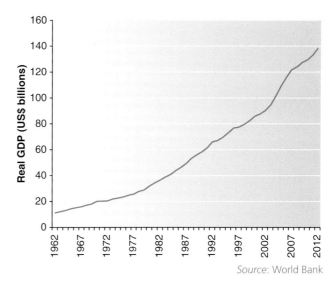

Source: World Bank

Figure 21.1 Real GDP in Pakistan, 1962–2012

Key term

GDP deflator: an implicit price index showing the relationship between real and nominal measures of GDP, providing an alternative measure of the general level of prices in an economy.

It is also sometimes useful to be able to convert nominal measurements into real terms. This can be done by dividing the nominal measurement by the price index, a process known as *deflating* the nominal measure.

Comparing the trends in real GDP over time between countries is not straightforward, if only because of differences in the size of countries. Figure 21.2 uses index numbers (based on 1962 = 100) to show the trends in real GDP in selected countries. This helps to put the performance of Pakistan's economy into context. You can see that Pakistan was outperformed by China and Malaysia when comparing real GDP at the end of the period with that in 1960. New Zealand expanded its GDP more slowly throughout, but started from a different baseline. China started more slowly, but expanded rapidly, especially after the mid-1980s. Malaysia slowed after about 1997.

These comparisons are only broadly indicative of the relative performance of these countries, as they neglect some key issues. In particular, they do not take into account the different starting points, or the relative magnitudes of the countries in terms of population. Furthermore, the data for GDP do not take into account the way in which income is distributed between groups in society; nor do they capture the range of factors that contribute to the quality of life, or the standard of living. These issues will be discussed in more detail in Chapter 22.

GDP can be interpreted as the amount of output produced in an economy during a period of time. It is then tempting to think of this as being the resources that residents of the economy have at their disposal. However, it is also important to recognise that there are income flows that take place between countries.

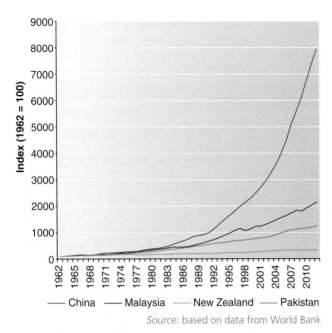

Source: based on data from World Bank

Figure 21.2 Index of real GDP, selected countries, 1962–2012

For example, there may be foreign workers in a country who remit part of their earnings back to their families – or there may be nationals of the country who work abroad and send income back to the domestic economy. **Gross national income (GNI)** is GDP plus net income from abroad. For some economies the difference is significant. For example, in 2011 net income from abroad amounted to more than 4% of GNI in Pakistan, reflecting the number of Pakistani nationals who were working abroad.

As time goes by, physical capital is used up – in other words, machinery and other equipment is subject to wear and tear. This process is known as depreciation, which also affects the calculation of total output. Depreciation cannot be directly observed, so national statistical offices make an estimate of it. **Net domestic product (NDP)** and **net national income (NNI)** are calculated by deducting depreciation from GDP and GNI respectively.

Key terms

Gross national income (GNI): GDP plus net income from abroad.
Net domestic product (NDP): GDP minus depreciation.
Net national income (NNI): GNI minus depreciation.

Figure 21.3 converts the data for GDP into annual growth rates for the period since 1990, which in some ways is revealing. One thing that stands out in this graph is the performance of

China's economy in this period, maintaining a rapid rate of growth since 1992. No other country in the world has matched its performance over this period. Malaysia has also had periods of rapid growth, especially in the early 1990s, but was strongly affected by the financial crisis that hit southeast Asia in 1997/98. Notice that all of the countries experienced a dip in the growth rate in 2008 at the time of the global crisis. Again, Malaysia seems to have been more strongly affected at this time, with GDP falling in 2009.

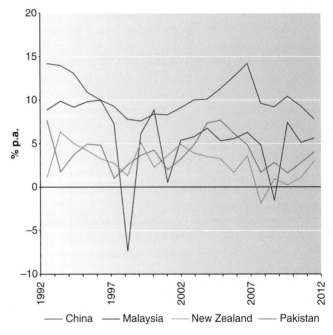

Source: Calculated from World Bank data

Figure 21.3 Annual growth rate of real GDP, selected countries, 1992–2012

Exercise 21.1

Table 21.1 shows GNI for each year between 2004 and 2010, measured in constant US$ (millions) for two countries. For each country, calculate the annual growth rate from 2005 to 2010. Which country was most affected by the world recession of 2008 and 2009? Which country grew by more in total over this period?

Table 21.1 Real GNI in Indonesia and Mauritius (US$ millions)

Year	Indonesia	Mauritius
2004	183 423.4	5252.5
2005	193 426.6	5323.5
2006	205 242.7	5584.9
2007	218 716.8	6038.6
2008	233 399.1	6297.4
2009	244 119.0	6414.5
2010	260 799.3	6773.9

Source: World Bank

Summary

- Gross domestic product (GDP) measures the total amount of goods and services produced in an economy during a time period.
- GDP can be measured through expenditure, income or output.
- Gross national income (GNI) is GDP plus net income from abroad.
- GDP is one way of trying to compare living standards across countries, but has some limitations for this purpose.
- The rate of growth of GDP or GNI provides information about how the economy is growing through time.

21.2 The government budget

Within a macroeconomic perspective, the government is an important influence. It raises revenue through various forms of taxation, and undertakes expenditure – comprising an important component in aggregate demand. In some economies, the government also participates directly in production through state-owned enterprises.

From a measurement perspective, the balance between expenditure and revenue (the **government budget**) is especially significant because it can influence the overall level of activity in the macroeconomy. When government expenditure exceeds revenue there is a **budget deficit**, whereas a situation in which revenue exceeds expenditure is known as a **budget surplus**.

Key terms

Government budget: the balance between government expenditure and revenue.

Budget deficit: a situation in which government expenditure exceeds government revenue.

Budget surplus: a situation in which government revenue exceeds government expenditure.

The government may choose to run a budget deficit because it has identified items of expenditure that it deems important for the economy – for example, it may wish to spend on providing education for its citizens, or on improving infrastructure such as roads. However, the government may also choose to run a budget deficit in order to stimulate aggregate demand. In some countries, the budget deficit may also reflect the difficulty of raising tax revenue, perhaps because of logistical or political problems. For example, Pakistan has experienced difficulties in this regard.

When the government faces a budget deficit situation, it needs to cover this. The deficit can therefore be seen as the **public sector net cash requirement (PSNCR)**, as it is known in the UK. Where can the government raise this needed cash? One option might appear to be getting the central bank to issue extra money (literally, cash) to cover the deficit. However, it will be seen in Chapter 24 that this causes problems for the macroeconomy. The alternative is to borrow the funds needed to cover the deficit.

Persistent borrowing by the government has important implications for the economy. In the short run, it can put upward pressure on interest rates – which may create problems for firms that will face a higher cost of borrowing. In the long term, persistent borrowing leads to the accumulation of *public debt*. The total accumulation of past borrowing is known as the **National Debt**.

Key terms

Public sector net cash requirement (PSNCR): the government budget deficit – the amount that needs to be covered by borrowing.

National Debt: the accumulated stock of past public debt.

The need for sustainability

One view is that, under normal conditions, current expenditure should be covered by the current generation, and borrowing should only be undertaken for projects that are intended to benefit future generations. The UK followed this principle in the last years of the Labour government. Figure 21.4 shows public

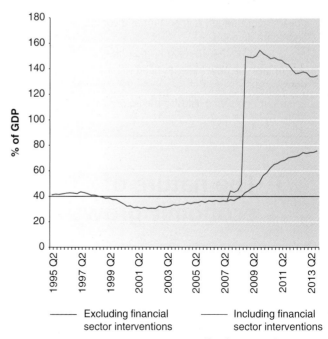

Source: Office for National Statistics

Figure 21.4 Public sector net debt in the UK (as a % of GDP), 1995–2013

sector net debt in the UK since 1995. The position seemed quite stable for most of this period until the credit crunch and financial crisis in the late 2000s. This is clearly visible in the figure. The financial support offered to Northern Rock and other banks in the bailout of 2008 had a noticeable effect on public sector net debt, as is all too clear in the figure.

Even without the financial sector interventions, net debt rose over the 40% mark in the last quarter of 2008 and continued to rise thereafter. This reflected other measures taken by the government to try to mitigate the effects of the recession. One example was the reduction in the rate of value-added tax (VAT) from 17.5 to 15%. This is tantamount to a fiscal expansion, but when it was introduced, it was made clear that it was intended as a temporary boost for a specified period. This statement enabled the government to maintain that it was not breaching its long-term fiscal commitment. The rate of VAT returned to 17.5% in January 2010, and was increased to 20% in January 2011.

Exercise 21.2

Discuss why a large accumulation of public debt might be a problem for a country.

Summary

- The government is an important player in the macroeconomy, raising revenue through taxation and undertaking expenditure.
- The balance between expenditure and revenue (the government budget) is important as a component of aggregate demand.
- The state of the government budget (deficit or surplus) determines the government's need to raise funds through borrowing.
- Persistent borrowing leads to the accumulation of public debt.

21.3 The nature of economic growth

Defining economic growth

From a theoretical point of view, economic growth can be thought of as an expansion of the productive capacity of an economy. If you like, it is an expansion of the potential output of the economy.

There are two ways in which this has been presented in earlier chapters. The first is in terms of the production possibility curve (PPC), which was introduced in Chapter 1. Figure 21.5 is a reminder – it is based on Figure 1.4, where economic growth was characterised as an outward movement of the production possibility frontier from PPC_0 to PPC_1. In other words, economic growth enables a society to produce more goods and services in any given period as a result of an expansion in its resources.

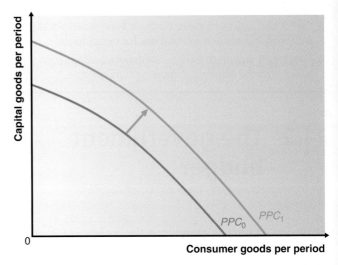

Figure 21.5 Economic growth

A second way of thinking about economic growth is to use the AD/AS model. In Figure 21.6, an increase in the skills of the workforce will enable firms to produce more output at any given price, so that the aggregate supply curve will shift outwards from AS_0 to AS_1. This entails an increase in full-employment output (or capacity output) from Y^* to Y^{**}. This again can be characterised as economic growth. But how can it be achieved?

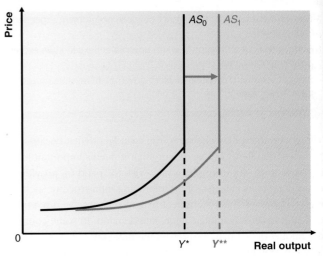

Figure 21.6 A shift in aggregate supply

If economists try to measure economic growth using the rate of change of GNI as an indicator, they are not necessarily measuring what they want to. GNI growth measures the *actual* rate of change of output rather than the growth in the *potential* output capacity of the economy.

In Figure 21.7, a movement from A to B represents a move to the frontier. This is an increase in actual output resulting from using up surplus capacity in the economy, but it is *not* economic growth in our theoretical sense, as moving from A to B does not entail an increase in productive capacity. On the other hand, a movement of the frontier itself, enabling the move from B to C, *does* represent economic growth. However, when economists observe a change in GNI they cannot easily distinguish between the two sorts of effect, especially if the economy is subject to a business cycle – in other words, if the economy is not always operating at full capacity. It is therefore better to think of economic growth in terms of the underlying trend rate of growth of real GNI.

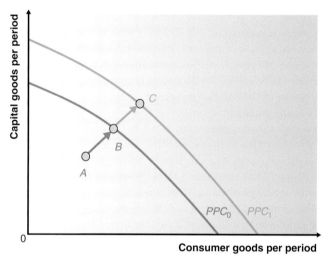

Figure 21.7 Economic growth?

The business cycle

Many economies are seen to experience fluctuations in levels of economic activity through time, a process known as the **business cycle**. During the cycle, the level of economic activity varies around an underlying trend rate of growth.

Key terms

Business cycle: a phenomenon whereby GDP fluctuates around its underlying trend, tending to follow a regular pattern.

Recession: a situation in which growth is negative for two or more consecutive quarters.

Output gap: the difference between actual real GDP and potential real GDP.

The low point of the cycle is known as the *trough*: if the growth rate is negative for two or more consecutive quarters, the economy

is said to be in **recession**. As the economy recovers from recession, it enters into a boom period, which lasts until the peak of the cycle, after which growth decelerates.

The **output gap** is the difference between actual real GDP and potential real GDP. You might think that the output gap could be measured as the difference between these two values. However, it is not so straightforward, as it could be that the economy never actually reaches its full capacity output, which means that potential real GDP cannot be observed directly. However, if the output gap is negative, this means that the economy is operating below its potential full capacity. The output gap will be positive during the boom period. Such fluctuations in economic activity may be damaging, but attempts to stabilise the economy can have adverse effects (this will be discussed in more detail in Chapter 27).

Sources of economic growth

At a basic level, production arises from the use of factors of production – capital, labour, entrepreneurship and so on. Capacity output is reached when all factors of production are fully and efficiently utilised. From this perspective, an increase in capacity output can come either from an increase in the quantity of the factors of production, or from an improvement in their efficiency or productivity. **Productivity** is a measure of the efficiency of a factor of production. For example, **labour productivity** measures output per worker, or output per hour worked. The latter is the more helpful measure, as clearly total output is affected by the number of hours worked, which varies somewhat across countries. **Capital productivity** measures output per unit of capital. **Total factor productivity** refers to the average productivity of all factors, measured as the total output divided by the total amount of inputs used.

Key terms

Productivity: a measure of the efficiency of a factor of production.

Labour productivity: a measure of output per worker, or output per hour worked.

Capital productivity: a measure of output per unit of capital.

Total factor productivity: the average productivity of all factors, measured as the total output divided by the total amount of inputs used.

An increase in productivity raises aggregate supply and the potential capacity output of an economy, and thus contributes to economic growth.

Capital

Capital is a critical factor in the production process. An increase in capital input is thus one source of economic growth. In order for capital to accumulate and increase the capacity of the economy to produce, investment needs to take place.

Notice that in economics 'investment' is used in this specific way. In common parlance, the term is sometimes used to refer to investing in shares or putting money into a deposit account at the bank. Do not confuse these different concepts. In economics, 'investment' relates to a firm buying new capital, such as machinery or factory buildings. If you put money into a bank account, that is an act of saving, not investment.

In the national income accounts, the closest measurement that economists have to investment is 'gross fixed capital formation'. This covers net additions to the capital stock, but it also includes depreciation. Some of the machinery and other capital purchased by firms is to replace old, worn-out capital: that is, to offset depreciation. It does not therefore represent an addition to capital stock. As depreciation cannot be observed easily, the convention in the accounts is to measure gross investment (i.e. including depreciation) and then make an adjustment for depreciation to arrive at **net investment**.

> ### Key term
>
> **Net investment**: gross investment *minus* depreciation.

Society has to decide between using resources for current consumption and using resources for investment. Investment entails sacrificing present consumption in order to have more resources available in the future. Different countries give investment very different priorities. Something of this can be seen in Figure 21.8, which shows gross capital formation in a selection of countries around the world in 2012. The diversity is substantial, ranging from just 15% in Pakistan to 49% in China. Given this high rate of investment, it is perhaps not surprising to discover that China is among the fastest-growing economies in the world in the early twenty-first century – but it must also be remembered that there is a cost to this, as it means sacrificing present consumption in China.

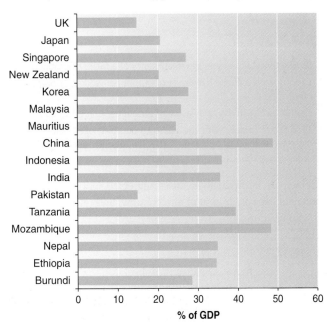

Note: Countries are in descending order of GNI per capita in 2012
Source: World Bank

Figure 21.8 Gross capital formation in 2012 (% of GDP)

The contribution of capital to growth is reinforced by technological progress, as the productivity of new capital is greater than that of old capital that is being phased out. For example, the speed and power of computers has increased enormously over recent years, which has had a great impact on productivity. Effectively, this means that technology is increasing the contribution that investment can make towards enlarging capacity output in an economy.

Innovation can also contribute, through the invention of new forms of capital and new ways of using existing capital, both of which can aid economic growth.

Labour

Capital has sometimes been seen as the main driver of growth, but labour too has a key contribution to make. There is little point in installing a lot of hi-tech equipment unless there is the skilled labour to operate it.

There is relatively little scope for increasing the size of the labour force in a country, except through international migration. (Encouraging population growth is a rather long-term policy!) Nonetheless, the size of the workforce does contribute to the size of capacity output. A number of sub-Saharan African countries have seen this effect in reverse in recent years, with the impact of HIV/AIDS. The spread of this epidemic had a devastating impact in a number of countries in the region; in some countries the percentage of adults affected rose to over 30% – nearly 40% in Botswana. This had a serious impact on capacity output because the disease affects people of working age disproportionately, diminishing the size of the workforce and the productivity of workers.

The quality of labour input is more amenable to policy action. Education and training can improve the productivity of workers, and can be regarded as a form of investment in **human capital**.

> ### Key term
>
> **Human capital**: the stock of skills and expertise and other characteristics that contribute to a worker's productivity; it can be increased through education and training, and improved nutrition and healthcare.

Education and healthcare may have associated externalities. In particular, individuals may not perceive the full social benefits associated with education, training and certain kinds of healthcare, and thus may choose to invest less in these forms of human capital than is desirable from the perspective of society as a whole. Another such externality is the impact of human capital formation on economic growth, which can be seen as a justification for viewing education and healthcare as merit goods.

For many developing countries, the provision of healthcare and improved nutrition can be seen as additional forms of investment in human capital, since such investment can lead to future improvements in productivity.

Exercise 21.3

Which of the following represent genuine economic growth, and which may just mean a move to the *PPC*?

a An increase in the rate of change of potential output.
b A fall in the unemployment rate.
c Improved work practices that increase labour productivity.
d An increase in the proportion of the population joining the labour force.
e An increase in the utilisation of capital.
f A rightward shift in the aggregate supply curve.

Summary

- Economic growth is the expansion of an economy's productive capacity.
- This can be envisaged as a movement outwards of the production possibility frontier, or as a rightward shift of the aggregate supply curve.
- Economic growth can be seen as the underlying trend rate of growth in real GNI.
- Economic growth can stem from an increase in the inputs of factors of production, or from an improvement in their productivity: that is, the efficiency with which factors of production are utilised.
- Investment contributes to growth by increasing the capital stock of an economy, although some investment is to compensate for depreciation.
- The contribution of capital is reinforced by the effects of technological progress.
- Labour is another critical factor of production that can contribute to economic growth: for instance, education and training can improve labour productivity. This is a form of human capital formation.

21.4 GNI and growth

GNI (gross national income) is a way of measuring the total output of an economy over a period of time. Although this measure can provide an indicator of the quantity of resources available to citizens of a country in a given period, as an assessment of the standard of living it has its critics.

GNI does have some things in its favour. First, it is relatively straightforward and thus is widely understood. Second, it is a well-established indicator and one that is available for almost every country in the world, so that it can be used to compare income levels across countries. For this purpose, it naturally helps to adjust for population size by calculating GNI per person (GNI *per capita*, as it is known). This then provides a measure of average income per head.

Figure 21.9a provides data on GNI per capita for the same countries that appeared in Figure 21.8. The extreme differences that exist around the globe are immediately apparent from the data. GNI per capita in Burundi was just $151 in 2011, whereas in the UK the figure was $38 530. In trying to interpret these data, there are a number of issues that need to be borne in mind, as the comparison is not as straightforward as it looks.

a

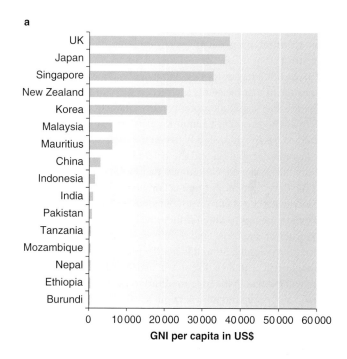

b

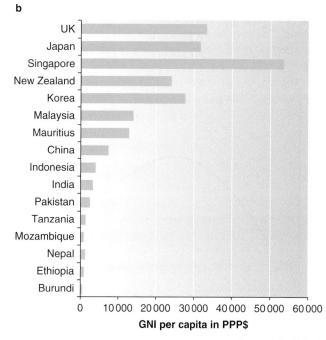

Source: World Bank

Figure 21.9 a GNI per capita in US$, 2011; **b** GNI per capita in PPP$, 2011

Inequality in income distribution

One important point to notice is that looking at the average level of income per person may be misleading if there are wide differences in the way in which income is distributed within countries. In other words, it cannot be assumed that every person living in Burundi receives $151, or that every person in the UK gets $38 530. If income is more unequally distributed in some countries, this will affect the perception of what the term 'average' means. For example, South Africa and Belarus had similar GNI per capita levels in 2010, but the income distribution in Belarus was far more equitable than in South Africa.

Weak institutions and poor governance in developing countries mean that measures such as taxation and transfers to influence the distribution of income are largely untried or ineffective. The economist Simon Kuznets argued that there is expected to be a relationship between the degree of inequality in the income distribution and the level of development that a country has achieved. He claimed that in the early stages of economic development, income is fairly equally distributed, with everyone living at a relatively low income level. However, as development begins to take off there will be some individuals at the forefront of enterprise and development, and their incomes will rise more rapidly. So in this middle phase the income distribution will tend to worsen. At a later stage of development, society will eventually be able to afford to redistribute income to protect the poor, and all will begin to share in the benefits of development.

This can be portrayed as the relationship between the Gini index and the level of development. The thrust of the Kuznets hypothesis is that this should reveal an inverted U-shaped relationship, as shown in Figure 21.10. Although the data do not strongly support this hypothesis, there is some evidence to suggest that the relationship does hold in some regions of the world.

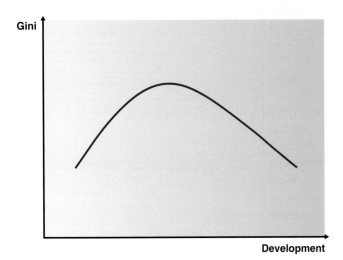

Figure 21.10 The Kuznets curve

The informal sector and the accuracy of data

A further problem with undertaking international comparisons is that it is never absolutely certain that the accuracy with which data are collected is consistent across countries. Definitions of GNI and other variables are now set out in a clear, internationally agreed form, but even when countries are working to the same definitions, some data collection agencies may be more reliable than others.

One particular area in which this is pertinent relates to the informal sector. In every economy there are some transactions that go unrecorded. In most economies, there are economic activities that take place that cannot be closely monitored because of their informal nature. This is especially prevalent in many developing countries, where often substantial amounts of economic activity take place without an exchange of money. For example, in many countries subsistence agriculture remains an important facet of economic life. If households are producing food simply for their own consumption, there is no reason for a money transaction to take place with regard to its production, and thus such activity will not be recorded as a part of GNI. Equally, much economic activity within the urban areas of less developed countries comes under the category of the 'informal sector'.

Where such activity varies in importance between countries, comparing incomes on the basis of measured GNI may be misleading, as GNI will be a closer indicator of the amount of real economic activity in some countries than in others.

Exchange rate problems

The data presented in Figure 21.9a were expressed in terms of US dollars. This allows economists to compare average incomes using a common unit of measurement. At the same time, however, it may create some problems.

Economists want to compare average income levels so that they can evaluate the standard of living, and compare standards across countries. In other words, it is important to be able to assess people's command over resources in different societies, and to be able to compare the purchasing power of income in different countries.

GNI is calculated initially in terms of local currencies, and subsequently converted into US dollars using official exchange rates. Will this provide information about the relative local purchasing power of incomes? Not necessarily.

One reason for this is that official exchange rates are sometimes affected by government intervention. Indeed, in many of the less developed countries exchange rates are pegged to an international currency – usually the US dollar. In these circumstances, exchange rates are more likely to reflect the government's policy and actions than the relative purchasing power of incomes in the countries under scrutiny.

Where exchange rates are free to find their own equilibrium level, they are likely to be influenced strongly by the price of internationally traded goods – which is likely to be a very different combination of goods than that typically consumed by residents in these countries. Again, it can be argued that the official exchange rates may not be a good reflection of the relative purchasing power of incomes across countries.

The United Nations International Comparison Project has been working on this problem for many years. It now produces an alternative set of international estimates of GNI based on purchasing power parity (PPP) exchange rates, which are designed to reflect more accura tely the relative purchasing power of incomes in different societies more accurately. Figure 21.9b shows estimates for the same set of countries.

Comparing this with Figure 21.9a, you will notice that the gap between the low-income and high-income countries seems a bit less marked when PPP dollars are used as the unit of measurement. In other words, the US dollar estimates exaggerate the gap in living standards between rich and poor countries. This is a general feature of these measurements – that measurements in US dollars tend to understate real incomes for low-income countries and overstate them for high-income countries compared with PPP-dollar data. Put another way, people in the lower-income countries have a stronger command over goods and services than is suggested by US-dollar comparisons of GNI per capita. You can also see that the relative rankings of countries in PPP$ are different in some cases – for example, compare Nepal with Mozambique, or Singapore with the UK.

Social indicators

A final question that arises is whether GNI can be regarded as a reasonable indicator of a country's standard of living. You have seen that GNI provides an indicator of the total resources available within an economy in a given period, calculated from data about total output, total incomes or total expenditure. This focus on summing the transactions that take place in an economy over a period can be seen as a rather narrow view of what constitutes the 'standard of living'. After all, it may be argued that the quality of people's lives depends on more things than simply the material resources that are available.

For one thing, people need to have knowledge if they are to make good use of the resources that are available. Two societies with similar income levels may nonetheless provide very different quality of life for their inhabitants, depending on the education levels of the population. Furthermore, if people are to benefit from consuming or using the available resources, they need a reasonable lifespan coupled with good health. So, good standards of health are also crucial to a good quality of life.

It is important to remember that different societies tend to set different priorities on the pursuit of growth and the promotion of education and health. This needs to be taken into account when judging relative living standards through a comparison of GNI per capita, as some countries have higher levels of health and education than other countries with similar levels of GNI per capita.

A reasonable environment in which to live may be seen as another important factor in one's quality of life, and there may be a trade-off between economic growth and environmental standards.

There are some environmental issues that can distort the GNI measure of resources. Suppose there is an environmental disaster – perhaps an oil tanker breaks up close to a beautiful beach. This reduces the overall quality of life by degrading the landscape and preventing enjoyment of the beach. However, it does not have a negative effect on GNI; on the contrary, the money spent on clearing up the damage actually adds to GNI, so that the net effect of an environmental disaster may be to *increase* the measured level of GNI!

Exercise 21.4

Below are some indicators for two countries, A and B. Discuss the extent to which GNI (here measured in PPP$) provides a good indication of relative living standards in the two countries.

	Country A	Country B
GNI per capita (PPP$)	4 943	6 206
Life expectancy (in years at birth)	74.9	62.5
Mean years of schooling	8.2	7.4
People living with HIV/AIDS (% of adults aged 15–49)	<0.1	13.1
Infant mortality rate (per 1000 live births)	15	48
% of population below national poverty line	15.2	38.0

Discuss what other indicators might be useful in this evaluation.

Summary

- GNI is a widely used measure of the total amount of economic activity in an economy over a period of time.
- The trend rate of change of GNI may thus be an indicator of economic growth.
- GNI is a widely understood and widely available measure, but it does have some drawbacks.
- Average GNI per person neglects the important issue of income distribution.
- There may be variation in the effectiveness of data collection agencies in different countries, and variation in the size of the informal sector.
- Converting from a local currency into US dollars may distort the use of GNI as a measure of the purchasing power of local incomes.
- GNI may neglect some important aspects of the quality of life.

21.5 The importance of economic growth

Expanding the availability of resources in an economy enables the standard of living of the country to increase. For developing countries this may facilitate the easing of poverty, and may allow investment in human capital that will improve standards of living further in the future. In the industrial economies, populations have come to expect steady improvements in incomes and resources.

In some less developed countries the perspective may be different, and there has been a long-running debate about whether a society in its early stages of development should devote its resources to achieving the growth objective or to catering for basic needs. By making economic growth the prime target of policy, it may be necessary in the short run to allow inequality of incomes to continue, in order to provide the incentives for entrepreneurs to pursue growth. With such a 'growth-first' approach, it is argued that eventually, as growth takes place, the benefits will trickle down: in other words, growth is necessary in order to tackle poverty and provide for basic needs. However, others have argued that the first priority should be to deal with basic needs, so that people gain in human capital and become better able to contribute to the growth process.

For the industrial countries, growth has become embedded as the main long-run objective of the economy, although the short-run objective of inflation control sometimes dominates media discussion.

The costs of economic growth

Economic growth also brings costs, perhaps most obviously in terms of pollution and degradation of the environment. In designing long-term policy for economic growth, governments need to be aware of the need to maintain a good balance between enabling resources to increase and safeguarding the environment. Pollution reduces the quality of life, so pursuing economic growth without regard to this may be damaging. This means that it is important to consider the long-term effects of economic growth – it may even be important to consider the effects not only for today's generation of citizens, but also for future generations. This is captured in the idea of **sustainable development**.

> ### Key term
>
> **Sustainable development**: 'development that meets the needs of the present without compromising the ability of future generations to meet their own needs' (Brundtland Commission, 1987).

China has experienced an unprecedented period of growth since 1978

These costs have been highlighted in recent years by the growing concerns that have been expressed about global climate change and the pressures on non-renewable resources such as oil and natural gas. For example, the rapid growth rates being achieved by large emerging economies such as China and India have raised questions about the sustainability of economic growth in the long run. China in particular has experienced a period of unprecedented growth since 1978, which is shown in Figure 21.11. This shows the average growth between 1978 and 1985 (when reforms began to affect the economy), and for each five-year period afterwards. No other economy in recent history has been able to achieve an average growth rate of 8.75% per annum over a 32-year period.

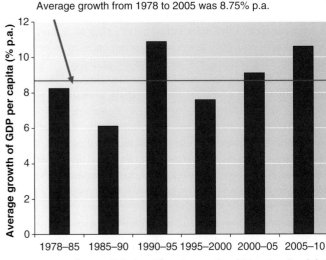

Source: Calculated from International Monetary Fund data

Figure 21.11 China's economic growth

These concerns have led to research into the development of renewable energy sources, but progress in promoting sustainability is impeded because of international externality effects. Where there are externality effects that cross international borders, it becomes difficult to ensure regulation or control.

Exercise 21.5

Discuss with your fellow students the various benefits and costs associated with economic growth, and evaluate their relative importance.

Summary

- The experience of economic growth has varied substantially in different regions of the world.
- There is a gap in living standards between countries that industrialised early and countries that are now classified as being less developed.
- Economic growth remains important for all countries, at whatever stage of development.
- There may be costs attached to economic growth, particularly in respect of the environment.

22 Economic and human development

One of the gravest economic challenges facing the world today is the global inequity in the distribution of resources. Worldwide, it is estimated that at the beginning of the twenty-first century more than a billion people were living in what the United Nations regards as absolute poverty. Furthermore, there were 114 million primary-age children who were not enrolled for school, more than a billion people without access to safe water, and 2.4 billion without access to sanitation. Progress since then has been slow. This chapter considers how to come to terms with such facts, and applies economic analysis in an attempt to understand what has gone wrong. Countries in different parts of the world have followed different paths to development – with varying degrees of success. Differences partly reflect the different characteristics of each country. Less developed countries (LDCs) do seem to share some characteristics, but each country also faces its own configuration of problems and opportunities. This chapter explores some of the common characteristics that LDCs display, but also examines some of the key differences between them.

Learning outcomes

After studying this chapter, you should:
- understand what is meant by economic and human development
- be familiar with the most important economic and social indicators that can help to evaluate the standard of living in different societies
- recognise the strengths and limitations of such indicators in providing a profile of a country's stage of development
- be aware of the importance of political and cultural factors in influencing a country's path of development
- be familiar with the common characteristics of less developed countries
- be aware of the diversity of experience of less developed countries
- be aware of significant differences between regions of the world in terms of their level and pace of development
- understand the importance of the structure of economic activity in an economy
- be familiar with the relative importance of different forms of economic activity in the process of development.

22.1 Defining development

The first step is to define what is meant by **development**. You might think that it is about economic growth – if a society can expand its productive capacity, surely that is development? But development means much more than this. Economic growth may well be a necessary ingredient, since development cannot take place without an expansion of the resources available in a society; however, it is not a sufficient ingredient, because those additional resources must be used wisely, and the growth that results must be the 'right' sort of growth.

Wrapped up with development are issues concerning the alleviation of poverty – no country can be considered 'developed' if a substantial portion of its population is living in absolute poverty. Development also requires structural change, and possibly changes in institutions and, in some cases, cultural and political attitudes.

In recognition of the multifaceted nature of development, the United Nations Millennium Summit in 2000 agreed a set of **Millennium Development Goals (MDGs)** that encapsulated their views of the main priorities for development. These were:
- eradicate poverty and hunger
- achieve universal primary education
- promote gender equality and empower women
- reduce child mortality
- improve maternal health
- combat HIV/AIDS, malaria and other diseases
- ensure environmental sustainability
- develop a global partnership for development.

Key terms

Development: a process by which real per capita incomes are increased and the inhabitants of a country are able to benefit from improved living conditions: that is, lower poverty and enhanced standards of education, health, nutrition and other essentials of life.

Millennium Development Goals (MDGs): targets set for each less developed country, reflecting a range of development objectives to be monitored each year to evaluate progress.

These eight goals represent key facets of development that need to be addressed. They constituted an enormous challenge for the period up to 2015, especially as progress in the early years was slow and uneven. In thinking about these goals, you can begin to understand the various dimensions of development, and realise that it is about much more than economic growth – although growth may be seen as a prerequisite for the achievement of the goals. At the same time, failure to achieve these goals will retard economic growth.

One of the Millennium Development Goals was to achieve universal primary education

To summarise, development is about more than just economic growth. Achieving higher real income per capita is a necessary part of development, but it is not all there is to it. A country will not be recognised as achieving development unless it is also able to alleviate poverty, improve education levels and health standards, and provide an enhanced physical and cultural environment. Furthermore, such improvements must reach all inhabitants of the country, and not be confined to certain groups within society. In other words, economic growth may be necessary for development to take place, but it is not sufficient. Expanding the resources available within a society is the first step, but those resources also need to be used well.

Summary

- Economic growth is one aspect of economic development, in that it provides an increase in the resources available to members of society in less developed countries.
- However, in addition, development requires that the resources made available through economic growth are used appropriately to meet development objectives.
- The Millennium Development Goals were set by the Millennium Summit of the United Nations in September 2000.
- These eight goals comprise a set of targets for each less developed country, to be achieved by 2015.

Exercise 22.1

Visit the Millennium Development Goals website at *http://www.undp.org/content/undp/en/home/mdgoverview/*. Discuss which of the goals you see to be of most importance for development and explore the extent to which progress is being made towards the goals in two or three countries of your choice.

22.2 Which are the less developed countries?

There is no single definitive list of which countries are regarded as being *less developed countries (LDCs)*, and it is important to be aware that this term is used to refer to a wide range of countries with differing characteristics. The discussion will be illustrated using indicators for a selection of countries from different regions of the world. Two economies that would now be regarded as being 'developed' countries (South Korea and Argentina) will be included for comparative purposes.

In broad terms, the countries regarded as LDCs are concentrated in four major regions: sub-Saharan Africa, Latin America, South Asia and South East Asia. This excludes some countries in the 'less developed' range, but relatively few. For some purposes it may be necessary to treat China separately, rather than including it as part of South East Asia, partly because of its sheer size, and partly because it has followed a rather different development path.

It is very important when discussing economic development to remember that there is wide diversity among the countries that are classified as LDCs, and although it is tempting to generalise, you need to be a little wary of doing so. Different countries have different characteristics, and face different configurations of problems and opportunities. Therefore, a policy that works for one country might fail totally in a different part of the world.

Summary

- Less developed countries (LDCs) are largely located in four major regions: sub-Saharan Africa, Latin America, South Asia and South East Asia.
- These regions have shown contrasting patterns of growth and development.

22.3 Indicators of development

GNI per capita

The first step is to be able to measure 'development'. One possible measure is GNI per capita – the average level of income per person in the population. This was discussed in Chapter 21. Figure 22.1 provides data on GNI per capita measured in PPP$ for a selection of countries from each of the four major regional

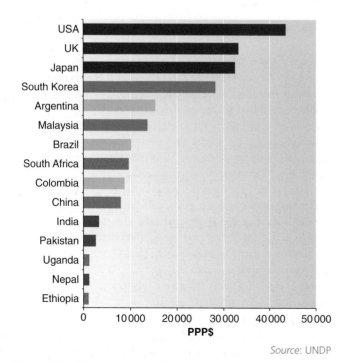

Source: UNDP

Figure 22.1 GNI per capita (PPP$), 2012

groupings. These countries will be used as examples throughout this discussion: they are colour-coded by region. Because of the diversity of countries in each of the regions, such a selection must be treated with a little caution. The USA, UK and Japan will not appear in the later figures.

The Human Development Index

To deal with the criticism that GDP per capita fails to take account of other dimensions of the quality of life, in 1990 UNDP devised an alternative indicator, known as the **Human Development Index (HDI)**. This was designed to provide a broader measure of the stage of development that a country had reached.

Key term

Human Development Index (HDI): a composite indicator of the level of a country's development, varying between 0 and 1.

The basis for the HDI is that there are three key aspects of human development: resources, knowledge of how to make good use of those resources, and a reasonable lifespan in which to make use of those resources (see Figure 22.2). The three components are measured by, respectively, GNI per capita in PPP$, indicators of education (mean years of schooling and expected years of schooling) and life expectancy. The measurements are then combined to produce a composite index ranging between 0 and 1, with higher values reflecting higher human development.

GNI per capita (in PPP$) represents resources in this set-up, and is intended to reflect the extent to which people have command over resources. The education indicators pick up two rather different aspects of this important component of human development. Mean years of education can be seen as a way of reflecting educational attainment, as it measures the average number of years of schooling that were received by people aged 25 and above in their lifetime. It thus tells us something about the extent to which there has been past investment in education.

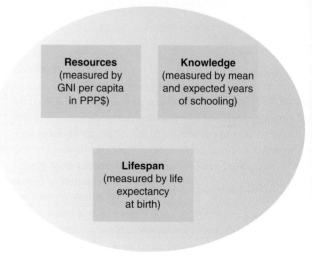

Figure 22.2 Components of the Human Development Index

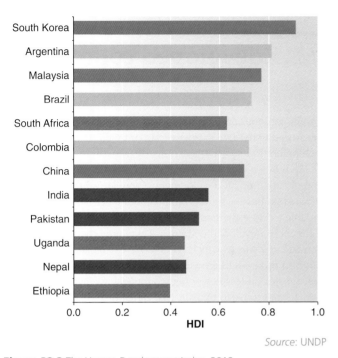

Figure 22.3 The Human Development Index, 2012

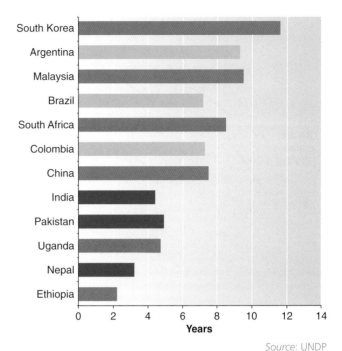

Figure 22.5 Mean years of schooling

Expected years of schooling, on the other hand, reveals something about the current state of education in an economy: that is, it identifies the number of years of schooling that a child of school entrance age can expect to receive, given current patterns of enrolment and access to education. Life expectancy is the natural indicator of expected lifespan, and is also closely related to the general level of health of people in the country.

Values of the HDI for 2012 are charted in Figure 22.3 for the selected countries. You can see that the broad ranking of the countries is preserved, but the gap between low and high human development is less marked. An exception is South Africa, which is ranked lower on the basis of the HDI than on GNI per capita: what this suggests is that South Africa has achieved relatively high income levels, but other aspects of human development have not kept pace. There are other countries in the world that share this feature.

Figures 22.4 and 22.5 show the levels of two of the measures that enter into the HDI: life expectancy and mean years of schooling. It is clear that life expectancy is primarily responsible for the low ranking of South Africa in the HDI, as its level of life expectancy is not very different from that of the other sub-Saharan African countries in the sample, even though its average income level is much higher. In contrast, Nepal performs quite well in terms of lifespan, but relatively poorly in terms of education. By comparing these data, you can get some idea of the diversity between countries that was mentioned earlier.

Another way of putting a country into perspective is to construct a development diamond. An example is shown in Figure 22.6. This compares Ethiopia's performance with the average for countries in its region, sub-Saharan Africa. On each axis, the value of the variable achieved by Ethiopia is expressed as a proportion of the value for sub-Saharan Africa. In this instance, Ethiopia is seen to have higher life expectancy but shows weaker achievement on the other indicators.

There is a view that growth should be the prime objective for development, since by expanding the resources available the benefits can begin to trickle down through the population. An opposing view claims that by providing first for basic needs, more rapid economic growth can be facilitated. The problem in

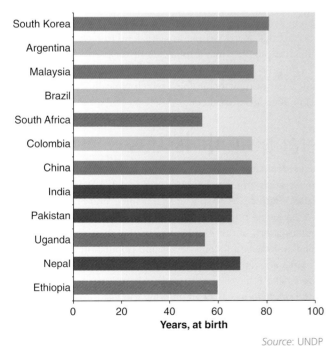

Figure 22.4 Life expectancy

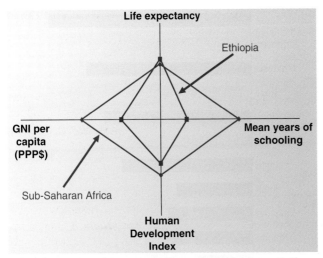

Figure 22.6 Development diamond for Ethiopia compared with all countries in sub-Saharan Africa

some cases is that growth has not resulted in the trickle-down effect, and inequality remains. It may be significant that countries such as Brazil and South Africa, where the GNI per capita ranking is high relative to the HDI ranking, are countries in which there remain high levels of inequality in the distribution of income.

The HDI may be preferred to GNI per capita as a measure of development on the grounds that it reflects the key dimensions of development as opposed to growth. However, it will always be difficult to reduce a complex concept such as development to a single statistic. The diverse characteristics of LDCs demand the use of a range of alternative measures in order to identify the configuration of circumstances and problems facing a particular country.

An alternative indicator was proposed by William Nordhaus and James Tobin in 1972, known as the *Measure of Economic Welfare (MEW)*. This began with GNP and then made various adjustments so that it only included the consumption and investment items that contribute positively to economic well-being. For example, they argued that the value of informal production should be added, but that there should be deductions for negative externalities such as environmental damage. An attempt was made to re-launch this as the *Index of Sustainable Economic Welfare (ISEW)*. It was hoped that this indicator would be able to capture key issues relating to the sustainability of economic growth, but it has yet to gain widespread support.

Summary

- GNI and GDP may neglect some important aspects of the quality of life.
- The Human Development Index (HDI) recognises that human development depends upon resources, knowledge and health, and therefore combines indicators of these key aspects.
- Different countries have different characteristics, and face different configurations of problems and opportunities.

Different countries are at different stages of development, as measured either by GNI per capita or by the Human Development Index (HDI). It seems clear that some countries have been much more successful than others in pursuing economic and human development. There are some countries in East Asia that have achieved rapid economic growth, and have been able to close the gap in living standards between them and the more developed countries. There are others, especially in sub-Saharan Africa, which seem to have stagnated, making little or no progress in growth terms since the 1960s. So what characteristics do less developed countries have in common? It is important to try to explain why different combinations of these characteristics may have joined with cultural, political and social influences to result in different experiences of growth and development.

The indicators that make up the HDI (namely, resources, knowledge and health) provide the first clues to the key characteristics of LDCs. LDCs have relatively low incomes, low levels of education in the population, and low levels of health. Education and health are important for many reasons. They are included in the HDI because they are seen as essential components of the quality of life, contributing directly to human development. However, they are also important because they are aspects of human capital. If an individual undertakes education, this can be viewed as an investment, gathering skills that can be used later to generate a flow of income. Health is also a form of human capital that influences a worker's productivity.

The fact that many people in LDCs tend to have low levels of human capital has major implications for productivity in those countries, and has also been seen as a critical factor in the adoption of new technology, which typically demands high levels of skills from workers.

Demographic issues

Some other characteristics of LDCs are important in setting the scene for analysing development. It is widely believed that population growth is of special significance, and Figure 22.7 shows projected population growth from 2010 to 2015. The irregular pattern of this graph suggests that there is no strong correlation between income levels and population growth. The prime concern about rapid population growth is felt by countries like Ethiopia and Uganda, where it has been suggested that the population has been growing too fast for education and healthcare services to keep up. Figure 22.8 shows one aspect of the problem: namely, the percentage of the population below 15 years of age in selected countries. In Uganda it amounts to almost half of the population, and in Ethiopia it is over 40%.

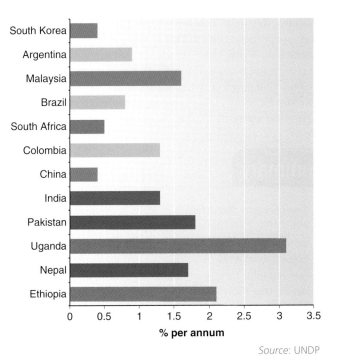

Source: UNDP

Figure 22.7 Average annual population growth, 2010–15

These children need to be supported by the working population, and in countries where HIV/AIDS is widespread this is particularly difficult because the disease is especially prevalent among those of working age. This is one example of dependency. People who are too young or too old to be part of the working population are in a state of dependency on those in work. If the proportion of dependants increases because of

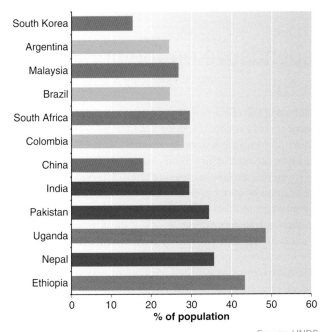

Source: UNDP

Figure 22.8 Population below 15 years old

shrinkage of the working population, this places added pressure on those remaining in work.

Poverty

A further characteristic of LDCs is the prevalence of poverty. One approach to measuring poverty is to define a basket of goods and services that is regarded as the minimum required to support human life: households that have incomes too low to allow them to purchase that basic bundle of goods are regarded as being in absolute poverty.

Research published in 2008 by the World Bank claimed that new data on incomes and prices in LDCs revealed that global poverty was more widespread than had been previously thought. It was estimated that households in which people were living on less than $1.25 per person per day (in PPP$) should be regarded as being in absolute poverty. In 2005, about 1.4 billion people in the world were said to be living below this threshold. Figure 22.9 shows a regional distribution of poverty. On a more positive note, the research showed that there had been substantial progress in the preceding years in reducing the number of people in poverty, although sub-Saharan Africa had made less progress than other regions.

The number of people living below the poverty line is not a perfect measure. In particular, it would also be useful to know how far below the poverty line people are living, which would indicate the intensity of poverty. However, this is not easy to measure. In 2010, the UNDP launched a new poverty index, the Multidimensional Poverty Index (MPI). The core idea of this index was that people may suffer deprivation in the three basic components of human development (resources, education and health). For example, households may have limited access to resources, such as clean water, sanitation, transport or assets such as a radio or refrigerator. They can also be deprived if children are unable to complete schooling, or if they are malnourished.

The new index is based on data relating to ten different deprivations, assembled from a single survey of households. The severity of poverty is also related to the number of dimensions in which a household is deprived – this reflects the intensity of poverty of people in a household. The index is interpreted as depicting the share of the population that is poor across the dimensions of deprivation, but adjusted by the intensity of the deprivations. Figure 22.10 shows the index for the LDCs included in our sample. For Ethiopia, the interpretation would be that nearly 40% of people suffer deprivation across the dimensions of poverty reflected in the index.

Poverty can also be defined in relative terms. If a household has insufficient income for its members to participate in the normal social life of the country, it is said to be in relative poverty. This too is defined in terms of a poverty line – this time it is 50% of the median (middle-ranked) household disposable income. Relative poverty can occur in any society.

Absolute poverty and relative poverty reflect different things. Absolute poverty is about whether people have enough to

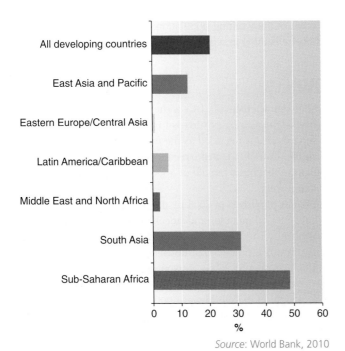

Source: World Bank, 2010

Figure 22.9 Percentage of population of developing countries living on less than $1.25 per day

survive, whereas relative poverty is more about inequality than about poverty. This is not to say that relative poverty should not be of concern to policy-makers, but people in absolute poverty clearly require urgent action.

An important part of development is the provision of infrastructure. In part, this is necessary to help alleviate poverty by providing essential services. But there are other vital aspects of infrastructure that are essential for markets

to operate effectively. This is particularly true of transport and communications and market facilities. Many areas of infrastructure display characteristics of public goods, so that government intervention is essential to ensure adequate provision. (Public goods were discussed in Chapter 6.)
A problem for many LDCs, however, is that the government does not have the resources to provide the necessary infrastructure.

Summary

- One common characteristic of LDCs is the relatively low levels of human capital in the population.
- Improvements in education, healthcare and nutrition are all needed in order to raise the skills and productivity of labour.
- Demographic factors are also important for LDCs, many of which have shown a more rapid rate of population growth than can readily be resourced.
- One result of the demographic situation is that many LDCs have a high proportion of the population who are aged below 15 years – in some cases, more than half.
- Poverty is widespread, and its alleviation is a key part of the development process.

22.5 The structure of economic activity in LDCs

Dependence on the primary sector

In evaluating the characteristics of LDCs, it is helpful to consider the structure of economic activity. One way of viewing this is to consider the separation between primary, secondary and tertiary production activities. The *primary sector* involves the extraction of raw materials and the growing of crops. It includes agriculture, the extraction of minerals (and oil), forestry, fishing and so on. The *secondary sector* is where these raw materials or crops are processed or transformed into goods. It includes various forms of manufacturing activity, ranging from the processing of food to the manufacture of motor vehicles or computer equipment. The *tertiary sector* is concerned with the provision of services. It includes transport and communication, hairdressing, financial services and so on. A subset of tertiary activity involves intellectual services. This is sometimes known as the *quaternary sector* and includes hi-tech industry, information technology, some forms of scientific research and other 'information products'.

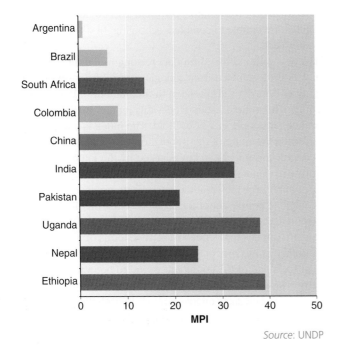

Source: UNDP

Figure 22.10 The Multidimensional Poverty Index

Figure 22.11 contrasts the structure of economic activity in two very different economies – Ethiopia and the UK. These data do not exactly correspond to the primary, secondary and tertiary divisions, as 'Industry' here includes not only manufacturing activity but also mining, construction, electricity, water and gas.

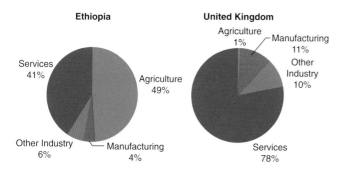

Figure 22.11 The structure of economic activity, 2009 (% of GDP)

Source: World Bank

Nonetheless, the contrast is striking. In the UK, the agricultural sector has dwindled almost to nothing, and services have become the dominant form of activity, although industry still accounts for more than a quarter of GDP. In Ethiopia, industry takes up only 10% of GDP – and remember this includes not only manufacturing (4%) but some other forms of activity (notably, utilities such as water and energy supply) as well. Agriculture, on the other hand, is the largest single sector.

Agriculture is the largest sector of economic activity in Ethiopia

Indeed, many LDCs have an economic structure that is strongly biased towards agriculture. Figure 22.12 shows the percentage of GDP coming from the agricultural sector (measured in terms of value added). In interpreting these data, it is important to be aware that labour productivity tends to be lower in agriculture than in other sectors. The data therefore understate the importance of agriculture in the structure of the economy, as the percentage of the labour force engaged in agriculture is higher than the agricultural share of output. This is further reinforced

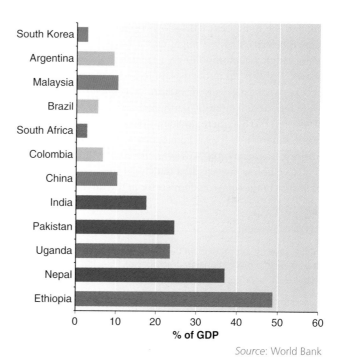

Figure 22.12 The importance of agriculture

Source: World Bank

by the importance of unrecorded agricultural production in the subsistence sector. In other words, if farmers produce food for their own consumption, this will not be included in GDP.

Figure 22.13 underlines the situation by showing the percentage of the population living in urban areas. It would appear that, for many of the low-income countries in the group, the majority of their people are relying on rural economic activities. In many LDCs, there is a stark contrast between the

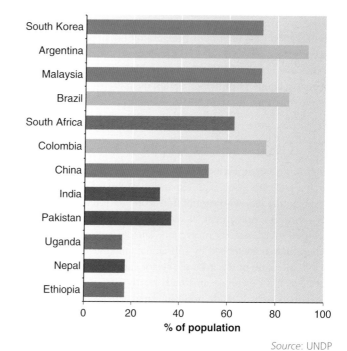

Source: UNDP

Figure 22.13 Urban population

urban and the rural areas. This shows up partly in terms of income differences, as you might expect from the different kinds of employment opportunity available in the urban areas. However, it shows up in other ways too – for example, in terms of access to education and healthcare, which tend to be better provided in the urban areas, partly because many teachers and doctors prefer to live there. In some countries, the inequality between different regions is tantamount to there being a **dual economy**. The economic activity in the country takes place in two quite different styles, and a traditional rural sector may co-exist with a burgeoning modern sector in the urban areas.

> ### Key term
>
> **Dual economy**: one in which a traditional (mainly rural) sector co-exists with a modern (mainly urban) sector.

This inequality between regions in a country may have the effect of encouraging migration towards the cities. There might be many reasons for this. It may be that workers head for the cities because they are attracted by the chance of obtaining higher wages or better living conditions. Alternatively, households might decide to send some members to earn in the city while the rest remain in the rural area. This might be seen as a way of diversifying risk rather than having all household members active in the same (rural) labour market.

Such movements of people are likely to pose severe problems. Consider Botswana, for example. In 1975 just 11% of its population lived in the urban areas. By 2010 this had risen to more than 60%. Botswana may not have a massively large population (about 2 million in 2010), but for a government needing to provide public goods, such rapid urban expansion puts significant pressure on urban infrastructure – roads, housing, water supply, sanitation and so on. Just as important, such migration puts enormous pressure on urban labour markets, so the provision of jobs for all these additional workers becomes a major challenge. The net result is that many rural workers exchange poor living conditions in the rural areas for unemployment in an urban environment.

The informal sector

Furthermore, as employment in the newer sectors cannot expand at such a rate, the result is an expansion of the informal sector. Migrants to the city who cannot find work are forced to find other forms of employment, as most LDCs do not have well-developed social security protection. The cities of many LDCs are therefore characterised by substantial amounts of informal activity. The scale of the informal sector can be seen in Figure 22.14: for example, in Ghana nearly 80% of employment in the urban areas is made up of informal activity.

Such informal activity covers a multitude of economic activities, such as hawkers selling food at the kerbside, roadside barbers and rickshaw drivers. However, in some cities, the informal sector has developed beyond such activities, and you

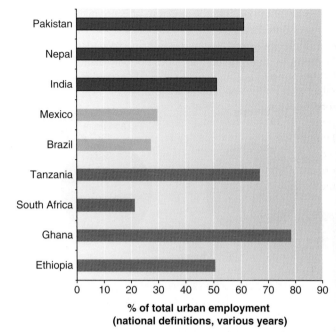

Source: International Labour Office

Figure 22.14 The urban informal sector

might find small manufacturing concerns recycling old car tyres as shoes, or packing cases as furniture.

The growth of the urban population may have externality effects on living standards in the urban areas. If there is rapid growth of the urban population, it is unlikely that the authorities will be able to ensure adequate infrastructure to cope with the growing numbers of residents: for example, in terms of housing, water supply or sanitation. This may lead to the growth of shanty towns – informal settlements in which new arrivals congregate, often in very poor conditions. Figure 22.15 illustrates this. The assumption here is that the marginal private costs faced by an individual migrant (MPC) are lower than the marginal social costs (MSC) because of the effects of congestion. Individual migrants will continue to come to the city up to the point where their

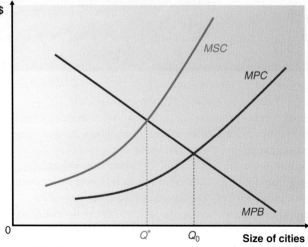

Figure 22.15 The externality effect of migration

marginal private benefits are equal to their marginal private costs (at Q_0), whereas Q^* would be better for society as a whole.

In some ways the existence of the informal sector may be seen as beneficial for an LDC, as it offers a coping strategy for the poor, and may even provide some training and skills that might later help workers to find employment in the modern or formal sector. These benefits need to be weighed against the potential costs arising from the externalities mentioned earlier. Furthermore, if the informal sector acts as a cushion for migrant workers, it is possible that it will be seen as reducing the opportunity cost of unemployment, which in turn could increase the flow of migrants.

Summary

- Economic activity can be classified into primary, secondary and tertiary production activities.
- Primary activity centres on agriculture and mineral extraction; secondary activity focuses mainly on manufacturing activity; tertiary activity is concerned with the provision of services.
- Many LDCs have an economic structure that is biased towards the primary sector.
- Agriculture is often characterised by low productivity.
- The importance of agriculture is also reflected in the high proportion of the population of many LDCs that live in rural areas.
- Inequality between rural and urban areas has led to rapid internal migration in some LDCs, and to the growth of the urban informal sector.
- Migration puts pressure on urban infrastructure.

22.6 The diversity of less developed countries

Although this chapter has identified a number of characteristics that many LDCs seem to have in common, it is difficult – and dangerous – to generalise too much when trying to analyse LDCs or to devise a policy to foster development. This is because every country has its own configuration of characteristics, strengths and weaknesses. To some extent, regional groupings of countries display some common features, but even here there remains an inherent diversity.

The East Asian experience

The rapid growth achieved by the East Asian **tiger economies**, as they came to be known, was undoubtedly impressive, and held out hope that other less developed countries could begin to close the gap in living standards. Indeed, the term 'east Asian miracle' was coined to describe how quickly these **newly industrialised economies** had been able to develop. At the heart of the success were four countries: Hong Kong, Singapore, South Korea and Taiwan; others, such as Malaysia and Thailand, were not far behind.

Key terms

Tiger economies: a group of newly industrialised economies in the East Asian region, including Hong Kong, Singapore, South Korea and Taiwan.

Newly industrialised economies: economies that have experienced rapid economic growth from the 1960s to the present.

None of these countries enjoys a rich supply of natural resources. Indeed, Hong Kong and Singapore are small city-states whose only natural resources are their excellent harbours and good positions – but they have small populations.

The tigers soon realised that to develop manufacturing industry it would be crucial to tap into economies of scale. This meant producing on a scale that would far outstrip the size of their domestic markets – which meant that they would have to rely on international trade. Only in this way would they be able to gain the benefits of specialisation.

By being very open to international trade and focusing on exports, the tigers were able to sell to a larger market, and thereby improve their efficiency through economies of scale. This enabled them to enjoy a period of **export-led growth**. In other words, the tiger economies expanded by selling their exports to the rest of the world, and building a reputation for high-quality merchandise. This was helped by their judicious choice of markets on which to focus: they chose to move into areas of economic activity that were being vacated by the more developed nations, which were producing new sorts of product.

Key term

Export-led growth: a situation in which economic growth is achieved through the exploitation of economies of scale, made possible by focusing on exports, and so reaching a wider market than would be available within the domestic economy.

The export-led growth hypothesis explains part of the success of the tiger economies, but there were other contributing factors. The tiger economies nurtured their human capital and attracted foreign investment. Their governments intervened to influence the direction of the economy, but also encouraged markets to operate effectively, fostering macroeconomic and political stability and developing good infrastructure. Moreover, these countries embarked on their growth period at a time when world trade overall was buoyant.

Sub-Saharan Africa

The experience of countries in sub-Saharan Africa is in total contrast to the success story of the tiger economies. Even accepting the limitations of the GDP per capita measure, the fact that in some countries it was lower in 2000 than it had been in 1975 (or even earlier) paints a depressing picture. Can sub-Saharan Africa learn from the experience of the tiger economies?

Part of the explanation for the failure of growth in this region lies in the fact that sub-Saharan Africa lacks many of the positive features that enabled the tiger economies to grow. Export-led growth is more difficult for countries that have specialised in the production of goods for which demand is not buoyant. Furthermore, it is not straightforward to develop new specialisations if human and physical capital levels are low, the skills for new activities are lacking and poverty is rife. On the other hand, continuing to rely on specialisation in agriculture when many of the potential export markets are characterised by strong protectionism is also fraught with difficulty. Encouraging development when there is political instability, and when markets do not operate effectively, is a major challenge.

The experience of the 2000s was rather more encouraging, as some economies in sub-Saharan Africa began to show signs of progress in terms of economic growth and development. This is evident in Figure 22.16, which shows annual growth rates for a selection of countries in sub-Saharan Africa since 1990. For these economies at least, the 2000s offered promise of improvement. Uganda consistently outperformed growth in the world as a whole, and Tanzania did so after the late 1990s. Furthermore, these economies maintained positive growth rates when the world as a whole showed negative growth in 2009. Cameroon went through a period in the early 1990s of continuous

recession, but then recovered in the 2000s. Sub-Saharan Africa as a whole experienced growth rates higher than in the world as a whole throughout the 2000s.

Although this may seem encouraging, it remains to be seen whether this performance can be maintained as the global economy struggles to recover – and whether this performance can be replicated by other economies in the region. Notice that the growth rates shown here are for GDP, not for GDP per capita, so average incomes were not rising as quickly as might be inferred from the figure.

Latin America

Countries in Latin America followed yet another path. There was a period in which the economies of Argentina, Brazil and Mexico, among others, were able to grow rapidly, enabling them to qualify as 'newly industrialised economies'. However, such growth could not be sustained in the face of the high rates of inflation that afflicted many of the countries in this region, especially during the 1980s. Indeed, many of them experienced bouts of hyperinflation, inhibiting economic growth.

In part this reflected fiscal indiscipline, with governments undertaking high levels of expenditure which they financed by printing money. In many cases, countries in this region have tended to be relatively closed to international trade. International debt reached unsustainable levels, and continues to haunt countries such as Argentina which, in 2005, wrote off its debt by offering its creditors about 33% of the value of its outstanding debt. Around three-quarters of the creditors accepted the deal, knowing that otherwise they would probably get nothing at all. However, whether anyone will be prepared to lend to Argentina in the future remains to be seen. Latin American economies also tend to be characterised by high levels of income inequality, and poverty remains a major problem.

The BRIC countries

In the early 2000s, a group of countries were identified as experiencing rapid economic growth and closing the gap on the developed economies. These were Brazil, Russia, India and China; they became known as the BRIC economies. Although originally the group was simply a set of countries identified as having some characteristics in common, the countries began forming a political group and having summit meetings, and in 2011 they invited South Africa to join them. At this point in time, the BRICs accounted for about 18% of world GDP and 15% of world trade, and contained about 40% of the world's population. If economic growth continues at current rates, the group will gain increasing economic and political influence relative to the G7.

Figure 22.17 shows economic growth in the original four BRIC countries since 1999, with the growth rate for the world as a whole to provide context. The consistency and rapidity of growth during the 2000s reveals why these countries were singled out

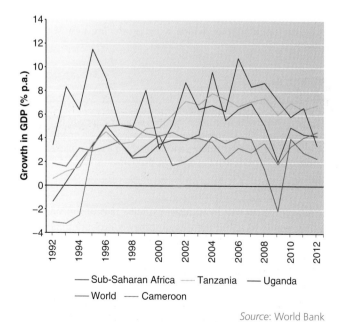

Source: World Bank

Figure 22.16 Growth in selected countries in sub-Saharan Africa

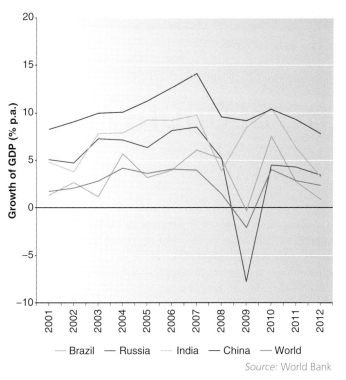

Figure 22.17 Growth in the BRIC countries

for attention, although Brazil was perhaps rather less successful in terms of its growth rates. What makes this performance more startling is the size of these economies, both in population and in the size of GDP. The achievements of the economies of China and India are especially impressive, in each case starting from a relatively low base – and for these two economies, the growth seemed robust in the face of the global recession. However, the factors underlying the growth performance were different in each case, as these economies are all at very different stages in terms of average incomes and display different characteristics, both politically and economically.

Exercise 22.2

Table 22.1 provides a selection of indicators for three countries. One of these is in sub-Saharan Africa, one is in southeast Asia and the other is in Latin America. See if you can identify which is which.

Table 22.1 Selected standard of living indicators for three countries

	Country A	Country B	Country C
Life expectancy at birth (years)	69.6	75.6	52.1
Adult literacy (%)	92.6	91.6	73.6
Population growth, 1975–2005 (% p.a.)	1.3	1.8	3.2
Urban population (% of total)	32.3	76.0	20.7
% of population under 15 years	21.7	30.8	42.6
% of population with access to safe water, 2004	99	97	61
% of adults aged 15–49 living with HIV/AIDS	1.4	0.3	6.1
Growth of GDP per capita, 1975–2005 (% p.a.)	4.9	1.0	0.1
Exports of primary goods (% of all merchandise exports)	22	23	79

Note: data are for 2005 unless otherwise stated.

Source: Human Development Report 2007/08

Sao Paulo, Brazil. Brazil has a rapidly growing economy and has been classified as a BRIC economy

Summary

- A small group of countries in South East Asia, known as the East Asian tiger economies, underwent a period of rapid economic growth, closing the gap on the more developed countries.
- This success arose from a combination of circumstances, including a high degree of openness to international trade, which was seen as crucial if economies of scale were to be reaped.
- However, the tigers are also characterised by high levels of human capital and political and macroeconomic stability.
- In contrast, countries in sub-Saharan Africa have stagnated; in some cases, real per capita incomes were lower in 2000 than they had been in 1975.
- Countries in Latin America began well, experiencing growth for a period, but then ran into economic difficulties.

23 Modelling the economy

In seeking to understand how the macroeconomy operates, we need to simplify the real world by the use of macroeconomic models that enable us to focus on the key relationships. This chapter begins with a reminder of the aggregate demand/aggregate supply (AD/AS) model first introduced in Chapter 7. Keynesian and Monetarist economists make different assumptions about the nature of aggregate supply, which have important implications for the nature of equilibrium in the macroeconomy. The Keynesian approach to macroeconomic equilibrium is illustrated by using the aggregate expenditure–income model, sometimes known as the 'Keynesian cross'. The chapter also discusses notions of full-employment income, the multiplier and the accelerator.

Learning outcomes

After studying this chapter, you should:

- be familiar with Keynesian and Monetarist approaches to aggregate supply
- appreciate the significance of these approaches for the nature of macroeconomic equilibrium
- be familiar with the aggregate expenditure–income approach to income determination
- understand the notion of full-employment income
- understand the nature of the multiplier and accelerator processes, and the interaction between them.

23.1 Monetarist and Keynesian approaches to the macroeconomy

Economists have adopted various approaches to modelling macroeconomic equilibrium, making different assumptions about how the economy operates at the aggregate level. Two important

schools of thought are the Monetarists and Keynesians, who came to very different views about the nature of macroeconomic equilibrium. A key point of difference is in their varying approach towards aggregate supply in the *AD/AS* model that was introduced during AS Economics.

Macroeconomic equilibrium in the short run

Figure 23.1 illustrates short-run macroeconomic equilibrium. Suppose that the economy begins in equilibrium with aggregate demand curve AD_0 and the **short-run aggregate supply curve** at SAS_0. Recall from Chapter 7 that the main components of aggregate demand are consumption, investment, government spending and net exports. The short-run aggregate supply curve shows how much output firms would be prepared to supply in the short run at any given overall price level. Macroeconomic equilibrium is achieved with real output given by Y_0 and with the overall price level at P_0.

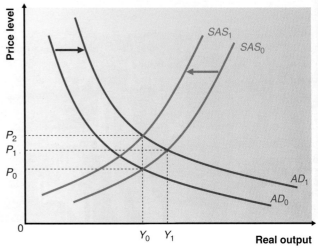

Figure 23.1 Short-run macroeconomic equilibrium

Key term

Short-run aggregate supply curve: a curve showing how much output firms are prepared to supply in the short run at any given overall price level.

Key terms

Full-employment income: the level of income achieved when all factors of production are fully employed.

Long-run aggregate supply curve: a curve that shows the amount of real output that will be supplied in the economy in the long run at any given overall price level.

If for some reason there is an increase in aggregate demand from AD_0 to AD_1, then the immediate response is a movement along the SAS curve, with real output increasing to Y_1 and the price level rising to P_1. What is happening here is that firms are responding to the increase in demand, expanding their production as prices rise.

The macroeconomy may not settle for long at this new position. As prices rise, there will be further adjustments. For example, workers may bid for higher wages to compensate for the higher prices, and firms may charge higher prices for the components that they supply to other firms. Or it may be that firms have to pay workers at overtime rates in order to induce them to work longer hours – especially if the economy is close to its full-employment position. These effects will feed back on to the costs faced by firms. As this happens, firms will be prepared to supply less output at any given overall price level, and the short-run aggregate supply curve will shift to the left.

In Figure 23.1, this is represented by the shift from SAS_0 to SAS_1. The overall price rises again, but real output now falls back. Indeed, in Figure 23.1, the level of real output returns to its original level at Y_0, but with a higher overall price level at P_2. This suggests that an increase in aggregate demand may lead to higher real output in the short run, but that this may not be a permanent increase.

Macroeconomic equilibrium in the long run

It was argued above that the adjustments to an increase in aggregate demand may offset the initial increase in real output. Indeed, it could be argued that there is a full-capacity level of real output beyond which no increase in real output can be sustained. This full-capacity level of output reflects full employment, and is known as the **full-employment income**. In the short run, output may rise beyond this, but only if firms are able to employ workers on overtime, which is not likely to be sustainable in the long term as it adds to the firms' labour costs. This suggests that the **long-run aggregate supply curve** is different in character from the short-run version.

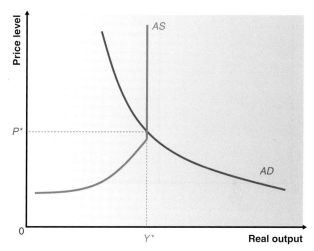

Figure 23.2 Macroeconomic equilibrium revisited

Figure 23.2 illustrates the situation. As before, AD is the aggregate demand curve, with the chief components of aggregate demand again being consumption, investment, government spending and net exports. AS is the aggregate supply curve, which becomes vertical at the full capacity level of output. In other words, Y^* represents the maximum amount of output that the economy can produce in a period if all its resources are being fully utilised. This is the full-employment level of output. The intersection of AD and AS provides the equilibrium position for the economy, with P^* in Figure 23.2 being the equilibrium price level. Remember that the AD curve is very different in nature from the individual demand curve for a commodity. Here the relationship is between the total demand for goods and services and the overall price level.

It is important to be aware of a debate that developed over the shape of the aggregate supply curve. This is important because it has implications for the conduct and effectiveness of policy options, which will be discussed in Chapter 27.

During the 1970s, an influential school of macroeconomists, which became known as the Monetarist school, argued that the economy would always converge on an equilibrium level of output that they referred to as the *natural rate of output*. They also argued that the adjustment to this natural rate would be rapid, perhaps almost instantaneous. Associated with this long-run equilibrium was a **natural rate of unemployment**. In this case, the long-run relationship between aggregate supply and the price level would be vertical, as shown in Figure 23.3. Here Y^* is the full-employment level of aggregate output – the natural rate of output. In this view of the world, a change in the overall price level does not affect aggregate output because the economy always readjusts rapidly back to full employment. Indeed, no change in aggregate demand can affect aggregate output, as it is only the price level that will adjust to restore equilibrium.

is operating below this level of output, aggregate supply is somewhat sensitive to the price level, becoming steeper as full employment is approached.

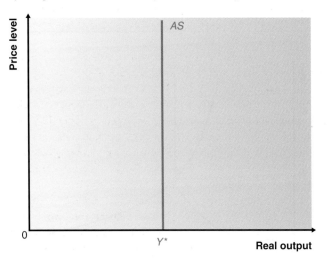

Figure 23.3 Aggregate supply in the long run ('Monetarist' view)

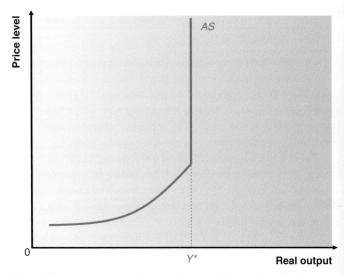

Figure 23.4 Aggregate supply in the long run ('Keynesian' view)

The policy implications of the Monetarist *AS* curve are strong. If the economy always converges rapidly on the full-employment level of output, no change of aggregate demand can have any effect except on the price level. This is readily seen in Figure 23.5 where, regardless of the position of the aggregate demand curve, the level of real output remains at Y^*. If aggregate demand is low at AD_0, then the price level is also relatively low, at P_0. An increase in aggregate demand to AD_1 raises the price level to P_1 but leaves real output at Y^*. In such a world, only a change that affects the position of the aggregate supply curve has any effect on real output.

Key term

Natural rate of unemployment: equilibrium full-employment level of unemployment.

An opposing school of thought (often known as the Keynesian school) held that the macroeconomy was not sufficiently flexible to enable continuous full employment. They argued that the economy could settle at an equilibrium position below full employment, at least in the medium term. In particular, inflexibilities in labour markets would prevent adjustment. For example, if firms had pessimistic expectations about aggregate demand, and thus reduced their supply of output, this would lead to lower incomes because of workers being laid off. This would then mean that aggregate demand was indeed deficient, so firms' pessimism was self-fulfilling. Pessimistic expectations would also affect investment, and thus have an impact on the long-run productive capacity of the economy.

Keynesian arguments led to a belief that there would be a range of outputs over which aggregate supply would be upward sloping. Figure 23.4 illustrates such an aggregate supply curve, and will be familiar from Chapter 7. In this diagram, Y^* still represents full employment; however, when the economy

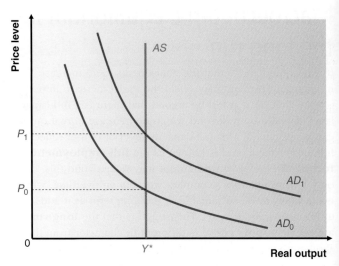

Figure 23.5 A demand-side shift with a vertical *AS* curve

Exercise 23.1

Using an *AD/AS* diagram, analyse the effect on macroeconomic equilibrium of an increase in the price of oil that causes the *AS* curve to shift. Conduct this experiment under Monetarist and Keynesian assumptions about the shape of the long-run *AS* curve.

Summary

- In using the *AD/AS* model, it is useful to distinguish between Monetarist and Keynesian views about the shape of aggregate supply.
- Monetarist economists have argued that the economy always converges rapidly on equilibrium at the natural rate of output, implying that changes in aggregate demand have an impact only on prices, leaving real output unaffected. The aggregate supply curve in this world is vertical.
- The Keynesian view is that the economy may settle in an equilibrium that is below full employment, and that there is a range over which the aggregate supply curve slopes upwards.

23.2 A Keynesian approach to macroeconomic equilibrium

Given the Keynesian view of aggregate supply, the position of the aggregate demand curve becomes significant. If *AD* is located in the upward-sloping part of the *AS* curve, then the macroeconomy is caught below the natural rate of output, and there will be unemployed resources in the economy. In the rest of this chapter, attention focuses on how income is determined relative to aggregate expenditure.

The circular flow of income, expenditure and output

Assume for the moment that there are just two types of economic agent in an economy: households and firms. In other words, ignore the government and assume there is no international trade. (These will be brought back into the picture soon.) We also assume that all factors of production are owned and supplied to firms by households.

In this simple world, assume that firms produce goods and hire labour and other factor inputs from households. Also assume that they buy investment goods from other firms, for which purpose they need to borrow in a financial market. Households supply their labour (and other factor inputs) and buy consumer goods. In return for supplying factor inputs, households receive income, part of which they spend on consumer goods and part of which they save in the financial market.

If you examine the monetary flows in this economy, you can see how the economy operates. In Figure 23.6 the blue arrow shows the flow of income that goes from firms to households as payment for their factor services (labour, land and capital). The red arrows show what happens to the output produced by firms: part of it goes to households in the form of consumer goods (*C*); the rest flows back to other firms as investment goods (*I*). The green arrows show the expenditure flows back to firms, part of which is for consumer goods (*C*) from households, and part for investment goods (*I*) from firms. The circle is closed by households' savings, by which part of their income is invested in the financial market; this is then borrowed by firms to finance their purchases of investment goods. These flows are shown by the orange arrows. This model is sometimes known as the circular flow model.

As this is a closed system, these flows must balance. This means that there are three ways in which the total amount of economic activity in this economy can be measured (indicated by the cross-lines in the figure): by the incomes that firms pay out, by the total amount of output that is produced, or by total expenditure. Whichever method is chosen, it should give the same result, as was discussed in Chapter 21.

A real-world economy is more complicated than this, so it is also necessary to take into account the economic activities of government and the fact that economies engage in international trade, so that some of the output produced is sold abroad and some of the expenditure goes on foreign goods and services.

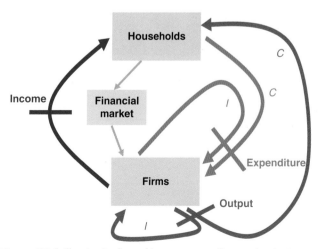

Figure 23.6 The circular flow of income, expenditure and output

The aggregate expenditure–income model

The full version of aggregate expenditure can be written as:

$$AE = C + I + G + X - M$$

where AE denotes aggregate expenditure, C is consumption, I is investment, G is government spending, X is exports and M is imports.

It is important to notice that when we observe the economy and measure these items of expenditure, inventory (stock) changes are included as part of investment. In this model, equilibrium is interpreted as a state in which the plans of economic agents in the economy (that is, households, firms and others) are fulfilled. If firms find that they have produced more output than is subsequently purchased, their inventory holdings increase. Thus, although after the event expenditure always equals output, this is because any disequilibrium is reflected in unplanned inventory changes.

Consumption

Consumption is the largest single component of aggregate demand. What factors could be expected to influence the size of total spending by households? John Maynard Keynes, in his influential book *The General Theory of Employment, Interest and Money*, published in 1936, suggested that the most important determinant is **disposable income**.

John Maynard Keynes was a very influential economist

Key term

Disposable income: the income that households have to devote to consumption and saving, taking into account payments of direct taxes and transfer payments.

In other words, as real incomes rise, households will tend to spend more. However, Keynes also pointed out that they would not spend all of an increase in income, but would save some of it. Keynes defined the **average propensity to consume** as the

ratio of consumption to income, and the **marginal propensity to consume** as the proportion of an *increase* in disposable income that households would devote to consumption.

Key terms

Average propensity to consume: the proportion of income that households devote to consumption.

Marginal propensity to consume: the proportion of additional income devoted to consumption.

Extension: other influences on consumption

Later writers argued that consumption does not necessarily depend upon current income alone. For example, Milton Friedman put forward the *permanent income hypothesis*, which suggested that consumers take decisions about consumption based on a notion of their permanent, or normal, income levels – that is, the income that they expect to receive over a five- or ten-year time horizon. This suggests that households do not necessarily vary their consumption patterns in response to changes in income that they perceive to be only transitory. An associated theory is the *life-cycle hypothesis*, developed by Ando Modigliani, who suggested that households smooth their consumption over their lifetimes, on the basis of their expected lifetime incomes. Thus, people tend to borrow in their youth against future income; then in middle age, when earning more strongly, they pay off their debts and save in preparation to fund their consumption in retirement. Consumption thus varies by much less than income, and is based on expected lifetime earnings rather than on current income.

However, income will not be the only influence on consumption. Consumption may also depend partly on the *wealth* of a household. As we have seen, income and wealth are not the same. Income accrues during a period as a reward for the supply of factor services, such as labour. Wealth, on the other hand, represents the stock of accumulated past savings. If you like, wealth can be thought of in terms of the asset holdings of households. If households experience an increase in their asset holdings, this may influence their spending decisions.

Furthermore, if part of household spending is financed by borrowing, the rate of interest may be significant in influencing the total amount of consumption spending. An increase in the rate of interest that raises the cost of borrowing may deter consumption. At the same time it may encourage saving, as the return on saving is higher when the interest rate is higher. The rate of interest may also have an indirect effect on consumption through its effect on the value of asset holdings. In addition, households may be influenced in their consumption decisions by their expectations about future inflation. Notice that some of these effects may not be instantaneous: that is, consumption may adjust to changes in its determinants only after a time lag.

This **consumption function** can be portrayed as a relationship between consumption and income. Figure 23.7 focuses on the relationship between consumption and household income, ceteris paribus: in other words, in drawing the relationship between consumption and income, it is assumed that the other determinants of consumption, such as wealth and the interest rate, remain constant. A change in any of these other influences will affect the *position* of the line. Notice that the marginal propensity to consume (*MPC*) is the slope of this line. For example, if the *MPC* is 0.7, this means that for every additional £100 of income received by households, £70 would be spent on consumption and the remaining £30 would be saved.

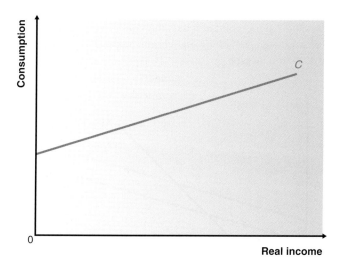

Figure 23.7 The consumption function

Key term

Consumption function: the relationship between consumption and disposable income; its position depends upon the other factors that affect how much households spend on consumption.

Investment

The rate of interest is also likely to be an important influence on firms' decisions about investment spending. Again, this is because the interest rate represents the cost of borrowing; so, if firms need to borrow in order to undertake investment, they may be discouraged from spending on investment goods when the rate of interest is relatively high.

Investment leads to an increase in the productive capacity of the economy, by increasing the stock of capital available for production. This capital stock comprises plant and machinery, vehicles and other transport equipment, and buildings, including new dwellings, which provide a supply of housing services over a long period.

Although important, the rate of interest is not likely to be the only factor that determines how much investment firms choose to undertake. First, not all investment has to be funded from borrowing – firms may be able to use past profits for this purpose. However, if firms choose to do this, they face an opportunity cost. Profits can be used to buy financial assets that will provide a rate of return dependent on the rate of interest. The rate of interest is thus still important, as it represents the opportunity cost of an investment project.

In considering an investment project, firms will need to form expectations about the future stream of earnings that will flow from the investment. Their expectations about the future state of the economy (and the demand for their products) will thus be an important influence on current investment. This is one reason why it is argued that inflation is damaging for an economy, as a high rate of inflation increases uncertainty about the future and may dampen firms' expectations about future demand, thereby discouraging investment.

Figure 23.8 shows the relationship between investment and the rate of interest. The investment demand function I_{D0} is downward sloping because investment is relatively low when the rate of interest is relatively high. An improvement in business confidence for the future would result in more investment being undertaken at any given interest rate, so the investment function would move from I_{D0} to I_{D1}.

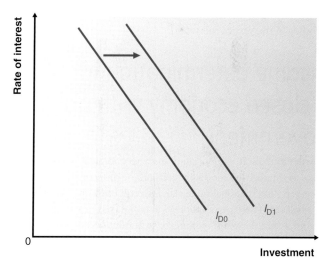

Figure 23.8 Investment and the rate of interest

Government expenditure

By and large, you might expect government expenditure to be decided by different criteria from those influencing private sector expenditures. Indeed, some aspects of government expenditure might be regarded as part of macroeconomic policy, as will be seen in Chapter 27. Some other aspects of government expenditure may vary automatically with variations in the overall level of economic activity over time. The effects of this will also be examined in Chapter 27.

From the point of view of investigating macroeconomic equilibrium, however, government expenditure can be regarded as mainly *autonomous*: that is, independent of the variables in the model that will be constructed in this chapter and the following one.

Trade in goods and services

Finally, there are the factors that may influence the level of exports and imports. One factor that will affect both of these is the exchange rate between the home and other currencies. This affects the relative prices of home-produced goods and those produced overseas. Other things being equal, an increase in the foreign exchange rate makes domestic exports less competitive and imports into the economy from overseas more competitive.

However, the demand for exports and imports will also depend upon the relative prices of goods produced in the domestic economy and the rest of the world. If domestic inflation is high relative to elsewhere, again this will tend to make exports less competitive and imports more competitive. These effects were examined in Chapter 9, where it was shown that movements in the exchange rate tend to counteract changes in relative prices between countries.

In addition, the demand for imports into the home economy will depend partly upon the level of domestic aggregate income, and the demand for exports will depend partly upon the level of incomes in the rest of the world.

Income determination in a closed economy with no government

In order to explore the notion of macroeconomic equilibrium, it helps to simplify the model by considering an economy in which there is no international trade (i.e. a closed economy) and no government. These assumptions will be relaxed in the next section.

In this simple world, aggregate expenditure has just two components – consumption (C) and investment (I). In other words:

$$AE = C + I$$

Income received by households (Y) is allocated to consumption and saving (S). So:

$$Y = C + S$$

As mentioned earlier, equilibrium is said to occur when the plans of households and firms are mutually compatible. In other words, equilibrium is where the production plans of firms are consistent with the consumption and saving plans of households. If we assume that consumption plans of households are always

fulfilled, this is tantamount to saying that equilibrium will occur when planned investment is equal to planned saving.

There are two ways of specifying this equilibrium – and of depicting it diagrammatically. First, equilibrium can be seen when planned aggregate expenditure (AE) is equal to real income (Y). Second, because consumption (C) is part of both income and expenditure, equilibrium occurs when planned investment is equal to planned saving.

In Figure 23.9, aggregate expenditure is shown on the vertical axis, and income (GDP) on the horizontal axis. The points at which $AE = Y$ can be represented by a line drawn at a 45° angle from the origin. In this simplified version of the model there are two items of expenditure, consumption (C), which varies with income, and investment (I), which does not. The $AE = C + I$ line thus shows how aggregate expenditure varies with income. The intersection of AE with the 45° line shows the unique point at which the equilibrium condition holds true, with AE^* being equilibrium aggregate expenditure and Y^* being income.

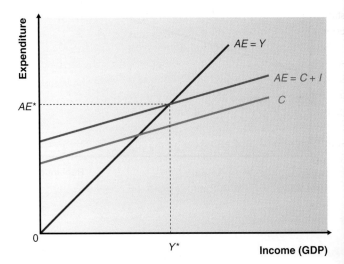

Figure 23.9 Equilibrium in the income–expenditure model

An important question is whether the economy will move towards this equilibrium, and by what mechanism. Figure 23.10 illustrates this. Y^* is the potential equilibrium point, but suppose that firms' production decisions result in income being below the equilibrium level at Y_0. In this situation, desired aggregate expenditure is AE_0 but this is higher than real income Y_0. The result of this is that firms will find that their inventories are being run down in order to meet demand. Another way of looking at this is that there is an *unplanned* fall in inventories – which indicates there is disequilibrium. Firms are likely to respond to this by increasing output, thus leading to an increase in income. The economy will thus move towards the equilibrium at Y^*.

A similar pattern emerges if real income is above the equilibrium. For example, suppose real income is at Y_1. Aggregate expenditure (at AE_1) is now too low to account for total output, and firms will find that their inventories start to

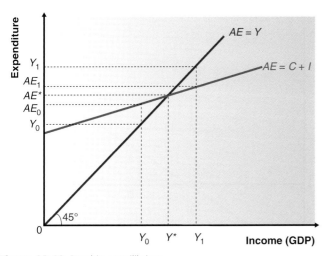

Figure 23.10 Reaching equilibrium

build up. The response is likely to be to reduce output, and thus income, again taking the economy towards the equilibrium.

This analysis shows that the equilibrium in the model is stable. In other words, if the economy finds itself away from the equilibrium position, it will move back towards it.

The same equilibrium position can be shown using the second way of specifying the equilibrium – namely, as planned investment equals planned saving. Figure 23.11 illustrates this approach. In this diagram, saving varies with income but planned investment is autonomous – in other words, it does not depend upon the level of income. The equilibrium position is shown by Y^*, which is the same equilibrium as was shown in the previous figures.

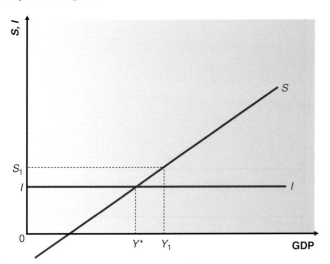

Figure 23.11 Savings = investment equilibrium

This equilibrium can also be seen to be stable. Suppose income is at Y_1, such that saving (S_1) is higher than planned investment. Firms find that there is an unplanned increase in their inventories because households are saving more and consuming less than is required to sustain the level of income. Firms will thus reduce output, leading to a fall in income, and the economy moves towards the equilibrium position.

Withdrawals and injections

One way of viewing saving within the circular flow of income, expenditure and output is that it is a **withdrawal** from the flow. Households receive income, but only spend a proportion on consumption. In the simple model, this gets recycled through the financial market. In other words, households save, depositing the saving in the financial market, and firms borrow in order to finance their investment expenditure. This investment expenditure constitutes an **injection** into the circular flow. Equilibrium can now be viewed as a situation in which planned withdrawals equal planned injections.

Key terms

Withdrawal: a leakage from the circular flow of income, expenditure and output; comprising saving, direct taxes and imports.

Injection: an addition to the circular flow, comprising investment, government expenditure and exports; these items are regarded as autonomous – that is, unrelated to the level of income.

Income determination in an open economy with government and international trade

In a world in which the government engages in economic actions, and where there is international trade, the pattern of withdrawals and injections changes.

The government raises revenue by imposing taxes (T), and undertakes expenditure (G) in the form of spending on goods and services and transfer payments to poor households. The taxes raised by government are seen to be a withdrawal from the circular flow, and in a simple model can be assumed to be proportional to income. Government expenditure is seen as an injection into the circular flow, and may be viewed as being autonomous – in other words, expenditure by government does not vary with real income. This may not always be the case, and this will be discussed later.

Bringing international trade into the picture, exports (X) can be seen to be an injection into the circular flow, and imports (M) as a withdrawal. Exports can be seen as being unrelated to domestic income, and thus will be treated as autonomous. However, imports are expected to vary with real income – at higher levels of real income, imports will tend to be higher. Aggregate expenditure is now:

$$AE = C + I + G + (X - M)$$

Equilibrium can again be seen as a situation in which planned withdrawals (W) are equal to planned injections (J):

$$S + T + M = I + G + X$$

Under the assumptions made, all three types of injection are autonomous – that is, unrelated to income. Figure 23.12 shows the equilibrium position.

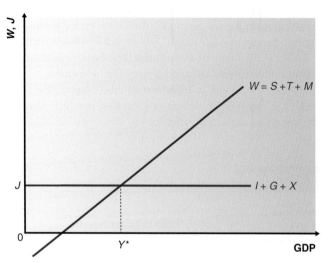

Figure 23.12 Equilibrium in the withdrawals–injection approach

Exercise 23.2

Use an income–aggregate expenditure diagram to show equilibrium in an economy with government and international trade. Discuss whether the economy will return to equilibrium if actual income is below equilibrium income, and explain the mechanism involved.

Full employment

The income–expenditure approach to income determination focuses very strongly on the demand side of the macroeconomy. The supply decisions of firms are relatively passive – firms are assumed to respond to unplanned changes in their inventories. As a result, there is no guarantee that the equilibrium that emerges will correspond to the full-employment level of real income, which was discussed earlier in the chapter. This is the level of real income at which all factors of production are fully employed. Keynes argued that an economy could settle at a level of income that was below full employment, meaning that there would be unemployment in that equilibrium position. This was a major point of disagreement with the Monetarist approach, which argued that the economy would naturally tend towards a full-employment equilibrium.

The situation that Keynes described can be depicted in Figure 23.13. Here the full-employment level of income is Y_f, but the equilibrium point at which injections equal withdrawals is lower, at Y^*. In this situation, the problem is that autonomous expenditure (injections) is insufficient to carry the economy to full employment. The shortfall is given in the figure by the distance AB, which is known as a **deflationary gap**.

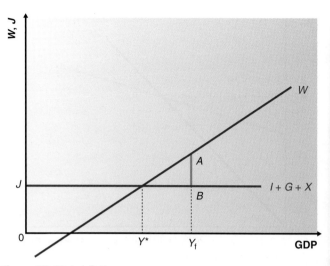

Figure 23.13 A deflationary gap

Figure 23.14 shows the opposite scenario. Here the equilibrium level of income is at Y^*, which is beyond the full-employment level Y_f. The problem now is that the equilibrium level Y^* cannot be reached, as it is beyond the capacity of the economy even when all factors of production are fully utilised. It is now the case that spending is beyond what can be delivered in terms of output. The distance QR is known as an **inflationary gap**. The reason for the term is straightforward – in this situation we have excess aggregate demand, and a natural response for the economy would be for the price level to rise to choke off that excess demand.

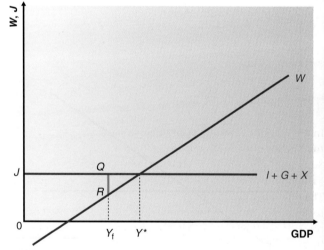

Figure 23.14 An inflationary gap

Key terms

Deflationary gap: a situation that arises when the equilibrium level of income is lower than the full-employment level.

Inflationary gap: a situation that arises when the equilibrium level of income is higher than the full-employment level, and thus cannot be reached.

Summary

- The circular flow of income, expenditure and output describes the relationship between these three key variables.
- The model suggests that there are three ways in which the total level of economic activity in an economy during a period of time can be measured: by total income, by total expenditure, and by total output produced.
- In principle, these should give the same answers, but in practice data measurements are not so accurate.
- Aggregate expenditure is the sum of consumption, investment, government expenditure and net exports.
- Consumption is the largest component, depending upon income and also upon household wealth and the rate of interest.
- Investment is likely to be influenced by the rate of interest.
- Government expenditure and exports are treated as autonomous in the simplified income–expenditure model.
- Equilibrium is attained where planned withdrawals are equal to planned injections.
- There is no guarantee that equilibrium income will occur at the full-employment level.

Governments may try to stimulate the economy by increasing building programmes – such as this flyover under construction in Kuala Lumpur, Malaysia

Key term

Multiplier: the ratio of a change in equilibrium real income to the autonomous change that brought it about; it is defined as 1 divided by the marginal propensity to withdraw.

23.3 The multiplier and accelerator effects

The multiplier

In his *General Theory*, Keynes pointed out that there may be **multiplier** effects in response to certain types of expenditure. Suppose that the government increases its expenditure by $1 billion, perhaps by increasing its road-building programme. The effect of this is to generate incomes for households – for example, those of the contractors hired to build the road. Those contractors then spend part of the additional income (and save part of it). By spending part of the extra money earned, an additional income stream is generated for shopkeepers and café owners, who in turn spend part of *their* additional income, and so on. Thus, the original increase in government spending sparks off further income generation and spending, causing the multiplier effect. In effect, equilibrium output may change by more than the original increase in expenditure. Investment and exports are also injections that will have similar effects.

Notice that it is the act of spending that allows these effects to be perpetuated. If the workers who receive additional income do not spend some of that income, the effects are diluted. The amounts that are not spent are referred to as 'withdrawals'. There are three ways in which these withdrawals take place. First, it may be that households decide to save some of the extra income that they receive instead of spending it. The amount of additional income that is saved is known as the marginal propensity to save (s). Second, some of the extra income will be spent on imports, and the marginal propensity to import (m) represents the fraction of extra income spent on imported goods or services. Third, a proportion of the extra income (t) is taken back by the government as taxes on income. The overall size of these induced effects will depend upon the marginal propensity to withdraw. The **marginal propensity to withdraw** (mpw) is thus the sum of these three effects ($s + m + t$).

Key term

Marginal propensity to withdraw: the sum of the marginal propensities to save, tax and import; it is the proportion of additional income that is withdrawn from the circular flow.

The size of the multiplier can then be calculated. For example, suppose that households save 5% of extra income ($s = 0.05$) and spend 10% of the extra income on imports ($m = 0.1$), and that 25% goes in tax ($t = 0.25$). The mpw is then $0.05 + 0.1 + 0.25 = 0.4$, and the multiplier is 2.5. An increase in the savings rate to 15% would increase the mpw to 0.5 and reduce the multiplier to 2.

It is worth noting that the size of the leakages may depend in part upon the domestic elasticity of supply. If domestic supply is inflexible, and therefore unable to meet an increase in demand, more of the increase in income will spill over into purchasing imports, and this will dilute the multiplier effect.

Exercise 23.3

In each case, indicate the direction of the multiplier effect.

a   Saving by households.
b   Expenditure by central government.
c   Spending by a country's residents on imported goods and services.
d   Expenditure by firms on investment.
e   Spending by overseas residents on home-produced goods and services.
f   Income tax payments.
g   The marginal propensity to save.

Exercise 23.4

Calculate the multiplier if households save 20% of any additional income that they receive and spend 10% on imports. Assume that the marginal tax rate is 10%. Check how the multiplier changes if the marginal tax rate increases to 20%.

The income–expenditure model revisited

The multiplier effect can be seen using the income–expenditure model. Figure 23.15 shows an economy that begins in equilibrium at Y_0, with injections composed of investment (I), government spending (G_0) and exports (X). If the government increases spending to G_1, injections increase from J_0 to J_1, and equilibrium income goes from Y_0 to Y_1. The effect of the multiplier is seen in the way that the increase in income ($Y_1 - Y_0$) is greater than the original increase in injections ($J_1 - J_0$).

An important implication of this is that it seems to give the government a way of controlling the level of equilibrium income. An increase in government expenditure is seen to have a multiplied impact on the level of equilibrium income. If an economy is trapped in a position with a deflationary gap – in other words, if equilibrium income is below the full-employment level – then the authorities can deal with it by manipulating expenditure. This sort of policy is known as **fiscal policy**, and will be discussed in Chapter 27. It is important to realise that this analysis rests on some key assumptions, not all of which may hold true in the real world. In particular, the effects of prices and interest rates have not been factored in.

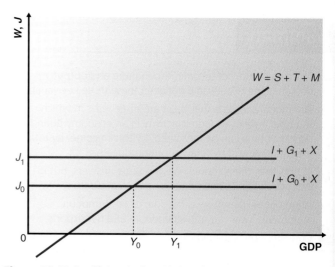

Figure 23.15 Equilibrium in the withdrawals–injections approach

---

Key term

Fiscal policy: decisions made by government on its expenditure, taxation and borrowing.

The paradox of thrift

It is often thought that the act of saving is good for the economy. Thriftiness rather than wastefulness is widely considered to be a virtue. However, in the income–expenditure model this is by no means so clear. An increase in saving by households means an increase in withdrawals, and a fall in equilibrium income, which may have the effect of taking the economy away from full employment, resulting in an increase in unemployment. Furthermore, the impact of such an increase in saving on equilibrium income is enhanced by the workings of the multiplier. This is known as the **paradox of thrift** – you would expect that an increase in saving would enable higher investment, which in turn would enable higher productive capacity in the economy. This does not happen in this model. However, it is important to remember that the model rests on some strong simplifying assumptions.

Key term

Paradox of thrift: a result from the income–expenditure model by which an increase in saving results in a fall in investment and aggregate income.

The accelerator

The idea of the multiplier is based on the induced effects of expenditure that spread the initial effects of an increase in spending. A similar notion is that of the **accelerator**. The notion of the accelerator arises from one of the driving forces behind firms' investment. Although some investment is needed to replace old equipment (known as depreciation), most investment is needed when firms wish to expand capacity. If there is an increase in demand for a firm's product (or if a firm expects there to be an increase in demand), it may need to expand capacity in order to meet the increased demand. This suggests that one of the determinants of the level of investment is a change in expected demand. Notice that it is the change in demand that is important, rather than the level, and it is this that leads to the notion of the accelerator.

Key term

Accelerator: a theory by which the level of investment depends upon the change in real output.

Suppose that the economy is in recession and begins to recover. As the recovery begins, demand begins to increase, and firms have to undertake investment in order to expand capacity. However, as the economy approaches full capacity, the growth

rate slows down – and hence investment falls, as it reacts to the change in output.

The multiplier and accelerator interact with each other. If there is an increase in output following an increase in aggregate demand, the accelerator induces an increase in investment. The increase in investment then has a multiplier effect that induces an additional increase in demand. In this way, the multiplier and accelerator reinforce each other. The downside to this is that the same thing happens when output slows, as this leads to a fall in investment, which has negative multiplier effects. This interaction between the multiplier and the accelerator can result in cyclical fluctuations in the level of output.

Summary

- The multiplier reinforces the effects of an increase in aggregate demand.
- The accelerator effect reinforces the multiplier when investment by firms responds to a change in output.
- The interaction between the multiplier and the accelerator can give rise to fluctuations in equilibrium output.

24 Money and the economy

This chapter explores the role of money in the economy. It has often been argued that the quantity of money in the economy – and its rate of growth – are crucial in influencing the rate of inflation, and hence the overall performance of the economy. However, it has also been noted that money stock is difficult to define, measure, monitor and control. This chapter explains why this is the case, setting out the various sources of money and credit creation in a modern economy. It also discusses the main theories that seek to explain the importance of money in the macroeconomy.

Learning outcomes

After studying this chapter, you should:

- appreciate the importance of money in the macroeconomy
- understand the distinction between narrow and broad measures of money supply
- be familiar with the sources of money in the economy, in particular noting the actions of commercial banks, the central bank and the government, and the influence of international financial transactions
- be aware of the determinants of the demand for money
- understand the way in which interest rates are determined
- be familiar with the liquidity preference theory and the loanable funds approach.

24.1 Money in the modern economy

The **money supply** is the quantity of money that is in circulation in the economy. Although this is an important macroeconomic variable, it is quite difficult to measure accurately.

An important characteristic of money is **liquidity**. This refers to the ease with which an asset can be spent. Cash is the most liquid asset, as it can be used for transactions. However, if you are holding funds in a savings account whereby you must either give notice of withdrawal or forfeit some return to withdraw it instantly, then such funds are regarded as being less liquid, as they cannot costlessly or instantly be used for transactions.

One traditional way of measuring the money stock in the UK was from the **monetary base**, which comprised all notes and coins in circulation. Together with the commercial banks' deposits at the Bank of England, this was known as **M0 or narrow money**. This was intended to measure the amount of money held for transactions purposes. However, with the increased use of electronic means of payment, M0 has become less meaningful as a measure, and the Bank of England stopped issuing data for M0 in 2005.

However, there are many assets that are 'near-money', such as interest-bearing current account deposits at banks. These are highly liquid and can readily be converted into cash for transactions. **M4 or broad money** is a measure of the money stock that includes M0 together with sterling wholesale and retail deposits with monetary financial institutions such as banks. In other words, it includes all bank deposits that can be used for transactions, even though some of these deposits may require a period of notice for withdrawal. However, M4 is held not only for transactions purposes, but also partly as a store of wealth.

Key terms

Money supply: the quantity of money in circulation in the economy.

Liquidity: the extent to which an asset can be converted to cash without the holder incurring a cost.

Monetary base: notes and coins in circulation.

Narrow money (M0): notes and coins in circulation and as commercial banks' deposits at the Bank of England.

Broad money (M4): M0 plus sterling wholesale and retail deposits with monetary financial institutions such as banks and building societies.

A problem if the monetary authorities want to control the money supply directly is that the complexity of the modern financial system makes it quite difficult to pin down a precise definition or measurement of money. It is also important to realise that the ending behaviour of the commercial banks can influence money supply, as by increasing their lending, banks can create credit. This makes it more difficult for the central bank to exert control over money supply. This could be achieved by forcing the banks to hold a proportion of their assets as cash or liquid assets.

The difficulty in measuring and monitoring money supply partly stems from the characteristics of money, which were discussed back in Chapter 1. Money performs four key roles – as a medium of exchange, store of value, a unit of account and a standard of deferred payment. There is a range of assets that can fulfil some or all of these roles, and this is at the core of the problem. These assets have varying degrees of liquidity. Cash and banknotes are liquid assets as they can be used for transactions directly. However, current (chequing) accounts are almost as liquid, but although savings accounts in banks may also be quite quickly converted to cash, there may be a time delay or a cost involved. Shares or government bonds are much less liquid as it takes time to convert them into cash. Nonetheless, they are several types of asset that can be regarded as being near-money. The central bank can control the quantities of some of these assets, but not all.

The central bank

All developed and most developing countries have a **central bank** that fulfils a range of roles, including having the responsibility for issuing currency (banknotes and coins). For example, the UK has the Bank of England to act as the country's central bank. Being the body responsible for issuing notes and coins, the central bank has some direct impact on the quantity of money in circulation in the country. However, this does not mean that it has complete control over the total stock of money.

Key term

Central bank: the banker to the government, performing a range of functions, which may include issue of coins and banknotes, acting as banker to commercial banks and regulating the financial system.

The central bank has other important roles to fulfil. The central bank acts as banker to the government, and may manage the government's programme of borrowing and the country's foreign exchange reserves. Furthermore, the central bank may act as a banker for the commercial banks and other financial institutions that operate in the economy. In addition, the central bank may act as the regulator of the financial system, monitoring the behaviour of the commercial banks and financial institutions. In some countries, the central bank has independent authority delegated from the government to pursue targets for inflation through the setting of interest rates or to promote growth and development.

In developing countries, the central bank may have an important role in establishing and consolidating the domestic financial system in order to build confidence in the currency and financial institutions. There may also be a developmental role in ensuring that credit can be made available for key development priorities. An example is the State Bank of Pakistan, which also has a responsibility for the 'islamisation' of the banking system, to recognise the importance to the country of developing Islamic forms of financial instrument. This activity is beyond the scope of this book.

The State Bank of Pakistan

The core activities, in terms of acting as banker to the government and financial institutions, managing the country's exchange reserves and supply of currency, and regulating the financial system, have strong implications for the supply of money and credit in the economy.

The commercial banks and credit creation

The operations of commercial banks can influence the quantity of money. Banks accept deposits from their customers, and issue loans. The way in which they undertake lending has an impact on the quantity of money.

The credit creation multiplier

Think first of all about the way in which the money supply is created. You might think that this is simply a question of controlling the amount of notes and coin issued by the central bank. However, because there are many different assets that act as near-money in a modern economy, the real picture is more complicated. The actions of the commercial banks also have implications for the size of money supply.

Consider the way that commercial banks operate. They accept deposits from customers, and supply them with banking services. However, they also provide loans – and this is how they make profits. Suppose that the government undertakes a piece of expenditure, and finances it by issuing money. The firms receiving the payment from the government are likely to bank the money they receive, so bank deposits increase.

From the perspective of the commercial banks, they know that it is unlikely that all their customers will want to withdraw their money simultaneously, so they will lend out some of the additional deposits to borrowers, who are likely to undertake expenditure on goods or services. As their expenditures work their way back into the banking system, the commercial banks will find that they can lend out even more, and so the process continues. In other words, an increase in the amount of money in the economy has a multiplied effect on the amount of credit created by the banks. This process is known as the **credit multiplier**.

> **Key term**
>
> **Credit multiplier**: a process by which an increase in money supply can have a multiplied effect on the amount of credit in an economy.

Consider the arithmetic example illustrated in Figure 24.1. Suppose that the commercial banks always act such as to hold 10% of their assets in liquid form – that is, as cash in the tills. If an extra $100 is lodged as deposits, the commercial banks will add $10 to the cash in tills, and lend out the remaining $90. When that $90 finds its way back into the hands of the bank, it will keep $9 as cash, and lend out the remaining $81. And so on. The process will stop when the bank is back to a cash ratio

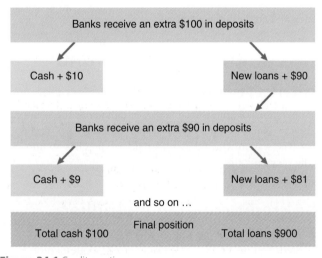

Figure 24.1 Credit creation

of 10%. The original extra $100 will have been converted into $100 in cash, and $900 in loans! The value of the multiplier is given by 1 divided by the desired cash ratio that the commercial banks decide to hold. The smaller this ratio is, the larger is the credit multiplier. If the commercial banks want to hold only 5% of their assets in the form of cash, then the credit multiplier will be 1/0.05 = 20.

The significance of this relationship is that changes in the supply of cash have a multiplied impact on the amount of credit in the economy. This makes monetary control through money supply a highly imprecise business, especially if the central bank does not know exactly what the commercial banks' desired liquidity ratio is.

Government deficit financing

Suppose the government chooses to run a deficit, by spending more than it collects in taxes. This possibility was raised in Chapter 21. In order to finance the deficit, the government needs to borrow if it does not wish to print money. The government borrows by issuing bonds (Treasury bills or gilt-edged securities), which it sells to the central bank, to the commercial banks or to the public. If the bonds are sold to the central bank or the commercial banks, there will be a multiplied effect on money stock. This is because when the government undertakes its expenditure, this releases new money into the system that then acts as an increase in the base on which credit creation takes place. Selling to the non-bank private sector does not have this effect, because the public draw down their bank deposits in order to pay for the bonds in the first place. Deficit financing by the government can thus have an impact on the size of money stock.

Open economy effects on the money stock

For an open economy, the domestic money supply can be affected by the central bank's operations in the foreign exchange market. This is most apparent when a country is operating a fixed exchange rate system, but can also occur in the case of a managed float, under which the central bank may intervene occasionally to influence the rate of exchange.

If the country is operating a fixed exchange rate, it decides to maintain the exchange rate against another currency (most often the US dollar). It may from time to time have to intervene to maintain the exchange rate. This will be necessary when the total currency flow between the domestic economy and the rest of the world is non-zero: in other words, when the demand and supply of domestic country are not equal.

For example, if there is a total currency flow deficit, such that the supply of domestic currency is higher than the demand, then the monetary authorities will need to sell foreign exchange in order to absorb the excess, thus reducing domestic money supply. On the other hand, if the demand for domestic currency exceeds the supply, the monetary authorities must buy foreign exchange, thus increasing domestic money supply, which will have a multiplied effect through the credit multiplier.

In other words, the central bank is not able to control both the exchange rate and money supply, and an imbalance on the balance of payments has implications for domestic money supply. In some circumstances, this imbalance in the total currency flow effectively acts as a source of domestic money supply.

Exercise 24.1

Suppose that the commercial banks in a country follow a rule such that they always aim to hold one-tenth of their assets in liquid form (i.e. as cash). Calculate the total increase in bank lending that would follow if government action leads to an extra $200 being lodged as bank deposits. Explain your answer.

Summary

- Liquidity is an important characteristic of financial assets.
- Traditional measures have distinguished between the monetary base (narrow money) and broad money.
- The difficulty of measuring money supply precisely creates problems if the monetary authorities wish to control the quantity.
- Money plays an important role in the macroeconomy.
- Most countries have a central bank that issues currency and may act as banker to the government and to commercial banks and other financial institutions.
- The central bank may also manage the government's programme of borrowing and the country's foreign exchange reserves.
- In many developing countries, the central bank also plays an important role in nurturing the domestic financial system and encouraging economic development.
- Money supply is difficult to control because money can be generated from a range of sources.
- Commercial banks can influence money supply through their lending policy via the credit multiplier.
- Government deficit financing and exchange rate policy can also affect the domestic money supply.

24.2 Money and inflation

The supply of money

Why should the quantity of money or credit in circulation be so important? Recall the quantity theory of money, which was introduced in Chapter 8. This quantity theory relationship suggests that prices can only increase persistently if money stock itself increases persistently, or if money stock persistently grows more rapidly than real output.

How can we interpret this in terms of aggregate demand and aggregate supply? If the money supply increases, then firms and households in the economy find they have excess cash balances – that is, for the given price level they have stronger purchasing power than they had anticipated. Their impulse will thus be to

increase spending, which will cause the aggregate demand curve to move to the right. They will probably also save some of the excess, which will tend to result in lower interest rates – which then reinforces the increase in aggregate demand. However, as the AD curve moves to the right, the equilibrium price level will rise, and return the economy to equilibrium.

Figure 24.2 illustrates this in the case of a monetarist long-run aggregate supply – recall from Chapter 23 that the AS curve would be vertical at the full-employment level. If aggregate demand begins at AD_0, and then shifts to AD_1, the figure shows that price increases from P_0 to P_1, but real output remains unchanged at Y^*.

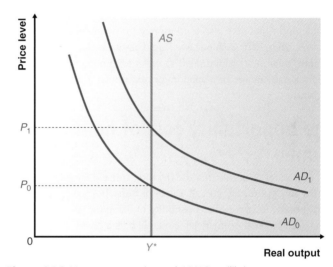

Figure 24.2 Monetary expansion and AD/AS equilibrium

If money supply continues to increase, the process repeats itself, with price then rising persistently. One danger of this is that people get so accustomed to the process that they speed up their spending decisions, and this accelerates the whole process. Inflation could then accelerate out of control.

To summarise, the analysis suggests that although a price rise can be triggered on either the supply side or the demand side of the macroeconomy, persistent inflation can only arise through persistent excessive growth in the money stock, which can be seen in terms of persistent movements of the aggregate demand curve.

Exercise 24.2

Sketch an AD/AS diagram with a Keynesian shape for aggregate supply. Discuss the extent to which this produces different results from those outlined above.

The demand for money

The discussion so far has focused on the importance of money supply, and how money supply is determined. However, it is also important to consider the demand for money. There are several reasons why individuals (people or firms) may choose to hold money balances.

The transactions demand for money

The first motive for holding money is clear – people and firms will hold money in order to undertake transactions. This is related to the need to use money when buying goods and services, and is closely associated with the functions of money as a medium of exchange and a unit of account. The demand for money for this purpose will probably be determined by the level of income.

The precautionary demand for money

People and firms may also hold money for precautionary reasons. They may wish to have liquid assets available in order to guard against a sudden need to cover an emergency payment or to take advantage of a spending opportunity at some point in the future.

The opportunity cost of holding money

It is important to notice that the decision to hold money balances carries an opportunity cost. If a firm or household chooses to hold money, it forgoes the possibility of using the money to purchase some other financial asset, such as a bond, that would yield a rate of return.

This means that the interest rate can be regarded as the opportunity cost of holding money: put another way, it is the price of holding money. At high rates of interest, people can be expected to hold less money, as the opportunity cost of doing so is high.

The speculative demand for money

The rate of interest may affect the demand for money through another route. If share (or bond) prices are low (and the rate of interest paid is high), then the opportunity cost of holding money is high, and people and firms will tend to hold shares. On the other hand, when the interest rate is low, and share prices are high, people will be more likely to hold money. This effect will be especially strong when people and firms see share prices to be unreasonably high, so that they expect them to fall. In this case, they may speculate by selling bonds in order to hold money in anticipation of taking advantage of future expected falls in the price of bonds.

Liquidity preference

If the interest rate may be regarded as being the opportunity cost of holding money, it can be argued that economic agents, whether households or firms, will display a demand for money, arising from the functions that money fulfils in a modern economy. This theory of **liquidity preference**, as it is known, was noted by Keynes in his *General Theory*.

Key term

Liquidity preference: a theory that suggests that people will desire to hold money as an asset.

Figure 24.3 illustrates what is implied for the money market. If the rate of interest is the opportunity cost of money, then it is expected that the demand for money will be lower when the rate of interest rate is relatively high, as the opportunity cost of holding money is high. People will be more reluctant to forgo the rate of return that has to be sacrificed by holding money. When the rate of interest is relatively low, this will be less of a concern, so the demand for money will be relatively high. This suggests that the money demand curve (MD) will be downward sloping. If money supply is fixed at M^* in Figure 24.3, then the money market will be in equilibrium at the rate of interest r^*.

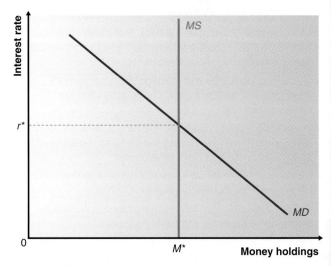

Figure 24.3 The money market

The existence of this relationship means that the monetary authorities have to be aware of the need to maintain (or allow) equilibrium in the money market. Interest rates and money supply cannot be fixed independently. This is a clear constraint on the use of monetary policy. An important question is the extent to which the demand for money is stable. If money demand were to be volatile, moving around from one time period to the next, then it would be virtually impossible for the monetary authorities to have any precise control over the market.

The situation is further complicated by the way that interest rates influence behaviour. The degree to which the demand for money is sensitive to the rate of interest will also be important. This will be reflected in the shape of the MD curve. Notice that because the level of income is also important in determining money demand, this will affect the *position* of the MD curve in the diagram. An increase in income will lead to a rightward shift in money demand, as people and firms will require larger money holdings when incomes are higher.

Analyse the effect on the rate of interest if there is an increase in the supply of money in an economy. Use a diagram such as Figure 24.3 as a starting point.

There are many reasons why people or firms like to hold on to money

The market for loanable funds

Although the rate of interest can be interpreted as being the opportunity cost of holding money, this is not the only way of viewing it. From a firm's point of view, it may be seen as the cost of borrowing. For example, suppose that a firm is considering undertaking an investment project. The rate of interest represents the cost of borrowing the funds needed in order to finance the investment. The higher the rate of interest is, the less investment projects will be seen as being profitable. If the firm is intending to finance its investment from past profits, the interest rate is still pertinent, as it then represents the return that the firm could obtain by purchasing a financial asset instead of undertaking the investment. Either way, the rate of interest is important in the decision-making process.

Key term

Market for loanable funds: the notion that households will be influenced by the rate of interest in making saving decisions, which will then determine the quantity of loanable funds available for firms to borrow for investment.

The rate of interest is also important to households, to whom it may represent the return on saving. Households may be encouraged to save more if the return on their saving is relatively high, whereas when the rate of interest is low, the incentive to save is correspondingly low. Within the circular flow of income, expenditure and output, it is the flow of saving from households that enables firms to find the funds needed to fund their investment expenditure. It is now apparent that the rate of interest may play an important role in bringing together these flows.

This is shown in Figure 24.4. The investment schedule is shown as downward sloping, because firms will find more investment projects to be worthwhile when the rate of interest rate is low. The savings schedule is shown to be upward sloping because a higher rate of interest is expected to encourage households to supply more saving. In other words, the supply of loanable funds will be higher when the rate of interest rate is relatively high.

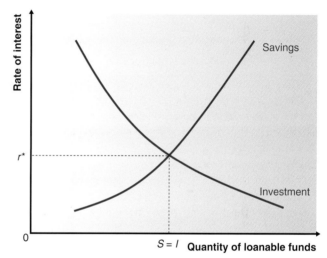

Figure 24.4 The market for loanable funds

Keynes believed that this could lead to instability in financial markets. He argued that investment and saving would be relatively insensitive to the rate of interest, such that the schedules in Figure 24.4 would be relatively steep. Investment would depend more crucially on firms' expectations about the future demand for their products, which could be volatile, moving the investment schedule around and thus leading to instability in the rate of interest. He thus came to the conclusion that governments should manage aggregate demand in order to stabilise the economy.

Suppose an economy begins with equilibrium in the market for loanable funds, as illustrated in Figure 24.4. Discuss how the market would be affected if the government decided to try to encourage more investment by holding the rate of interest below r^*. Do you think that such a policy would be effective?

Summary

- The quantity theory of money suggests that there is a close relationship between money supply and the overall price level.
- Under the quantity theory, persistent shifts in aggregate demand result in persistent inflation.
- People and firms within the economy choose to hold money for certain purposes.
- The demand for money reflects transactions, and precautionary and speculative motivations.
- The rate of interest can be regarded as the opportunity cost of holding money.
- Keynes developed liquidity preference theory, showing how the demand for money would be related to the rate of interest.
- It has been argued that both investment and saving depend upon the rate of interest.
- The rate of interest is important in determining the equilibrium of saving and investment within the market for loanable funds.

25 Policies to promote development

This chapter focuses on some of the obstacles that have hindered development in less developed countries, especially in sub-Saharan Africa, where very little progress seems to have been made after several decades of development efforts. This is in contrast to some countries in East Asia, which have experienced such rapid growth since the 1960s that they have successfully closed the income gap with countries that developed in earlier periods. The governments of LDCs that wish to stimulate development need to devise policies that will make the best possible use of the resources available to them domestically. However, in many cases, domestic resources are lacking, so it is important to consider the alternative possibility of mobilising resources from outside the country by attracting foreign direct investment, accepting overseas assistance or borrowing on international capital markets. Trade policy is also seen to be crucial.

Learning outcomes

After studying this chapter, you should:

- be aware of important obstacles to economic growth and development in less developed countries
- understand the causes and significance of rapid population growth
- understand the dangers of continued dependence on primary production, especially on low-productivity agriculture
- appreciate the importance of missing markets, especially financial markets
- be aware of the importance of social capital in promoting long-term development
- be aware of the need for less developed countries to mobilise external resources for development
- understand the significance of trade policy for less developed countries
- be familiar with the potential use of overseas assistance for promoting development, and the effectiveness of such flows of funds in the past.

25.1 Problems facing less developed countries

Chapter 22 highlighted some of the characteristics of less developed countries (LDCs). In order to devise policies that will help to stimulate a process of development, it is first important to identify whether some of these characteristics constitute obstacles to development that will need to be overcome. These may be regarded as *internal* problems – problems that arise because of domestic issues. However, it is apparent that LDCs have also faced obstacles from outside. Such *external* problems arise in an international context because of the interactions between countries in global markets, and through political ties. Such international linkages have become more important with the spread of globalisation.

Internally, one group of issues arises in relation to the balance of factors of production available in LDCs, which tend to be characterised by a relative abundance of labour resources and a lack of capital. A second group of issues relates to the underdevelopment of markets – especially financial markets, which may be of particular importance given the stress on saving and investment in many of the models. There are also issues arising from government failure. Externally, issues arise from trade interactions and from the trend towards globalisation.

Population growth

Early writers on development were pessimists. For example, Thomas Malthus argued in the late eighteenth century that real wages would never rise above a bare subsistence level. This was based on his ideas about the relationship between population growth and real incomes.

Malthus believed that it was not possible for a society to experience sustained increases in real wages, basically because the population was capable of exponential growth, while the food supply was capable of only arithmetic growth as a result of diminishing returns.

Although he was proved wrong (he had not anticipated the improvements in agricultural productivity that were to come), the question of whether population growth constitutes an obstacle to growth and development remains. At the heart of this is the debate about whether people should be regarded as key contributors to development, in their role as a factor of production, or as a drain on resources, consuming food, shelter, education and so on. Ultimately, the answer depends upon the quantity of resources available relative to the population size.

In global terms, world population is growing at a rapid rate: by more than 80 million people per year. In November 1999, global population went through the 6 billion mark, and in 2012, the 7 billion mark was reached – that is, about seven times as many people as there were in 1800. However, the growth is very unevenly distributed: countries such as Italy, Spain, Germany and Switzerland are projected to experience declining populations in the period 2000–15, while the population of sub-Saharan Africa continues to grow by 2.4% per annum, and that of 'low human development' countries (according to the UNDP definition) by 2.5%. A country whose population is growing at 2.5% per annum will see a doubling in just 28 years.

Figure 25.1 shows fertility rates for the group of countries selected in Chapter 22. The fertility rate records the average number of births per woman. Thus, in Uganda the average number of births per woman is about 6. Of course, this does not mean that the average number of *children* per family is so high, as not all the babies survive.

In Uganda, the average number of births per woman is about 6

the availability of resources. Indeed, it could be argued that there is an *optimum population* for a country, given its resource allocation. Too few people means that the country cannot make the best use of its resources, but too many causes problems.

Exercise 25.1

Discuss the way in which the age structure of a population may influence its rate of economic growth and development.

Dependence on primary production

Another common characteristic of LDCs that was identified in Chapter 22 is the way that many LDCs, especially in sub-Saharan Africa, continue to rely heavily on the agricultural sector to provide employment and incomes. Because labour productivity in agriculture tends to be relatively low, this may keep rural incomes low. The pressures of population growth tend to reinforce this dependence. It is worth being aware that one of the driving forces behind the Industrial Revolution in Britain was an increase in agricultural productivity, enabling more workers to shift into manufacturing activity. In an LDC context, this transition may run into a number of problems.

Unemployment and underemployment

With the rural areas experiencing low incomes and high population growth, it is perhaps natural that people should want to migrate to the urban areas in search of higher incomes and an escape from poverty – a process known as **urbanisation**.

Key term

Urbanisation: a process whereby an increasing proportion of the population comes to live in cities.

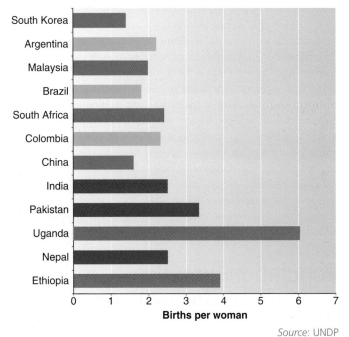

Figure 25.1 Total fertility rate

Source: UNDP

This pattern of high fertility has implications for the age structure of the population, leading to a high proportion of young dependants. It puts a strain on an LDC's limited resources because of the need to provide education and healthcare for so many children, and in this sense high population growth can prove an obstacle to development. This argument might be countered by pointing out that people themselves are a resource for the country. However, it is a question of the balance between population and

Migration occurs in response to a number of factors. One is the attraction of the 'bright lights' of the cities – people in rural areas often perceive urban areas as offering better access to education and healthcare facilities, and better recreational opportunities. Perhaps more important are the economic gains to be made from migrating to the cities, in terms of the wage differential between urban and rural areas.

Urban wages tend to be higher for a number of reasons. Employment in the manufacturing or service sectors typically offers higher wages, in contrast to the low productivity and wages in the agricultural sector. In addition, labour in the urban areas tends to be better organised, and governments have often introduced minimum wage legislation and social protection for workers in the urban areas – especially where they rely on them for electoral support.

Such wage differentials attract a flow of migrants to the cities. However, in practice there may not be sufficient jobs available, as the new and growing sectors typically do not expand quickly enough to absorb all the migrating workers. The net result is that rural workers exchange poor living conditions in the rural areas for unemployment in the urban environment.

Structural change and financial markets

Given the difficulties caused by over-reliance on primary production and the burgeoning urban informal sector, a key question concerns structural change. A transformation of the structure of economic activity seems crucial for growth and development to take place, but how can this be initiated? A major problem is that the rate of growth that would be needed in the industrial sector to absorb the number of workers looking for employment is far in excess of what has been – or could be – achieved. This poses a substantial challenge for LDCs.

The expansion of the industrial sector requires physical capital, which most LDCs must import as they do not have the capacity to produce capital goods domestically. Furthermore, the process requires investment – which in turn requires saving. Generating a flow of savings that can be made available for investment requires a sacrifice of current consumption, which may be problematic when domestic incomes are low. Furthermore, in order for a flow of funds for investment to be mobilised, and in order for those funds to be appropriately channelled into productive investment, fully functioning financial markets are needed. The undeveloped nature of financial markets is especially problematic in rural areas, where the lack of formal financial markets makes borrowing to invest in agricultural improvements almost impossible.

One of the problems is that the cost of establishing rural branches of financial institutions in remote areas is high; the fixed costs of making loans for relatively small-scale projects are similarly high. This is intensified by the difficulty that banks have in obtaining information about the creditworthiness of small borrowers, who typically may have no collateral to offer.

Attempts have been made to remedy this situation through *microfinance* schemes. This approach was pioneered by the Grameen Bank, which was founded in Bangladesh in 1976. The bank made small-scale loans to groups of women who otherwise would have had no access to credit, and each group was made corporately responsible for paying back the loan. The scheme has claimed great success, both in terms of the constructive use of the funds in getting small-scale projects off the ground and in terms of high payback rates.

Other schemes have involved groups of households pooling their savings in order to accumulate enough funds to launch small projects. Members of the group take it in turns to use these joint savings, paying the loan back in order for the next person to have a turn. These are known as *rotating savings and credit schemes (ROSCAs)*, and they have had some success in providing credit for small schemes. In spite of some successful enterprises, however, such schemes have been found to be less sustainable than Grameen-style arrangements, and have tended to be used to obtain consumer durable goods rather than for productive investment and innovation.

In the absence of such schemes, households may be forced to borrow from local moneylenders, often at very high rates of interest. For example, a survey by the Bank of Uganda found that households were paying rates between 0% (when borrowing from family members) and 500%. In part this may reflect a high risk of the borrower's defaulting, but it may also reflect the ability of local moneylenders to use market power. The absence of insurance markets may also deter borrowing for productive investment, especially in rural areas.

Macroeconomic instability

In the World Bank's market-friendly view of the growth process, macroeconomic stability is highlighted as one of the key conditions that enable markets to work effectively. There are two aspects to this argument. One is that firms will be reluctant to undertake investment if they find it difficult to predict future market conditions. If inflation is high and volatile, it will not be easy for firms to form expectations about the future, so this will discourage investment. Second, it is argued that prices will fail to act as reliable signals to guide resource allocation when inflation is either high or unstable. This may then distort the pattern of resource allocation, which may be especially important for LDCs that are trying to improve the allocation of resources, and to encourage a process of structural change.

Inflation has been a feature of some – but not all – LDCs. It was a prominent feature of many Latin American economies, peaking during the 1980s at annual rates above 1000%. However, the relationship between inflation and economic growth is a complex one. It is true that few countries that have experienced very high inflation rates have been successful in terms of economic growth. It is also the case that countries that have experienced rapid growth have maintained relatively low inflation rates. Nonetheless, there are countries that have maintained low inflation rates, but have then experienced slow (or even negative) growth rates. A tentative conclusion might be that low inflation is necessary for rapid growth to take place, but not sufficient. In other words, low inflation may be a crucial part of a growth strategy, but achieving it does not guarantee rapid growth.

Government failure

Such periods of hyperinflation partly reflected government failure. Many Latin American economies ran large fiscal deficits in this period, financing these through money creation, which led inexorably to galloping inflation. It was claimed by some (mainly Latin American) writers that inflation could be of benefit to economic growth, by redistributing income towards those in the economy with a high marginal propensity to save – namely, the government and the rich. However, there is no conclusive evidence that this does lead to higher growth, as governments cannot always be relied upon to use the funds wisely, and the rich have a tendency to indulge in luxury consumption, rather than undertaking productive investment.

Government failure has been important in many LDCs, and not only in relation to fiscal indiscipline. Governments that depend upon being re-elected may be tempted to introduce policies that are more designed to keep them in power than to foster long-term economic development. One common manifestation of this has been observed in relation to food prices. In a number of cases, governments depend primarily on the urban population to vote them back into office. Governments then may be tempted to introduce policies that are pro-urban. This might mean, for example, imposing low prices for food in order to combat urban poverty. This has undesirable effects as it affects the incentives for farmers and may thus inhibit growth. Similarly, minimum wage legislation may have the effect of leading to higher unemployment – again, mainly in the urban areas, where such legislation is likely to bite more strongly.

Sustainability

Economic growth may have important effects on the environment, and in pursuing growth, countries must bear in mind the need for sustainable development, safeguarding the needs of future generations as well as the needs of the present.

These issues have been widely discussed in the context of the more developed countries. However, the issue is equally important for LDCs. Deforestation has been a problem for many LDCs that have areas of rainforest. In some cases, logging for timber has destroyed large areas of valuable land; in other cases, land has been cleared for unsuitable agricultural use. This sort of activity creates relatively little present value, and leaves a poorer environment for future generations.

Another aspect of environmental degradation concerns *biodiversity*. This refers to the way in which misuse of the environment is contributing to the loss of plant species – not to mention those of birds, insects and mammals – which are becoming extinct as their natural habitat is destroyed. Some of the lost species may not even have been discovered yet. Given the natural healing properties of many plants, this could mean the destruction of plants that might provide significant new

Deforestation is a problem for many LDCs that have areas of rainforest and it has become a global issue

drugs for use in medicine. But how can something be valued when its very existence is as yet unknown?

One way of viewing the environment is as a factor of production that needs to be used effectively, just like any other factor of production. In other words, each country has a stock of *environmental* capital that needs to be utilised in the best possible way.

However, if the environmental capital is to be used appropriately, it must be given an appropriate value and this can be problematic. If property rights are not firmly established – as they are not in many LDCs – it is difficult to enforce legislation to protect the environment. Furthermore, if the environment (as a factor of production) is underpriced, then 'too much' of it will be used by firms.

There are externality effects at work here too, in the sense that the loss of biodiversity is a global loss, and not just something affecting the local economy. In some cases there have been international externality effects of a more direct kind, such as when forest fires in Indonesia caused the airport in Singapore to close down because of the resulting smoke haze.

As countries like China and India enter a period of rapid economic growth, it is likely that there will be effects on the environment because of the trade-off between rapid growth and the environment. There are many aspects to this issue, of which protecting the environment is just one. Sustainable development also entails taking account of the depletion rates of non-renewable resources, and ensuring that renewable resources *are* renewed in the process of economic growth. So, although economic growth is important to a society, the drive for growth must be tempered by an awareness of the possible trade-offs with other important objectives.

External obstacles to growth and development

Not all of the obstacles facing LDCs in their quest for growth and development arise from domestic factors. The law of comparative advantage highlights the fact that countries can gain through specialisation. It is not necessary to have an *absolute* advantage to benefit from specialisation and trade, so long as there is some source of *comparative* advantage. In the case of most LDCs, it may be crucial to be able to import some goods that cannot be produced domestically. For example, there are few LDCs that are capable of producing capital goods, although these are extremely important if a process of industrialisation is to be initiated.

However, although the law of comparative advantage identifies the potential gains from international trade, it does not guarantee that those gains can actually be made, and the terms under which trade takes place may place limits on the extent to which LDCs can benefit. There may thus be external obstacles that will affect LDCs. LDCs that rely on specialising in the production and exporting of primary goods tend to suffer from volatility of export earnings in the short run and a deterioration of their terms of trade in the long run.

International debt

For some LDCs, these problems have been compounded by strategies adopted to cope with balance of payments problems. The origins of this date back to the time of the first oil price crisis in 1973/74, when oil prices were suddenly raised by a substantial percentage. For many oil-importing countries, this posed a major problem, as the demand for oil was relatively inelastic, so the increase in the price of oil led immediately to a deficit on the current account of the balance of payments. Borrowing from the International Monetary Fund (IMF) was one solution, as offering help with short-run balance of payments problems is exactly the role that the IMF was designed to fulfil. However, IMF loans come with strings attached, so many LDCs in the late 1970s looked elsewhere for funds, borrowing from commercial sources. Such loans were often on variable interest rate terms. In the 1980s, oil prices rose again. Furthermore, interest rates rose worldwide when governments in North America and western Europe adopted strict monetary policies. This created problems for many LDCs that had borrowed heavily – especially those that had not perhaps used the funds as wisely as they might have. Some countries in Latin America threatened to default on their loans, and various plans had to be devised to salvage the financial system.

The problems of debt have proved a major obstacle to development in many countries. Latin American countries were affected strongly, as they had borrowed large amounts in US dollar terms. Countries in sub-Saharan Africa had borrowed less in money terms, but accumulated debts that were substantial relative to GDP or exports. They thus found that a high share of their export revenues were being used to make payments on past debts, and so were not available for promoting development at home. The problem reached a point at which it was clear that the debt burdens of many LDCs were unsustainable, and the World Bank launched an initiative to tackle the problem.

Diversity in development

With all these obstacles to growth and development, from both internal and external sources, it would be easy to despair of ever being able to tackle poverty in the world. However, it is important to remember that not all countries face all of the obstacles. Countries face different configurations of characteristics and problems, and such diversity needs to be matched by diversity in the design of policies to promote growth and development.

Summary

- Early writers such as Malthus were pessimistic about the prospects for sustained development, believing that diminishing returns to labour would constrain economic growth.
- Globally, population is growing rapidly, with most of the increase taking place in less developed countries.
- Coupled with the age structure of the population, rapid population growth can create difficulties for LDCs because of the pressure on resources.
- The pattern of existing comparative advantage suggests that LDCs should specialise in the production of primary commodities such as agricultural goods, minerals or other raw materials.
- However, the prices of such goods tend to be volatile in the short run, varying from year to year as a result of instability arising from either the supply side or the demand side.
- Furthermore, the nature of demand for such products and the development of artificial substitutes for some raw materials may be expected to lead to a long-run deterioration in the terms of trade for primary producers.
- These factors will limit the extent to which LDCs benefit from international trade in primary commodities.
- International debt also grew to be a major obstacle to development for many countries.

25.2 The Harrod–Domar model

Returning to the issue of economic growth, if it is seen in terms of a shift in aggregate supply, then the focus must be on investment, which enables an increase in productive capacity. This idea is supported by the **Harrod–Domar model** of economic growth, which first appeared in separate articles by Roy Harrod in the UK and Evsey Domar in the USA in 1939. This model was to become significant in influencing LDCs' attitudes towards the process of economic growth. It was developed in an attempt to determine how equilibrium could be achieved in a growing economy.

Key term

Harrod–Domar model: a model of economic growth that emphasises the importance of savings and investment.

The basic finding of the model was that an economy can remain in equilibrium through time only if it grows at a particular rate. This unique *stable growth path* depends on the *savings ratio* and the *productivity of capital*. Any deviation from this path will cause the economy to become unstable. This finding emphasised the importance of savings in the process of economic growth, and led to the conclusion that a country seeking economic growth must first increase its flow of savings.

Figure 25.2 illustrates the process that leads to growth in a Harrod–Domar world. Savings are crucial in enabling investment to be undertaken – always remembering that some investment will have to be used to replace existing capital that has worn out. Investment then enables capital to accumulate and technology to be improved. The accumulation of capital leads to an increase in output and incomes, which leads to a further flow of savings, and the cycle begins again. This figure highlights a number of problems that may prevent the Harrod–Domar process from being effective for LDCs.

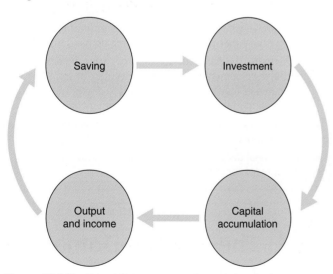

Figure 25.2 The Harrod–Domar process of economic growth

Generating a flow of savings in an LDC may be problematic. When incomes are low, households may have to devote most of their resources to consumption, and so there may be a lack of savings. Nonetheless, some savings have proved possible. For example, in the early 1960s South Korea had an average income level that was not too different from that of countries like Sudan or Afghanistan, but it managed to build up the savings rate during that decade.

Setting aside the problem of low savings for the moment, what happens next?

Will savings lead to investment and the accumulation of capital?

If a flow of savings can be generated, the next important step is to transform the savings into investment. This is the process by which the sacrifice of current consumption leads to an increase in productive capacity in the future.

Some important preconditions must be met if savings are to be transformed into investment. First, there must be a way for potential borrowers to get access to the funds. In developed countries this takes place through the medium of financial markets. For example, it may be that households save by putting their money into a savings account at the bank; then with this money the bank can make loans to entrepreneurs, enabling them to undertake investment.

In many LDCs, however, financial markets are undeveloped, so it is much more difficult for funds to be recycled in this way. For example, a study conducted in 1997 by the Bank of Uganda found that almost 30% of households interviewed in rural Ugandan villages had undertaken savings at some time. However, almost none of these had done so through formal financial institutions, which did not reach into the rural areas. Instead, the saving that took place tended to be in the form of fixed assets, or money kept under the bed. Such savings cannot readily be transformed into productive investment.

In addition, governments in some periods have made matters worse by holding down interest rates in the hope of encouraging firms to borrow. The idea here is that a low interest rate means a low cost of borrowing, which should make borrowing more attractive. However, this ignores the fact that, if interest rates are very low, there is little incentive to save because the return on saving is so low. In this case, firms may wish to invest but may not be able to obtain the funds to do so.

The other prerequisite for savings to be converted into investment is that there must be entrepreneurs with the ability to identify investment possibilities, the skill to carry them through and the willingness to bear the risk. Such entrepreneurs are in limited supply in many LDCs.

Will investment lead to higher output and income?

For investment to be productive in terms of raising output and incomes in the economy, some further conditions need to be met. In particular, it is crucial for firms to have access to physical capital, which will raise production capacity. Given their limited capability of producing capital goods, many LDCs have to rely on capital imported from the more developed countries. This may be beneficial in terms of upgrading home technology, but such equipment can be imported only if the country has earned the foreign exchange to pay for it. A shortage of foreign exchange may therefore make it difficult for the country to accumulate capital.

The importance of human capital

If the capital *can* be obtained, there is then a need for the skilled labour with which to operate the capital goods. Human capital, in the form of skilled, healthy and well-trained workers, is as important as physical capital if investment is to be productive.

In principle, it might be thought that today's LDCs have an advantage over the countries that developed in earlier periods. In particular, they can learn from earlier mistakes, and import technology that has already been developed, rather than having to develop it anew. This suggests that a *convergence* process should be going on, whereby LDCs are able to adopt technology that has already been produced, and thereby grow more rapidly and begin to close the gap with the more developed countries.

However, by and large this has not been happening, and a lack of human capital has been suggested as one of the key reasons for the failure. This underlines the importance of education in laying the foundations for economic growth as well as contributing directly to the quality of life.

Harrod–Domar and external resources

Figure 25.3 extends the earlier schematic presentation of the process underlying the Harrod–Domar model of economic growth. This has been amended to underline the importance of access to technology and human capital.

The discussion above has emphasised the difficulty of mobilising domestic savings, both in generating a sufficient flow of savings and in translating such savings into productive investment.

The question arises as to whether an LDC could supplement its domestic savings with a flow of funds from abroad. Figure 25.3 identifies three possible injections into the Harrod–Domar process. First, it might be possible to attract flows of overseas assistance from higher-income countries. Second, perhaps the amount of investment could be augmented directly by persuading multinational corporations to engage in foreign direct investment. Third, the LDC might be able to borrow on international capital markets to finance its domestic investment. It is worth noting that the tiger economies took full advantage of these external sources of funds. However, each of these ways of attracting external resources has a downside associated with it. As far as overseas assistance is concerned, in the past such flows have been seen by some donor countries as part of trade policy, and have brought less benefit to LDCs than had been hoped. In the case of the multinational corporations, there is a tendency for the profits to be repatriated out of the LDC, rather than recycled into the economy. Finally, international borrowing has to be repaid at some future date, and many LDCs have found themselves burdened by debt that they can ill afford to repay.

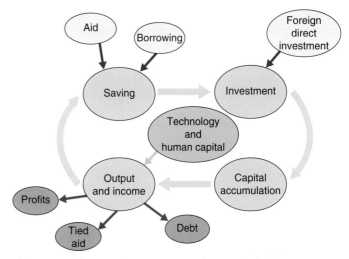

Figure 25.3 The Harrod–Domar process of economic development augmented

Summary

- Although development is a broader concept than economic growth, growth is a key ingredient of development.
- The Harrod–Domar model of economic growth highlights the importance of savings, and of transforming savings into productive investment.
- However, where markets are underdeveloped, this transformation may be impeded.
- Human capital is also a critical ingredient of economic growth.
- If resources cannot be generated within the domestic economy, a country may need to have recourse to external sources of funding.

25.3 Institutions and development

The design of economic policy must be considered in the context of the economic and institutional environment within which policy measures are implemented. The role of institutions in the development process has increasingly been seen as an important one in recent years. LDC governments, multilateral institutions such as the World Bank, non-governmental organisations and major trade groupings like the European Union all contribute to the policy environment. The interactions between them are also extremely important.

LDC governments

The governments of LDCs have the ultimate responsibility for designing their domestic economic and development policy, but it has often been argued that many are ill-equipped to devise and implement the sorts of policy that are required to stimulate the process of development. This is partly related to the level of development of the political and cultural systems in LDCs, and may also depend upon the existence (or absence) of a reliable and non-corrupt bureaucracy that would enable policies to be set in motion. Another major factor to remember is the constraint that LDC governments face in terms of resources. Where average incomes are low and tax collection systems are undeveloped, governments have difficulty in generating a flow of revenue domestically, which is needed in order to launch policies encouraging growth and development.

In some cases, governments have tended to rely on taxes on international trade, which are relatively easy to administer, rather than on domestic direct or indirect taxes. Naturally, this has not helped to stimulate international trade.

Some LDC governments have responded to the problem by borrowing funds from abroad. However, in many cases such funds have not been best used. They have sometimes been used for prestige projects, which impress lenders (or donors) but do little to further development.

Corruption and the legal framework

The legal framework is a key part of the infrastructure needed to support development. Where this is weak, development is likely to be hindered. In the case of international borrowing, there have been instances where funds have been diverted into private use by government officials, and there are well-documented examples of politicians, officials and civil servants accumulating personal fortunes at the expense of their countries' development.

Tendencies towards corruption are likely to be more significant in countries where there is relatively little political stability, so that the government knows it will not remain in power for long. In this situation, it is not only corruption that may be problematic, as in general the incentives for such governments are weak. There is little reason to expect a government to take a long-term view of the development process, and to introduce policies that will only bring benefits in the distant future, if it only faces a short period in office, or if it perceives that it needs to bring in populist policies to ensure re-election. In other words, even in the absence of corruption, there may be little incentive for governments to take a long-term perspective.

The lack of a strong legal framework can be a serious obstacle to development. If the rule of law is fragile, then corruption and political instability are more likely. Also important is the existence of strong property rights for individuals. For example, if a peasant farmer does not hold not secure property rights over the land being farmed, then the incentives for making improvements to the land or the production methods are weak. Furthermore, in the absence of secure property rights, a farmer may not be able to borrow funds from the commercial banking sector in order to make improvements or undertake investment, as without secure ownership of land it may not be possible to provide collateral against loans. Hence the importance of a strong legal framework to allow financial and other markets to operate effectively.

Markets or state planning?

The World Bank and IMF have taken the view that countries should adopt **market-friendly growth**, allowing markets to work more effectively to allocate resources where this is possible. This notion was embodied in a set of policies that came to be known as the *Washington Consensus*, which LDCs were encouraged to follow. This approach was not as successful as had been hoped, and there has been a growing recognition of the need to tailor policies to the particular configuration of characteristics and problems faced by individual LDCs, rather than trying to impose a one-size-fits-all policy package.

> **Key term**
>
> **Market-friendly growth:** economic growth in which governments intervene less where markets can operate effectively, but more strongly where markets are seen to fail.

An extreme alternative to this approach is to rely on *central planning*. This view of the development process was attractive to many countries, with the Soviet Union being seen as a role model for many years. The breakdown of the Soviet bloc has discredited this approach to some extent, although there are still a few countries that adhere to central planning, such as Cuba and North Korea. Elsewhere, governments have come to see the benefits that derive from allowing market forces to play at least some role in resource allocation. For example, market reforms in China have contributed to that country's outstanding success in achieving rapid economic growth.

Allowing market forces to lead resource allocation has some key advantages over central planning for many LDCs. These arise from the problems mentioned above relating to the lack of reliable bureaucracy in many LDCs and the temptations to corruption. Central planning relies very heavily on bureaucratic structures in order to manage the process of development. It also relies on reliable and detailed information about the economy. Without these, central planning cannot operate effectively. In contrast, a market system is efficient because it devolves decision-making to individuals, and uses prices to provide signals and to coordinate the allocation of resources.

Problems arise where institutions do not enable the free operation of markets, and an early priority in seeking to promote development is to ensure that measures are in place that will allow markets to work. These measures would include such things as secure property rights and the provision of appropriate infrastructure. Indeed, intervention may be needed in various parts of the economy in order to counter problems arising from *market failure*.

Domestic policies for development

The objective of domestic policy is to make the best use of the resources that are available within a society. Policy must also try to balance the need to tackle short-term problems with devising a strategy that will cater for the long run.

A strategy for the long run must bear in mind the need for balance in the *structure* of economic activity. This means reducing the dependence on primary production and moving towards a more diversified economy. A precondition for this is to bring about improvements in agricultural productivity. This enables food production to be secured and may then permit some release of surplus labour into new types of economic activity.

It is important to be aware of areas of potential market failure that may inhibit development, growth and structural transformation. Of particular importance may be the provision of *infrastructure*. Intervention here is justified because of the public goods characteristics of much infrastructure, which means that there will be insufficient provision if it is left to the private sector. Improved roads and communication links, and market facilities, are examples of public goods that are essential for economic development.

Another area of potential market failure relates to aspects of *human capital*. The presence of information failures and externality effects may combine to prevent efficient provision of education and healthcare. However, these are of vital importance, not only for short-run purposes of alleviating poverty, but also because the improvement of human resources contributes to productivity improvements, and hence to economic growth. To the extent that households make inappropriate decisions on family size, there may also be a need to try to influence the rate of population growth.

LDC governments should also take steps to ensure a *stable macroeconomic environment* in order to enable the private sector to take good decisions. Only in a stable macroeconomic environment will firms be able to form reliable expectations about the future, and thus take good decisions about investment.

Given the parlous state of many LDC economies, such domestic measures are unlikely to be sufficient to stimulate self-sustained development. This partly reflects the severe scarcity of resources faced by many LDC governments. An implication of this is that LDCs must also attempt to mobilise resources from external sources.

Summary

- Governments in LDCs have limited resources with which to encourage a more rapid rate of economic growth and development.
- Corruption and poor governance have meant that some of the resources that have been available have not been used wisely in some LDCs.
- The World Bank has argued that markets should be encouraged to work where this is possible, but that governments should intervene in the presence of market failure.
- The steps needed for LDCs to achieve development and growth using domestic resources may be limited.

25.4 The role of external resources in development

The shortage of resources in many LDCs has been a severe obstacle to their economic growth and development. This was emphasised by the Harrod–Domar model of economic growth which was introduced earlier in the chapter.

The underlying process by which growth can take place requires the generation of a flow of savings that can be transformed into investment in order to generate an increase in capital, which in turn enlarges the productive capacity of the economy. This then enables output and incomes to grow, which in turn feeds back into savings and allows the process to become self-sustaining.

However, the process will break down if savings are inadequate, or if markets do not operate sufficiently well to maintain the chain. In considering the possibility that the process could be initiated by an inflow of resources from outside the economy, there are three possible routes: foreign direct investment, overseas aid and international borrowing. A country's attitude towards international trade is also important.

Trade policy

An important area in which policy may be important in contributing to economic development is in the area of trade policy. If a country is short of foreign exchange, there are two broad approaches that it can take in drawing up its trade policy to deal with the problem. One is to reduce its reliance on imports in order to economise on the need for foreign currency – in other words, to produce goods at home that it previously imported. This is known as an **import substitution** policy. An alternative possibility is to try to earn more foreign exchange through **export promotion**.

Key terms

Import substitution: a policy encouraging domestic production of goods previously imported in order to reduce the need for foreign exchange.

Export promotion: a policy encouraging domestic firms to export more goods in order to earn foreign exchange.

Import substitution

The import substitution strategy has had some appeal for a number of countries. The idea is to boost domestic production of goods that were previously imported, thereby saving foreign exchange. A typical policy instrument used to achieve this is the imposition of a tariff.

The effect of tariffs and non-tariff barriers were discussed in Chapter 10.

The benefits from implementing such policies rarely seem to be worth the costs. A major problem with an import substitution policy is that to be successful it requires a large effective domestic market if producers are to be able to tap into economies of scale. This is not often possible for many LDCs.

Export promotion

Export promotion requires a more dynamic and outward-looking approach, as domestic producers need to be able to compete with producers already established in world markets. The choice of which products to promote is critical, as it is important that the LDC develops a new pattern of comparative advantage if it is to benefit from an export promotion strategy.

For primary producers, a tempting strategy is one that begins with existing products and tries to move along the production chain. For example, in 1997 (under encouragement from the World Bank), Mozambique launched a project whereby, instead of exporting raw cashew nuts, it would establish processing plants that would then allow it to export roasted cashew nuts. In the early 1970s Mozambique was the largest producer of cashew nuts in the world, but by the late 1990s the activity had stagnated, and the country had been overtaken by producers in Brazil and India.

This would seem to have been a good idea because it makes use of existing products and moves the industry into higher value-added activity. However, the project ran into a series of problems. On the one hand, there were internal constraints: processing the nuts requires capital equipment and skilled labour, neither of which was in plentiful supply in Mozambique. In addition, tariff rates on processed commodities are higher than on raw materials, so the producers faced more barriers to trade. They also found that they were trying to break into a market that was dominated by a few large existing producers, which

were reluctant to share the market. Furthermore, the technical standards required to sell processed cashew nuts were beyond the capability of the newly established local firms. Indeed, the setting of high technical specifications for imported products is one way in which countries have tried to protect their own domestic producers – it is an example of a non-tariff barrier.

These are just some of the difficulties that face new producers from LDCs wanting to compete in world markets. The east Asian tiger economies pursued export promotion strategies, making sure that their exchange rates supported the competitiveness of their products and that their labour was appropriately priced. However, it must be remembered that the tiger economies expanded into export-led growth at a time when world trade itself was booming, and when the developed countries were beginning to move out of labour-intensive activities, thereby creating a niche to be filled by the tigers. If many other countries had expanded their exports at the same time, it is not at all certain that they could all have been successful.

As time goes by, it becomes more difficult for other countries to follow this policy. It is particularly difficult for countries that originally chose import substitution, because the inward-looking attitudes fostered by such policies become so deeply entrenched.

It should also be remembered that there will always be dangers in trying to develop new kinds of economic activity that may entail sacrificing comparative advantage. This is not to say that LDCs should remain primary producers for ever, but it does suggest that it is important to select the new forms of activity with care in order to exploit a *potential* comparative advantage.

Exercise 25.2

Discuss the relative merits of import substitution and export promotion as trade strategies. Under what conditions might import substitution have a chance of success?

Summary

- Governments in LDCs have limited resources with which to encourage a more rapid rate of economic growth and development.
- Corruption and poor governance have meant that some of the resources that have been available have not been used wisely in some LDCs.
- In designing a trade policy, an LDC may choose to go for import substitution, nurturing infant industries behind protectionist barriers in order to allow them to produce domestically goods that were formerly imported.
- However, such infant industries rarely seem to grow up, leaving the LDC with inefficient producers, which are unable to compete effectively with world producers.
- Export promotion requires a more dynamic and outward-looking approach, and a careful choice of new activities.

25.5 Foreign direct investment

One possible source of external funding that has been attractive to many LDCs is **foreign direct investment (FDI)**. This entails encouraging **multinational corporations (MNCs)** to set up part of their production in an LDC.

Key terms

Foreign direct investment (FDI): investment undertaken by foreign companies.

Multinational corporation (MNC): a company whose production activities are carried out in more than one country.

MNCs by their nature tend to be large-scale enterprises, in business to make profits. This can influence the way in which they operate when they choose to locate in an LDC, not always in ways that are beneficial for the LDC.

MNCs may engage in FDI in order to reach new markets, to take advantage of some key resource, such as natural gas, or they may be looking to improve efficiency by locating part of their production in a favourable location.

The motivation for LDCs in seeking to attract MNCs is to obtain an injection of investment that may stimulate economic growth and human development. This may occur through the physical capital to which MNCs have access, but they may also bring skills to the local labour force, management expertise and entrepreneurial skills – and access to global markets. The spillover effects may be seen to be potentially important for local businesses. The LDC may also hope to be able to raise tax revenue.

All too often, these benefits have not materialised. The size of MNCs is likely to give them substantial economic and political influence in an LDC, the technology that they utilise may not be appropriate for local market conditions, and if profits are repatriated to shareholders overseas, then the LDC will not gain as much as it hoped. After all, MNCs are in business to make profits. What is important is that LDCs are able to negotiate reasonable deals with the MNC, perhaps through agreements to increase the employment of local labour or to limit the tax holidays often offered to MNCs as an inducement.

It has also been difficult for some countries to attract FDI, especially in sub-Saharan Africa, where low levels of human capital and social and physical infrastructure are low, and where political stability may not be high.

Exercise 25.3

Draw up a list of the potential benefits and costs of MNC involvement in an LDC, and evaluate the benefits relative to the costs.

Summary

- Multinational corporations (MNCs) are companies whose production activities are carried out in more than one country.
- Foreign direct investment (FDI) by MNCs is one way in which an LDC may be able to attract external resources.
- MNCs may be motivated by markets, resources or cost effectiveness.
- LDCs hope to benefit from FDI in a wide range of ways, including capital, technology, employment, human capital, tax revenues and foreign exchange. There may also be spillover effects for local firms.
- However, MNCs may at times operate in ways that do not maximise these benefits for LDCs.

25.6 Overseas assistance

If LDCs could enter a phase of economic growth and rising incomes, one result would be an increase in world trade. This would benefit nations around the world, and the more developed industrial countries would be likely to see an increase in the market for their products. This might be a reason for the governments of more developed countries to help LDCs with the growth and development of their economies. Of course, there may also be a humanitarian motive for providing assistance – that is, to reduce global inequality.

Indeed, there may be market failure arguments for providing aid. For example, it may be that governments have better information about the riskiness of projects in LDCs than private firms have. In relation to the provision of education and healthcare, it was argued earlier that externality effects may be involved. However, LDC governments may not have the resources needed to provide sufficient education for their citizens. Similarly, it was argued that some infrastructure may have public good characteristics that require intervention.

Official aid is known as overseas development assistance (ODA), and is provided through the Development Assistance Committee of the Organisation for Economic Cooperation and Development (OECD). Notice that the discussion here focuses not on short-run aid to deal with an emergency, such as a drought or tsunami, but rather on funds that are provided to foster long-term development.

A contentious issue is whether ODA should be channelled to those countries most in need of it, or focused on those countries best equipped to make good use of the funding. If humanitarian motives are uppermost, then you would expect there to be a strong relationship between flows of overseas assistance and average income levels. However, if other motives are important, this relationship might be less apparent. In 2006, Iraq and Pakistan came high up the list of the highest recipients of ODA in dollar terms, which may reflect the importance of these countries in terms of US foreign policy in the aftermath of 9/11 and the Iraq war. It is important also to realise that some countries rely very heavily on ODA: for some this makes up almost half of their GDP.

At a meeting of the United Nations in 1974, the industrial countries agreed that they would each devote 0.7% of their GNP to ODA. This goal was reiterated at the Millennium Summit as part of the commitment to achieving the Millennium Development Goals. Progress towards this target has not been impressive, although the late 2000s saw some improvement from some countries. Figure 25.4 shows the performance of donor countries relative to this target, and you can see that only five countries had achieved the 0.7% UN target by 2012. The amount of ODA provided by the UK as a percentage of GNI increased after 1997, but the USA's share has fallen. However, it should be borne in mind that in terms of US$, the USA is by far the largest contributor.

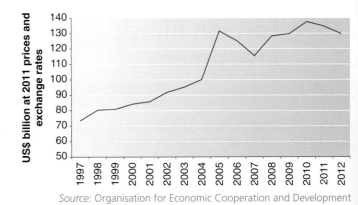

Source: Organisation for Economic Cooperation and Development

Figure 25.5 Flows of ODA, 1997–2012

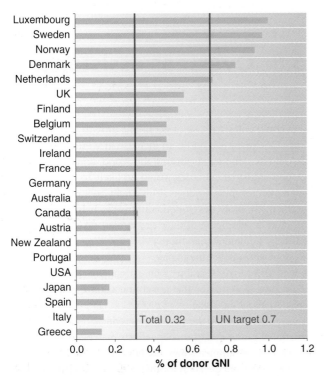

Source: Organisation for Economic Cooperation and Development

Figure 25.4 Overseas development assistance in 2012

An encouraging sign is that total ODA flows increased in the late 1990s and the early years of the new millennium, as can be seen in Figure 25.5. This seemed to represent an enhanced awareness of the importance of such flows for many LDCs. Indeed, at the summit meeting of the G8 (the governments of eight of the world's largest economies) at Gleneagles in July 2005, the commitment to the UN target for ODA was reiterated.

A World Bank study of the effectiveness of aid, published in 1997, reported that 'foreign aid to developing countries since 1970 has had no net impact on either the recipients' growth rate or the quality of their economic policies'. Some evidence was found to suggest that aid was more effective in countries where 'sound economic management' was being practised. In other words, it was argued that aid might prove effective in

stimulating growth only if the country were also implementing 'good' economic policies – particularly in terms of openness to trade, low inflation and disciplined fiscal policy.

There are many possible reasons for the ineffectiveness of aid. It may simply be that providing aid to the poorest countries reduces its effectiveness, in the sense that the resources of such countries are so limited that the funding cannot be efficiently utilised. In some cases it may be related to the fact that aid flows are received by LDC governments, which can be inefficient or corrupt, so there are no guarantees that the funds are used wisely by these governments. Or it might simply be that the flows of aid have not been substantial enough to have made a difference.

There are other explanations, however. For example, some donor countries in the past have regarded aid as part of their own trade policy. By tying aid to trade deals, the net value of the aid to the recipient country is much reduced: for instance, offering aid in this way may commit the recipient country to buying goods from the donor country at inflated prices.

In other cases, aid has been tied to use in specific projects. This may help to assure the donor that the funds are being used for the purpose for which they were intended. However, it is helpful only if appropriate projects were selected in the first place. There may be a temptation for donors to select prestige projects that will be favourably regarded by others, rather than going for the LDC's top-priority development projects.

Such deals are becoming less common, as now more ODA is being channelled through multilateral organisations than bilaterally between donor and recipient directly. This may mean that aid flows will be more effective in the future. An important issue for all sorts of aid is that it should be provided in a way that does not damage incentives for local producers. For example, dumping cheap grain into LDC markets on a regular basis would be likely to damage the incentives for local farmers by depressing prices.

Trade and aid

There has been debate in some quarters about the relative merits of trade and aid as a way of stimulating economic growth and development in less developed countries. Economic analysis reveals that countries do not face a choice between trade and aid, and that both trade and aid could contribute to growth and development.

Proponents of aid argue that it can be used to provide the foundations needed for development to take place. Critics argue that aid can foster a state of dependency, such that the recipient countries do not have the incentive to take their own initiative in development and that funds often get diverted to unproductive uses.

There is potential for aid to have a beneficial effect on LDCs, when it is wisely utilised. The debt relief received by many LDCs in recent years has released funds to be used in poverty alleviation and in improving human capital and social infrastructure. The shift towards more multilateral aid transfers has reduced the political motivation for aid donors. Aid can be harnessed to promote development without leading to dependency, but it must be carefully directed.

Proponents of trade argue that encouraging LDCs to open up their markets and adopting a more open stance towards trade provides better incentives for LDCs to adopt good macroeconomic policies and thus promote economic growth. Critics argue that a more open stance towards trade opens up LDCs to exploitation by rich countries and powerful multinational corporations. Again, there may be elements of truth in both positions. For LDCs to gain fully from engaging in international trade, there must be a willingness amongst the developed nations to open their markets to LDC goods, and not adopt too protectionist a stance. There have been encouraging signs in recent years, even in the face of global recession. In the long run, some combination of trade and aid is needed to allow development to take off.

Summary

- Overseas development assistance (ODA) comprises grants and concessional funding provided from the OECD countries to LDCs.
- The countries most in need of ODA may not be in a position to use it effectively.
- In some cases, the direction of ODA flows is influenced by the political interests of the donor countries.
- The more developed countries have pledged to devote 0.7% of their GNPs to ODA, but few have reached this target so far.
- Some evidence suggests that aid has been ineffective except in countries that have pursued 'good' economic policies.
- The tying of aid to trade deals or to specific projects can limit the aid's benefits to recipient LDCs, but the vast majority of bilateral aid is now untied.

Examination questions

1 How far do you agree with the proposition that the main aims of economic government policy should be low unemployment and low tax rates? [25]

Cambridge AS and A Level Economics 9708, Paper 4, Q7, June 2007

2 A World Bank report in 2007 commented on the continuing need for major spending worldwide on infrastructure on everything from roads and railways to water and electricity generation.

Source: Wall Street Journal, June 2007

a Explain the effect on national income when there is an increase in spending on infrastructure. [10]

b Discuss whether an efficient allocation of resources can be obtained only if large-scale investment is undertaken by the public sector rather than the private sector. [15]

Cambridge AS and A Level Economics 9708, Paper 4, Q7, June 2009

3 Some Japanese economists have argued that higher interest rates would, unusually, improve Japan's economic growth.

a Explain why it might be said that this link between interest rates and economic growth is unusual. [12]

b Discuss whether economic growth is good for an economy. [13]

Cambridge AS and A Level Economics 9708, Paper 41, Q5, November 2009

4 For some years governments of developed countries have been promoting Fair Trade, which means paying a fair price for primary products bought from African developing countries. Now the governments in developed countries, anxious to conserve resources, are complaining that the transport of products around the world increases pollution and should be limited. They support instead the purchase of goods produced at home. These are often more expensive to produce. African farmers may be left with products that their local people do not eat.

a Explain what might determine whether a country is classified as developed or developing. [12]

b Discuss whether the old and the new approaches to trade of the developed countries would help achieve the conservation of resources. [13]

Cambridge AS and A Level Economics 9708, Paper 41, Q5, June 2010

5 Economic analysis states that the aims of the government include economic growth and economic efficiency.

a Explain how achieving economic growth might conflict with other government macroeconomic aims. [12]

b Is economic efficiency better achieved by the market mechanism rather than by government microeconomic policy? [13]

Cambridge AS and A Level Economics 9708, Paper 41, Q7, November 2010

6 a A firm undertakes a major investment. Analyse why in a closed economy without a government the increase in national income from this investment might be higher than in an open mixed economy. [12]

b Discuss the policies that a government might use to influence the level of investment in an economy. [13]

Cambridge AS and A Level Economics 9708,
Paper 41, Q6, June 2010

7 National income statistics are used to calculate a country's GDP. The table shows the GDP for five countries for 2008.

Discuss how far the table might be used to determine whether one country has higher living standards than another. [25]

Country	GDP $m
USA	14 580 000
India	3 319 000
Singapore	244 000
Mauritius	14 060
Swaziland	5 626

Cambridge AS and A Level Economics 9708,
Paper 41, Q5, November 2010

8 Emerging economies and the way out of a recession
During the recession of 2009 several economists forecast that some emerging (fast developing) economies would perform better than the developed economies. One indicator of this, they said, was the strength of the exchange rate of the currency of some emerging economies against the US dollar. For example, between November 2008 and July 2009, the Brazilian currency rose 11.4% against the dollar and the Indonesian currency rose 10.2%. Another indicator was the forecast growth rate in GDP as shown in Table 1.

Table 1 Forecast growth rate in GDP for selected countries

Forecast growth rate in GDP		
	2009 %	2010 %
US	−2.7	+1.4
UK	−3.5	+0.3
Germany	−4.3	+0.3
Japan	−6.5	+0.4
Hong Kong	−5.9	−0.3
China	+6.0	+7.0
Singapore	−7.5	+1.9
Brazil	−1.5	+2.7
Columbia	−1.0	+1.5
India	+5.0	+6.4
Indonesia	−1.3	+0.6

Emerging economies are often dependent on exports to achieve an increase in GDP. Some economists suggested that it would be better for their economic growth if these countries were to concentrate on domestic demand rather than exports. China, in particular, they said could lead the world out of the recession if it relied increasingly on domestic demand. Indeed, the Chinese government encouraged a shift from export-led industries to programmes aimed at improving the Chinese infrastructure in order to create jobs and thus increase consumption of Chinese goods. Banks were encouraged to make borrowing easier in order to create more credit for consumers and businesses. The government started a massive fiscal stimulus and increased its forecast of GDP to a growth rate of 8.3% in 2009 and 10.9% for 2010 (previous forecast figures were 6.0% and 7.0% as in Table 1).

However, other economists do not accept that there should be an emphasis on domestic demand. They argue that trading links are the strongest evidence of the emerging economies' ability to grow. They state 'no emerging market that adopted an export-led growth model has subsequently needed to break away from it – including China'. China's exports as a percentage of GDP are 32% compared with only 13% for the US. Smaller Asian countries are even more dependent on exports; Singapore's ratio of exports to GDP is 234%, Hong Kong's is 169%. It will be difficult for economies such as these to increase domestic demand and reduce their dependence on export-led growth.

Source: Financial Times, 12 June 2009.
Table source: Economist, p. 105, 18–24 April 2009

a Explain what is meant by GDP. [3]

b The article says that banks were encouraged to make borrowing easier. Explain what this might mean and why the government might have thought this was necessary. [3]

c Is there enough evidence in the article to support the view that there has been an improvement in the economic situation of emerging economies? [6]

d Identify the **two** policy approaches suggested by economists in the article and discuss whether there is a conflict between them. [8]

Cambridge AS and A Level Economics 9708,
Paper 43, Q1, June 2011

26 Macroeconomic performance

The discussion of macroeconomics so far has drawn attention to a number of problems faced by the economy as a whole – inflation, instability in the balance of payments, and the need to achieve economic growth and development. For many countries, especially in the developing world, a key problem is unemployment. For many countries, people are their most valuable resource, and yet they are often underutilised, because they are either unemployed or in occupations that do not make full use of their potential. This chapter thus begins by looking at the problem of unemployment. A complication when trying to assess the performance of an economy is that very often the problems that can afflict an economy are interrelated. The chapter concludes by examining some of these key interrelationships between macroeconomic problems.

Learning outcomes

After studying this chapter, you should:

- understand the meaning of unemployment
- be familiar with the main causes of unemployment in an economy
- be aware of the costs of unemployment for individuals and for society as a whole
- understand the distinction between voluntary and involuntary unemployment
- appreciate the particular problems caused by unemployment in less developed countries
- be familiar with the way in which macroeconomic problems may be interrelated
- be aware of the Phillips curve relationship between unemployment and inflation.

26.1 Unemployment

For an economy to be operating on its production possibility curve, the factors of production need to be fully employed. From society's point of view, surplus capacity in the economy represents waste. In the macroeconomic policy arena, attention in this context focuses on unemployment. For example, Figure 26.1 shows that under Keynesian assumptions about aggregate supply, it is possible for an economy to be in macroeconomic equilibrium at a level of output Y_1 that is below the potential full-employment level at Y^*. This may be seen as an unnecessary waste of potential output. In addition, there may be a cost suffered by the people who are unemployed, and who could have been productively employed.

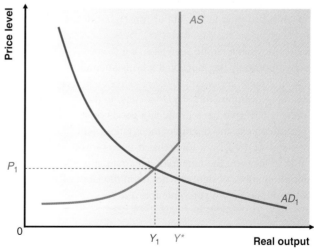

Figure 26.1 Macroeconomic equilibrium below full employment

The way in which people earn a living is an important aspect of any economy. One measure on which governments are judged is whether people who want to work can find jobs – and find jobs that are appropriate to their talents and training. In order to evaluate this, it is necessary to explore the composition of the population, and the way in which unemployment is measured.

The first step is to define what is meant by the **working population**. In any society, there are individuals who are either too young or too old to work. The working population is defined as the number of people of working age – often taken to be those aged between 16 and 65. Notice that the minimum and maximum ages at which people may work vary between countries. Indeed, in a number of developed countries, the retirement age is beginning to be increased.

Amongst those people of working age, there may be some who choose not to participate in work. The **participation rate** measures the percentage of the working population who choose to join the labour force or workforce, by becoming **economically active**.

Key terms

Working population: that part of the population made up of people of working age.

Participation rate: the percentage of people of working age who choose to join the labour force.

Economically active: those people who are active in the labour force.

The participation rate varies significantly between countries, and between males and females. Female participation rates tend to be lower, partly because of child-care responsibilities, but also because of cultural differences between societies.

Within the labour force, it is important to distinguish between different categories of people. Some are employed, accepting a wage or salary from an employer. Others are self-employed, working for themselves. There are also those who are unemployed, being willing to work (because they regard themselves as being in the labour force), but unable to find a job.

Unemployment can be seen as a cost to society. There are the costs borne by the individual who is unemployed, but in addition, if there are unemployed resources within the economy, this is an opportunity forgone by society, in the sense that those workers could have been producing goods or services.

In this context, the unemployment rate is defined as the percentage of the labour force that is unemployed. In order to be able to measure the unemployment rate, it is necessary to count the number of people who are in the labour force and the number of people who are unemployed.

Unemployment in the UK

Historically in the UK, unemployment was measured by the number of people registered as unemployed and claiming unemployment benefit (the Jobseeker's Allowance (JSA)). This measure of employment is known as the **claimant count of unemployment**. People claiming the JSA must declare that they are out of work, capable of, available for and actively seeking work, during the week in which their claim is made.

Key term

Claimant count of unemployment: the number of people claiming the Jobseeker's Allowance each month.

One of the problems with the claimant count is that although people claiming the JSA must declare that they are available for work, it nonetheless includes some people who are claiming benefit, but are not actually available or prepared for work. It also excludes some people who would like to work, and who are looking for work, but who are not eligible for unemployment benefit, such as women returning to the labour force after childbirth.

Because of these problems, the claimant count has been superseded for official purposes by the so-called **ILO unemployment rate**, a measure based on the *Labour Force Survey*. This identifies the number of people available for work, and seeking work, but without a job. This definition corresponds to that used by the International Labour Organization (ILO), and is closer to what economists would like unemployment to measure.

It defines as being unemployed those people who are:

> without a job, want a job, have actively sought work in the last four weeks and are available to start work in the next two weeks; or out of work, have found a job and are waiting to start it in the next two weeks.

Labour Market Statistics, September 2004

Key term

ILO unemployment rate: a measure of the percentage of the workforce who are without jobs, but are available for work, willing to work and looking for work.

However, a major difference between the two alternatives from a measurement perspective is that the claimant count is a full count of all those who register, whereas the ILO measure is based on a sample. Figure 26.2 shows both the claimant and ILO measures for the period since 1986. You can see that the difference between the two measures is narrower when unemployment is relatively high, and wider when unemployment is falling. This may be partly because low unemployment encourages more people who are not eligible for unemployment benefit to look for jobs, whereas they withdraw from the workforce when unemployment rises and they perceive that finding a job will be difficult. This is said to affect women in particular, who may not be eligible for the Jobseeker's Allowance because of their partner's earnings.

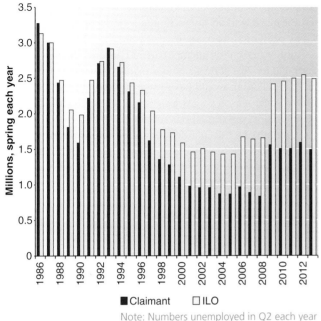

Figure 26.2 Alternative measures of unemployment in the UK, 1986–2012

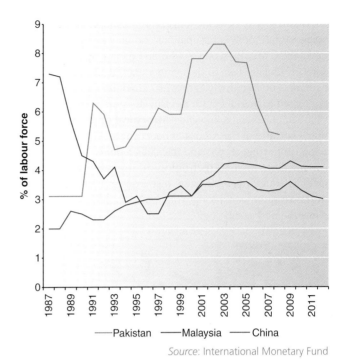

Source: International Monetary Fund

Figure 26.3 Unemployment in selected Asian countries

Unemployment in Asia

Comparing unemployment across countries can be problematic, even when a standard definition is adopted. Recall that two key things need to be counted in order to measure the unemployment rate – the number of people in the labour force, and the number of people who are unemployed.

It may not always be straightforward to count either of these things. In particular, if there is no provision for a job seeker's allowance or unemployment benefit in a country, then there is no possibility of counting those who register as unemployed – because they have no incentive to do so. It is then necessary to rely on a labour force survey in order to be able to count the number of unemployed – and the number of people in the labour force. Such surveys are expensive, and more difficult to undertake in a country that covers a large geographic area, and in which there may be remote rural areas to be covered. Furthermore, there are some countries in which there remains substantial subsistence agriculture, and a large informal sector. The informal sector covers largely unregulated economic activity, which is endemic in many less developed countries. In this context, the very concepts of the labour force and of unemployment become difficult to pin down, and the reliability of data may be expected to vary between countries.

Nonetheless, data on open unemployment are published for many countries around the world, using the ILO definition. Figure 26.3 presents data for three Asian countries, showing the unemployment rate since 1987.

Exercise 26.1

Discuss the time patterns for unemployment in Asian countries shown in Figure 26.3. Discuss why the patterns may vary between countries.

Causes of unemployment

There will always be some unemployment in a dynamic economy. At any point in time, there will be workers transferring between jobs. Indeed, this needs to happen if the pattern of production is to keep up with changing patterns of consumer demand and relative opportunity cost. In other words, in a typical period of time there will be some sectors of an economy that are expanding and others that are in decline. It is crucial that workers are able to transfer from those activities that are in decline to those that are booming. Accordingly, there will be some unemployment while this transfer takes place, and this is known as **frictional unemployment**.

Key term

Frictional unemployment: unemployment associated with job search: that is, people who are between jobs.

In some cases, this transfer of workers between sectors may be quite difficult to accomplish. For example, coal mining may be on the decline in an economy, but international banking may be booming. It is clearly unreasonable to expect coal miners to turn themselves into international bankers overnight. In this sort of situation there may be some longer-term unemployment while workers retrain for new occupations and new sectors of activity. Indeed, there may be workers who find themselves redundant at a relatively late stage in their career and for whom the retraining is not worthwhile, or who cannot find firms that will be prepared to train them for a relatively short payback time. Such unemployment is known as **structural unemployment**. It arises because of the mismatch between the skills of workers leaving contracting sectors and the skills required by expanding sectors in the economy. **Technological unemployment** is a type of structural unemployment that arises from the introduction of technology, when existing workers do not have the skills to operate the new technology.

High levels of unemployment can cause unrest, such as this protest in Hyderabad, Pakistan

Key terms

Structural unemployment: unemployment arising because of changes in the pattern of activity within an economy.

Technological unemployment: a type of structural unemployment that arises from the introduction of technology.

Figure 26.1 showed a different form of unemployment, one that arises because the economy is trapped in an equilibrium position that is below full employment. This is sometimes referred to as **demand-deficient unemployment** – and a solution to it might be to boost aggregate demand. This possibility will be discussed in Chapter 27.

Key term

Demand-deficient unemployment: unemployment that arises because of a deficiency of aggregate demand in the economy, so that the equilibrium level of output is below the full-employment level.

There may also be *seasonal unemployment*, when there are regular fluctuations in the level of economic activity. For

example, this could occur in agriculture, where there may be a need for more workers at certain times of the agricultural cycle, such as planting or harvesting.

A further reason for unemployment concerns the level of wages. Figure 26.4 shows a labour market in which a free-market equilibrium would have wage W^* and quantity of labour L^*. If for some reason wages were set at W_0, there would be disequilibrium between labour supply (at L_s) and labour demand (at L_d). Expressing this in a different way, here is a situation in which there are more workers seeking employment at the going wage (L_s) than there are firms prepared to hire at that wage (L_d). The difference is unemployment.

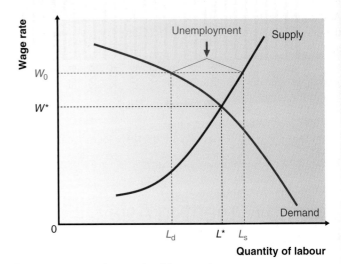

Figure 26.4 Unemployment in a labour market

There are a number of reasons why this situation might arise. Trade unions might have been able to use their power and influence to raise wages above the equilibrium level, thereby ensuring higher wages for their members who remain in employment, but denying jobs to others. Alternatively, it could be argued that wages will be inflexible downwards. Thus, a supply shock that reduced firms' demand for labour could leave wages above the equilibrium, and they may adjust downwards only slowly. Chapter 6 mentioned that in some situations the imposition of a minimum wage in a low-wage competitive labour market could also have the effect of institutionally setting the wage rate above its equilibrium level, thus causing unemployment.

Finally, if unemployment benefits are set at a relatively high level compared with wages in low-paid occupations, some people may choose not to work, thereby creating some **voluntary unemployment**. From the point of view of those individuals, they are making a rational choice on the basis of the options open to them. From society's point of view, however, there needs to be a balance between providing appropriate social protection for those unable to obtain jobs and trying to make the best use of available resources for the benefit of society as a whole.

Costs of unemployment

The costs of unemployment were mentioned earlier. From society's perspective, if the economy is operating below full capacity, then it is operating within the production possibility curve, and therefore is not making the best possible use of society's resources. In other words, if those unemployed workers were in employment, society would be producing more aggregate output; the economy would be operating more efficiently overall.

Furthermore, there may be costs from the perspective of prospective workers, in the sense that **involuntary unemployment** carries a cost to each such individual in terms of forgone earnings and the need to rely on social security support. At the same time, the inability to find work and to contribute to the family budget may impose a cost in terms of personal worth and dignity.

Key terms

Voluntary unemployment: the situation arising when an individual chooses not to accept a job at the going wage rate.

Involuntary unemployment: the situation arising when an individual who would like to accept a job at the going wage rate is unable to find employment.

Unemployment in less developed countries

For less developed countries in which there is no social security system providing benefits or protection for the unemployed, the consequences of unemployment are more severe, and those who find themselves unable to find formal employment may be forced to enter the informal sector. Such informal economic activity is widespread in many LDCs. Migration into the cities puts added pressure on the employment situation, and makes it difficult to provide sufficient jobs in the formal sector.

The nature of employment and economic activity in many LDCs creates additional forms of unemployment – in particular, there may be disguised unemployment or underemployment in many cases.

One example of underemployment occurs in countries in which there is substantial subsistence-level agriculture. It may be that a family-based household lives by farming a piece of land that is not sufficiently large to provide employment for all household members. The work to be done may be divided between all members of the household, meaning that none of them is fully employed.

Another form of hidden unemployment occurs where there are skilled workers who cannot find a job that reflects their skill levels. They may then find employment in lower-skilled occupations – but they are clearly working below their potential. University graduates who work as taxi drivers are not making full use of their human capital, and therefore cannot be regarded as being fully employed.

Exercise 26.2

Classify each of the following types of unemployment as arising from frictional, structural, demand-deficient or other causes, and decide whether they are voluntary or involuntary.

a Unemployment arising from a decline of the coal mining sector and the expansion of financial services.
b A worker leaving one job to search for a better one.
c Unemployment that arises because the real wage rate is held above the labour market equilibrium.
d Unemployment arising from slow adjustment to a fall in aggregate demand.
e Unemployment arising because workers find that low-paid jobs are paying less than can be obtained in unemployment benefit.
f A situation in which a qualified engineer takes a job as a taxi driver.

Summary

- Full employment occurs when an economy is operating on the production possibility curve, with full utilisation of factors of production.
- An economy operating below full capacity is characterised by unemployment.
- Some unemployment in a dynamic economy is inevitable, as people may have to undergo short spells of unemployment while between jobs – this is known as frictional unemployment.
- Structural unemployment occurs when there is a mismatch between the skills that workers have to offer and the skills that employers want. This occurs when the economy is undergoing structural change, with some sectors expanding and some contracting.
- Demand-deficient unemployment may occur if the macroeconomy is in equilibrium below full employment.
- If wages are held above the equilibrium level – for example, by minimum wage legislation or trade union action – then unemployment may occur.
- High levels of unemployment benefit may encourage some workers not to accept jobs, as the opportunity cost of not working is low.
- Other forms of unemployment occur in less developed countries, where there may be hidden unemployment or underemployment.

26.2 Interrelated macroeconomic problems

Key term

Phillips curve: a trade-off relationship between unemployment and inflation.

Many macroeconomic problems are interrelated. One example is that there may be a conflict between economic growth and the environment, so that the pursuit of economic growth may need to be tempered by concern for the environment. Policy must therefore be designed bearing in mind that there may be a trade-off between these two objectives – at some point, it could be that more economic growth is possible only by sacrificing environmental objectives.

Unemployment and inflation

This notion of trade-off between macroeconomic variables applies in other areas too. One important trade-off was discovered by the Australian economist Bill Phillips. In 1958 Phillips claimed that he had found an 'empirical regularity' that had existed for almost a century and that traced out a relationship between the rate of unemployment and the rate of change of money wages. This was rapidly generalised into a relationship between unemployment and inflation (by arguing that firms pass on increased wages in the form of higher prices).

Figure 26.5 shows what became known as the **Phillips curve** (*PC*). Although Phillips began with data, he also came up with an explanation of why such a relationship should exist. At the heart of his argument was the idea that, when the demand for labour is high, firms will be prepared to bid up wages in order to attract labour. To the extent that higher wages are then passed on in the form of higher prices, this would imply a relationship between unemployment and inflation: when unemployment is low, inflation will tend to be higher, and vice versa.

The 1970s provided something of a setback to this theory, when suddenly a number of economies including the UK economy started to experience both high unemployment and high inflation simultaneously, suggesting that the Phillips curve had disappeared. This combination of stagnation and inflation became known as **stagflation**.

Key term

Stagflation: a situation in which an economy simultaneously experiences stagnation (high unemployment) and high inflation.

One possibility is that the Phillips curve had not in fact disappeared, but had moved. Suppose that wage bargaining takes place on the basis of *expectations* about future rises in retail prices. As inflation becomes embedded in an economy, and people come to expect it to continue, those expectations will be built into wage negotiations. Another way of viewing this is that expectations about price inflation will influence the *position* of the Phillips curve.

Figure 26.6 shows how this might work. PC_0 represents the initial Phillips curve. Suppose we start with the economy at the *natural rate of unemployment*, U_{nat}. If the economy is at point A, with inflation at π_0 and unemployment at U_{nat}, the economy is in equilibrium. If the government then tries to exploit the Phillips curve by allowing inflation to rise to π_1, the economy moves in the short run to point B. However, as people realise that inflation is now higher, they adjust their expectations. This eventually begins to affect wage negotiations; the Phillips curve then moves to PC_1, and unemployment returns to the natural

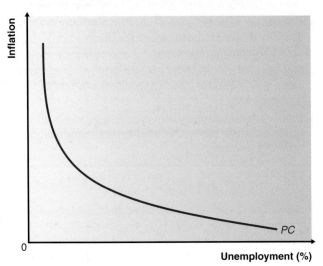

Figure 26.5 The Phillips curve

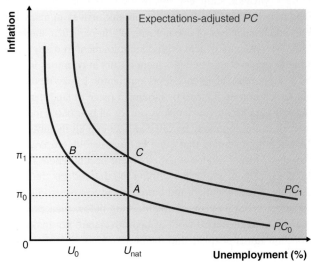

Figure 26.6 The expectations-augmented Phillips curve

rate. The economy settles at *C* and is again in equilibrium, but now with higher inflation than before – and the same initial rate of unemployment. For this reason, the natural rate of unemployment is sometimes known as the **non-accelerating-inflation rate of unemployment (NAIRU)**.

> **Key term**
>
> Non-accelerating-inflation rate of unemployment (NAIRU): the rate of unemployment in an economy at which inflation will be stable.

The problem that arises with this is how to get back to the original position with a lower inflation rate. This can happen only if people's expectations adjust so that lower inflation is expected. This means that the economy has to move down along PC_1, pushing up unemployment in order to reduce inflation. Then, once expectations adjust, the Phillips curve will move back again until the natural rate of unemployment is restored. If this takes a long time, the cost in terms of unemployment will be high.

Economic growth and the current account

In some circumstances, conflict can also arise between achieving economic growth and attaining equilibrium on the current account of the balance of payments. An increase in economic growth resulting in higher real incomes could lead to an increase in imports of goods and services, if domestic residents spend a high proportion of their additional income abroad. This was seen as a major problem in the UK during the fixed exchange rate era of the 1950s and 1960s, when any deficit on the current account had to be met by running down foreign exchange reserves. This led to a 'stop–go' cycle of macroeconomic policy, where every time growth began to accelerate, the current account went into deficit, and policy then had to be adjusted to slow down the growth rate to deal with the deficit. The situation arose partly from the nature of the fixed exchange rate system, as the authorities were committed to intervening in order to maintain the value of the pound.

Inflation and the balance of payments

Another example of the interrelated nature of macroeconomic problems is the connection between inflation and the balance of payments. If the domestic economy enters a period of inflation

that is high relative to its trading partners, then problems are likely to follow for the balance of payments. If prices rise more rapidly in the domestic economy than in the country's trading partners, the result will be a loss in international competitiveness, making it more difficult for firms to export their goods, and leading to a rise in imports. This is likely to lead to a deficit on the current account of the balance of payments, putting pressure on the exchange rate. Effectively, the difference in inflation rate in the domestic economy leads to a divergence between the internal and external value of money.

Implications for macroeconomic policy

These interrelationships between macroeconomic variables have implications for when policy-makers set out to try to influence or control the macroeconomy. In other words, the nature of trade-offs between macroeconomic problems will influence the effectiveness of alternative macroeconomic policies, as a policy designed to influence one variable may have an impact on other variables. For example, a policy designed to reduce unemployment in a country may have undesirable effects on other policy objectives, such as inflation. These issues will be discussed in the next chapter.

> **Summary**
>
> - Many macroeconomic problems are interrelated, and there may be trade-offs between them.
> - Rapid economic growth may conflict with the need to sustain and conserve the environment.
> - Phillips argued that there was a long-established relationship between unemployment and inflation, such that high unemployment tended to be associated with low inflation, and vice versa.
> - Economic growth and inflation are also seen to be connected to the balance of payments.
> - This has implications for the design of macroeconomic policy.

27 Designing macroeconomic policy

Previous chapters have identified a number of problems that can arise at the macroeconomic level. This chapter examines the policy options available to tackle these problems. Analysis of the multiple objectives of macroeconomic policy reveals some important sources of conflict, as policies designed to meet one objective can be seen to jeopardise the meeting of other targets. The multiplicity of objectives also means that there are multiple dimensions over which the performance of the economy has to be monitored and measured. Given the trade-offs that exist between some objectives, it is also important to prioritise them appropriately.

Learning outcomes

After studying this chapter, you should:

- be familiar with the prime aims of macroeconomic policy
- understand the alternative types of fiscal policy instrument, including the use of alternative tax instruments and government spending
- be aware of the effect of automatic stabilisers
- be able to analyse the impact of changing fiscal instruments on the distribution of income
- understand the consequences of a fiscal budget deficit or surplus
- appreciate the difference between direct and indirect taxation as means of raising revenue
- be familiar with the prime instruments of monetary policy
- be able to understand the monetary transmission mechanism
- be familiar with the operation of monetary policy and its effectiveness in helping to manage the economy
- be aware of the importance of exchange rate policy in influencing the effectiveness of monetary policy and affecting international competitiveness
- be able to evaluate the contribution of supply-side policies to the improvement of economic performance
- understand the potential conflicts that may arise between the targets of macroeconomic policy.

27.1 Objectives of macroeconomic policy

There are a number of problems that can affect the macroeconomic performance of an economy. The previous chapter pointed out that these problems can be interrelated – which in turn means that the policies that can be used to tackle the problems may have complex and sometimes conflicting effects. It is also important to remember, when comparing the performance of different countries, that they may have set out to achieve different objectives or set different priorities. The first stage in analysing policy options is to identify the key objectives that governments wish to achieve.

Price stability

The control of inflation has been the prime target of macroeconomic policy in many countries around the world, including the UK, since the mid-1970s. Prices play a key role in an economy, acting as signals that guide the allocation of resources. When prices are unstable, firms may find it difficult to interpret these price signals, which may lead to a misallocation of resources. Furthermore, instability of prices creates difficulties for firms in trying to forecast future expected demand for their products, which may discourage them from undertaking investment. This in turn means that the economy's capacity to produce may expand by less than it could otherwise have done – in other words, high or unstable inflation may dampen economic growth through its effect on investment. Chapter 8 identified some other costs of inflation, and you might want to look back to remind yourself of them. However, the effects on resource allocation and investment are widely accepted to be the most important damaging effects of inflation.

Full employment

A second key policy objective is full employment. Unemployment imposes costs on society and on the individuals who are unemployed. From society's point of view, the existence of substantial unemployment represents a waste of resources and indicates that the economy is working below full capacity.

The balance of payments

Under a flexible exchange rate system, the overall balance of payments will always be zero because the exchange rate adjusts to ensure that this is so. Nevertheless, the balance of payments remains an objective, not so much to ensure overall balance as to maintain an appropriate balance between the current account and the financial account. If the current account is in persistent deficit, this could cause problems in the long run, as the implication is that the country is selling off its assets in order to obtain goods for present consumption. Under a fixed exchange rate system, the need to maintain the exchange rate acts as a constraint upon economic growth, which tends to lead to an increase in imports, creating a current account deficit.

Economic growth

It is through long-run economic growth that the productive capacity of the economy is raised, and this in turn allows the living standards of the country's citizens to be progressively improved over time. In a sense, this is the most fundamental of the policy objectives. However, attaining other policy objectives may be a prerequisite for success in achieving growth.

Environmental considerations

It must be recognised that it is not only resources that contribute to living standards: conserving a good environment is also important. Sustainable growth and development means growth that does not prejudice the consumption possibilities of future generations, and this consideration may act as a constraint on the rate of economic growth.

Income redistribution

Another macroeconomic policy objective concerns attempts to influence the distribution of income within a society. This may entail transfers of income between groups – that is, from the rich to the poor – in order to protect the vulnerable. Such transfers may take place through progressive taxation (whereby those on higher incomes pay a greater proportion of their income in tax) or through a system of social security benefits such as the Jobseeker's Allowance or Income Support in the UK.

Correcting market failure

At the microeconomic level there are policy measures designed to deal with various forms of market failure. Competition policy is one example of this; it is designed to prevent firms from abusing monopoly power, and to improve the allocation of resources. Although such policies operate at the microeconomic level, they have consequences for macroeconomic objectives such as economic growth.

Productivity

A further measure of the performance of the economy is productivity, which may be regarded as a measure of the efficiency with which factors of production are being utilised in the economy. This is important if the economy's performance is to be judged relative to that of other countries. For example, if the UK's trading competitors were all experiencing greater improvements in productivity, this would have potentially damaging effects on the competitiveness of UK goods and services in international markets.

Exercise 27.1

Discuss which of the above objectives you consider to be of most importance. Can you see reasons why it might not be possible to achieve all of the objectives simultaneously?

Economic policy objectives – an overview

You will realise from the discussion above that there are several targets for macroeconomic policy. However, we can put these into perspective by recognising that policy is aimed at a relatively small number of ultimate objectives, which we can summarise as:

- economic stability
- economic growth
- international competitiveness.

We could argue that the most important of these overarching objectives is economic growth. It is through economic growth that it becomes possible to improve the quality of life of a nation's citizens, as it is only through economic growth that the quantity of resources available to citizens can be expanded. This is not to say that the other two objectives are unimportant. Economic stability is important – but partly because it creates an environment within which economic growth can take place. For example, if we have price stability, then firms will have more confidence to invest in the future, thus stimulating economic growth. Similarly, maintaining or improving the international competitiveness of domestically produced goods also contributes to economic stability and provides a solid demand base to encourage firms to expand by selling in global markets – again helping to increase economic growth. In the next chapters, we will examine a range of different policy approaches, and you will find that some of these are likely to be more useful in achieving some of the objectives.

Summary

- The macroeconomic performance of an economy can be affected by a number of problems, which may then be targets of policy.
- Price stability (the control of inflation) has been central to macroeconomic policy in many countries in recent years.
- Full employment is also viewed as being important, as is the need to maintain balance on the balance of payments.
- The most fundamental target for policy is economic growth, as it is through growth that people living in an economy can have the potential to become better off.

27.2 Fiscal policy

The term fiscal policy covers a range of policy measures that affect government expenditures and revenues through the decisions made by the government on its expenditure, taxation and borrowing. Fiscal policy is used to influence the level and structure of aggregate demand in an economy. The effectiveness of fiscal policy also depends crucially on the whole policy environment in which it is utilised. In other words, fiscal policy covers a range of policy measures that affect government expenditures and revenues. As the government has discretion over the amount of expenditure that it undertakes and the amount of revenue that it chooses to raise from taxation, these can be manipulated in order to influence the course of the economy.

What is the role of fiscal policy in a modern economy? Following Keynesian analysis, traditionally fiscal policy was used to affect the level of aggregate demand in the economy. The overall balance between government receipts and outlays affects the position of the aggregate demand curve, which is reinforced by multiplier effects. A budget deficit occurs when the revenues raised through taxation are not sufficient to cover the government's various types of expenditure.

The overall size of the budget deficit may limit the government's actions in terms of fiscal policy. In addition, the overall pattern of revenue and expenditure has a strong effect on the overall balance of activity in the economy. A neutral government budget can be attained either with high expenditure and high revenues, or with relatively low expenditure and revenues. Such decisions affect the overall size of the public sector relative to the private sector. Over the years, different countries throughout the world have adopted different approaches.

Figure 27.1 shows the share of total (current and capital) expenditure by governments in a range of developed countries.

This reveals something of a contrast between, on the one hand, Switzerland, Australia, Japan and North America, and on the other hand, many European countries, where governments have been more active in the economy. In part this reflects the greater role that government plays in some countries in providing services such as education and healthcare, whereas in other countries the private sector takes a greater role, often through the insurance market.

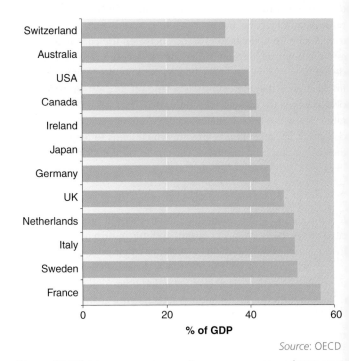

Source: OECD

Figure 27.1 Total government expenditure as a percentage of GDP, 2013

Direct and indirect taxes

Fiscal policy, and taxation in particular, has not only been used to establish a balance between the public and private sectors of an economy. In addition, taxation remains an important weapon against some forms of market failure, and it also influences the distribution of income. In this context, the choice of using direct or indirect taxes is important.

Direct taxes are taxes levied on income of various kinds, such as personal income tax. Such taxes are designed to be progressive and so can be effective in redistributing income: for example, a higher income tax rate can be charged to those earning high incomes. In contrast, indirect taxes – taxes on expenditure, such as VAT and excise duties – tend to be regressive. As poorer households tend to spend a higher proportion of their income on items that are subject to excise duties, a greater share of their income is taken up by indirect taxes. Even VAT can be regressive if higher-income households save a greater proportion of their incomes.

Sustainability of fiscal policy

An issue that came to the fore in the UK during the 1990s concerned the sustainability of fiscal policy. This is wrapped up with the notion that current taxpayers should have to fund only expenditure that benefits their own generation, and that the taxpayers of the future should make their own decisions, and not have to pay for past government expenditure that has been incurred for the benefit of earlier generations.

In this context, what is significant is the overall balance between receipts and outlays through time. If outlays were always larger than receipts, the spending programme could be sustained only through government borrowing, thereby shifting the burden of funding the deficit to future generations. This could also be a problem if it made it more difficult for the private sector to obtain funds for investment, or if it added to the national debt. In the UK, the Labour government introduced a so-called **'Golden Rule' of fiscal policy**, which stated that, on average over the economic cycle, the government should borrow only to invest and not to fund current expenditure. This was intended to help achieve equity between present and future generations. It should perhaps be noted that this was a self-imposed guideline, so there would be no penalty for breaking the rule other than loss of political credibility. The Coalition Government that followed was less committed to the concept of the Golden Rule, and the onset of the financial crisis – and the need to bail out commercial banks in order to safeguard the financial system – rendered the Golden Rule impossible to follow.

> **Key term**
>
> **'Golden Rule' of fiscal policy**: a rule stating that, over the economic cycle, net government borrowing will be for investment only, and not for current spending.

If receipts and outlays more or less balance over the economic cycle, the economy is not in a position whereby the current generation is forcing future generations to pay for its consumption. However, it is not practical to impose this rule at every part of the cycle, so the Golden Rule was intended to apply over the economic cycle as a whole. There was also a commitment to keep public sector net debt below 40% of GDP – again, on average over the economic cycle. Figure 21.4 on page 195 shows data for this since 1993. The Golden Rule seemed secure until the onset of the credit crunch. However, the financial support offered to Northern Rock and other banks in the bailout of 2008 had a noticeable effect on public sector net debt, as is all too clear in the figure. Even without the financial sector interventions, net debt rose over the 40% mark in the last quarter of 2008 and continued to rise thereafter. This reflected other measures taken by the government to try to mitigate the

effects of the recession. One example was the reduction in the rate of VAT from 17.5 to 15%. This is tantamount to a fiscal expansion, but when it was introduced, it was made clear that it was intended as a temporary boost for a specified period. This statement enabled the government to maintain that it was not breaching its long-term fiscal commitment. The rate of VAT returned to 17.5% in January 2010, and was increased to 20% in January 2011.

Taxes and current expenditure around the world

Tax collection and government expenditure presents a challenge to many less developed countries. In many cases, the institutions needed to collect taxes are absent, or are ineffective. This is reflected in the data shown in Figure 27.2, which depicts tax revenue in a range of countries as a percentage of GDP.

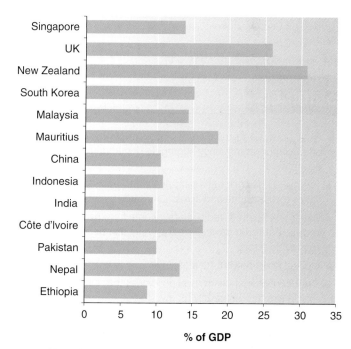

Note: Countries are in descending order of GDP per capita in PPP$.
Source: World Bank

Figure 27.2 Tax revenue as a percentage of GDP

Notice how the UK and New Zealand in this group are able to raise a significantly higher proportion of GDP in the form of tax revenue. Of course, there may also be countries that could raise a higher level of taxes, but which choose not to do so. However, there are also countries such as Pakistan that are not able to collect taxes efficiently and effectively. This is then reflected in the extent to which they can undertake expenditure, as seen in Figure 27.3. (Notice that this figure only includes consumption spending, so is not comparable to Figure 27.1, which also included capital spending.)

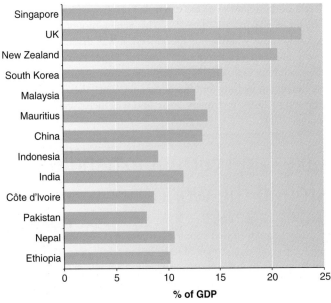

Source: World Bank

Figure 27.3 Government consumption expenditure as a percentage of GDP

Summary

- Fiscal policy concerns the use of government expenditure and taxation to influence aggregate demand in the economy.
- The overall balance between private and public sectors varies through time and across countries.
- Direct taxes help to redistribute income between groups in society, but if too progressive they may dampen incentives to provide effort.
- Indirect taxes tend to be regressive.
- The UK's Golden Rule of fiscal policy was that the government should aim to borrow only for investment, and not for current expenditure (averaged over the economic cycle).
- There was also a commitment to keep the national debt below 40% of GDP; this commitment did not survive the financial crisis and recession of the late 2000s.

27.3 Fiscal policy and the *AD/AS* model

It is important to understand how fiscal policy can be analysed using the *AD/AS* model. As already noted, the overall balance between government receipts and outlays affects the position of the aggregate demand curve, which is reinforced by multiplier effects. When government outlays exceed government receipts, the result is a budget deficit. This occurs when the revenues raised through taxation are not sufficient to cover the government's various types of expenditure. An increase in the fiscal deficit has the effect of shifting the aggregate demand curve to the right.

Figure 27.4 shows that shifting the aggregate demand curve in this way affects only the overall price level in the economy when the aggregate supply curve is vertical – and remember that the Monetarist school of thought argued that it would always be vertical. Hence a key issue for a government considering the use of fiscal policy is knowing whether there is spare capacity in the economy, because otherwise an expansion in aggregate demand from increased government spending will push up prices, but leave real output unchanged.

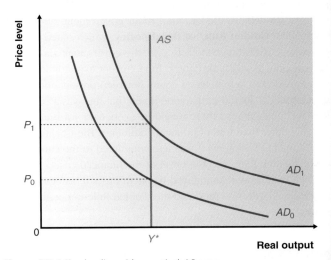

Figure 27.4 Fiscal policy with a vertical *AS* curve

Chapter 23 introduced the concept of the multiplier, which suggested that for any increase in autonomous spending, there would be a multiplied increase in equilibrium output. The idea of the multiplier is that, if there is an increase in (say) government expenditure, this provides income for workers, who will then spend that income and create further expenditure streams. The size of these induced effects will depend upon the marginal propensity to withdraw.

In terms of the *AD/AS* diagram, the existence of the multiplier means that if there is an increase in government expenditure, the *AD* curve moves further to the right than it otherwise would have done, because of the multiplier effects. However, this does not mean that equilibrium income will increase by the full multiplier amount. Looking more closely at what is happening, you can see that there are some forces at work that are acting to weaken the multiplier effect of an increase in government expenditure. One way in which this happens is through interest rates. If the government finances its deficit through borrowing, a side effect is to put upward pressure on interest rates, which then may cause private sector spending – by households on consumption and by firms on investment – to decline, as the cost of borrowing has been increased. This process is known as the **crowding out** of private sector activity by the public sector. It limits the extent to which a government budget deficit can shift the aggregate demand curve, especially if the public sector activity is less productive than the private sector activity that it replaces.

Automatic and discretionary fiscal policies

It is important to distinguish between automatic and discretionary changes in government expenditure. Some items of government expenditure and receipts vary automatically with the economic cycle. They are known as **automatic stabilisers**. For example, if the economy enters a period of recession, government expenditure will rise because of the increased payments of unemployment and other social security benefits, and revenues will fall because fewer people are paying income tax, and because receipts from VAT are falling. This helps to offset the recession without any active intervention from the government.

Key terms

Crowding out: a process by which an increase in government expenditure 'crowds out' private sector activity by raising the cost of borrowing.

Automatic stabilisers: a process by which government expenditure and revenue vary with the economic cycle, thereby helping to stabilise the economy without any conscious intervention from government.

More important, however, is the question of whether the government can or should make use of discretionary fiscal policy in a deliberate attempt to influence the course of the economy. As already mentioned, the key issue is whether or not the economy has spare capacity, because attempts to stimulate an economy that is already at full employment will merely push up the price level.

There are many examples of how excessive government spending can create problems for the economy. Such problems arose in a number of Latin American economies during the 1980s. In Brazil, a range of policies was brought to bear in an attempt to reduce inflation – including direct controls on prices. However, with no serious attempt to control the fiscal deficit, inflation continually got out of control – reaching almost 3000% in 1990. Only when the deficit was reduced did it become possible to bring inflation to a more reasonable level. More recently, the collapse of the economy of Zimbabwe was accompanied by inflation at such a high level that the printing presses could not keep up with the need for banknotes.

Balance between the public and private sectors

Economic analysis supports the view that fiscal policy should not be used as an active stabilisation device. However, this does not mean that there is no role for fiscal policy in a modern economy. Decisions about the size of government expenditure and revenue influence the overall balance between the public and private sectors. The balance that is achieved can have an important influence on the overall level of economic activity, and upon economic growth, so the importance of designing an appropriate fiscal policy should not be underestimated. An important theme that runs through much economic analysis is that governments may be justified in intervening in the economy in order to correct market failure. Some of this intervention requires the use of fiscal policy: for example, taxes to correct for the effects of externalities, or expenditure to ensure the provision of public goods. In other words, fiscal policy can be an instrument that operates at the microeconomic level, as well as having macroeconomic implications.

Take infrastructure as an example. Infrastructure covers a range of goods that are crucial for the efficient operation of a market economy. Businesses need good transport links and good communication facilities. Households need good healthcare, education and sanitation facilities, not only in order to enjoy a good standard of life, but also to be productive members of the labour force. Both public goods and externality arguments come into play in the provision of infrastructure, so there needs to be appropriate government intervention to ensure that such goods are adequately provided. The consequence of failing to do this will be to lower the productive capacity of the economy below what would otherwise have been possible. In other words, the aggregate supply curve will be further to the left than it need be.

On the other hand, too much government intervention may also be damaging. One of the most compelling arguments in favour of privatisation was that when the managers of public enterprises are insufficiently accountable for their actions, X-inefficiency becomes a major issue, so public sector activity tends to be less efficient than private sector enterprise. On this argument, too large a public sector may have the effect of lowering aggregate productive capacity below its potential level.

These arguments suggest that an important role for fiscal policy is in affecting the supply side of the economy, ensuring that markets operate effectively to make the best possible use of the economy's resources. Some further aspects of this will be discussed in the context of supply-side policies later in the chapter.

Income distribution

The other key role for fiscal policy is in affecting the distribution of income within society. Taxes and transfers can have a large effect on income distribution. This in turn may have effects on the economy by affecting the incentives that people face in choosing their labour supply.

Benefits

There are two forms of benefit that households can receive to help equalise the income distribution. First, there are various types of *cash benefit*, designed to protect families whose income in certain circumstances would otherwise be very low. Second, there are *benefits in kind*, such as health and education. These accrue to individual households depending on the number of members of the household and their age and gender. Again, the extent to which a country can provide these sorts of benefits will depend in part upon its ability to raise revenue through taxation.

Taxation

Direct taxes (taxes on incomes) tend to be progressive. In other words, higher income groups pay tax at a higher rate. With a tax such as income tax, its progressive nature is reflected in the way the tax rate increases as an individual moves into a higher income range. In other words, the marginal tax rate increases as income increases. The progressive nature of the tax ensures that it does indeed help to reduce inequality in income distribution – although its effects are less than the cash benefits discussed earlier.

The effect of indirect taxes, on the other hand, can sometimes be regressive: in other words, indirect taxes may impinge more heavily on lower-income households.

Indirect taxes are levied on expenditure rather than income. They include sales taxes, which may be calculated on a value-added basis (the value added tax, VAT), excise duties levied on particular goods or a service tax. For example, Pakistan has a sales tax that covers most goods; Malaysia has a sales tax and a service tax, and in addition imposes excise duty payments on alcohol, tobacco, motor vehicles and playing cards. Some countries also impose customs duties. The UK has the value added tax (VAT), tobacco taxes, excise duties on alcohol and oil duties. Chapter 6 analysed how the incidence of a tax is related to the price elasticity of demand of a good or service. It explained how, where demand is price inelastic, producers are able to pass much of an increase in the tax rate on to consumers, whereas if demand is price elastic, producers have to absorb most of the increase as part of their costs.

Why are some of these taxes regressive? Take the tobacco tax. In the first place, the number of smokers tends to be higher among lower-income groups than among the relatively rich –

research in the UK has shown that only about 10% of people in professional groups now smoke compared with nearly 40% of those in unskilled manual groups. Second, expenditure on tobacco tends to take a lower proportion of income of the rich compared with that of the poor, even for those in the former group who do smoke. Thus, the tobacco tax falls more heavily on lower-income groups than on the better-off.

As pointed out earlier, achieving a balance of taxation between direct and indirect taxes is an important aspect of the government's redistributive policy. A switch in the balance from direct to indirect taxes will tend to increase inequality in a society. The incentive effects must also be kept in mind. High marginal tax rates on income can have a disincentive effect; if people know that a large proportion of any additional work they undertake will be taxed away, they may be discouraged from providing more work. In other words, cutting income tax can encourage work effort by reducing marginal tax rates. This is yet another reminder of the need for a balanced policy – one that recognises that, while some income redistribution is needed to protect the vulnerable, disincentive effects may arise if the better-off are over-taxed. For many less developed countries, there may be a need to balance the need to raise revenue against the incentive and distributional effects.

For a country that is concerned to increase tax revenue, it may be tempting to consider raising the tax rate. However, there may be situations in which raising the tax rate may actually lead to a fall in tax revenue. This effect is captured in the Laffer curve, shown in Figure 27.5. The curve plots tax revenue on the vertical axis against the tax rate on the horizontal. As the tax rate increases from zero, tax revenue initially increases. However, after a certain point, revenue begins to decline because of people's reactions. If the figure relates to income tax, for example, it is likely that at some point a higher tax rate has disincentive effects, such that people will not supply additional labour hours if a high portion of the income they earn is being taxed away.

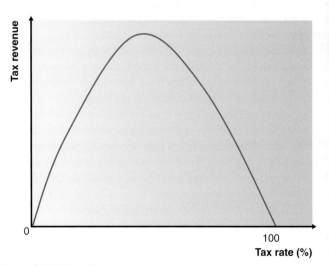

Figure 27.5 The Laffer curve

Summary

- Fiscal policy entails changes in taxation and in the government's expenditure to influence the level or pattern of aggregate demand.
- Fiscal policy retains a key role in ensuring an appropriate balance between private and public sectors, and ensuring the provision of public goods and tackling externality effects.
- It also plays a key role in influencing the distribution of income between groups within society.
- In doing this, an appropriate balance needs to be found between achieving a desired level of equity between individuals, and providing incentives to work.

27.4 Monetary policy

Monetary policy entails the use of monetary variables such as money supply and interest rates to influence aggregate demand. It will be shown that under a fixed exchange rate system, monetary policy becomes wholly impotent, as it has to be devoted to maintaining the exchange rate. So, the effectiveness of monetary policy depends upon the policy environment in which it is used. In many less developed countries, monetary policy may also aim to encourage the development of the financial sector and to promote confidence in it.

Monetary policy has become the prime instrument of government macroeconomic policy in many developed countries, with the interest rate acting as the key control variable. Monetary policy involves the manipulation of monetary variables in order to influence aggregate demand in the economy, with the intention of meeting the government's inflation target.

Key term

Monetary policy: decisions made by the government regarding monetary variables such as money supply and interest rates.

Although the previous paragraph talked about 'the interest rate', this is a simplification. In the real-world economy, there are many different interest rates. For example, if you borrow from a bank, you will pay a higher interest rate than would be paid to you on your savings. Indeed, it is this difference between the rates for savers and borrowers that enables the banks to make a profit.

Similarly, interest rates on financial assets differ depending on the nature of the asset. In part, these differences reflect different degrees of risk associated with the assets. A risky asset pays a higher interest rate than a relatively safe asset. A long-term asset tends to pay a higher interest rate than a short-term asset, although the differences have been quite small in the first few years of the twenty-first century.

How does monetary policy work?

In evaluating the tools of monetary policy, it is important to understand the route by which a change in a monetary variable can have an effect on the real economy. In other words, how can a change in money supply, or the interest rate, affect the level of equilibrium output in the economy?

The monetary transmission mechanism

In drawing this analysis together, an important issue concerns the relationship between the rate of interest and the level of aggregate demand. This is critical for the conduct of monetary policy. Indeed, the interest rate has been seen as the prime instrument of monetary policy in recent years – and monetary policy is seen as the prime instrument of macroeconomic policy. By setting the interest rate, monetary policy is intended to affect aggregate demand through the so-called **monetary transmission mechanism**.

Key term

Monetary transmission mechanism: the channel by which monetary policy affects aggregate demand.

At a higher interest rate, firms undertake less investment expenditure because fewer projects are worthwhile. In addition, a higher interest rate may encourage higher saving, which also means that households undertake less consumption expenditure. This may then reinforce the impact on investment because if firms perceive consumption to be falling, this will affect their expectations about future demand, and further dampen their desire to undertake investment. Furthermore, if domestic interest rates are high relative to elsewhere in the world, they will attract overseas investors, increasing the demand for local currency. This will tend to lead to an appreciation in the exchange rate, which in turn will reduce the competitiveness of domestic goods and services, reducing the foreign demand for exports and encouraging domestic residents to reduce their demand for domestic goods and buy imports instead. All these factors lower the level of aggregate demand, shifting the AD curve to the left.

This can be seen by looking at Figure 27.6. The initial equilibrium is with real output at Y_0, the price level at P_0 and the rate of interest at r_0. An increase in the rate of interest to r_1 will need to be balanced by a decrease in money supply to maintain money-market equilibrium. However, more significant is the effect on investment, which is shown in the middle panel

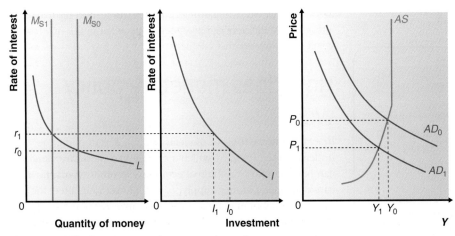

Figure 27.6 The interest rate and aggregate demand

of the figure. The increase in the rate of interest leads to a fall in investment from I_0 to I_1. This will cause the aggregate demand curve to move from AD_0 to AD_1, resulting in a lower overall price level P_1 and a lower real output level at Y_1. The lower level of real output arises because the AS curve was drawn with an upward-sloping segment.

Notice that this may not be the end of the story. If one of the effects of the higher interest rate is to discourage investment, this will also have long-term consequences. Investment allows the productive capacity of the economy to increase, leading to a rightward drift in the AS curve. With lower investment, this process will slow down, leaving the economy with lower productive capacity than it otherwise would have had.

The AD/AS graph is drawn in terms of the overall price level. However, in a dynamic context, such a policy stance may be needed in order to maintain control of inflation. A reduction in interest rates would, of course, have the reverse effect. However, notice that the interaction of the money supply, interest rates and the exchange rate makes policy design a complicated business.

In creating a stable macroeconomic environment, the ultimate aim of monetary policy is not simply to keep inflation low, but to improve the confidence of decision-makers, and thereby encourage firms to invest in order to generate an increase in production capacity. This will stimulate economic growth and create an opportunity to improve living standards.

Exercise 27.2

Outline the mechanism by which an increase in the rate of interest affects aggregate demand in an economy.

Monetary policy in practice

The monetary transmission mechanism explains the way in which a change in the interest rate affects aggregate demand in the economy. In summary, suppose there is a reduction in

the interest rate. From firms' point of view, this lowers the cost of borrowing, and would be expected to encourage higher investment spending. Furthermore, consumers may also respond to a fall in the interest rate by increasing their expenditure, both because this lowers the cost of borrowing – so there may be an increase in the demand for consumer durable goods – and because households may perceive that saving now pays a lower return, so may decide to spend more. Thus a fall in the interest rate is expected to have an expansionary effect on aggregate demand. In terms of the AD/AS model, this has the effect of shifting the aggregate demand curve to the right. The effectiveness of this will depend upon the shape of the aggregate supply curve and the starting position of the aggregate demand curve.

An expansionary monetary policy intended to stimulate aggregate demand would be damaging if the economy were close to (or at) full employment, as the main impact would be on the overall price level rather than real output. This suggests that monetary policy should also not be used to stimulate aggregate demand. However, monetary policy can still play an important role in managing the economy. This arises through its influence on the price level and hence the rate of change of prices – that is, inflation.

Monetary policy in the UK is the responsibility of the Bank of England, which has been the case since 1997. The Bank's responsibility is to meet the government's target for inflation. The Bank's Monetary Policy Committee (MPC) meets each month to decide whether or not the interest rate needs to be altered. The objective of this exercise is to ensure that the government's inflation target is met. If the rate of inflation threatens to accelerate beyond the target rate, the Bank of England can intervene by raising interest rates, thereby having a dampening effect on aggregate demand and reducing the inflationary pressure. In reaching its decisions, the MPC takes a long-term view, projecting inflation ahead over the next two years.

However, decisions to change the rate of interest are not taken solely in the light of expected inflation. In its deliberations about the interest rate, the MPC takes a wide variety of factors into account, including developments in:

- financial markets
- the international economy
- money and credit
- demand and output
- the labour market
- costs and prices (e.g. changes in oil prices).

A good example was in 2008, when the UK and other countries were struggling to cope with the financial crisis. At this time, inflation was accelerating, and had reached a rate that was more than 1 percentage point above the target. This being so, it might have been expected that the Bank of England would raise interest rates in order to stem aggregate demand and bring inflation back into line with the target. However, this would have been damaging in other ways, pushing the economy further into recession. With house prices falling, an increase in interest rates could have damaged this sector too. It was also thought that there were other pressures affecting the world economy that would in any case mean that the rate of inflation was likely to slow down of its own accord. In the event, inflation accelerated way beyond its target range, but the MPC refrained from raising the bank rate because of fears that the recession would become even deeper, or that the economy would recover more slowly. This was a good example of how different policy targets may come into conflict, and of how it may be prudent not to stick to a rule just for its own sake.

It is also important to remember that the transmission mechanism has a third channel in addition to the effects of the change in interest rate on consumption and investment. This third channel arises through the exchange rate, so that monetary policy cannot be considered in isolation from exchange rate policy. The channels of the transmission mechanism are summarised in Figure 27.7.

Evaluation of monetary policy

For a decade after the responsibility for monetary policy was delegated to the Bank of England, monetary policy was seen to be highly effective in enabling the achievement of the inflation target. Inflation stayed within the required 1 percentage point of its target, moving outside that range in only one month between May 1997 and April 2008. However, matters then took a turn for the worse with the onset of the financial crisis and the ensuing recession, and inflation accelerated beyond its limit, then plummeted dramatically before accelerating again.

The need to combat recession led to the bank rate being reduced to 0.5% in March 2009. Having fallen to this level, further reductions become ineffective, so the Bank announced that it would start to inject money directly into the economy, effectively switching the instrument of monetary policy away from the interest rate and towards the quantity of money. This would be achieved by a process known as **quantitative easing**, by which the Bank purchases assets such as government and corporate bonds, thus releasing additional money into the system through the banks and other financial institutions from which it buys the assets. The hope was that this would allow banks to increase their lending and thus combat the threat of deflation – and perhaps help to speed recovery.

Key term

Quantitative easing: a process by which liquidity in the economy is increased when the central bank purchases assets from banks.

The UK was not alone in facing this combination of circumstances. A number of countries had also enjoyed relative stability for several years, followed by a more turbulent period. This in itself suggests that the conduct of monetary policy cannot claim full responsibility for the period of calm; nor perhaps be entirely blamed for the subsequent problems. The process of globalisation that has been taking place means that the UK economy cannot be viewed in total isolation from events occurring elsewhere in the world, and macroeconomic policy is interconnected – through movements in the exchange rate and through trading links.

This is illustrated by Figure 27.8, which shows monthly inflation (in % per annum) from the beginning of 2000 for the world as a whole and for two country groupings. You can see how inflation in the world as a whole began to accelerate from mid-2007 onwards after a period of relative stability, only to plummet as the recession set in during 2008 and 2009. Latin America displays higher inflation – and more instability than the world as a whole – whereas the advanced economies experienced inflation rates below the world average throughout the period, but also began to see inflation rates creeping up towards the end of the period.

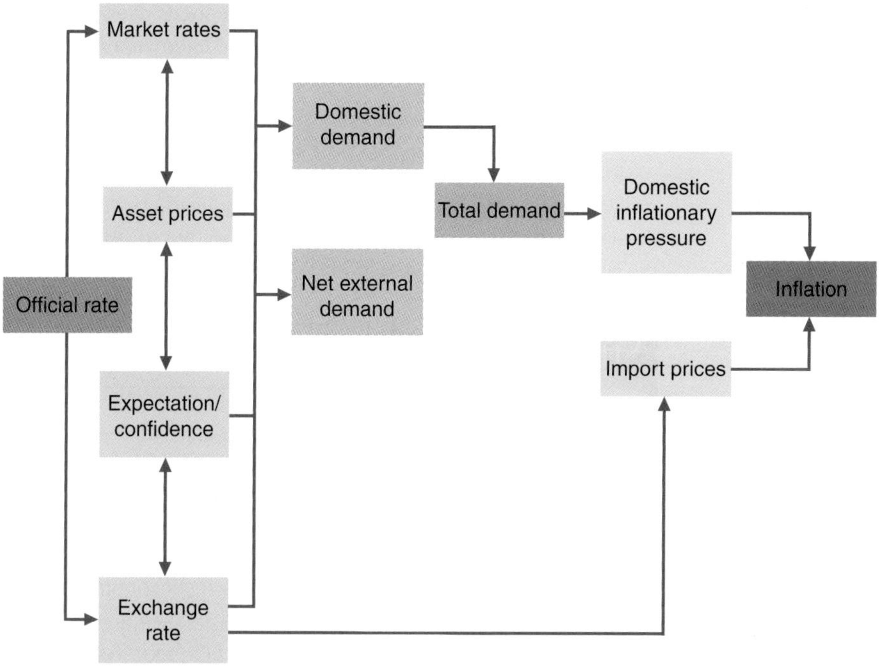

Figure 27.7 The transmission of monetary policy

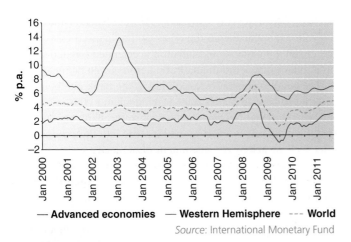

— **Advanced economies** — **Western Hemisphere** --- **World**

Source: International Monetary Fund

Figure 27.8 World inflation

Summary

- Monetary policy is the use of financial variables, such as money supply or the rate of interest, to influence the performance of the economy.
- Money supply does not provide a reliable control mechanism, so the prime instrument of monetary policy is the interest rate.
- The transmission mechanism from the interest rate to aggregate demand works through investment and consumption and indirectly via the exchange rate.
- Monetary policy cannot focus solely on meeting the inflation target, but must also operate with an awareness of other developments in the macroeconomy.
- It is also important that monetary policy is coordinated with other policy measures being implemented that affect the macroeconomy.

27.5 Exchange rate policy

In considering the tools of monetary policy, it is also important to consider the **exchange rate** – that is, the rate at which one currency exchanges against another. This is because the exchange rate, the interest rate and the money supply are all intimately related. If interest rates in the domestic economy are high relative to elsewhere in the world, they will attract overseas investors, increasing the demand for domestic currency. This will tend to lead to an appreciation in the exchange rate – which in turn will reduce the competitiveness of domestic goods and services, reducing the foreign demand for exports and encouraging residents to reduce their demand for domestic goods and buy imports instead.

Indeed, under a fixed exchange rate regime, the monetary authorities are committed to maintaining the exchange rate at a particular level, so could not allow an appreciation to take place.

In this situation, monetary policy is powerless to influence the real economy, as it must be devoted to maintaining the exchange rate. Under a floating exchange rate system, monetary policy is freed from this role, but even so it must be used in such a way that the current account deficit of the balance of payments does not become unsustainable in the long run. In other words, the use of interest rates to target inflation has implications for the magnitude of the current and financial accounts of the balance of payments.

Most developed countries operate under floating exchange rates, but many less developed countries have chosen to peg their currencies – mainly to the US dollar. Exchange rates in this context have been used in different ways. Some countries have chosen to overvalue their exchange rate relative to the equilibrium level, in order to encourage domestic production. Others have chosen the reverse strategy, undervaluing the exchange rate in order to stimulate exports. China has been much criticised by the USA in this context.

The exchange rate and international competitiveness

In analysing the balance of payments, the relative competitiveness of domestically produced goods and services is an important issue. If an economy persistently shows a deficit on the current account, does that imply that its goods are uncompetitive in international markets?

The demand for exports in world markets depends upon a number of factors. In some ways, it is similar to the demand for a good. In general, the demand for a good depends on its price, on the prices of other goods, and on consumer incomes and preferences. In a similar way, you can think of the demand for exports as depending on the price of exported goods, the price of other countries' goods, incomes in the rest of the world and foreigners' preferences for one country's goods over those produced elsewhere. However, in the case of international transactions the exchange rate is also relevant, as this determines the purchasing power of domestic incomes in the rest of the world. Similarly, the demand for imports depends upon the relative prices of domestic and foreign goods, incomes in the domestic economy, preferences for foreign and domestically produced goods and the exchange rate. These factors will all come together to determine the balance of demand for exports and imports.

Summary

- The exchange rate plays an important role in macroeconomic policy because the exchange rate, the interest rate and money supply are closely interrelated.
- Under a fixed exchange rate system, monetary policy has to be devoted to maintaining the exchange rate, so it cannot be used independently to influence the real economy.
- The exchange rate is also important in influencing the international competitiveness of domestic goods in overseas markets – and of foreign goods in the domestic market.

27.6 Supply-side policy

Supply-side policies comprise a range of measures intended to have a direct impact on aggregate supply – specifically, on the potential capacity output of the economy. These measures are often microeconomic in character and are designed to increase output and hence economic growth.

> ## Key term
>
> **Supply-side policies:** a range of measures intended to have a direct effect on aggregate supply – and specifically on the potential capacity of the economy.

Supply-side policies are directed at influencing the position of the aggregate supply curve. In Figure 27.9, Y^* represents full-employment output before the policy, with the equilibrium overall price level at P_0. Supply-side policies, which lead to an increase in the economy's productive capacity, shift equilibrium output to Y^{**} and the overall price level to P_1.

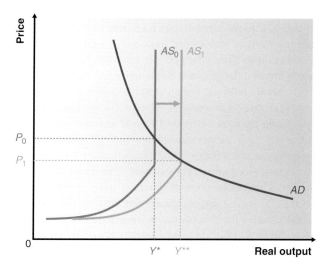

Figure 27.9 A shift in aggregate supply

Notice that the effect on real output is achieved from supply-side policies whether the equilibrium is in the vertical segment of the Keynesian *AS* curve (or with a Monetarist *AS* curve), as shown in Figure 27.9, or in the upward-sloping segment of the Keynesian *AS* curve, as in Figure 27.10. Here the shift in aggregate supply raises equilibrium real output from Y_0 to Y_1.

Supply-side policies include encouraging education and training, improving the flexibility with which markets operate and promoting competition. Notice that it is quite difficult to quantify the effects of these supply-side policies. In the case of education and training, the idea is that by increasing education and training, the human capital of the labour force is increased, thus resulting in improvements in productivity,

which enable an increase in the overall productive capacity of the economy – in other words, this will lead to a rightward shift of the aggregate supply curve. However, some of the effects of increased spending become evident only after very long time lags.

In the case of competition policy, again, it is not easy to identify the effects on productive capacity, although it is argued that the use of competition policy will provide incentives for firms to be more productively efficient, and will reduce the loss of allocative inefficiency through the abuse of market power.

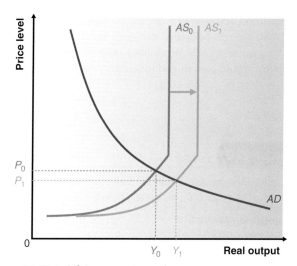

Figure 27.10 A shift in aggregate supply

It is particularly difficult to isolate the impact of these policies when so much else in the economy is changing through time. Nonetheless, these policies do have the effect of stimulating economic growth without inflationary pressure.

Another example that is important to examine is the effect of changing the rate of income tax. When people face high marginal rates of income tax, there is a disincentive to offer additional labour hours, or even to participate in the labour force at all. A reduction in income tax rates would therefore provide an incentive for people to work more hours or to participate in the labour force. This would then lead to higher employment, and a higher potential capacity output for the economy as a whole.

Such high marginal tax rates are normally found at the high end of the income distribution, but there may also be disincentive effects to consider at low incomes. These effects may arise where unemployment benefits are set at such a level that individuals would be little better off if they accepted a low-paid job – a situation sometimes known as the 'unemployment trap'. This effect may be reinforced if the search costs for jobs are relatively high – for example, if the jobs available are not in areas where unemployment is high. There may then be people who do not find it worth their while undertaking a costly search for jobs, especially if the wage they could command would be only marginally better than the benefits that they can receive.

In this situation, a reduction in the rate of unemployment benefits or social security benefits could have the effect of increasing people's willingness to accept jobs. This would reduce unemployment and again lead to an expansion of the economy's potential productive capacity. However, there is a need to keep an appropriate balance between providing incentives to work and protecting the vulnerable.

Supply-side policies may also have an effect on the balance of payments current account. Policies that affect trade and competitiveness fall into this category: for example, supply-side policies to improve the flexibility of the labour market could be seen to improve the international competitiveness of domestic firms, and thus to improve the current account deficit. In addition, it might be argued that steps taken to increase the productive capacity of the economy would allow an increase in exports that would (ceteris paribus) reduce the current account deficit.

Exercise 27.3

For each of the following, analyse the effect on the productive capacity of the economy, explaining how this happens.

a The government introduces subsidies for firms to train unskilled workers.
b Immigrant workers are encouraged to return to their home countries.
c A monopoly firm is forced to reduce barriers to the entry of new firms into its market.
d There is a reduction in the highest rate of income tax.
e There is an increase in the threshold of income below which no income tax is payable.
f There is a decrease in the rate of social security payments for the unemployed.

Summary

- Supply-side policies are directed at influencing the position of the aggregate supply curve by increasing the potential productive capacity of the economy.
- Such policies include policies to affect the flexibility of labour markets, including education and training.
- Policies that promote competition may also lead to efficiency improvements.
- Changes in income tax rates, or in social security benefits, can also have an effect on potential capacity by affecting incentives to work.
- Improvements in efficiency may have spillover effects on the balance of payments if they improve the international competitiveness of domestic goods in world markets.

27.7 Conflicts between policy objectives

Having reviewed the main macroeconomic policy objectives and instruments, it should be clear that the designing of economic policy is likely to be something of a juggling act. This is especially so because there may be conflict and trade-offs between some of the targets of policy.

Unemployment and inflation

Chapter 26 introduced the *Phillips curve*, a trade-off relationship between unemployment and inflation. This trade-off is important when it comes to designing policy. If the Phillips curve relationship holds, attempts to reduce the rate of unemployment are likely to raise inflation. On the other hand, a reduction in inflation is likely to result in higher unemployment. This suggests that it might be difficult to maintain full employment and low inflation at the same time. For example, Figure 27.11 shows a Phillips curve that is drawn such that to achieve an unemployment rate of 5%, inflation would need to rise to 15% per annum; this would not be acceptable these days, when people have become accustomed to much lower inflation rates. Furthermore, to bring inflation down to zero would require an unemployment rate of 15%. Having said that, as recently as 1990 the UK economy was experiencing inflation of nearly 10% and unemployment of 7%, which is not far from this example.

Nonetheless, the Phillips curve trade-off offers a tempting prospect to policy-makers. For example, if an election is imminent, it should be possible to reduce unemployment by allowing a bit more inflation, thereby creating a feel-good factor. After the election the process can be reversed. This suggests that there could be a political business cycle induced by governments seeking re-election. In other words, the conflict between policy objectives could be exploited by politicians who see that in the short run an electorate is concerned more about unemployment than inflation.

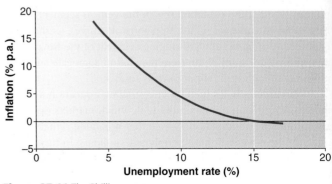

Figure 27.11 The Phillips curve

Economic growth and sustainability

It is clear that there may be conflict between achieving economic growth and the environment. Nowhere is this better seen than in the case of China in the early part of the twenty-first century. China's persistently rapid growth has had consequences for the quality of the environment. Figure 27.12 shows one aspect of this – the emissions of carbon dioxide, which is one of the key so-called greenhouse gases that contribute to the process of global warming. The acceleration of emissions in China in the early years of the century is very apparent in the figure, and China overtook the USA to become the largest emitter of carbon dioxide in the early 2000s.

The link between economic growth and environmental degradation is a clear one. In the case of China, there are several aspects to notice. During the process of industrialisation, it is crucial to ensure that energy supplies keep pace with the demand, as factories cannot operate effectively without reliable electricity and other energy sources. China has become the world's second biggest oil importer (behind the USA), and is the world's largest producer of coal, which accounts for some 80% of its total energy use – and is not the cleanest of energy technologies. It is also possible that inadequate regulation can add to environmental degradation, as in the case of the explosion at a chemical plant that caused pollution in the Songhua river, which not only affected the city of Harbin, but also part of Russia, which was downstream from the incident.

For economic growth to be sustainable, these environmental effects must be taken into account, or there is a real danger that the improved standard of living that flows from the growth process will be obtained only at the expense of the quality of life of future generations. This may require growth to be slowed in the short run in order to devote resources to the development of renewable and cleaner energy sources. However, it is difficult to impose this on newly emerging societies in which there is widespread poverty, especially when the richer nations of the world continue to enjoy high standards of living whilst causing pollution of their own.

Economic growth and the current account of the balance of payments

As noted in the previous chapter, a country operating under a fixed exchange rate system may find that a growth strategy may be thwarted by the need to avoid a problem with the current account of the balance of payments. If there is an increase in real incomes resulting from an acceleration of economic growth, there may be an increase in the demand for imports, as a proportion of the increase in incomes is spent on imported goods. This can lead to a deficit building on the current account of the balance of payments. The action needed by the authorities to maintain the exchange rate and correct the deficit is likely to be contractionary, thus preventing the improvement in economic growth from being sustained.

Government failure in macroeconomic policies

The notion of government failure was introduced in the context of microeconomic intervention, where well-intended policy interventions can sometimes have adverse effects on resource allocation. In similar fashion, intervention at the macroeconomic level can sometimes have unintended negative effects. There are many possible reasons for this, arising from the complexity of policy design at the economy-wide level and the interactions between policy measures and objectives.

China has become the largest emitter of carbon dioxide

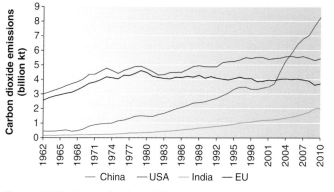

Figure 27.12 Carbon dioxide emissions

One particular problem faced by the government is the time lag that exists between initiating a policy and its effects on the economy. It may sometimes be that by the time a policy has an effect, the economy has moved on, so that the original issue which required a solution has gone away. In some cases, problems are triggered by external shocks that are beyond the government's control. In other situations, an attempt to make financial markets more flexible may mean that lax regulation results in unanticipated problems. The financial crisis that began in the late 2000s has been partly attributed to this. Alternatively, it may simply be that firms and households do not react to policy interventions in the way that governments expect, so that adverse consequences follow.

At the heart of many of these explanations is the idea that governments do not have enough knowledge about how the macroeconomy operates, or do not have sufficient up-to-date information about the economy to take perfect decisions. This is sometimes known as *bounded rationality*: a situation in which a government takes decisions with the best intentions and with the best possible information available, but still fails to produce the required effects because knowledge and information are inadequate. This is partly what makes economics such an exciting challenge – we are still learning about how the world around us works.

Exercise 27.4

Given the following list of policy objectives, discuss the possible conflicts that may arise between them, and discuss how these might be resolved:

- low inflation
- low unemployment
- high economic growth
- a low deficit on the current account of the balance of payments
- maintenance of a high environmental quality
- equity in the distribution of income.

Summary

- Macroeconomic variables are inherently interconnected.
- This means that there are also likely to be interrelationships between policy instruments.
- Policy design must therefore take into account the possibility of trade-offs between variables, and conflicts between alternative policies.

Examination questions

1 Tourism and the local workers

Here are two accounts of the tourist industry in Africa.

Article 1

The Gambia, on the west coast of Africa, is ranked 160th out of 173 on the United Nations Human Development Index. Over half the population live on less than one US dollar a day and survive on subsistence agriculture and cannot compete with subsidised American farmers.

However, things are changing as The Gambia expands its tourist sector, which is now a significant part of the national economy, accounting for 7.8% of GDP. It employs 5000 directly and creates work for 6000 others. Large European tour operators play a vital role in marketing, assuring quality, and providing flights and accommodation. Tourism has the major advantage that developed countries cannot place tariff barriers on tourist exports. Tourists spend on average US$40 to US$50 a day on meals, souvenirs, crafts and tours. One third is spend in the informal sector, where income is not recorded, providing a livelihood for taxi drivers, craft workers and local guides.

However, there are disadvantages. Tourism is highly seasonal, and tour operators negotiate low prices which keep profit margins low – so low, in fact, that many hotels have closed because they could not cover costs.

Article 2

A union official in Tanzania said that the tourism sector is expanding in Tanzania but the return to the country's economy is low and the benefit to the workers is about 0.5% of the total industry's income. In the hotels the lowest wages are around US$50 a month, from which tax and rent have to be deducted. Someone who has been working for 5 years or more receives no extra pay or promotion. Contracts are short-term, lasting for a year.

Hotel operators oppose workers joining trade unions. Most tour operators come from outside Tanzania. Only 10% of each US dollar earned by the tourist industry remains in the country, and most of that goes to the management not the workers. Top managers are usually foreign workers paid two or three times as much as a Tanzanian manager.

Source: Development Magazine, Issue 27, 2004

a What evidence is there that The Gambia is a developing country? [4]

b What does Article 1 mean when it says that tourism created work for 6000 others? [3]

c Article 2 mentions the low pay of hotel workers. Why might many hotel workers receive low pay? [5]

d Does the evidence provided enable you to conclude that tourism merely exploits resources and is of little benefit? [8]

Cambridge AS and A Level Economics 9708, Paper 4, Q1, November 2007

2 Analyse why the aims of government policy might conflict with each other and discuss which of the aims ought to be given priority. [25]

Cambridge AS and A Level Economics 9708, Paper 4, Q7, November 2007

3 In 2006 it was reported that a country's unemployment rate has remained steady and that its central bank, through its interest rate policy, had prevented an increase in inflation despite a sharp rise in oil prices.

Source: *The Guardian*, 6 September 2006

a Explain what might cause unemployment. [12]

b Discuss how interest rate policy might prevent a rise in inflation. [13]

Cambridge AS and A Level Economics 9708, Paper 4, Q5, June 2009

4 Counting the cost

India has transformed itself from a primarily agricultural economy into a major industrial one in less than 60 years. Some argue that industrialisation results in increased wealth and a better standard of living. Certain areas of India are better suited to this industrialisation than others. The state of Orissa is one.

Orissa is a state of contrasts – 48% of its people live below the poverty line; it is the most heavily indebted Indian state; its literacy level is below the national average; the level of infectious disease is high and malnutrition is alarming; it is subject to natural disasters such as floods. But it has unrivalled natural resources including one of Asia's largest deposits of coal, large areas of forest and extensive mineral reserves. These attract big industrial companies. A new steel plant has been established which will produce six million tonnes of steel a year.

In Orissa, a balance has to be achieved between potential profits and benefits from industrialisation and its cost to the people and the environment. The steel company is recruiting from local engineering colleges and is able to offer employment and new opportunities. People have increased incomes. Farm workers earn less than half what the factory pays its workers. One worker said 'I used to work on the land and was at the mercy of the weather. Now I do not have to pray for rain. The company also employs my sons and we are much better off.'

However, the factory is not labour-intensive and is unlikely to employ the huge numbers of people seeking work. Also, mining and infrastructure development destroyed some of the forest. Industrial production results in soil erosion and pollutes the air with the dark smoke from factory chimneys which causes acid rain. The rivers have also become contaminated with toxic waste which is posing a threat to wildlife, such as elephants, tigers and deer, as well as to local people.

The industrialisation meant that some people lost their homes and had to be resettled elsewhere. The new houses had safe water provision and drainage, unlike some of the original homes, but people complained about the poor way the houses were built. In 2007, 13 were killed during a protest about the lack of compensation for the loss of their homes.

Source: *Developments*, Issue 38, 2007

a What is meant by industrialisation? [2]

b Why might some argue that the economic costs of the exploitation of the natural resources in Orissa are too high? [5]

c Comment on whether the development of the steel plant is likely to have been a benefit for the workers in Orissa. [5]

d It is said that the standard of living in Orissa continues to be very low. Discuss whether the evidence you have been given is sufficient to support this view. [8]

Cambridge AS and A Level Economics 9708, Paper 41, Q1, November 2009

5 a An increase in investment will raise national income but an increase in the desire by consumers to save will reduce national income. Explain why this is the case. [12]

b To increase national income, interest rates should be lowered; indeed lowering interest rates is the only policy available to increase national income. Discuss whether you support this opinion. [13]

Cambridge AS and A Level Economics 9708, Paper 43, Q6, June 2011

6 Interest rates, inflation and growth

Between 1 July and 1 October 2007, the GDP of the US rose at an annual equivalent rate of 4.0%. This was faster than the forecast rate of 3.1%. The rise was caused by an increase in consumer spending and by rising exports.

By November 2007, however, there were increased signs of a housing market slump, a rise in oil prices and a fall in the value of the US dollar. These changes presented the Federal Reserve (the US central bank) with a problem about interest rates.

The Federal Reserve had already cut interest rates in October 2007 and it reduced the interest rate again in November in order to help defend the US economy against the worsening housing market. Further interest rate cuts were thought unlikely, as there was anxiety over the rising price of oil, which by November 2007 had reached a record level. The Federal Reserve said 'recent increases in energy and commodity prices may result in further inflation'.

Source: *The Times Business Section*, 1 November 2007

a Name **two** components of aggregate demand **not** mentioned in the first paragraph of the extract. [2]

b Calculate the percentage increase in the GDP of the US between 1 July and 1 October 2007. [2]

c   Why does Figure 4 refer to a 'falling dollar' when the
    trend of the line is upward?   [2]
d   Discuss the likely effectiveness of a reduction in interest
    rates as a solution to a housing market slump.   [6]
e   To what extent does the data support the view that the
    US economy was facing 'conflicting policy objectives'?   [8]

Cambridge AS and A Level Economics 9708,
Paper 41, Q1, June 2010

A difficult balance: conflicting policy objectives

America's housing market
is slumping ...

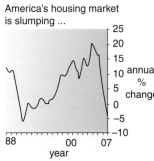

Figure 1 House price index

... so the Federal Reserve acted
to cut borrowing costs

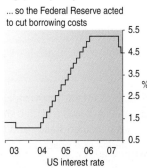

Figure 2 US interest rate

but soaring oil prices pose
an inflation threat ...

Figure 3 US crude oil price

... and so does the falling
dollar

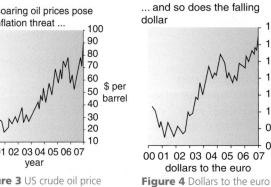

Figure 4 Dollars to the euro

Glossary of key terms

Terms in black are first mentioned in the AS course, terms in blue relate to the A level course.

abnormal, supernormal or economic profits: profits above normal profits

absolute advantage: the ability to produce a good more efficiently (e.g. with less labour)

absolute poverty: the situation of a household whose income is insufficient to purchase the minimum bundle of goods and services needed to sustain human life

accelerator: a theory by which the level of investment depends upon the change in real output

ad valorem tax: a tax on expenditure set at a percentage of the price

aggregate demand: the total amount of effective demand in the economy

aggregate demand curve (AD): a curve showing the relationship between the level of aggregate demand in an economy and the overall price level; it shows planned expenditure at any given overall price level

allocative efficiency: achieved when society is producing an appropriate bundle of goods relative to consumer preferences

appreciation: a rise in the exchange rate within a floating exchange rate system

arbitrage: a process by which prices in two market segments will be equalised by a process of purchase and resale by market participants

asymmetric information: a situation in which some participants in a market have better information about market conditions than others

automatic stabilisers: process by which government expenditure and revenue vary with the economic cycle, thereby helping to stabilise the economy without any conscious intervention from government

average cost: total cost divided by the quantity produced, sometimes known as unit cost or **average total cost**

average propensity to consume: the proportion of income that households devote to consumption

average revenue: the average revenue received by the firm per unit of output; it is total revenue divided by the quantity sold

balance of payments: a set of accounts showing the transactions conducted between residents of a country and the rest of the world

barrier to entry: a characteristic of a market that prevents new firms from readily joining the market

behavioural economics: a branch of economics that builds on the psychology of human behaviour in decision making

broad money (M4): M0 plus sterling wholesale and retail deposits with monetary financial institutions such as banks and building societies

budget deficit: a situation in which government expenditure exceeds government revenue

budget line: shows the boundary of an individual's consumption set, given the amount available to spend and the prices of the goods

budget surplus: a situation in which government revenue exceeds government expenditure

business cycle: a phenomenon whereby GDP fluctuates around its underlying trend, tending to follow a regular pattern

capital account of the balance of payments: account identifying transactions in (physical) capital between the residents of a country and the rest of the world

capital productivity: measure of output per unit of capital

capitalism: a system of production in which there is private ownership of productive resources, and individuals are free to pursue their objectives with minimal interference from government

cartel: an agreement between firms on price and output with the intention of maximising their joint profits

central bank: the banker to the government, performing a range of functions, which may include issue of coins and banknotes, acting as banker to commercial banks and regulating the financial system

centrally planned economy: decisions on resource allocation are guided by the state

ceteris paribus: a Latin phrase meaning 'other things being equal'; it is used in economics when we focus on changes in one variable while holding other influences constant

claimant count of unemployment: the number of people claiming the Jobseeker's Allowance each month

common market: a set of trading arrangements in which a group of countries remove barriers to trade among them, adopt a common set of barriers against external trade, establish common tax rates and laws regulating economic activity, allow free movement of factors of production between members and have common public sector procurement policies

comparative advantage: the ability to produce a good *relatively* more efficiently (i.e. at lower opportunity cost)

Glossary of key terms

comparative static analysis: examines the effect on equilibrium of a change in the external conditions affecting a market

competition policy: a set of measures designed to promote competition within markets to encourage efficiency and protect consumer interests

competitive market: a market in which individual firms cannot influence price of the good or service they are selling, because of competition from other firms

complements: two goods are said to be complements if people tend to consume them jointly, so that an increase in the price of one good causes the demand for the other good to fall

conglomerate merger: a merger between two different firms operating in different markets

constant returns to scale: found when long-run average cost remains constant with an increase in output – in other words, when output and costs rise at the same rate

consumer price index (CPI): a measure of the general level of prices in the UK, adopted as the government's inflation target since December 2003

consumer surplus: the value that consumers gain from consuming a good or service over and above the price paid

consumption: household spending on goods and services in the economy

consumption externality: an externality that impacts on the consumption side of a market, which may be either positive or negative

consumption function: the relationship between consumption and disposable income; its position depends upon the other factors that affect how much households spend on consumption

contestable market: a market in which the existing firm makes only normal profit, as it cannot set a price higher than average cost without attracting entry, owing to the absence of barriers to entry and sunk costs

cost efficiency: the appropriate combination of inputs of factors of production, given the relative prices of those factors

cost-push inflation: inflation initiated by an increase in the costs faced by firms, arising on the supply–side of the economy

credit multiplier: a process by which an increase in money supply can have a multiplied effect on the amount of credit in an economy

cross-price elasticity of demand (*XED*): a measure of the sensitivity of quantity demanded of a good or service to a change in the price of some other good or service

crowding out: process by which an increase in government expenditure 'crowds out' private sector activity by raising the cost of borrowing

current account of the balance of payments: account identifying transactions in goods and services between the residents of a country and the rest of the world

customs union: a group of countries that agree to remove restrictions on trade between the member countries, and set a common set of restrictions (including tariffs) against non-member states

deadweight loss: loss of consumer surplus that arises when a monopoly restricts output and raises price

deflation: a period in which the general level of prices in an economy falls

deflationary gap: a situation that arises when the equilibrium level of income is lower than the full-employment level

demand: the quantity of a good or service that consumers choose to buy at any possible price in a given period

demand curve: a graph showing how much of a good will be demanded by consumers at any given price

demand-deficient unemployment: unemployment that arises because of a deficiency of aggregate demand in the economy, so that the equilibrium level of output is below the full-employment level

demand-pull inflation: inflation initiated by an increase in aggregate demand

demerit good: a good that brings less benefit to consumers than they expect, such that too much will be consumed by individuals in a free market

depreciation: a fall in the exchange rate within a floating exchange rate system

depreciation: the fall in value of physical capital equipment over time as it is subject to wear and tear

derived demand: demand for a good not for its own sake, but for what it produces – for example, labour is demanded for the output that it produces

devaluation: a process whereby a country in a fixed exchange rate system reduces the price of its currency relative to an agreed rate in terms of a foreign currency

development: a process by which real per capita incomes are increased and the inhabitants of a country are able to benefit from improved living conditions: that is, lower poverty and enhanced standards of education, health, nutrition and other essentials of life

direct tax: a tax levied directly on income

discount: a process whereby the future valuation of a cost or benefit is reduced (discounted) in order to provide an estimate of its present value

diseconomies of scale: occur for a firm when an increase in the scale of production leads to higher long-run average costs

disposable income: the income that households have to devote to consumption and saving, taking into account payments of direct taxes and transfer payments

division of labour: a process whereby the production procedure is broken down into a sequence of stages, and workers are assigned to particular stages

dominant strategy: a situation in game theory where a player's best strategy is independent of those chosen by others

dual economy: one in which a traditional (mainly rural) sector co-exists with a modern (mainly urban) sector

dynamic efficiency: a view of efficiency that takes into account the effect of innovation and technical progress on productive and allocative efficiency in the long run

economic and monetary union: a set of trading arrangements the same as for a common market, but in addition having fixed exchange rates between the member countries and a common monetary policy

economic growth: an expansion in the productive capacity of the economy

economic rent: a payment received by a factor of production over and above what would be needed to keep it in its present use

economically active: those people who are active in the labour force

economies of scale: occur for a firm when an increase in the scale of production leads to production at lower long-run average cost

economies of scope: economies arising when average cost falls as a firm increases output across a range of different products

effective exchange rate: the exchange rate for a country relative to a weighted average of currencies of its trading partners

elasticity: a measure of the sensitivity of one variable to changes in another variable

equi-marginal principle: that a consumer does best in utility terms by consuming at the point where the ratio of marginal utilities from two goods is equal to the ratio of their prices

excess burden of a sales tax: the deadweight loss to society following the imposition of a sales tax

exchange controls: a policy under which the authorities regulate the amount of foreign currency available for domestic residents to import goods, services or assets from abroad

Exchange Rate Mechanism (ERM): a system which was set up by a group of European countries in 1979 with the objective of keeping member countries' currencies relatively stable against each other

exchange rate: the price of one currency in terms of another

expenditure dampening: a reduction in domestic demand for imports so that the supply curve for the domestic economy shifts

expenditure switching: a situation in which the demand for exports of a country increases because some foreign consumers switch to buying from that country, thus shifting the demand for the domestic currency

export-led growth: a situation in which economic growth is achieved through the exploitation of economies of scale, made possible by focusing on exports, and so reaching a wider market than would be available within the domestic economy

export promotion: policy entailing encouraging domestic firms to export more goods in order to earn foreign exchange

external benefit: a benefit that is associated with an individual's (a firm or household's) production or other economic activities, which is borne by a third party

external cost: a cost that is associated with an individual's (a firm or household's) production or other economic activities, which is borne by a third party

externality: a cost or a benefit that is external to a market transaction, and is thus not reflected in market prices

factors of production: resources used in the production process; *inputs* into production, including labour, capital, land and entrepreneurship

financial account of the balance of payments: account identifying transactions in financial assets between the residents of a country and the rest of the world

firm: an organisation that brings together factors of production in order to produce output

fiscal policy: decisions made by the government on its expenditure, taxation and borrowing

fixed costs: costs that do not vary with the level of output

fixed exchange rate system: a system in which the government commits to maintaining the exchange rate at a specific level against another currency

floating exchange rate system: a system in which the exchange rate is permitted to find its own level in the market

foreign direct investment (FDI): investment undertaken by foreign companies

foreign exchange reserves: stocks of foreign currency and gold owned by the central bank of a country to enable it to meet any mismatch between the demand and supply of the country's currency

free-rider problem: when an individual cannot be excluded from consuming a good, and thus has no incentive to pay for its provision

free-market economy: one in which resource allocation is guided by market forces without intervention by the state

free trade area: a group of countries that agree to remove tariffs, quotas and other restrictions on trade between the member countries, but have no agreement on a common barrier against non-members

frictional unemployment: unemployment associated with job search: that is, people who are between jobs

full-employment income: the level of income achieved when all factors of production are fully employed

game theory: a method of modelling the strategic interaction between firms in an oligopoly

GDP deflator: an implicit price index showing the relationship between real and nominal measures of GDP, providing an alternative measure of the general level of prices in an economy

Glossary of key terms

General Agreement on Tariffs and Trade (GATT): the precursor of the WTO, which organised a series of 'rounds' of tariff reductions

Gini index: a measure of the degree of inequality in a society

globalisation: a process by which the world's economies are becoming more closely integrated

'Golden Rule' of fiscal policy: rule stating that, over the economic cycle, net government borrowing will be for investment only, and not for current spending

government budget: the balance between government expenditure and revenue

government failure: a misallocation of resources arising from government intervention

gross domestic product (GDP): a measure of the economic activity carried out in an economy during a given time period

gross national income (GNI): GDP plus net income from abroad

Harrod–Domar model: a model of economic growth that emphasises the importance of savings and investment

horizontal merger: a merger between two firms at the same stage of production in the same industry

hot money: stocks of funds that are moved around the globe from country to country in search of the best return

human capital: the stock of skills and expertise and other characteristics that contribute to a worker's productivity; it can be increased through education and training, and improved nutrition and healthcare

Human Development Index (HDI): a composite indicator of the level of a country's development, varying between 0 and 1

Hyperinflation: occurs when inflation is very high, sometimes defined as being above 50% per month

ILO unemployment rate: measure of the percentage of the workforce who are without jobs, but are available for work, willing to work and looking for work

import substitution: policy encouraging domestic production of goods previously imported in order to reduce the need for foreign exchange

incidence of a tax: the way in which the burden of paying a sales tax is divided between buyers and sellers

income effect of a price change: reflects the way that a change in the price of a good affects purchasing power

income elasticity of demand (*YED*): a measure of the sensitivity of quantity demanded to a change in consumer incomes

index number: a device for comparing the value of a variable in one period or location with a base observation (e.g. the retail price index measures the average level of prices relative to a base period)

indifference curve: shows the combinations of two goods that give equal utility to a consumer

indirect tax: a tax levied on expenditure on goods or services (e.g. VAT)

industry long-run supply curve: under perfect competition, a curve that is horizontal at the price which is the minimum point of the long-run average cost curve for the typical firm in the industry

inferior good: one where the quantity demanded decreases in response to an increase in consumer incomes

inflation: the rate of change of the average price level: for example, the percentage annual rate of change of the CPI

inflationary gap: a situation that arises when the equilibrium level of income is higher than the full-employment level, and thus cannot be reached

injection: an addition to the circular flow, comprising investment, government expenditure and exports; these items are regarded as autonomous, that is, unrelated to the level of income

insider–outsider phenomenon: where existing workers can protect their position against newcomers because they have inside information about how the firm operates

internalising an externality: an attempt to deal with an externality by bringing an external cost or benefit into the price system

investment: expenditure undertaken by firms to add to the capital stock; an increase in the capital stock

invisible hand: term used by Adam Smith to describe the way in which resources are allocated in a market economy

invisible trade: trade in services

involuntary unemployment: situation arising when an individual who would like to accept a job at the going wage rate is unable to find employment

Keynesian school: a group of economists who believed that the macroeconomy could settle in an equilibrium that was below the full employment level

labour productivity: measure of output per worker, or output per hour worked

law of comparative advantage: a theory stating that there may be gains from trade arising when countries (or individuals) specialise in the production of goods or services in which they have a comparative advantage

law of demand: a law that states that there is an inverse relationship between quantity demanded and the price of a good or service, ceteris paribus

law of diminishing marginal utility: states that the more units of a good that are consumed, the lower the utility from consuming those additional units

law of diminishing returns: law stating that if a firm increases its inputs of one factor of production while holding inputs of other factors fixed, eventually the firm will get diminishing marginal returns from the variable factor

liquidity: the extent to which an asset can be converted to cash without the holder incurring a cost

liquidity preference: a theory that suggests that people will desire to hold money as an asset

long run: the period over which the firm is able to vary the inputs of all its factors of production

long-run aggregate supply curve: a curve that shows the amount of real output that will be supplied in the economy in the long run at any given overall price level

Lorenz curve: a graphical way of depicting the distribution of income within a country

luxury good: one for which the income elasticity of demand is positive, and greater than one, such that as income rises, consumers spend proportionally more on the good

macroeconomics: the study of the interrelationships between economic variables at an aggregate (economy-wide) level

managed floating exchange rate system: a system under which the exchange rate is permitted to find its own level in the market, but within limits, with the government intervening in certain situations

marginal cost: the cost of producing an additional unit of output

marginal cost of labour (MC_L): the additional cost to a firm of an additional unit of labour input

marginal physical product of labour (MPP_L): the additional quantity of output produced by an additional unit of labour input

marginal principle: the idea that firms (and other economic agents) may take decisions by considering the effect of small changes from an existing situation

marginal productivity theory: an approach based on the assumption that the demand for labour depends upon the marginal revenue product of labour

marginal propensity to consume: the proportion of additional income devoted to consumption

marginal propensity to withdraw: the sum of the marginal propensities to save, tax and import; it is the proportion of additional income that is withdrawn from the circular flow

marginal revenue: the additional revenue received by the firm if it sells an additional unit of output

marginal revenue product of labour (MRP_L): the additional revenue received by a firm as it increases output by using an additional unit of labour input, i.e. the marginal physical product of labour multiplied by the marginal revenue received by the firm

marginal social benefit: the additional benefit that society gains from consuming an extra unit of a good

marginal tax rate: tax on additional income, defined as the change in tax payments due divided by the change in taxable income

marginal utility: the additional utility gained from consuming an extra unit of a good or service

market: a set of arrangements that allows transactions to take place

market economy: market forces are allowed to guide the allocation of resources within a society

market equilibrium: a situation that occurs in a market when the price is such that the quantity that consumers wish to buy is exactly balanced by the quantity that firms wish to supply

market failure: a situation in which the free market mechanism does not lead to an optimal allocation of resources – for example, where there is a divergence between marginal social benefit and marginal social cost

market-friendly growth: economic growth in which governments intervene less where markets can operate effectively, but more strongly where markets are seen to fail

market for loanable funds: the notion that households will be influenced by the rate of interest in making saving decisions, that will then determine the quantity of loanable funds available for firms to borrow for investment

market structure: the market environment in which a firm operates

means-tested benefit: a benefit (in cash or in kind) paid to people or households whose income falls below a certain level

merit good: a good that brings unanticipated benefits to consumers, such that society believes that it will be under-consumed in a free market

microeconomics: the study of economic decisions taken by individual economic agents, including households and firms

Millennium Development Goals (MDGs): targets set for each less developed country, reflecting a range of development objectives to be monitored each year to evaluate progress

minimum wage: legislation under which firms are not allowed to pay a wage below some threshold level set by the government

mixed economy: resources are allocated partly through price signals and partly on the basis of direction by government

model: a simplified representation of reality used to provide insight into economic decisions and events

Monetarist school: a group of economists who believed that the macroeconomy always adjusts rapidly to the full-employment level of output; they also argued that monetary policy should be the prime instrument for stabilising the economy

monetary base: notes and coins in circulation

monetary policy: decisions made by the government regarding monetary variables such as money supply and interest rates

monetary transmission mechanism: the channel by which monetary policy affects aggregate demand

money stock: the quantity of money in the economy

money supply: the quantity of money in circulation in the economy

monopolistic competition: a market that shares some characteristics of monopoly and some of perfect competition

monopoly: a form of market structure in which there is only one seller of a good

monopsony: a market in which there is a single buyer of a good, service or factor of production

Glossary of key terms

multinational corporation (MNC): a company whose production activities are carried out in more than one country

multiplier: the ratio of a change in equilibrium real income to the autonomous change that brought it about; it is defined as 1 divided by the marginal propensity to withdraw

n-firm concentration ratio: a measure of the market share of the largest n firms in an industry

narrow money (M0): notes and coins in circulation and as commercial banks' deposits at the Bank of England

Nash equilibrium: a situation occurring within a game when each player's chosen strategy maximises payoffs given the other player's choice, so no player has an incentive to alter behaviour

National Debt: the accumulated stock of past public debt

nationalisation: a process whereby an enterprise is taken into state ownership.

natural monopoly: arises in an industry where there are such substantial economies of scale that only one firm is viable

natural rate of unemployment: equilibrium full-employment level of unemployment

negative income tax: a system whereby support for people on low incomes is provided through the tax system rather than by the direct payment of benefits

net domestic product (NDP): GDP *minus* depreciation

net investment: gross investment *minus* depreciation

net national income (NNI): GNI *minus* depreciation

net present value: the estimated value in the current time period of the discounted future net benefit of a project

newly industrialised economies: economies that have experienced rapid economic growth from the 1960s to the present

NIMBY (not in my back yard): a syndrome under which people are happy to support the construction of an unsightly or unsocial facility, so long as it is not in their neighbourhood (back yard)

nominal exchange rate: the price of one currency in terms of another, with no account being taken of changes in relative prices in the two countries

nominal GDP: GDP measured at current prices

nominal value: value of an economic variable based on current prices, taking no account of changing prices through time

non-accelerating-inflation rate of unemployment (NAIRU): the rate of unemployment in an economy at which inflation will be stable

non-pecuniary benefits: benefits offered to workers by firms that are not financial in nature

non-tariff barrier: an obstacle to free trade other than a tariff (for example, quality standards imposed on imported products)

normal good: one where the quantity demanded increases in response to an increase in consumer incomes

normal profit: the rate of return that a firm needs in order to remain in business – it is the opportunity cost of being in a market

normative statement: a statement about what *ought to be*

nudge theory: a notion based on behavioural economics suggesting that people can be nudged towards behaviour that is beneficial for society

oligopoly: a market with a few sellers, in which each firm must take account of the behaviour and likely behaviour of rival firms in the industry

opportunity cost: in decision-making, the value of the next-best alternative forgone

paradox of thrift: a result from the income–expenditure model by which an increase in saving results in a fall in investment and aggregate income

Pareto optimum: an allocation of resources is said to be a Pareto optimum if no reallocation of resources can make an individual better off without making some other individual worse off

participation rate: the percentage of people of working age who choose to join the labour force

perfect competition: a form of market structure that produces allocative and productive efficiency in long-run equilibrium

Perfect/first-degree price discrimination: a situation arising in a market whereby a monopoly firm is able to charge each consumer a different price

Phillips curve: a trade-off relationship between unemployment and inflation

policy trade-off: the situation arises when a policy that improves performance in relation to one policy target damages performance in relation to another

positive statement: a statement about what *is*, i.e. about *facts*

poverty trap: a situation in which an individual has no incentive to take a job, because any additional income will be taken away in taxes and lost benefits, thus leaving them worse off

predatory pricing: an anti-competitive strategy in which a firm sets price below average variable cost in an attempt to force a rival or rivals out of the market and achieve market dominance

price elasticity of demand (*PED*): a measure of the sensitivity of quantity demanded to a change in the price of a good or service. It is measured as: $\dfrac{\%\ \text{change in quantity demanded}}{\%\ \text{change in price}}$

price elasticity of supply (*PES*): a measure of the sensitivity of quantity supplied of a good or service to a change in the price of that good or service

price taker: a firm that must accept whatever price is set in the market as a whole

prinicipal – agent problem: a situation in which people (principals) cannot be sure that those who act on their behalf (agents) will act in their best interests, as a result of asymmetric information

prisoners' dilemma: an example of game theory with a range of applications in oligopoly theory

private benefit: a benefit incurred by an individual (firm or consumer) as part of its production or other economic activities

private cost: a cost incurred by an individual (firm or consumer) as part of its production or other economic activities

private good: a good that, once consumed by one person, cannot be consumed by somebody else; such a good has excludability and is rivalrous

privatisation: a process whereby an enterprise is transferred from public into private ownership

producer surplus: the difference between the price received by firms for a good or service and the price at which they would have been prepared to supply that good or service

product differentiation: a strategy adopted by firms that marks their product as being different from their competitors'

production externality: an externality that impacts on the production side of a market, which may be either positive or negative

production function: relationship that embodies information about technically efficient ways of combining labour and other factors of production to produce output

production possibility curve: a curve showing the maximum combinations of goods or services that can be produced in a set period of time given available resources

productive efficiency: attained when a firm operates at minimum average total cost, choosing an appropriate combination of inputs (cost efficiency) and producing the maximum output possible from those inputs (technical efficiency)

productivity: measure of the efficiency of a factor of production

progressive tax: a tax in which the marginal rate rises with income

prohibition: an attempt to prevent the consumption of a demerit good by declaring it illegal

public good: a good that is non-exclusive and non-rivalrous – consumers cannot be excluded from consuming the good, and consumption by one person does not affect the amount of the good available for others to consume

public sector net cash requirement (PSNCR): the government budget deficit – the amount that needs to be covered by borrowing

purchasing power parity theory: a theory stating that, in the long run, exchange rates (or a floating rate system) are determined by relative inflation rates in different countries. It argues that the exchange rate will adjust to maintain the real competitiveness of domestic goods and services

quantitative easing: a process by which liquidity in the economy is increased when the central bank purchases assets from banks

real exchange rate: the nominal exchange rate adjusted for differences in relative inflation rates between countries

real GDP: GDP measured at constant prices (the prices prevailing in a base year) such that inflation has been taken into account

real value: value of an economic variable taking account of changing prices through time

recession: a situation in which growth is negative for two or more consecutive quarters

regressive tax: a tax bearing more heavily on the relatively poorer members of society

regulatory capture: a situation in which the regulator of an industry comes to represent its interests rather than regulating it

relative poverty: the situation in which household income falls below 50% of median adjusted household income

reserve assets: stocker of foreign assets (e.g. foreign currency or gold) owned by the central bank of a country to enable it to meet any mismatch between the demand and supply of the country's currency

retail price index (RPI): a measure of the average level of prices in the UK

revaluation: a process whereby a country in a fixed exchange rate system raises the price of the domestic currency in terms of a foreign currency

satisficing: behaviour under which the managers of firms aim to produce satisfactory results for the firm – for example, in terms of profits – rather than trying to maximise them

scarcity: a situation that arises because people have unlimited wants in the face of limited resources

shadow price: an estimate of the monetary value of an item that does not carry a market price

short run: the period over which a firm is free to vary its input of one factor of production (labour) but faces fixed inputs of the other factors

short-run aggregate supply curve: a curve showing how much output firms are prepared to supply in the short run at any given overall price level

short-run supply curve: for a firm operating under perfect competition, the curve given by its short-run marginal cost curve above the price at which $SMC = SAVC$; for the industry, the short-run supply curve is the horizontal sum of the supply curves of the individual firms in the industry

social benefit: the sum of private and external benefits

social cost: the sum of private and external costs

social cost–benefit analysis: a process of evaluating the worth of a project by comparing its costs and benefits, including both direct and social costs and benefits – including externality effects

specific tax: a tax of a fixed amount imposed on purchases of a commodity

stagflation: a situation in which an economy simultaneously experiences stagnation (high unemployment) and high inflation

structural unemployment: unemployment arising because of changes in the pattern of activity within an economy

subsidy: a grant given by the government to producers to encourage production of a good or service

Glossary of key terms

substitutes: two goods are said to be substitutes if consumers regard them as alternatives, so that the demand for one good is likely to rise if the price of the other good rises

substitution effect of a price change: reflects the way that a change in the price of a good affects relative prices

sunk costs: costs incurred by a firm that cannot be recovered if the firm ceases trading

supply curve: a graph showing the quantity supplied at any given price

supply-side policies: a range of measures intended to have a direct effect on aggregate supply – and specifically on the potential capacity of the economy

sustainable development: 'development that meets the needs of the present without compromising the ability of future generations to meet their own needs' (Brundtland Commission, 1987)

tacit collusion: a situation occurring when firms refrain from competing on price, but without communication or formal agreement between them

tariff: a tax imposed on imported goods

technical efficiency: attaining the maximum possible output from a given set of inputs

technological unemployment: a type of structural unemployment that arises from the introduction of technology

terms of trade: the ratio of export prices to import prices

tiger economies: a group of newly industrialised economies in the East Asian region, including Hong Kong, Singapore, South Korea and Taiwan

total cost: the sum of all costs that are incurred in producing a given level of output

total factor productivity: the average productivity of all factors, measured as the total output divided by the total amount of inputs used

total physical product of labour (TPP_L): in the short run, the total amount of output produced at different levels of labour input with capital held fixed

total revenue: the revenue received by a firm from its sales of a good or service; it is the quantity sold, multiplied by the price

trade balance: the balance between expenditure on exports and on imports

trade creation: the replacement of more expensive domestic production or imports with cheaper output from a partner within the trading bloc

trade diversion: the replacement of cheaper imported goods by goods from a less efficient trading partner within a bloc

trade union: an organisation of workers that negotiates with employers on behalf of its members

trading possibilities curve: shows the consumption possibilities under conditions of free trade

transfer earnings: the minimum payment required to keep a factor of production in its present use

transfer payment: occurs where the government provides benefits (in cash or in kind) to poor households; hence there is a transfer from taxpayers to the recipients of the benefits

unemployment: results when people seeking work at the going wage cannot find a job

universal benefit: a benefit (in cash or in kind) paid without reference to the income of the receiving person or household

urbanisation: process whereby an increasing proportion of the population comes to live in cities

utility: the satisfaction received from consuming a good or service

variable costs: costs that vary with the level of output

velocity of circulation: the rate at which money changes hands: the volume of transactions divided by the money stock

vertical merger: a merger between two firms in the same industry, but at different stages of the production process

visible trade: trade in goods

voluntary export restraint: an agreement by a country to limit its exports to another country to a given quantity (quota)

voluntary unemployment: situation arising when an individual chooses not to accept a job at the going wage rate

withdrawal: a leakage from the circular flow of income, expenditure and output; comprising saving, direct taxes and imports

working population: that part of the population made up of people of working age

World Trade Organization (WTO): a multilateral body responsible for overseeing the conduct of international trade

X-inefficiency: occurs when a firm is not operating at minimum cost, perhaps because of organisational slack

Index

Note: page numbers in *italics* indicate exercises and examination questions.

Index

Index

Index